Article 356 of the Constitution of India

PROMISE AND PERFORMANCE

Article 356 of the Constitution of India

PROMISE AND PERFORMANCE

Revised and Expanded
Second Edition

Dr. K. SURYAPRASAD

Synergy Books India
(A Unit of M/s Bookwell Publication)
New Delhi

Article 356 of the Constitution of India
Promise and Performance

First Published, 2012
ISBN:978-93-82059-06-6

Published by:
Synergy Books India
(A Unit of M/s Bookwell Publication)
24/4800 Ansari Road, Darya Ganj
New Delhi-110002
Phone: 011-23268786, 23257264
Fax: 011-23281315
E-Mail: synergybooks@gmail.com
bookwell@vsnl.net

Printed in India at Mudrak, 30-A Patparganj, Delhi-110091

Karmanye – vaadhika – raste
Maa phaleshu Kadachana
Maa Karma – phala – hetur – bhoormaa
Te Sangostwokarmini.
(Bhagavadgita 2:47)

Your right is to work only,
But never to its fruits;
Let not the fruits of action be thy motive,
Nor let thy attachment be to in action.

This Book is Dedicated to the
Beloved Memories of
My Father,
Shri. K.Karunakaran and
My Brother- in-law,
Dr. S. Chandramohan

Foreword

The Constitution of India is a lengthy document consisting of 395 articles and 12 schedules. Among the various articles of the Constitution, no other articles has been the subject of serious controversy during the last sixty years as that of Article 356 dealing with the imposition of President's Rule in the states.

When this article was discussed in the Constituent Assembly several members expressed apprehension about the possibility of its misuse because of the vague expressions and the use of the word "otherwise". A perusal of the discussions in the constituent Assembly makes it clear that the framers of the Constitution intended Article 356 as a remedy for exceptional cases where the failure of the constitutional machinery in any state necessitated the intervention of the central authority for the limited purpose of carrying on the civil administration and the interregnum of President's Rule was to provide a breather for the re induction of an elected government. It is well recognized by constitutional experts that lawlessness, maladministration, corruption, and bad governance cannot be valid grounds for invoking this article.

Replying to the acrimonious debate in the Constituent Assembly on 4 August 1949, Ambedkar said, "I share the sentiments expressed by honourable friend Mr. Gupta yesterday that the proper thing we ought to expect is that such articles will never be called into operation and that they would remain a dead letter. If at all they are brought into operation, I hope, the President who is endowed with these powers will take proper precautions before actually suspending the administration of the provinces. I hope the first thing he will do would be to issue a mere warning to a province that has erred, that things were not happening in the way in which they were intended to happen in the Constitution. If that warning fails, the second thing for him to do will be to order an election allowing the people of the province to settle matters by themselves. It is only when the two remedies fail that he would resort to this article. I do not think we could then say that these articles were imported invain or that the president had acted wantonly". (Constituent Assembly Debates Vol IX, p.p. 176 – 177)

However, unfortunately, this expectation of Ambedkar did not prove to be true and its misuse started immediately after the adoption of the new Constitution in 1950. From Jawaharlal Nehru onwards every regime at the Union has abused these provisions mercilessly. So far it has been invoked as many as 110 times during the last six decades. Every single major political party has been a major victim of President's Rule. Each instance has resulted in loud protest and a fervent promise by the victim to abolish Article 356. Once in power the very same political parties, exalt in the pleasure of abusing the President's Rule provisions for party political gains.

Morarji Desai's Janata government upstaged his predecessors by dissolving nine state assemblies in 1977, a compliment returned by Indira Gandhi in 1980, on her return to power. All this was blessed by the Supreme Court's astonishing decision in 1977. The Supreme Court's interpretations of Article 356 has widened its scope without making way for a full-fledged Judicial review in the dissolution case (1977) allowed the suspension of state democracy in half of India, paving the way for future suspensions.

In Actual practice Article 356 has been misused by Union Governments by: a) dismissing state governments having majority in the Assembly; (b) Suspending and dissolving the Assemblies on partisan considerations; (c) Not giving a chance to the opposition to form a government.; (d) Denying opportunity to the opposition to form government where ministry resigned in anticipation of defeat on the floor of the House and; (e) Not allowing the opposition to form government even after the defeat of the ministry on the floor of the House.

The wording of the Article raises certain pertinent questions: What is meant by failure of the constitutional machinery?

Breakdown of law and order is totally different from failure of constitutional machinery. The former is failure or inability of the Home department to resolve a law and order problem but the latter is collapse of the entire administration of the state in all spheres. In the case of law and order it is the constitutional duty of the Centre to extend all cooperation and help to curb violence or disorders by deploying armed forces or any other measures sought by the state government. If the situation continues to be anarchic and uncontrollable, the question of failure of the constitutional machinery arises for invoking article 356. Seldom do we witness such situations in any states.

The apex court has been refusing to admit any case challenging the proclamation under articles 356 up to late 1970s. After the 44 amendment in A.K Ray's case, the Supreme Court, held that the proclamation under Articles 356 (1) was now open to judicial review on the ground of illegality, impropriety or *mala fide* or in short abuses of power. If the proclamation is struck down by the court the dismissed state government can be restored (Sunderlal Patwa v. Union of India). It has also been suggested that the Assembly be not dissolved until the proclamation is approved by the Houses of Parliament.

So far as the limited questions of the use of Article 356 is concerned, most often than not the provision is resorted to as the only panacea for all the evils affecting a state government. Several other articles available to the Union government are ignored and remain unutilized. The last remedy becomes the first entirely against the intentions of the frames of the Constitution.

Drawing attention to the repeated abuse of article 356, the Sarkaria Commission observed. "Article 356 should be used sparingly in extreme cases as a measure of last resort when all available alternatives fail to prevent or rectify a breakdown of the constitutional machinery in the state". All attempts should be made to resolve the crisis at the state level" and a warning should be issued to the errant state in specific terms that it is not carrying on the government of the state in accordance with the Constitution. Before taking actions any explanation received from the state should be taken into account".

The Supreme Court in its judgment in S.R. Bommai Case (1994) enumerated certain situations which may not amount to failures of the constitutional machinery in the states and where the use of Articles 356 will be improper. Some of them are:-

1. Imposition of President's Rule in a situation of maladministration by a ministry enjoying majority support in the Assembly will be extraneous to the purpose for which the power under articles 356 has been conferred. The framers of the constitutions has made it clear that Article 356 is not meant to be exercised for the purpose of securing good government.

2. Just because the ruling party in the state has suffered a defeat in the elections to the Lok Sabha, Article 356 cannot be invoked for dissolving the state Legislative Assembly.

3. In a situation of internal disturbances not amounting to abdication of governmental powers of the state government, possible measures should be taken by the Union under articles 355. Before invoking Articles 356, the union should exhaust the powers under articles 355.

4. In the case of internal subversion, physical breakdown and non–compliance with constitutional directions of the Union government, the use of power under articles 356 will be in proper if the President gives no prior warning to the state government to correct itself. Such a warning can be dispensed with only in cases of extreme urgency.

5. Article 356 cannot be invoked where response to the warning or notice or direction under article 256, 257 etc to state government applied the corrective measures and complied with the directions or satisfied the Union executions that the warning or direction was based on incorrect facts.

Above all, the Supreme Court unambiguously declared that the dissolution of the Assembly prior to the approval of the proclamation by the Parliament under clauses (3) of the said article would be invalid"

The standing committee of the Inter - State Council at its meeting on 17 July 1996 suggested certain safeguards against possible misuse of Articles 356. These included reliance on Governor's report, issue of show cause notice to the state, granting a week's time to the state to reply, approval of the proclamation within one month by the Parliament and that too by 2/3 majority.

The report of the Governor to the Union government should be a speaking document containing a precise and clear statement of all material facts and grounds to enable to President to satisfy himself.

The decision of the United Front government at the Centre to dismiss the BJP government in U.P (1997) was reversed following a direction from President K.R. Narayanan. In the case of Bihar (1998) also the President exercised his constitutional discretion to show disapproval of the Union government's move to dismiss the Rabari Devi government in Bihar.

President Narayanan's minutes of September 25, 1998 returning Union Cabinet's recommendation for reconsideration will act as a guideline for future Presidents as well as future governments at the Centre. Its significance will be realized by the future chronicles of constitutional history. No centre government in future would lightly think of removing a duly constituted state government enjoying the majority support. The minutes makes it clear that any imposition of Articles 356 barring exceptional or extreme situations must be preceded by nonconformational efforts to sort out Centre - State differences and conflicts and there by issuing warnings and directions and eliciting explanations form the state. The minute draws the government's attention to the Presidents address to Parliament in March 1998 in which he articulated his government's intensions to implement the Sarkaria Commissions recommendations.

In short, Article 356 should be used sparingly and as a last resort when all other measures to restores constitutional propriety failed. In actual practice these are situations which warrant the use of Articles 356. They are:

(a) When immediately after the election none of the parties is prepared to form the government;
(b) When parties are equally balanced and none of the parties is prepared to put - up a candidate for the Speaker ship as it happened in Manipur 1967;
(c) When the coalition or a majority government resigned opposition is not prepared to form a government;
(d) When the state government violates the constitutions by 1) indulging in secessionist and other activities which

adversely affect national unity and integrity 2) exercising the executive power in a manner which impedes the exercise of executive powers of the Union or the implementation of central laws; and (3) not implementing judicial decisions.

The paradox about Article 356 is that even its worst critics do not want to scrap it. The controversy centres around the misuse of this article for gaining political mileage against adversaries and thereby subverting the basic principles of federation and democracy. The misuse of Article 356 can be prevented by strictly following the recommendations of the Sarkaria Commission, the guidelines laid down by the Supreme Court in the Bommai case and the safeguards suggested by the standing committee of the Inter-State-Council. President Narayanan has strictly followed all of them while returning the recommendations of the Union cabinet regarding the dismissal of the Bihar government and thereby created a very healthy convention which would go a long way in strengthening the fabric of federalism in India and upholding the Constitution.

II

The book 'Article 356 of the Constitution of India: Promise and Performance' by K. Suryaprasad is a scholarly work on the relevance and working of Article 356. In this comprehensive work he attempts an analytical study of the exercise of this presidential power in the six decades following the adoption of the Constitution. He has meticulously examined the hundred and eleven odd instances of the use of Article 356 in the post 1950 period and also the various suggestions made by different Commissions sofar for plugging the loopholes in the provision.

The major objectives of the study are: 1) to ascertain whether the founding fathers of the Constitution were justified in incorporating Article 356 in the Constitution of India 2); to analyse the real scope and ambit of the term 'failure of the constitutional machinery in the state; 3) to find out real reasons for the proclamations of Article 356 in the states and examine whether these reasons are in conformity with the constitutional provisions;

(4) to examine whether the Parliament can rectify the defects, if any, in case excesses are committed by the Union executive; (5) to discuss whether the Court can adjudicate on the validity of the presidential proclamations and; (6) if the article has been misused for mere politicking, whether the situations could be rectified in any other way including amendment to the Article barring the scrapping of the Article.

The study is designed to find answer to the above questions and to suggest feasible and viable remedies to prevent the misuses of the provision. This book is organized under eight chapters of equal importance besides an introduction. He observes that in 70 cases out of 111 the decisions to impose President's rules was motivated by political considerations of the Centre and not inspired by its responsibility and obligations to uphold the Constitution. Thus it becomes clear that in a large number of instances, the invoking of Articles 356 has not been in accordance with the assurance given by Ambedkar in the Constituent Assembly though in a few cases the power has been properly used. Thus the apprehension and doubt expressed by the founding fathers regarding the possibility of the Article "being abused or employed for political purpose" proved prophetic, he remarks.

The basic problem, according to him, is that no political party has a definite stand in the utility of Article 356. It is precisely for this reason that despite several meetings, the standing committee of the Interstate Council could not reach a consensus on Article 356. All this shows that no safeguards whether constitutional or conventional or even judicial will ensure a centpercent guarantee against misuse or abuse of the constitutional provisions unless the political parties are committed to democratic ideology, principles and practice. Further no existing political party has consistently demanded the deletion of Article 356.

As a result of this analytical study, Suryaprasad comes to the conclusion that as things stand today, the only effective safeguard against the misuse of Article 356 appears to be the judiciary. As and when the power is unilaterally used against a state government, the Courts apart from considering the case should also be able to come out with a verdict within a short period of times. It is suggested that the power to issue writs in this regard will enable the Supreme

Court and High Courts to deliver such timely verdicts. This will help to put the constitutional process back on the rails without further damage, he observes.

Suryaprasad has left no stone unturned in the task of collecting relevant data for this study. The debates of the Constituent Assembly, Archival materials, government reports, recommendations of the various Commissions appointed by the governments, suggestions of constitutional experts like H.M Seervai, Rajeev Dhavan, Soli J. Sorabjee, Justice H.R. Khanna , Justice V. R. Krishna Iyer etc.-all these have been judiciously utilized for the study. This path breaking study has opened up a new vista to the proper understanding of the presidential powers in the correct perspective. The study also reflects his perceptual clarity and reveal, his ability for perceptive analysis. He has succeeded in the task of presenting the politico - legal aspects of Article 356 in a unique manner. As such the study is extremely useful to all students of Indian Constitution. Written in a simple and lucid style the book provides a treasure house of information on some of the critical areas of Indian Constitution. This book should not be missed by any serious student of Indian Constitution. It is, indeed, a valuable addition to the existing literature on Indian Constitution. It gives me great pleasure and pride in presenting this pioneering work to a wider audience.

15 August 2011.

Prof. (Dr.) K. Raman Pillai,
Former Professor and Head,
Dept. of Political Science,
University of Kerala.
Thiruvananthapuram

Preface to the Second Edition

I am very happy to know that the first edition of this book has been well received by academic community and general public. This encouraged me to bring out the present edition. In this edition almost all chapters in the first edition have been thoroughly revised, suitably enlarged and systematically updated, incorporating new developments in the area along with necessary comments. This revision has been made keeping in view that it should continue to satisfy the information requirements of the scholars in the light of the latest developments since the first edition in 2001. The author has carefully taken note of all such developments in the present edition. While doing so a special attempt has been made to critically examine the office and functions of Governors, the changing role of the President, decline of the Parliament, among other things. Further, a comparative study of Indian provisions with some other federal Constitutions has been undertaken to pin-point the basic differences and similarities in approaches. Articles 365 has a close bearing with Article 356. Therefore, attention is given to undertake a discussion of its scope and ambit. Gujarat Imbroglio in 2002, Article 356 in the age of coalition and growing importance of regional parties in the working of the Indian Federal System are some other highlights of this edition. In addition, a thorough analysis of the latest Supreme Court decision in Rameshwarprasad and ors. v. Union of India has also been discussed at length. This has been done with a view to enrich the chapter entitled 'Safeguards against the Abuse of power: The Judiciary'.

Divided into nine chapters, the author categorically analyses various dimensions of the problem in a clear, concise and well organised style that the academic community can follow and understand. Description of the topics is simple and direct. Analysis is critical yet objective. Relevant historical facts have been adduced wherever necessary to facilitate an easy understanding of the problem. Over and above, a large number of headings, subheadings, tables, figures and charts have been given at appropriate places to get a bird's eye view of the multi-dimensional problem. Bibliography has also been updated and in number of places new references and notes have been added. The readers of this book can enhance their knowledge and seek allied and additional information by referring to the specific documents mentioned in the comprehensive and exhaustive bibliography.

In the preparation of this book, the author has benefited greatly from critical readings of authentic documents by many authorities. The author would like to record his deep sense of gratitude to all the authors whose works have been consulted in the preparation of this book. Certainly, his indebtedness goes far beyond the one specifically mentioned in the notes and references.

The author shall consider himself successful, if this edition of this book would serve Students, Research Scholars, Teachers, Lawyers, Judges as well as the general public interested in the constitutional issues and political questions for the furtherance of their information needs.

Thiruvananthapuram,
15 August 2011.

Dr. K. Suryaprasad
University of Kerala,
Kariavattom Campus,
Thiruvananthapuram.

Acknowledgements

Gratitude is the language of the heart. When the language is from the heart, emotions prevail; and when emotions prevail words fail.

It gives me immense pleasure to acknowledge my deep sense of gratitude to my respected and most dear supervising teacher, Dr. R.K. Suresh Kumar, Reader and Head of the Department of Political Science, University College, Thiruvananthapuram. It was under his valuable guidance that I embarked upon this work. His unassuming suggestions and advice, practical and simple solutions to even most complex problems and the unfailing interest in my work throughout have always been a source of constant inspiration to me. My gratitude and indebtedness to him and his wife Smt.Maya and his children Veena and Mahesh are beyond words.

I express my deep sense of gratitude and indebtedness to my respected professor, Dr. K. Ramanpillai, former professor and head of the department of Political science, University of Kerala, who had helped me a great deal in my work. He proved to be a great source of inspiration to me through out my studies. I extend my heart-felt respect, love and regard to him and thanks him for the foreword graciously awarded to this edition.

I wish to aknowledge my sincere thanks and respect to Prof. N.K. Jayakumar, Vice-Chancellor, National University of Advanced Legal Studies, Kochi (Kerala), for his unassuming encouragement, informative advice and necessary suggestions. Though I am not privileged to be a student under him, I am fortunate enough to be associated with him throughout the present work.

My extreme thanks and gratitude are also due to Prof. G. Gopakumar, Professor and head of the department of Political Science, University of Kerala, who was my teacher and guide both in my M.A and M. Phil courses. I am happy to say that whenever I approached him for his advice and suggestions, he was kind enough to offer them in plenty.

I am pleased to record and register my deep sense of gratitude and indebtedness to Shri. K. Sukumaran Nair, former Director, Survey Research Centre, University of Kerala, for his sincere encouragement, critical and informative advice and worthy suggestions during the initial stage of my endeavour.

I wish to acknowledge my deep sense of gratitude to Smt. C.S. Laila, the University Librarian, Smt. Saraswathy and Smt. Gayathri, the Deputy Librarians of the Kerala University for their good wishes, constant encouragement and timely direction.

I express my deep sense of gratitude to Prof. K.C. Sunny, Head of the Department of Law, University of Kerala, Prof. P.P. Ajaya Kumar, Director IDE, University of Kerala, Prof. N.K. Baskaran, former professor and head of the department of Political Science, Prof. M. Baskaran Nair, Prof. T.S Anirudhan, Prof. Nagappan Nair, Shri. C. Muraleedharan, Shri. C.P. Suresh, Dr. Shaji Varkey, Dr. Bismi Gopala Krishnan for their good wishes.

My extreme thanks and gratitude are also due to Prof. G.M. Nair, Professor and Head of the Department of Biotechnology, University of Kerala, and Prof. Ashalatha, S Nair, Professor and Head of the Department of Botany, University of Kerala whose good wishes gave me impetus to undertake and finish this work successfully. My deep sense of gratitude and indebtedness to them are beyond words.

I cannot but remember and acknowledge the sincere and everlasting encouragement received from Prof. N. Omanakumari, the former Professor and Head of the Department of Botany, University of Kerala.

I would like to make a special mention to the sincere help and encouragement given to me by Shri. Somanpillai, a leading educationalist in Kerala. His critical readings and advice at the final stage of the manuscript preparation is thankfully remembered.

Words fail me to express my sincere thanks to Dr. S. Unnikrishnan, Dr. Valsaladevi, Smt. Rasheeda Beevi, Shri. Hamsa, A. Shri Aravindakshan, Shri. Raj Kishan Nair S.S, Smt. Jayammal K.R, Dr. Satheesh Kumar (Statistics) , Dr. Suresh Kumar P, Smt. SushamaPillai, Dr. Shaiju, Shri. Harikumar S, Dr.Anirudhan *Dreamtech* Ajith and *Springer* Rajendran who have inspired me, encouraged me and many a time helped me of various problems. Their heart-felt love, affection, blessings and good wishes showered upon me are affectionately remembered.

In the preparation of this book, I was sustained and carried forward by the encouragement and assistance I received in abundance from my colleagues. I would particularly like to thank Smt. G. Radhamony teacher, Dr. P.M. Radhamony Dr. GangaPrasad, , Dr. Suhara Beevi, Dr. Bindu. R. Nair, Dr. Raja Lekshmi, Smt. Sreelaraj, Smt. Shylajakumary, Smt. Parvathy, Shri. Gilbert, Smt. Radhamony and Smt. Rama Devi.

I take this opportunity to record my obligation and gratitude to Prof. Jayakrishnan, the honourable Vice-chancellor of the University of Kerala, Prof. J. Prabash, the Pro-Vice-chancellor, Shri Ragavan P. the Registrar, and Prof. A.R. Rajan, University of Kerala for all the facilities provided to me.

Many generous individuals took their valuable time to help me for information search and retrieval. Special mention must be made of Smt. Sreekumari T.S (campus library), Smt. Lekha, Smt. Marry Leela, Shri. Girikumar, Shri. Hari Kumar and Smt. Indu (Library professionals in the Kerala Legislators' Library) Shri Vamadevan (Dept. of Law) Smt. Lakshmi Devi and Smt. Preetha (Dept. of Political Science) Shri. Joythi babu, Shri.Madhusoodhanakurup and Shri. Anil kumar (campus library) I would be failing in my duty if I do not record and register my indebtedness to them. I take this opportunity to express my sincere and heart-felt love and regards to each and every one of them.

I have received valuable help from friends and colleagues who have read the draft and made a large number of correction and clarifying comments that enriched this book. I am particularly obliged to, Shri. Harikumaramenon, Shri Freedy pious, Shri. A.K Ampoty, Dr. V.A. Gangadharan and Dr. Pradeep.

There are many others who helped me with encouragement and good wishes and it is difficult to name all of them. Yet I would be showing ingratitude unless I mention some of them like Shri. Pratapa Chandran-Kartha, Shri. Sisubalan S. Dr. A.K. Prasad (Eco), Ranjeev V.K, Dr. Sheeja (IDE), Dr. P.F. Gopakumar, Dr. Asha, Hashim, Shri Abdul Mageed Shri Mageed H, Shri. Justin Bright, Dr. Raju Abraham, Dr. D. Pradeep, Shri. Deerendra Singh, Shri. Jayachandran, Shri Gee-Verghese and Smt. Madhumathy.

I accord my earnest gratitude to all my friends and neighbours in general and Shri. Santhosh S, Shri. Jayachandra Das, Shri. Arivandakshan, Dr. Mohankumar, Shri Prabhakaran Nader, Shri Stanley George, Shri. Arul Raj, Shri. GopalaKrishnan Chettiyar and Shri. George in particular for their love, help and cooperation extended to me.

I shall be showing ingratitude unless I remember my respected and ever-loving teachers in Manoor L.P.S and V.T.M. N.S.S. College, Dhanuvachpuram. Mention in this regard may be made of Shri. Kuttan Pillai, Shri. Yeshudasan, Shri. Krishnankutty Nair, Shri. Thankayan, Prof. K.K. Nair, Shri. G. Bahuleyan Nair, Shri Gopinathapillai and Shri R. Prabhakaran Thampi. Their encouragement and everlasting influence are affectionately remembered and acknowledged.

I wish to thank Rakesh M.R, Shri. G Aneesh Kumar, the Manager of Ganish Design, Shri. Uma Sankar for the dedication in making this excellent version of the book.

As a matter of pleasant duty, I must also record here my profound appreciation for my esteemed publisher, *Book well publishers*, New Delhi for bringing out this book at an early date with all sincerity.

Finally, I owe a debt of gratitude to my beloved parents and the Almighty for blessing me to tide over every stage of my career.

Dr. K. Suryaprasad

List of Tables

List of Figures

List of Abbreviations

AcLR	Academy Law Review
AGP	Assam Gana Parishad
AIADMK	All India Anna Dravida Munnetta Kazhagam.
AIR	All India Reporter
All.	Allahabad
Anr.	Another
AP	Andhra Pradesh
ARC	Administrative Reforms Commission
AWR	Andhra Weekly Reporter.
BJP	Bharatiya Janata Party.
BKD	Bharatiya Kranti Dal.
BSP	Bahujan Samaj Party
CAD	Constituent Assembly Debates
Cal.	Calcutta.
CJ	Chief Justice.
CM	Chief Minister.
CPI	Communist Party of India.
CPI (M)	Communist Party of India (Marxist).
CRPF	Central Reserve Police Force.
CULR	Cochin University Law Review.
CWC	Congress Working Committee
DMK	Dravida Munnetta Kazhagam
EPW	Economic and Political Weekly.
Gahu.	Gauhati.
HP	Himachal Pradesh.
IIPA	Indian Institute of Public-Administration.

INC	Indian National Congress
ISDA	Institute for the Study of Developing Areas
ISS	Islamic Sevak Sangh.
J.	Justice.
(J).	Journal
JCPS	Journal of Constitutional and Parliamentary Studies.
JD	Janata Dal.
JD(S)	Janata Dal (Secular)
JD (U)	Janata Dal (United)
JILI	Journal of Indian Law Institute.
J&K	Jammu and Kashmir.
Kart.	Karnataka.
Ker.	Kerala.
Lah.	Lahore.
LDF	Left Democratic Front.
LF	Left Front
LJ	Law Journal.
LSD	Lok Sabha Debates.
LTTE	Liberation Tigers of Tamil Elam.
Mal.	Malayalam.
MLA	Member of Legislative Assembly.
MP	Madhya Pradesh.
NC	National Conference.
NDA	National Democratic Alliance
NNO	Naga National Organization.
NNP	Naga National Party.
Ori.	Orissa.
Ors.	Others
OUP	Oxford University Press.
PAC	Provincial Armed Constabullery.
PC	Privy Council.
PDF	Progressive Democratic Front.
PEPSU	Patiala and East Punjab States Union.
PandH	Punjab and Haryana.
PSP	Praja Socialist Party.
Punj.	Punjab.

PVD	Progressive Vidhayak Dal.
RJD	Rashtriya Janata Dal.
RSD	Rajya Sabha Debates.
RSP	Revolutionary Socialist Party.
RSS	Rashtriya Swayam Sevak Sangh.
SC	Supreme Court.
SCC	Supreme Court Cases.
SP	Samajwadi Party
Supp.	Supplement
SVD	Samyukta Vidhayak Dal.
TDP	Telungu Desam Party
UCJPS	University College Journal of Political Science
UDF	United Democratic Front.
UF	United Front.
ULF	United Liberation Front.
ULFA	United Liberation Front of Assam.
UNI	United News of India.
UP	Uttar Pradesh.
UPA	United Progressive Alliance.
USA	United States of America.
v.	Versus.
VHP	Vishva Hindu Parishad.

Contents

Chapter 1

Introduction

This study is an attempt to understand the relevance and working of Article 356 of the Constitution of India, which empowers the Union government to dismiss a State government, dissolve a State legislature and bring the State under President's Rule. The study examines the mechanisms relevant to Article 356 as "in action" and not "at rest". An empirical and analytical study of the exercise of this presidential power in the six decades following the adoption of the Constitution is attempted. Through an exhaustive study of the hundred and eleven odd instances of the use of Article 356 in the post-1950 period, an effort is also made to systematically present the emerging model of President's Rule in the States. The scope of the study also includes a serious look into the suggestions made so far for plugging the loopholes, if any, in the provision for President's Rule.

The founding fathers of the Constitution were convinced that the President must have enough power to deal with a situation which may pose threat to the unity and integrity of the country and to see that the governments of various States are carried on in accordance with the provisions of the Constitution. Article 356 empowered the President to impose President's Rule in case of the failure of the constitutional machinery of the state. The basic philosophy behind the incorporation of this Article is to maintain national unity and integrity and as such the Article is more positive in essence than its negative application.

At the time when the Constituent Assembly discussed the need to incorporate the Article in the Constitution, stout opposition to it was put forth by some members and it was argued that if power was given to the Centre to intervene, there was a possibility of this Article "being abused or employed for political purposes or being resorted to for 'unnecessary or intolerant action through political prejudice'. Also they apprehended that the Centre might 'intervene in petty provincial matters' on the 'slightest pretext' 'on the pretext of purifying or reforming maladministration obtaining in a particular state' or on the ground of 'mismanagement or inefficiency or corruption in a province' or for resolving 'a mere crisis or a vote of non-confidence in the ministry by the Legislature' or for ensuring 'good government' thus reducing 'provincial autonomy to a farce'. Accepting the apprehension of the members, Ambedkar admitted that these Articles were 'liable to be abused' and 'employed for political purposes'. But he reasoned that such an 'objection applied to every part of the Constitution which gives power to the Centre to override the provinces' and expressed the hope that the occasion for invoking these power under the relevant article would be very rare and that 'they would remain a dead letter' and that a mere possibility of abuse cannot be ground for not incorporating it". However, the Constitutional practice shows that this Article has been invoked one hundred and eleven times during the last six decades. As a result, it is now a subject of controversy and with every invocation of Article 356 the controversy scales new heights.

It is true that till 1967, with a few exceptions as in Punjab, Pepsu, Andhra, Travancore-Cochin and Kerala, the Article had not assumed controversial proportions so as to cause any stresses and strains in Centre-State relations. That has been due to the prevalence of single party dominant system or Congress dominant system both at the Centre and in the States. The situation has changed radically since 1967. The instances of the imposition of Article 356 started showing a sharp increase in the post 1967 period. The fourth general elections effected a major change in the political map of India by ending the twenty years of Congress monopoly of legislature. The 1967 general elections marked the beginning of the transformation of the Indian political system to a multi-party system. The Congress majority in the Lok Sabha was greatly reduced and in eight of the sixteen State legislatures, the Congress failed to secure majority. Coalition ministries were formed in a number of States for the first time. But these coalitions of convenience were unstable and President's Rule was imposed by the Union government in many of these States. It was during this period that the opposition parties started expressing dissatisfaction over the emerging state of Centre-State relations. The State leaders of these parties started using the languages of conflicts and confrontations, threats and warnings and complaints and grievances. They also started rallying the people for the redressal of their grievances. Thus, Article 356 emerged as a key issue in the Union-State relations. A bitter controversy arose on the nature of Article 356 and the manner in which the provision was applied.

In spite of the clamour for applying brakes, change of government at the Centre witnessed a crescendo of the misuse of Article 356. Since the eighties there have been many instances of its use by different political parties which came to power at the Centre. The opposition political parties continued to criticise the manner in which the provision was put into operation. In 1984, a Commission headed by Justice Sarkaria was appointed to look into the thorny problem of Centre-State relations, including Article 356. The Commission observed that in great majority of cases, the imposition lacked constitutional validity. The Commission after a critical analysis of various controversies and issues relating to this provision, made certain constructive suggestions within the existing constitutional scheme for the Union government to adhere to. The Government of India, however, did not accept these recommendations. Had the recommendations of the Sarkaria Commission been accepted, the unpleasant situations in Karnataka in 1989 in Madhya Pradesh, Himachal Pradesh and Rajasthan in 1992, in Bihar 2005 and again in Karnataka in 2011 could have been avoided. Rajeev Gandhi dismissed the Janata Dal ministry led by S.R.

Bommai in Karnataka without giving the Chief Minister an opportunity to prove his majority on the floor of the House, despite his repeated requests. Narasimha Rao removed three BJP governments in the aftermath of the demolition of Babri-Masjid even though they enjoyed the confidence of the respective Houses. Again, the dissolution of Bihar Assembly without the members taking oath has given rise to another controversy that was wholly avoidable.

At the time of the Bommai judgement, the Article was one of the key issues in Union-State relations and also in the political realm. Despite the recommendations of the Sarkaria Commission and the rulings of the Supreme Court in the Bommai and Rameshwar Prasad cases, the attempts to dismiss Kalyan Singh government in Uttar Pradesh in 1997, the R.J.D government of Rabri Devi in Bihar in 1998 and Mulayam government again in UP in 2007 (in the first two cases the Presidential activism came to the help of the State governments) and the dissolution of Bihar Assembly in 2005, brought the matter again to the fore. Despite its misuse, the provision continues to be the corner stone of Indian Constitution in the backdrop of the emerging competitive nature of our polity. The highly volatile political situation of the present coalition era compels a serious student of Indian Constitution and political system to re-read the relevant provisions regarding Presidents Rule and to have a fresh look at it from the experiences gained so far.

The most important criticism with regard to the use *of* Article 356 is that, more often than not, it has been interpreted and applied differently in similar situations to suit the political interest of the ruling party at the Centre. It has also been alleged that opposition parties or groups had not been given a chance to form alternative governments. Similarly, it has been pointed out that there have been instances of Legislative Assemblies being dissolved or being kept in a state of suspended animation for purposes like buying time to realign party strength or to sort out problems arising out of intra-party alliances and to resolve leadership issues. Further, it was also alleged that President's Rule was used to dislodge State governments run by political parties or coalitions other than the ruling party at the Centre on the plea of corruption, maladministration and deterioration of law and order, even though the governments commanded the confidence of the respective Assemblies. It was also criticised that during the period of coalition politics, the Governors acted as agents and representatives of the Centre and they were looked upon as the chief instruments of Union governments alleged conspiracy to topple opposition led governments in the States. In this context it is worthwhile to find out how far there is truth or substance in the above mentioned charges and to attempt to define the present relevance of Article 356 from the experiences gained so far.

The main objectives of the study may be summarised as:

1. to ascertain whether the founding fathers of the Constitution were justified in incorporating Article 356 in the Constitution of India;
2. to analyse the real scope and ambit of the term "failure of the constitutional machinery in the State";
3. to find out the real reason or reasons for the proclamation of Article 356 in the States and examine whether these reasons are in conformity with the constitutional provisions;
4. to examine whether the Parliament can rectify the defects, if any, in case excesses are committed by the Union executive;
5. to discuss whether the Court can adjudicate on the validity of the Presidential proclamation and;
6. if the Article has been misused for mere politicking, whether this situation could be rectified in any other way, including amendment to the Article, barring scrapping of the Article.

The study is designed to find answers to the above questions and to suggest feasible and viable remedies to prevent the misuse of the provision.

As has been stated earlier, the study is interdisciplinary in its nature and scope. Since the topic has both political and legal connotations, insights from these disciplines have been used wherever necessary. The methodology used for the study is analytical, and historical. Case study method is also widely used. Some official documents relating to the subject like the Constituent Assembly Debates, the Administrative Reforms Commission Report, the Governors' Committee Report, the Sarkaria Commission Report, Report of the NCRWC etc. serve as the background for the study. Newspaper reports, articles published in the journals, books and the documents of political parties and organised groups also provided information. In addition to these, the decisions of various High Courts and the Supreme Court of India have been extensively used as primary data. These different sources are clearly noted and acknowledged in the footnotes of the respective chapters and mentioned again in the bibliography given at the end of the book.

The present study is organised under nine chapters of equal importance, including an introduction. While analysing a constitutional provision, the historical setting is crucial to the process. To a large extent, Constitutions are unique plants that need the proper historical soil and sociological climate to grow and flower. As such the second chapter is concerned primarily with the evolution of Article 356 and the incorporation of emergency provisions under the Article. In chapter third, the orbit of operation of the provision and its implications and promises are analysed. This chapter also gives special attention to the analysis of the concept 'failure of the constitutional machinery in the States'. A brief survey of all presidential proclamations made under the Article has been attempted in the fourth chapter. It gives a clear picture of the political situations which prevailed in the affected States on the eve of the application of the Article. This is followed by an analytical survey which examines the reasons for the imposition of President's Rule, with comments on major issues. An attempt has also been made in this chapter to draw an emerging model on the basis of the analysis of previous chapters. In the next chapter a close scrutiny of the emerging model is under taken. Subsequently the role of the Parliament as a safeguard against the abuse of power is taken up for discussion in the seventh chapter. Judiciary is the only branch which is immune from populist pressure. No doubt, the Judiciary has stepped into prevent the misuse of this provision. Therefore, chapter eight of the study discusses the progressively developing and increasingly gratifying role of the judiciary in this regard. In the concluding chapter along with the summary of the study, a few suggestions are also made with a view to check the misuse of Article 356 in future.

The study does not cover Governor's Rule in Jammu and Kashmir under section 92 of the Constitution of Jammu and Kashmir and also the imposition of President's Rule in Union territories under section 51 of the Union Territories Act, 1963.

Many books, pertaining to the study of the President's Rule in the states, have been produced by eminent political scientists and constitutional experts. However, several developments have taken place in the field since these publications appeared. The last few years have witnessed the growing role and influence of regional parties at the Centre and their demand for imposing President's Rule against their political enemies, increased judicial activism, an assertive Presidency, a vigilant public opinion and compulsions on all political parties to stick to healthy convention in this regard as a result of the emerging plural centres of political power in different parts of the country. All these warrant a fresh look into this thorny problem.

Associated with the above task, it is also to be accepted that constitutional provisions and political institutions are not made up of mechanical parts, nor do they operate by themselves. They are composed of and operated by people coming from different socio-cultural milieu. This explains why different constitutional offices and provisions are not conforming to the set patterns. The consequence is that this field (Article 356) remains an evergreen pasture for serious students of Indian constitutional system. This fact has motivated the author to undertake an exhaustive study of Article 356 and its mechanisms as 'in action' and to draw a clear picture of the emerging model. It is this uniqueness of approach that distinguishes this work from the rest.

Chapter 2

The Genesis of Article 356 of The Constitution of India: A Retrospect

This chapter discusses the historical and constitutional genesis of the provision for President's Rule in the States as incorporated in the Constitution of India, which grants "extremely extensive and unusual power"[1] to the Centre to meet an extraordinarily exceptional situation where breakdown of constitutional machinery occurs in a state. This would provide a spectacle of the origin of the Article, changes effected in it, its development and final transformation into its present form. This is examined chronologically with reference to the Government of India Act of 1909, Act of 1919, Act of 1935 and the Draft Constitution of India as discussed by the founding fathers of the constitution in the Constituent Assembly. It would also be noteworthy that this provision was introduced and incorporated as an insignificant provision which would never be called into operation and that "remains a dead letter"[2] or is rarely used. But gradually this has transformed itself into an established, integral and highly controversial provision of the Constitution, that no established political party of the country which has come to power at the Centre either as a majority party or as a partner of a coalition unequivocally or wholly opposed.[3]

The Colonial Roots of the Article

Imposition of central rule in a province was an imperial power introduced by the British colonialists. That is, the seeds of the Article can very well be traced back to the pre-Independence days, when the Government of India Act of 1909 or Minto-Moreley Reforms were introduced.

Before the introduction of the Act, the native people had no role in administration and legislation. The affairs of the provinces were carried on by the Governor-General through his Executive Councillors. However, the Act marked the beginning of a new phase in the constitutional history of India by inaugurating a new era characterised by the growth of responsible government by delegating some powers to the Indian Legislatures, Indian politicians and the Indian people.[4] As the projected legislative bodies under the reforms had no real powers, the Britishers did not care to devise ways and means to keep these legislatures under their control in the true sense of the term.

The changes introduced by the Act were, however, one of degree and not of kind. Even Lord Moreley himself emphatically repudiated that the measures were in no sense a step towards parliamentary government. There was disappointment, and frustration among Indian leaders who initially hailed Moreley-Minto Reforms. In response to their agitations and demand for more changes, the Government of India Act of 1919 or Montague-Chelmsford Reforms were enacted.

The Act introduced Dyarachy in the provinces.[5] Under this system, the provinces were mere administrative units having no independent status of their own. Though the ultimate responsibility still rested with the British Parliament yet, this phase witnessed the introduction of a modicum of responsibility in the working of government which was made possible by the constitutional arrangement of Dyarachy. The Act aimed at the gradual development of self governing institutions in India "with a view to the progressive realization of responsible government". In addition, a major attempt was made to initiate a policy of devolution "as a means of giving greater scope to the provincial governments and of forming a half-way house between the old centralization and federalism".[6] The centre's basic power of interference was also incorporated under sections 12 and 13 of the Act.[7] These provision imposed a considerable check on the legislative activities of the central and provincial legislative bodies. Thus the seeds of central interference in provincial autonomy in British India were sown.

The reforms of 1919 fell far short of satisfying the Indians who had been struggling for self government. The Indian National Congress condemned it as "inadequate, unsatisfactory and disappointing". The failure of reforms was due to external circumstances as well as some inherent defects of the system of Dyarachy. It was just an experiment carried out by the Britishers in constitution making process. In theory also, dyarachy was unsound and India continued to be unilaterally governed. No occasion arose for the take over of the provincial governments.

When India's struggle for independence was at its peak, a Commission headed by John Simon, a leading constitutional lawyer of Britain and member of the British Parliament, was appointed to look into the question of constitutional reforms for India and to make suitable recommendations. Though all political parties in India rejected its report outright, the Government of India Act of 1935 was based on the recommendations of the Simon report.[8] The act contained an emergency provision, the spirit of which subsequently found its way into the present Indian Constitution.

The Commission discussed at length several vital issues like the breakdown of law and order in Bombay, Madras, United Provinces and Punjab and the exercise of special powers vested in the Governors. The Commission realised that Governors, interfered a fair bit in provincial matters especially at the instance of political instability. The most important recommendation of the commission was the special provision for a state of emergency. The Simon Report noted that:

> Experience in the past has shown that, howsoever carefully a provincial constitution may be framed, a breakdown occurs through such causes as complete inability to form or maintain in office any ministry enjoying support from the legislature. A situation equally grave would arise if there was widespread refusal to work the normal constitution of the province, or general

> adoption of a policy which aimed at bringing government to a standstill. We hope that the extended trust now to be placed in representative institutions will bring about such a change of atmosphere and attitude as will make such developments unlikely. But if such an emergency were to arise, it is essential to insert into the Constitution provision to make the situation secure. This is no denial of self government, it is an ultimate recourse if self government is repudiated.[9]

This is the origin of the concept of Emergency provision in the states. It was ironic that similar provisions were not enacted in the case of Ireland within the United Kingdom in the Government of Ireland Act, 1920. This special power appears to have been reserved for meeting the Indian situation in the spirit that "the King's government must go on".

This imperial provision was retained by the White Paper of 1931 which enjoined that the Governor should be endowed with special powers and responsibilities to ensure smooth governance of the country, hoping that the use of this unhappily granted power would never be necessary because "a constitutional breakdown implies no ordinary crisis".[10]

The Joint Parliamentary Committee on 'Indian Constitutional Reforms' was also convinced that the Imperial government needed special powers, responsibilities and emergency powers.[11] While commenting on the Reports of the Joint Parliamentary Committee on Indian Constitutional Reforms and Simon Commission, M.C. Setalvad observed that:

> "These recommendations were clearly an attempt to meet a situation which may arise as a result of the intense agitation of the Indian people for self government and independence, which had frequently advocated and led to the practice of complete non-co-operation with governmental measures and policies which the people did not approve of."[12]

The political and administrative unification of the entire subcontinent of India, before and during the British rule remained a distant dream because of its socio-political, geographical, linguistic and cultural diversities. These complexities were so irreconcilable that any attempt at bringing about a unified state was deemed to fail. This was the background convenient for the Britishers to consolidate their control over India through the policy of Divide and Rule. India was further divided into Presidencies for the sake of administrative convenience and a centralized system of governance was set up. Native participation in the legislature was just a political device conceived by the British government to satisfy the rising political aspirations of the Indian people. Thus, the twin objectives of self preservation and administrative expediency necessitated the existence of a strong centre.

The Indian National Congress as a mark of protest passed several resolutions against the Simon Commission, White paper and Joint Committee recommendations and demanded the setting up of a Constituent Assembly. However, the British government went ahead with the enactment of the Government of India Act of 1935.[13]

The Act aimed at the completion of the process of devolution. It introduced certain new principles-federal principles- along with its corollary of provincial autonomy and the principle of popular responsible government in the provinces subject to certain "safeguards", as they were "called in political parlance in India". The scheme of provincial autonomy as envisaged in the Act was accompanied by a constitutional delimitation of legislative and executive jurisdiction between the federation and the units. With the creation of autonomous provinces, two questions arose; *first,* how to enable the centre to direct and control provincial policies and act in an emergency such as war or internal disturbance; the *second,* how to make provision for carrying on the administration if the machinery of ministerial government failed to function. In this context, the recommendations of the Statutory Commission manifested themselves in clause 45 and 93 of the Act.[14] These provisions were highly significant since they became the forerunners to the President's Rule provision in the Constitution of independent India.

Section 45 of the Act dealt with the situation of the failure of the constitutional machinery of the federation. It said:

If at any time the Governor General is satisfied that a situation has arisen in which the government of the federation cannot be carried on in accordance with the provisions of this Act, he may by proclamation:

a. declare that his functions shall to such extent, as may be specified in the proclamation, be exercised by him in his discretion.
b. assume to himself all or any of the powers vested in or exercisable by any Federal body or authority...

Likewise, section 93 enabled the Governors of the province to issue a proclamation enabling them *inter alia* to "assume to himself all or any of the powers vested in or exercisable by any provincial body or authority" if he "is satisfied that a situation has arisen in which the government of the province cannot be carried on in accordance with the provisions of this Act".[15] It is to be noted that these powers vested in the Governor General and Governors under the above sections were not contemplated to be "Emergency powers".

The Indian National Congress opposed these sections tooth and nail and after its landslide victory in the 1937 election, the Congress asked for an assurance from Linlithgow, the then Governor General of India, that the Governor of a province would not be allowed to exercise powers under section 93.[16] But the answer from the Governor was negative. However, the Congress asserted that it would fight against the excessive use of such power from within and assured the nation that it would never incorporate such a section in the Constitution of independent India. Contrary to its stand, the Congress introduced the clause for taking over the administration of the States by the Centre. What is alarming is that Article 356 turned out to be more dangerous and despotic than section 93 of the Government of India Act of 1935. Durga Das Basu observed that:

> "the object of 1935 Act, was simply to withdraw power from popular control and to place it on an irresponsible executive when it was found either at the Centre or in any Province that the machinery of the responsible government which was introduced by the Act of 1935 could not function".[17]

These provisions made it abundantly clear that though the Britishers experimented with a federal system in India by the 1935 Act, they were not ready to forgo their control over the provinces under their jurisdiction. They were equally apprehensive of a possible 'collapse' of the new experimental system of parliamentary democracy either at the centre or in the provinces. Hence they incorporated many provisions like section 93 in the Act which would enable the Governors to resume and to take back the very few powers entrusted to the elected governments in the provinces as and when, in their opinion, the government of the province could not be carried on in accordance with the provisions of the Act. As far as the British colonialists were concerned, it was incumbent on them to include a provision of this sort because the British Parliament was not prepared to trust the political parties in India. Many of them were opposed to the British rule and some of the parties like the Indian National Congress had declared openly that they would enter the legislatures and the government with a view to wrecking the system[18] from within by using constitutional and extra-constitutional means.

This kind of check envisaged by section 93 of the Act was applied in the provinces during freedom struggle.[19] The motive of self preservation of the British Raj appears to be very dominant in these invocations. Also the socio-political climate was highly disturbed, which further accentuated the imperial instincts of oppressive dominance over Indian representative institutions.

These provisions were not introduced in the Indian (provincial Constitution) order, 1947.[20] The Indian Independence Act of 1947 virtually ended the British rule in India and 'enabled the Constituent Assembly to frame and adopt a new Constitution and to supersede the Indian Independent Act without any further legislation from the British Parliament.

Constituent Assembly Deliberations

An examination of the discussion in the Constituent Assembly is necessary to get a true perspective of the Article.[21] It is a key to an understanding of the socio-economic and political context in which it was decided to adopt the emergency provisions. The framers of the Constitution had before them the examples and experiences of different countries seeking to solve the national crises faced by them through constitutional and legal means. They were also deeply concerned with the holocaust of partition, war in Kashmir, Communist subversion, the recalcitrant attitude of some princely states towards joining the Union, armed insurrection in the Telungana region of the Hyderabad state, worsening law and order situation and deteriorating economic conditions. Further, the Assembly started its work in the midst of pulls and counter pulls by divisive forces and fissiparous tendencies which were operating in different parts of the country and even shaking the very foundation of the newly formed Union. Above all these came the assassination of U. Aungsan and most of his cabinet colleagues in the neighbouring Burma in July 1947. The possibilities of a state government coming under the influence of an extremist ideology or a regional ethnic upsurge, which might endanger the unity and integrity of the nation could not be ruled out. In such situations, unified, speedy and effective action was necessary. In this context, the founding fathers followed section 93 of the Government of India Act of 1935 as if it were a sacred gospel. However, the authors of the Constitution did not entirely copy down the Government of India Act, 1935.

The crystallization of emergency provisions through the Constituent Assembly began with the discussion, under Nehru's chairmanship, by the Union Power Committee in February 1947. It was generally felt that the Union should have power similar to those under sections 126-A and 102 of the Act of 1935, to effectively carry out its defence responsibilities and to deal with grave economic crisis in any part of the Union. Keeping the recommendations of the Committee in mind B.N. Rao drafted his memorandum on the Union Constitution and his model Provincial Constitution, in which he considered Emergency situations. At the Union level, Rao suggested that, the President had a special responsibility, which he was to fulfil in his discretion, to prevent grave menace to the peace and tranquillity of the union and safeguard its financial stability and credit. Regarding the crisis at the state level, he suggested that the Governors shall have discretionary power to prevent any grave menace to the peace and tranquillity of their provinces or any part thereof.[22] However, Rao did not present a detailed picture of how the president and the Governors were to fulfil these special responsibilities.

The Union and the Provincial Constitution Committee both separately and jointly examined Rao's suggestions. In the latter, the division of functions between the President and the Governor became a contentious issue. The primary question debated was whether the Governor of a state should have the authority to declare an emergency on his own initiative and without prior consultation with his ministers, or was he merely to report to the President the existence of an emergency leaving it to the President to take necessary action. In view of the far reaching importance of this issue and the point of common interest of the Union and the Provincial Constitution Committee, it was decided to have a joint discussion. The joint committee after a strenuous discussion recommended that the Governor's power should be limited to reporting a grave menace to the peace of the province to the President, who would take action under his own powers. The Provincial Constitution Committee accepted this view. It was made clear that in sending his report it would not be necessary for the Governor to get the concurrence of his ministers. The Hindustan Times in an editorial interpreted this as tacitly recognizing "the right of the Union to directly administer the affairs of the Province on emergent occasion".[23]

When this report was presented to the Constituent Assembly, K.M. Munshi moved an amendment which altered this position. The amendment envisaged that in case of grave menace to the peace of the province, the Governor might assume to himself by a proclamation all or any of the powers vested in any body or authority. The Governor had to communicate his proclamation to the President immediately for appropriate action to be taken by the latter. The proclamation would cease to operate after two weeks. The President was expected to take suitable action within this period. This amendment was carried though it was attacked by Kunzru, Pant and others. It appears that this view got majority support at the time of preliminary consideration due to the tragic happenings in Burma, where a prime minister along with his colleagues were murdered in a sudden manner. In the event of such a thing happening in a province, it was thought advisable to invest the Governor with sufficient powers to take action pending presidential intervention.

Finally, in October 1947, a Draft Constitution was prepared by the constitutional adviser to be placed before the Constituent Assembly.[24] The strategy of these draft articles was to give the Governor the power to declare an emergency for a maximum period of two weeks and then leave it to the President to take further action to extend the emergency beyond the period of two weeks or to revoke it within two weeks. This was a shift from the strategy of the Act of 1935 which gave the Governor the power to declare an emergency but required him to procure the concurrence of the Governor General. Now the Governor could declare emergency himself. The President then could act on his general emergency powers which were mentioned elsewhere in the draft Constitution. These draft articles were redrafted and renumbered as Article 188 and Article 278.

When the Draft Constitution was presented in the Constituent Assembly, there ensured a long and lively discussion on the implications of these provisions.[25] Significantly, the mode of selection of the Governor received vital attention and became a bone of contention among the members. The question debated was whether there should be an elected Governor. Some members suggested that the Governor should, as in U.S.A, have complete executive authority in a province, nominating his cabinet, which would be answerable to him and not to the legislature and that he should be elected by people under a system of adult franchise. Some others suggested that the Governor should be a constitutional head, acting on the advice of the Prime minister, who would be responsible to the legislature and that he should be appointed by a system of indirect election. Some other members suggested that the central government should have wide range of authority over the province, the Governor should function as a liaison between the Central government and the provincial executive and that he should be nominated by the Central Government. Some even expressed doubts regarding the relevance of the post of Governor.[26] Therefore, a joint meeting of the Union Constitution Committee and the Provincial Constitution Committee was held on 7 June 1947. Eventually, the special committee of Constituent Assembly overwhelmingly accepted the concept of a nominated Governor rather than an elected one on the ground that the co-existence of an elected Governor and a Chief Minister responsible to the legislature might lead to friction and consequent weakness in administration.[27]

On 3 August, when the final debate of President's Rule Provision took place, a series of amendments were moved. In this connection, Ambedhkar moved three important amendments. The three amendments were: (1) That Article 188 be deleted; (2) That after draft Article 277, a new draft Article be inserted; Article 277 (A) and (3) That for old draft Article 278 the new Article 278(1) and 278(A) be substituted. All the amendments put together made considerable changes in the broad strategy. They were:

1. The Governor was to be stripped of his power to declare a temporary two weeks' emergency;
2. The President was to be given the power to declare an emergency on a report from the Governor "or otherwise";
3. A duty or obligation was cast on the Union in express terms to protect states against external aggression and internal disturbance and to ensure that the government of the state is carried on in accordance with the provisions of the constitution;
4. The new provision reduced the time period for which an emergency could be declared by the President without the approval of Parliament from "six months" to "two months"; and
5. The new Article 278 A clarified allocation of responsibilities between parliament and the administration during pendency of emergency.

All these noteworthy changes were the focus of a heated discussion which lasted over five hours spreading over two working days.[28] The debate that took place as regards important draft Articles are summarized below.

Article 188 of the Draft Constitution

In the discussion on the future of Article 188, Ambedkar made it very clear that the Union must have a clear constitutional responsibility to intervene in a province. Therefore, he pleaded for the deletion of the Article. In support of his argument he stated that no useful purpose would be served if there was a real emergency in which the President is required to act, by giving the Governor in the first instance, the power of suspending the Constitution merely for two weeks. "If the President is ultimately to take responsibility of entering into the provincial field in order to sustain the Constitution", he said, "then it is much better that the President should come into field right at the very beginning".[29] The amendment was supported by G.M. Gupta (who was the author of an earlier amendment which constituted Article 188). Supporting the amendment, Pant suggested that a Governor should not be permitted to take action in emergencies without President's consent or advice of his ministers. Santhanam opined that it was a "wrong provision" which allowed the Governor to proclaim emergency. Hunzru believed that it was inconsistent with the establishment of responsible government in the provinces and the new position of the Governor.

On the other hand, stalwarts like P.S. Deshmukh, Krishna Swamy Bharathi, Nazirudeen Ahmad and Alga Rai Sastri strongly opposed Ambedkar and stood for the retention of the provision on the ground that the amendment sought to divest the Governor, the man on the spot, of emergency power to act at the opportune moment and that it was inconsistent with the principle of federalism.[31] In the final reply to the debate, Ambedkar did not significantly dwell on this amendment and it was finally adopted. Therefore, Article 188 was deleted from the Draft Constitution. Why such an important departure was made from the scheme as envisaged in the earlier draft. As would appear from the debate in the Constituent Assembly, it is definite that an important reason for the shift of strategy was the altered position of the mode of selection of the Governor. Originally, the office of the Governor was to be an elective office but when the provision was changed in favour of the Governor being appointed by the President, the original draft article became unacceptable.

Draft Article 277 – A (Now Article 355)

The underlying principle and purpose for insertion of this Article was described by Ambedkar during his opening remarks. According to him, Article 277A was not merely a pious declaration. While explaining the reasons for its incorporation, he stressed the fact that our Constitution was a federal one, notwithstanding the many provisions bestowing overriding powers on the centre, since the provinces were given plenary authority to make any law for their peace, order and good government. In that case, intervention by the centre in the administration of the affairs of the provinces would amount to an invasion of sovereign authority. It follows that if the centre is to interfere in the administrative affairs of the provinces, it must do so only under some obligation which the Constitution has imposed upon the Centre. Ambedkar also emphasized that the invasion must not be an invasion which is wanton, arbitrary or unauthorized by law and hence the incorporation of Article 277-A. He sought to further justify his position by pointing out the incorporation of similar provisions in the American and Australian Constitutions.[32] Thus Ambedkar made it quite clear that any intervention by the Union in the provincial affairs would be an act in fulfilment of the constitutional duty and obligation and that it could not be treated as a wanton, arbitrary and unauthorized act.

The above words of Ambedkar reveal that, not with standing the many provisions in the Constitution where the Centre has been given sufficient power to override the states, our Constitution is of federal nature and the States are sovereign with regard to those fields which are left to them. The States are neither satellites nor agents of the Union. But during emergencies and certain other eventualities of that kind, powers of the States are overridden or invaded by the Centre.

The invasions of power under such circumstances, it must be noted, were exceptions and have to be resorted to in order to meet exigencies of the situations and as such there is nothing wrong in concluding that such acts on the part of the Centre do not constitute a normal feature of the Constitution.

In the Constituent Assembly, views were expressed both to support and to oppose Ambedkar. Alladikrishna Swamy Ayyar observed that the primary thing concerning the nation and the union government was to maintain the Constitution. If responsible government as contemplated in the Constitution functioned properly in the provinces, the Union would not and could not interfere. The provision according to him, was not an impediment to the growth of healthy provincial or state autonomy, but a bulwark in its favour because the primary obligation was cast upon the union to see that the Constitution was maintained.[33]

Thakur Das Bhargava, another supporter of the Article was of the view that the provision removed a great lacuna in the Constitution and stated that he was for granting of more powers to the Centre to effectively perform its duties. He asked: "How can a province by itself be able to meet the situation when the use of army and other forces is required by the state".[34]

H.Y Kamath, Naziruddin Ahamad and several others were opposed to the above contention. According to the former, the incorporation of the draft Article would result in the subversion of state autonomy by the Union on the pretext of averting or quelling internal disturbance. He further suggested that the words 'internal disturbance' in the draft Article 277-A should be substituted by "internal insurrection or chaos", since the word disturbance, which is a very wide and elastic term, might be interpreted to range from two people coming to blows to a full-fledged insurrection.[35]

P.S. Deshmukh viewed the Article as a "very intriguing provision" which has no connection whatsoever with any emergency.[36] Naziruddin Ahamad, who almost on all occasions, took a strong provinciality posture was very much critical of Article 277(A) as a record of 'pious wishes' rather than a constructive provision, which lacked clarity and enabled the centre to interfere on the slightest pretext of protecting the State from external aggression and internal disturbance and it might also enable the centre to refuse to interfere on the gravest occasion. He pointed out that "so gracefully guarded is its vagueness so elusive is its craftsmanship that we cannot but admire the Drafting Committee for its vagueness and evasion".[37] He was of the opinion that the Constituent Assembly by inserting draft Article 277-A, was deliberately providing excuses through vagueness of language to interfere with the domestic management of the provinces. Finally, the provision was adopted and Article 277-A was inserted in the draft Constitution.

Draft Article 278 (Now Article 356)

Article 278 of the Draft constitution (now Article 356) is the logical corollary of Article 277(A) (now 355). Being ambiguous and anachronistic, this Article was a bone of contention among the founders of the Constitution. The main supporters of this Article were Alladikrishna Swamy Ayyar, Santhanam Brajeshwar Prasad, T.S. Bhargave and Ambedkar. Ayyar's principal argument was that in view of grave dangers facing the infant republic, some check by the Centre was inevitable so that people might realize their responsibility and work towards responsible government properly.[38] Brajeshwar Prasad, another supporter pinpointed the fact that the forces of disorder and lawlessness were increasing and spreading fast in the country. He observed "I see no harm, no irreparable damage will be done, no wrong done to the people of the country or to the Constitution, if for a short time, for a limited period, the legislative powers as well are vested in the hands of the President".[39]

K. Santhanam, while describing the Article as an important one, wanted that the possibilities of the failure of the constitutional machinery be based on the ground of "physical breakdown", "political breakdown", or "Economic break down". Of course, he did assert that if the Centre acted upon the strict letter of the law, anything might be deemed to constitute a breakdown of Constitution and it was possible that the interference of the centre might be frequent and objectionable. In this context, he stressed the need for healthy conventions as a remedy. He had no doubt in his mind that these would grow and this Article would be utilized for the legitimate purpose for which it was intended.[40]

Some supporters of this provision defended it on another ground, namely danger of secession, which they characterized as a still greater danger than even chaos. It was argued by B.H. Zaidi that the danger of fissiparous tendencies and secession came from the units and not from the centre. He emphatically asked: "Have the various units, not tried to break away from the centre again and again?"[41]

In contrast, the provision appeared to many of the members as the very negation of the principle which they visualised for building up a great democracy. H.V. Kamath, H.N. Hunzru, K.T. Shaw, Shibanlal Saxena, PS. Desmukh etc... vehemently opposed the inclusion of the provision which according to them was virtually a vestige of the colonial rule, in the Constitution of free India. Perhaps the most scathing criticism came from H.V. Kamath. He apprehended that there was a possibility of this Article being used or employed for political purposes on the pretext of resolving ministerial crisis or on the pretext of purifying or reforming maladministration obtaining in a particular state. He even went to the extent of terming it as criminal transaction and informed the Assembly that he foresaw the possible end of democracy in India in the form of Hitler like take-over by the Union Government. According to him, it was dishonest on the part of the Constituent Assembly to say in one article that public order shall be the responsibility of the states and then in another article to confer powers upon the Union Government to intervene in the internal affairs of the state on the slightest pretext of any internal disturbance.[42]

PS. Deshmukh believed that the bestowing of such powers on the President was both impractical and unfederal because it placed too great a burden on Parliament and gave the President authority to override "at his own sweet will the provisions of the Constitution itself".[43] To Hridaynath Kunzru the instability resulting from a large number of political groups in a state legislature would not justify central intervention. He saw the possibility of misuse of the power under the Article. According to him, if the powers were given to the Centre to intervene, there was clear danger and whenever there was dissatisfaction in a State, appeal would be made to the Central government to come to its rescue and the provincial electorate would be able to transfer its responsibility to the central government. This would also, he says, create serious discontent. To him the draft Article was "nothing but the undiluted autocracy of the centre".[44]

Naziruddin Ahamed, another strong opposer, criticized the provision because he saw in the enlarged jurisdiction of the Centre "a drift towards dictatorship" and destruction of provincial autonomy.[45] Shibbanlal Saksena described the power under this provisions as "far too sweeping" thus reducing—if not abolishing "the provincial autonomy to a farce"[46]

At the end of the two days debate, it was clear that the Assembly was going to accept this provision and that it did. To allay the fears and apprehensions raised during the general debate in the Constituent Assembly, Ambedkar stated as follows:

> I do not altogether deny that there is a possibility of these articles being abused or employed for political purposes. But that objection applies to every part of the Constitution which gives power to the centre to override the provinces. In fact I share the sentiments...that the proper thing we ought to expect is that such articles will never be called into operation and that they remain a dead letter. If at all they are brought into operation; I hope the president who is endowed with these powers, will take proper precautions before actually suspending the administration of the provinces. I hope the first thing he will do would be to issue a mere warning to a province that has erred, that things were not happening in the way in which they were intended to happen in the Constitution. If that warning fails, the second thing for him to do will be to order an election allowing the people of the province to settle matters by themselves. It is only when these two remedies fail that he would resort to this article. I do not think that we could

then say that these articles were imported in vain or that the President had acted wantonly.[47]

The above words of Ambedkar testify to the fact that he was not very happy with these drastic provisions. It is evident from what he said while replying to the final debate on the Emergency provisions. He said: "My friends who have spoken against the article will, I hope understand that I am in no sense an opponent of what they have said- In fact, I respect their sentiments very much. All the same, I remain quite unconvinced".[48] However, as he was the chairman of the Drafting Committee he had no option but to go along with the Articles. He had the Government of India, Act 1935 before him, in addition to the reports of various committees appointed by the Constituent Assembly. Moreover, he was required to convince his colleagues in the Drafting Committee about the need for this particular provision in the Constitution.[49] His innate faith in democracy and rule of law enabled him to insist that rules of democracy must be based on justice and fair play. Hence, he underlined the need for giving directions and warning and the necessity of holding election before acting under Article 356.[50]

Thus the concept of Centre's basic power of interference in the provincial field started reappearing constantly in the constitutional history of India from Minto-Moreley Reforms of 1909 onwards. The Montague-Chelmsford Reforms of 1919, the Simon Commission report of 1928, the Report of the Joint Parliamentary Committee on Indian Constitutional Reforms in 1933-34, the Government of India Act of 1935 and the present Constitution widened the concept by carrying it forward. Though Article 356 is not the exact carbon copy of section 93 of the Government of India Act of 1935, the parallelism between these two documents is not merely incidental but of design. Notwithstanding the metamorphosis of section 93 through a number of revocations, modifications, and additions, it still remains the mainstay of the Article 356 and 357 of the present Constitution.

We should take into account the fact that the Indian National Congress became heir to all the advantages and disadvantages of its predecessor, the British Government. Even though the governance of the country passed into the hands of the Indian National Congress, separatist tendencies, fissiparous tendencies, geography, poverty, illiteracy, secessionist forces—everything—remained the same as before or posed even greater problems. The centuries old problems were the same, they had not changed. The complex nature of Indian society and polity provided a fertile ground for disagreement and conflicts between the numerous groups and different regions occupying the land. These problems, sometimes, assumed serious proportions threatening the very unity and integrity of the country. This necessitated strong and at the same time drastic state action to preserve the unity and integrity of the country. The constitutional fathers, who knew this historic reality more than anybody else, recognized the fact that in a grave emergency due to external aggression or internal disturbances the Union must have adequate and even over-riding powers to deal quickly and effectively with any threat to the existence of the nation and also to control and direct all aspects of administration and legislation throughout the length and breadth of the country. The states as such did not possess the capacity or resources to deal with such a situation. Only the intervention and the aid by the Union could give adequate protection to every state in times of emergency[51]

The progenitors of the Constitution were also alive to the fact that several regions of our country had no experience of parliamentary form of Government, and as such failure or break down of the constitutional machinery could never be ruled out as an impossibility. Thus the founding fathers of the Constitution thought that the President must have some powers to deal with such a situation which may pose threat to the unity and integrity of the country and to ensure that the government of every state is carried on in accordance with the provisions of the Constitution.

The above realities of the Indian context acted as a moving

spirit behind the incorporation of this provision in the Constitution of free India.

References

1. Rajeev Dhavan, *President's Rule in the States* (Bombay : N.M. Tripathi, 1979) 14.
2. *Constituent Assembly Debates,* (Hereinafter it is referred to as CAD) Vol. IX, 177.
3. Regional parties like DMK., TDP, Akali Dal and National Conference demanded that the Article be scrapped.
4. Minto Morley suggested that: One seat on the Governor-General's and one on each of the provincial executive councils were in practice reserved for Indian members. All the legislative councils were enlarged and all were given a real and substantial elected element while the provincial legislative councils were also given non-official majority. The right of discussing questions of public interest was also conceded to the councils. This gave members a real opportunity of exercising some influence on questions of administration and finance, and though the executive government was left free to act up on such recommendations as it thought fit, the concession was regarded by persons of insight as perhaps the most important of these changes. (See Rajeev Dhavan 15)
5. Dyarachy was a system of double government. The provincial subjects were divided into two classes : the '*reserved subjects*' and the '*transferred subjects*'. With regard to the reserved subjects the governor exercised control through the executive council and was responsible to the Governor-General in council. The transferred subjects were administered by the Governor and his ministers selected from among the members of the Provincial Legislative Council and were responsible to the latter.
6. Percival Spear, *The Oxford History of Modern India* (Oxford: Clarendon Press, 1965) 343.
7. Section 12 gave Governors, Lieutenant—Governors and chief commissioners the power to return a Bill passed by the provincial legislature to the latter and in certain cases reserve such legislation for the consideration of the Governor General. Section 13 further gave the Governor the power to certify the

passage of a Bill on a Reserved subject which "is essential for the discharge of his responsibility for the subject" and which his legislative council refused leave to introduce or failed to pass. Such a Bill would become an Act after being reserved for consideration by His Majesty-in-council, proviso to section 13(2) also added: provided that, where in the opinion of the Governor-General a state of emergency exists which justifies such action, he may instead of reserving such Act, signify his assent thereto and thereupon the Act shall have such force and effect as aforesaid, subject however to disallowance by His Majesty in Council. Similar provisions were also enacted under section 26 for the central legislature (See *Montague Chelmsford, Report on Indian Constitutional Reforms* (1919)).

8. It may, not be out of place to recall that the genesis of Article 356 goes back to the Simon Commission Report wherein both the phrases viz., "*breakdown of constitutional system*" and "*the government of a province cannot be carried on in accordance with the provisions of the statute*" were used together as though they were linked to one another.

9. *Report of the Indian Statutory Commission (Simon Commission)* (1930) Vol. II, para 65.

10. The White Paper of 1931 observed that .... *if at any time he (Governor) is satisfied that a situation has arisen which renders it for the time being impossible for the Government of the province to be carried on in accordance with the provisions of the Constitution Act, by proclamation to assume to himself all such powers vested in law in any provincial authority as appear to him to be necessary for the purpose of securing that the Government of the province shall be carried on effectively. A proclamation so issued will have the same force and effect as an Act of parliament; will be communicated forthwith to the Governor General and to a Secretary of State and laid before Parliament; will cease to operate at the expiry of six months unless before the expiry of that period it has been approved by Resolutions of both Houses of parliament; and may at any time be revoked by Resolution of both Houses of parliament.* (See *White Paper, proposals for Indian Constitutional Reform,* (1931) para 105, 328.

11. The Joint Parliamentary Committee said: *Lastly, it is proposed to give the Governor power at his discretion, if at any time he is satisfied that a situation has arisen which for the time being render it impossible for the government of the province to be carried on in accordance with the provisions of the Constitution Act, to assume to himself by proclamation all such powers vested in any provincial authority as*

appeared to him to be necessary for the purpose of securing that government of the province shall be carried on effectively. Events in more than one province since the reforms of 1919 have shown that powers of this kind are unhappily not yet unnecessary, and it is soon to predict that even under responsible government their existence will never be necessary. We do not read the White Paper as meaning that Governor, in event of a breakdown of the constitutional machinery, is bound to take over the whole government of the province and administer it himself on his own undivided responsibility. We conceive that the intention is to provide also for the possibility of a partial breakdown and to enable the Governor to take over part only of the machinery of government ...Thus the Governor might, if the breakdown were in the legislative machinery of the province alone, still carry on the government with the aid of his ministers, if they were willing to support him. we are speaking of course of such a case as the refusal of the Legislature to function at all, and merely of lesser conflicts or disputes between it and the governor. (See *Report of the Joint Committee on Indian Constitutional Reform* (1933-34) V.I, para 109, p. 60-61).

12. M.C Setalvad, *Grave Emergency and Emergency arising out of the Failure of the Constitutional Machinery in a State* (Madras: University of Madras, 1965) 14.
13. The importance of the legislative history of the president's Rule provisions, *vis-a-vis* the government of India Act of 1935 has been pointed out by Venkatarama Iyer J. "... *our Constitution was not written on a tabula rasa, that a Federal Constitution had been established under the Government of India Act of 1935 and though that has undergone considerable change by way of repeal, modification and addition it still remains the framework on which the present constitution is built and that the provisions of the constitution must accordingly be read in the light of the provisions of the Government of India Act, 1935" (M.P.V. Sundararamier v. A.P. (1958)* SCR 1422).
14. As a result of extensive discussion of these clauses in the British Parliament certain minor changes were brought about in the original clauses. In the House of Commons, Colonial Wedgwood expressed the fear of abuse of these provisions when he wondered aloud whether a breakdown of constitutional machinery would be real or contrived. S. Hoare another member moved an amendment which would give Parliament the power to extend an emergency for six months at a time subject to a maximum of 3 years. In the House of Lords the Marquess of Zealand moved amendment to continue emergency without parliamentary

approval for twelve months at a time (instead of 6 months), to make computation of three years as a continuous period and to insert a new sub clause to ensure that any legislation enacted by the Governor-General would continue in force even after the proclamation of emergency has been revoked, similar amendments were made in clause 93. These amendments were by and large adopted by both Houses. (See Rajeev Dhavan 27-28).

15. *See Appendix.I.*
16. Jawaharlal Nehru, the then president of the Indian National Congress, mercilessly criticised the nefarious provision of the Act by saying that it was "*a new chapter of slavery to strengthen the bonds of imperialistic domination.* (See Michael Breecher, *Nehru—A political biography,* (London: Oxford University press, 1959) 22. On a different occasion, he wrote, "*it was the old constitutional conflict between an autocratic king and parliament which had so often taken place elsewhere leading to revolution and suppression of the king*". (See Jawaharlal Nehru, *the Discovery of India* (New York: Doubleday and Co., 1960) 285.
17. D.D. Basu, *Commentary on the Constitution of India,* 6th ed.. Vol. O (Calcutta: Kamal Law House, 1990) 11.
18. While the Act of 1919 was in operation in the central province, the Swaraj Party under E. Raghavendra Rao refused office and did not allow any other ministry to function, *thus wrecking the constitution.* In fact, it was to meet such a situation that section 93 was emphatically introduced in the 1935 Act.
19. In 1937 in the Congress ruled eight provinces when the Congress ministries resigned the viceroy declared Section 93 of the Act of 1935. (See Subash C. Kashyap, *History of Parliamentary Democracy,* Delhi: Shipra, 1991), 97). This kind of situation also occurred in Punjab on 4 March 1946 when the coalition ministry headed by Malik Khizar Hyat Khan Tiwane resigned and no alternative ministry could be formed. Central rule was imposed in Bengal simply because a non-confidence motion was tabled by one of the parties in the legislature. This happened when the Chief Minister Fazlul Haq, was induced or forced to resign in March 1943 by the Governor, John Herbert. It was alleged that the resignation was forced upon the Chief Minister owing to want of good relations between the Chief Minister and the Governor. Constitutionally, however, the use of Section 93 after resignation had been tendered could not be said to be improper, because the

Chief Minister had resigned, and, shortly after the imposition *of* Governor's rule it was, in fact, possible to form an alternative ministry under Naziruddin. (See Basu 12).

20. Pandit H.N. Kunzru's explanation for this in the Constituent Assembly is significant. He observed: *"I suppose it was omitted because it was thought to be inconsistent with the new order of things"*. The learned Pandit who gave political reasons for the existence of Section 93 believed that the section was no longer needed as 'antagonisms' between the Government of India and its people no longer existed. (See *CAD*, Vol. IX 156-7).
21. The Constituent Assembly was entrusted with the task of framing a Constitution for India. It was mainly an elected body which represented almost all shades of public opinion. It was constituted with the representatives elected by the popular provincial legislatures and those of the princely states according to a scheme evolved by the British Cabinet Mission in consultation with the leaders of India in 1946. The broad ideological spectrum of the Assembly provided by the Indian National Congress was enlarged by the inclusion of non-congress experts from various disciplines and walks of life. Thus constituted and organized, it settled down to frame a constitution for free Indian in a pragmatic way with a view to ensuring the welfare of the people. The Assembly was first convened on 9 December 1946. (See Shivraj B. Nakade, *Emergency in Indian Constitution, New Delhi: Cosmo, 1990,* 27).
22. See Granville Austin, *The Indian Constitution: Cornerstone of a Nation*

(Madras: OUP, 1966) 210.

23. *The Hindustan Times,* 11 June 1947 Granville Austin, 210.
24. B.N. Rao, the constitutional adviser thrashed out a draft constitution on the basis of detailed discussion of the concerned provisions in the provincial committee and the union committee. (See B. Shiva Rao, ed. *The framing of India's Constitution: Select Documents,* Vol. 3 (Bombay: N.M. Tripathi, 1966) 311.
25. The discussions mainly centerd around the general principles underlying the Constitution especially Federalism and Emergency Provisions.
26. See K.P. Singh, *The Governor in the Constituent Assembly, The Indian Journal of Political Science 26* (1965): 38-39.
27. This view was the product of mature thought and abundant caution, and the framers of the constitution have been justified in their decision when we look at the events in some of the states

during last few years. It would be worthwhile to note here that the Canadian constitution which has a strong centre seems to have influenced the framers in this connection. In Canada, the Governor of the province is appointed by the Governor General and he holds office during the pleasure of the Governor General. (See PL. Mathur, *Role of Governor in Non-Congress States* (Jaipur: Rawat, 1988)
28. The debate took place on 3 and 9 of August 1949. (See *CAD, V.IX 130-180).*
29. *CAD* 132-133.
30. *Ibid.,* 130-180.
31. See the arguments of P.S. Deshmukh, Krishna Swamy Bharathi, Naziruddin Ahamed and Algu Rai Sastri, *(Ibid.).*
32. *Ibid.* 133.
33. *Ibid.* 150.
34. *Ibid.* 169-170.
35. *Ibid.* 135-138.
36. *Ibid.* 147.
37. *Ibid.* 162.
38. *Ibid.* 150.
39. *Ibid.* 170.
40. *Ibid.* 153-54.
41. *Ibid.* 145.
42. *Ibid.* 141.
43. *Ibid.* 146.
44. *Ibid.* 156.
45. *Ibid.* 165.
46. *Ibid.* 142-43.
47. *Ibid.* 177.
48. *Ibid.* 548.
49. T.K. Tope, *Dr. Ambedkar and President's Rule in a State: Some Reflections, Dr. Ambedkar and Empowerment: Constitutional Vicissitudes,* ed. K.I. Vibhute (Poona : University of Poona, 1993) 286-287.
50. As the constitutional expert H.M Seervai points out, his speech does throw some light on the nature of power conferred by the Article 356 on the president First, the Article was meant to be a last resort as Article IV, Section 4 of the U5 Constitution, which requires the United States to guarantees to every state a republican form of government, was to be, and had provided to be, a last resort, secondly, Ambedkar's observation that the President would issue a warning is important because such a warning serves several purposes. It would compel the centre to

specify in what respect the state government was not being carried on in accordance with the constitution. On receipt of the warning, the state government may set things right It may also be able to show mat the warning was based on imperfect information and unreasonable inferences or is otherwise unjustified. The need for giving a warning would show that the power is not arbitrary. Thirdly, the necessity of holding an election before acting under Article 356 emphasis the fact that the President's Rule cuts at the root of parliamentary government to which our country is fortunately committed. (H.M. Seervai, *Constitutional Law of India,* Vol. 3, 4th ed. (Bombay: N.M. Tripathy; 1996) 3088-89.

51. The press in India also came out in support of the new provision. *The Hindustan Times* in one of its editorials wrote: *critics of the provision must remember that in the face of unconstitutional challenge to any authority within the union, the only power in a position to safeguard the states, the Union, and the Constitution is the Central Executive and there is no escape from it. (The Hindustan Times.* 4 August 1949. See Granville Austin 210).

Chapter 3

Article 356: The Operational Orbit

A discussion on the scope of Article 356 should begin with Article 355, which has a great bearing on Article 356 of the Constitution of India. The power conferred on the Union under Article 355 is purposive: the purpose is to ensure that 'the government of a state is carried on in accordance with the provisions of the Constitution'. To make the power of the Union effective, Article 356 enables the President to impose what is commonly known as the President's Rule. Thus it is clear from Article 355 that it is not an independent source of power for interference in the functioning of the state governments but it is in the nature of a justification for the measures to be adopted under Articles 356 and 357.

Article 355: Scope and Ambit

> Article 355 says: "It shall be the duty of the Union to protect every state against external aggression and internal disturbances and to ensure that the government of every state is carried on in accordance with the provisions of the Constitution".[1]

It is worthwhile to note here that neither the Government of India Act of 1935 nor the first draft of the Constitution prepared by the Drafting Committee contained a provision analogous to Article 355 of the present Constitution. It was inserted later on the request of princely states. On the basis of the provisions in the federal Constitutions of U.S. A, Australia and Switzerland, it was argued that the Union should protect the States against external aggression, domestic violence and insurrection. The ingenious suggestion was apparently based on the apprehension of those in power in the Indian States that pressure might be brought to bear on them by democratic forces in the then provinces to introduce responsible government in the Indian States. Presumably, the suggestion was made to prevail upon the centre to deal with such pressure, if and when it manifested itself.[2]. Thus 'they planted the embryo of Article 355' [3] Hence, the seed of the Article 355 can be traced to the retrogressive, anti-people, anti-democratic power statusquoism of the then native princes. The Drafting Committee accepted the suggestions but ingeniously and deliberately and with farsightedness omitted the reference to "request by the state for invocation of central assistance against domestic violence". The Constituent Assembly Debates give no explanation for this omission. But it can be safely concluded that the founding fathers were guided by the American and Australian Constitutions which provided for central intervention into state affairs even without any request by the state concerned.[4]

In short, Article 355 is an afterthought, which was introduced to ensure that the centre has been given authority, by the Constitution itself to interfere in state matters even to the extent of suspending the states normal functioning during times of grave exigencies.

Article 355: Essential Elements

A preliminary analysis of the Article suggests that the Constitution imposes three obligations[5] upon the Union Government in respect of states. They are:

1. The duty of the Union to protect every state against external aggression;
2. The duty of the Union to protect every state from internal disturbance; and
3. The duty of the Union to ensure that the government of the state is carried on in accordance with the provisions of the Constitution.

Provisions in other Constitutions

Other federal Constitutions also contain similar provisions analogous to Article 355 of our Constitution. It would be appropriate and relevant to make a brief discussion of such provisions so as to get a comparative perspective.

1. The Constitution of United States of America

The American Constitution imposes an obligation upon the federal government to guarantee to every State in the Union a republican form of Government, and shall protect each of them against invasion, on application of the Legislature, or of the Executive when the Legislature is not in session or when the legislatures cannot be convened, against domestic violence. On close examination, it would be seen that the provision incorporates three essential elements. They are: (1) Federal guarantee to ensure republican form of government in the States, (2) Protection against invasion, and (c) protection against domestic violence [6] The object of the first part of the clause is to protect the Union against aristocratic and monarchical invasions in its units. However, during the civil war this power was used by the Congress against southern states which attempted to secede by setting up alternative governments in those states.

The guarantee of protection against invasion or external aggression is not of much significance for an invasion of a state will *ipso facto* be an invasion of the Union which will be resisted with 'the entire strength of the nation' as observed by the U.S. Supreme Court. The third clause implies that if the working of a state government becomes impossible owing to domestic violence, the federal government will come to the aid and help of the state authorities with its military forces, if required, only on the application for such aid by the State Legislature or Executive. However, federal interference in the internal affairs of the state without its request is permissible under certain circumstances. In this context, the U.S Supreme Court observed that 'if internal disturbance in any state interfered with the operation of national government itself or the process of federal court or with the movement of inter-state commerce or federal property in danger, the centre can send forces on its own initiative, without waiting for the application of State authorities [7]

The Federal guarantee with regard to the maintenance of republican form of government in the State is similar to the last part of Article 355 i.e. obligation of the Union to ensure that the government in every state is carried on in accordance with the provisions of the Constitution. In the US, the courts have held that 'maintenance of representative form of Government will be sufficient to ensure Republican form of Government.' This is definitely a very restricted interpretation when compared to our situation which encompasses a wider gamut of constitutional obligations. The responsibility for invoking the power guaranteed by the Article vests with the Congress in the case of America while it is vested in the Union executive in the case of India. As regards guarantee against domestic violence a glaring difference is that the power can be invoked in the U.S only on the request of a state Government but in India the power of central interference is allowed even without the request or application for the same by the state.

2. The Constitution of Commonwealth of Australia

A parallel to Article 355 is also found in the Australian Constitution. Section 114 of the Commonwealth Constitution provides that the states shall not, without the consent of Common wealth Parliament, raise or maintain any naval or military force. An obligation to protect the states is therefore reposed in the commonwealth. Section 119 thus provides: The common wealth shall protect every state against invasion and also against domestic violence on application by the executive government of the state[8] As in the case of the Constitution of America, a request from the state concerned is mandatory for the intervention of the Commonwealth in case of domestic violence in the states.

Section 119 of the Australian Constitution is similar to that of Article 355 of the Indian Constitution. As has already been stated, the Article reposes a duty on the Union 'to protect every state against external aggression and internal disturbance'. A similarity between the Australian and Indian provision should be noted. It seems that, the Australian provision is somewhat parallel to the latter part of Article 355 of our Constitution. In India, however, execution and maintenance of central laws are not effected through Article 355.

The Constitution of Switzerland

In Switzerland, the federal authority can intervene on its own initiative if the disorder within the cantons endanger the safety of the nation. Articles 5, 15 and 16 are relevant provisions in the present context[9] Article 5 imposes an obligation upon the Confederation to guarantee to the Cantons their territorial integrity and sovereignty, their Constitution, the liberty and rights of their people....' Article 15 provides that' in case of sudden danger from without, the government of the canton threatened must invoke the assistance of the confederated states and immediately notify federal authority the measures which may subsequently be taken by the latter not being prejudiced thereby. The canton so called upon are bound to give their assistance. The cost shall be borne by the Confederation . Article 16 says that 'in case of internal disorder or danger being threatened from another canton, the government of the canton threatened must immediately notify the Federal Council, in order that the body may take the necessary measures within the limits of its competence, or convene the Federal Assembly. In case of urgency, the cantonal government while immediately notifying the Federal Council, may call for the assistance of the other confederated states, which the latter are bound to render.

A comparative study of the provisions in Switzerland and India reveals striking similarities as well as apparent differences. The most important difference is that in Switzerland when a Canton is threatened from without, it must invoke assistance of other Cantons and they are bound to help. The cost will be borne by the Swiss Confederation. In India interstate assistance in case of external aggression is not envisaged. Again, unlike the Indian Constitution the Swiss Constitution has provided for threats from fellow Cantons also. However, a striking similarity is that like in our Constitution the Federal authority can intervene in its own initiative when there is grave disorder endangering the safety of Switzerland.

Similar provisions are also seen in the Weimar Constitution of Germany 1919. One may also compare our constitutional provisions with the provision of the Weimar Constitution. Article 48 is the relevant provision in the present context.

Article 48(1) provides that: if any state does not perform the duty imposed upon it by the constitution or by national laws, the National President may hold it to the performance thereof by force of arms.

Article 48(2) Says: 'If public safety and order in the German Commonwealth is metrically disturbed or endangered, the national President may take the necessary measures to restore public safety and order, and, if necessary, to intervene the force of arm [10]

In Canada, there is no specific provision in the Constitution in this regard, but in times of national emergency, the federal government may take such action as it may deem necessary under its residuary powers. Similar provisions are also found in the Constitutions of West Germany (1949) and Malaysia (1957).

From the above analysis, it seems that, an important distinction between the American and Australian provisions on the one hand, and the Indian provisions on the other, is that while in America and Australia application by the state to the centre is necessary for the protection against domestic violence, no such conditions is laid down in India. Article 355 does not stipulate that a state should request the centre before it could send its forces into a state to counter the breakdown of law and order. In India, the Union Government is not bound to wait for a request from the states before intervening in the affairs of the units.

The first limb of Article 355 explicitly puts a duty on the Centre to protect the state government in case of external aggression. It is not possible to define precisely the expression "external aggression". The expression is also used in Article 352 in the context of grave emergency. Hence, it is necessary to distinguish between the contextual connotations and the scope of the expression in Article 352 from its use in Article 355. "External aggression" is a valid ground for action under

Article 352 (1), only if it threatens the security of India or any part thereof. If the external aggression is not a gravity calling for action under Article 352 or does not involve a situation of failure of Constitution, then the Union will be competent to take all appropriate steps, other than action under 352 and 356, that it may consider necessary in the fulfilment of its duty under Article 355.

The concept of 'external aggression' takes different shapes and forms. It need not necessarily be an overt act of forcibly crossing the internationally recognised boundaries of India by regular forces of an outside power. It may even be a covert act of sending trained irregulars or agent provocateurs by a foreign country to indulge in acts of sabotage with a view to overthrow the government of any state in India, or by clandestinely and actively supporting with money and material any guerrilla activity or disgruntled section of people in a state etc.[11]

The expression "internal disturbance" also provides a ground for action under Article 356. Article 352 of the Constitution of India which deals with national emergency has originally contained a similar reference. But the 44th amendment initiated by the Janata Government replaced the word "internal disturbance" by "armed rebellion"[12] in Article 352. Internal disturbance is, therefore, no longer a ground for taking action under the Article. The expression "internal disturbance" is certainly of larger connotation than "armed rebellion". In other words, while proclamation of emergency can be made for internal disturbance only if it is created by armed rebellion, neither such a proclamation can be made for internal disturbance caused any other situation nor a proclamation can be issued under Article 356 unless the internal disturbance gives rise to a situation in which "the government of the State is not carried on in accordance with the provisions of the Constitution".[13]

When this provision was introduced in the Constituent Assembly, critics characterised this provision as too vague. This vagueness, it was argued, allowed the President to interfere in provincial matters even when no emergency existed. H.V. Kamath wanted these words substituted with the words "internal insurrection or chaos" as the word disturbance "was very elastic and capable of being interpreted in different ways"[14] He wanted the President to intervene only when the President was satisfied that there was a grave danger to the peace and tranquility of the state and not merely in cases of constitutional breakdown.[15] In the absence of such a limitation, he foresaw the destruction of provincial autonomy by the government on the pretext of averting or quelling internal disturbance.[16] Despite these apprehensions so emphatically expressed by many members, the Constituent Assembly accepted the expression as it stood.

As in the case of external aggression, it is also hard to define what does and what does not constitute internal disturbance. As has been discussed earlier, similar provisions, however, occur in other federal Constitutions as those of Switzerland (internal disorder) and USA (domestic violence) However, the Sarkaria report see it as 'domestic chaos taking the colour of security threat and leading to the breakdown of constitutional machinery of the state. 'Instead of domestic chaos' as is used in other Constitutions, the framers of the Indian Constitution used the expression "internal disturbance". Obviously, they have done so as they intended to cover not only domestic violence, but some thing more.

The scope of "internal disturbance" is relatively wider than that of the expression 'domestic chaos'. It may be man - made or the result of natural calamities. Thus large scale public disorder endangering the security of state is regarded as one such instance of human made internal disturbance. In this regard, satyagraha, a civil disobedience movement, a general strike, a political stir, a mass-upsurge and a unified and concerted effort of a political agitation to paralyze the government to coerce the ministry to resign are not political conditions which amount to and constitute an internal disturbance that warrants the President's emergency rule; or justifies union intervention unless the state government deems it so and invites Union intervention, unable to cope with the situation.[17] The natural calamities of unprecedented magnitude, such as flood, cyclone, earthquake, epidemic etc.... which paralyse the government of the state and put its security in jeopardy are treated as nature -created 'internal disturbance'.

A distinction between 'internal disturbance' and ordinary problems relating to law and order[18] is highly warranted to remove the ambiguity and to avoid its misuse for political convenience. In India, law and order is a state subject, vide Entry 1, List II and it is the responsibility of the state concerned to handle the ordinary problems of law and order, excepting where it requires the use of armed forces of the Union. Section 129 and 130 of the criminal procedure code enable the state to seek the aid of the armed forces of the union to disperse an unlawful assembly. If the Army, the CRPF or the BSF need to be deployed, it ceases to be a state subject.

It is important to note here that Article 257-A, inserted in the Constitution by the 42nd amendment was deleted by 44th amendment. It reads 'the government of India may deploy any armed forces of the Union or any other force subject to the control of the Union for dealing with any grave situation of law and order in any state'. The insertion of this provision in the Constitution raised a flood gate of criticisms. It was interpreted as a move causing domination of the Centre even in the limited autonomy given to the states. As a result, of the clamour for its removal, the 44th amendment deleted Article 257-A from the Constitution but entry 2.A (still remains a part) of list 1, giving legislative and executive powers to take necessary action to deploy armed forces in a state in the aid of civil power. It is now almost agreed, internal disturbance within the contemplation of Article 355 cannot be equated with mere breaches of public peace. In the context of Article 355, the internal disturbance should be of such serious gravity and magnitude that the local government is unable to control it. It should be a case of more serious magnitude than the ordinary breaches of public peace such as affray or riots which can be quelled by police force with the help of the law and order machinery of the state concerned. Therefore, the difference between a situation of public disorder and internal disturbance is not only one of degree but also of kind. While the latter is an aggravated form of public disorder, which endangers the security of the state, the former involves relatively minor breaches of peace of purely local significance.[20] As a matter of fact, what internal disturbance means and when the Union should invoke the said Article is a matter that has been left to the pure discretion of the Union government.[21]

As has already been mentioned, the scope of the Article is very wide and it does not requires the Union to obtain the prior consent of the state government before the exercise of its executive power, nor does it mean that the duty placed on the Union is required to be discharged by the Union only at the request of the state. Entry 2A read with Article 355 empowers the Centre to send its forces on its own accord and deploy them even against the wishes of the state government, provided that the situation is one of 'internal disturbance', 'domestic chaos', or 'armed rebellion'. Any isolated incident or aberration cannot be considered 'breakdown of constitutional machinery'. However, a convention has arisen that ordinarily the Centre sends help to a State on request by the state government. In view of the specific constitutional obligation placed on the Centre, it will be unjustifiable for the Centre to refuse a request for help by the states. But it cannot be ascerted that the Centre never intervenes in the state *suo moto* without its request or against the wishes of the state government.[22] For instance, whenever the internal safety and tranquillity of the state is threatened, the duty-bound Union government will come forward to render aid to the state for the purpose of maintaining public order and protecting the life and property of the people of the state, particularly when the resources of the state governments are not sufficient to cope with the situation of such disturbance. In such situations, irrespective of the fact whether any request from a state for help for the purpose of maintaining peace, tranquillity and public order has been received or not the centre intervenes. Thus, in a sense, it enables the Union government to make interferences in the internal affairs of the state. The Constitution, however, does not specifically state as to how the Centre could discharge its obligation. Obviously, it is left to the judgement of the Union. Ordinarily the Centre should discharge its obligation through advice, assistance in the form of of material and finance and through deployment of armed forces.

In this context, the following well considered observation of the Sarkaria Commission is very pertinent. The Commission recommend that the Centre could not deploy its armed forces in contravention of the wishes of the state government in order to deal with a less serious situation of public disorder which is unlikely to escalate and that the state government is confident of tackling it[23] The Commission, however, held that in the unusual event where a situation is 'fast drifting towards anarchy' or a 'physical breakdown of administration' the Centre may *suo moto* deploy its armed forces to restore public order. In adopting this view, the Commission could foresee the possibility of a state government is both ' unable or unwilling' to suppress an internal disturbance and may refuse ' to seek the aid of armed forces of the Union in this matter' [24] Ordinarily, however, the Commission held that it is desirable to consult the state concerned whenever feasible before deploying its armed forces, otherwise than at the request of the state. In case the armed forces are deployed, the Commission continues, ' the Union government cannot assume the sole responsibility for dealing with an internal disturbance by superseding or excluding the state police and other authorities responsible for maintaining public order[25]. This position is further supported by the Inter State Council which agreed with the Commission that in an emergency situation threatening the country's security prior consultation with the state government concerned before deploying troops there *suo moto* would not possible. However, the Council observed, in other circumstances of domestic trouble, it would be desirable to consult the state concerned as recommended by the Sarkaria commission.

The Commission's and Council's recommendations are the result of a comprehensive and deep study of the history of the deployment of armed forces of the Centre in the past and also of the observation on the criticism of the exercise of that power by constitutionalists, eminent men and politicians on the issue. The past may not repeat itself if their recommendations are followed.

The third limb of the Article 355 casts a duty on the union to ensure that "the government of every state is carried on in accordance with the provisions of the Constitution". This leads us to an in-depth analysis of Art. 356.

Article 356: Import and Ambit

Article 356 reads: "If the President, on receipt of a report from the Governor of a state or otherwise, is satisfied that a situation has arisen in which the government of the state cannot be carried on in accordance with the provisions of the Constitution", the President may by proclamation assume to himself all or any of the functions of the government of the state and all or any of the powers of the state vested in the Governor of the state and declare that the powers of the legislature of the state shall be exercised by the parliament. However, the President is not authorized to assume to himself any of the powers vested in the High Court of the state or to suspend the operation of any provision of the Constitution relating to the High Court.[26]

Before making a detailed study, inorder to provide a proper focus and perspective of this Article a brief Comparison of other two Articles viz. Article 352 and Article 360 with Article 356 is be attempted.

Article 356 differentiated from Article 352[27]

A distinction may be made between Emergency under Article 356 and Emergency under 352. A proclamation of Emergency under Article 352 may be made by the President at any time if he is satisfied that the security of India or any part thereof is threatened by war, external aggression and armed rebellion, while an emergency is proclaimed under Article 356 on the ground of 'breakdown of constitutional machinery in a state. The essential difference between these two provisions in the Constitution were explained by Dr. Ambedkar in the Constituent Assembly. He pointed out thus:

> "I should like, first of all, to draw the attention of the house to the fact that the occasions on which the two sets of Articles will come into operation are quite different. Article 275 limits the intervention of the Centre to a state of affairs

> when there is war or aggression internal or external. Article 278 refers to the failure of the machinery by reason other than war or aggression. Consequently the operative clauses, as I said, are different. For instance, when a proclamation of emergency has been issued under Article 275 you get no authority to suspend the provincial Constitution. The provincial Constitution would continue in operation. The Legislature will continue to function and possess the powers which the Constitution gives it; the Executive will retain its executive powers and continue to administer the province in accordance with the law of the province. All that happens under Article 276 is that the centre also gets concurrent power of Legislation and concurrent power of administration. This is what happens under Article 276. But when Article 278 comes into operation the situation would be totally different. There will be no legislature in the provinces because the legislature would have been suspended. There will be practically no executive authority in the provinces unless any is left by the proclamation by the President or the Parliament or by the Governor. The two situations are quite different. I think it is essential that we ought to keep the demarcation which we have made by component words of Article 275 and Article 278. I think mixing the two things up would cause a great deal of confusion.[28]

An incisive observation of the speech of Ambedkar, and a detailed analysis of the relevant constitutional provision reveal that when a proclamation is made under Article 352 the State government cannot be suspended. The State legislature and State executive continue to function normally and exercise all the powers assigned to them under the constitutional provision. The only effect is that the Centre gets the concurrent power of legislation and administration in the State matters and thus it can make the State to follow a uniform policy through out India. In a proclamation under Article 356, on the other hand, the state government is dismissed and the state Legislature is either dissolved or kept in a state of suspended animation. Further, the executive as well as the legislative powers of the state are exercised by the Centre.

Another point of difference is that under Article 352, the relationship of all the states with the Centre undergo a change whereas in the case of Article 356 the relationship of the concerned states with the centre alone is affected. The effect of proclamation under Article 352 are vast when compared to a proclamation made under Article 356. Furthermore, the initial tenure of operation of a proclamation without the parliamentary approval is one month in the case of National Emergency whereas it is two months in the case of breakdown of constitutional machinery in states.

Article 356 and Article 360

Article 360[29] of the Constitution provides that if the President is satisfied that a situation has arisen whereby financial stability or credit of India or any part of India is threatened, he can declare Financial Emergency. The ground of issuance of proclamation under Article 356 is broad and exhaustive while compared to the ground of issuance of proclamation under 360 which is specific and narrow. The power of the President under Article 360 is confined to the issuance of directives to the state concerned as regards to financial prosperity and to the giving of such other directions as the President may deem necessary and adequate for the purpose. In the case of Emergency under Article 356 the President can exercise wide powers which includes the power to assume to himself the functions of the Governor or state Government authorities excluding the legislative power, power to grant the Parliament authority to legislate for the state and the power to suspend the provisions of the Constitution with regard to that state.

Article 356 of the Constitution of India is a provision un paralleld. Constitution of no other country contains a similar provision though other federal states like United States and Australia have an obligation to ensure that the constitutional provisions are followed. The only other Constitution that includes a somewhat similar provision is the 1973 Constitution of Pakistan, vide, Article 58(2) b [30] and 112(2) b. Under these provisions, the President/Governor can in his discretion dissolve the National/Provincial Assembly and dismiss the National/Provincial ministry if in his opinion a situation has arisen in which the government of the federation/ province cannot be carried on in accordance with the provisions of the Constitution and an appeal to the electorate is necessary Both these provisions appear to be inspired by Sections 45 and 93 of the Government of India Act of 1935.

A perusal of Articles 58(2) b and 112 (2) b of the Constitution of Pakistan and our Article 356 (1) will reveal similarities as well as differences. The most striking similarity is with regard to the justification or ground for invoking this provision. In both the Constitutions, the justification is the same. The Constitution of Pakistan goes on to add a further ground expressly that an appeal to the electorate is necessary. As such, what is implicit in our Constitution is made explicit in their Constitution.

Regarding differences, the first aspect is about the President's mode of functioning. Under Article 58(2) b of the Pakistan Constitution, the President exercises this power in his own personal discretion. This is not the position under our Constitution. Under Article 356, the President has to act in accordance with the advice of the cabinet. The second distinguishing feature is that the Pakistan Constitution provides for declaration of emergency at the central and provincial levels by the President and the Governor respectively. The Indian Constitution contemplates only an emergency at the state level but that is proclaimed by the President.

In the final analysis, it can be stated that Article 356 is truly a unique and extraordinary provision unparalleled in the history of federal Constitutions.

A close scrutiny and analysis of clause (1) of Article 356 suggests the following ingredients:

1. A report from the Governor of the state;
2. "or otherwise" than the Governor's Report;
3. The President must be satisfied;
4. Breakdown of constitutional machinery in a state.[31]

In order to get a proper focus on the orbit of its operation a brief analysis of each ingredient becomes imperative.

A Report from the Governor

We have seen that the Constitution of India in its Article 355 casts an obligation upon the government at the Centre to ensure that the government of every State is carried on in accordance with the provisions of the Constitution. It has no agency in the state other than the Governor, to keep it informed of the happenings and to see whether the government is being carried on as per the directions of the Article. Here comes the role of the Governor in the declaration of Article 356 in a state. He is duty bound to see that the government of the state is being carried on in accordance with the constitutional provisions and when he discovers that the state government is not functioning in accordance with the Constitution, it is his duty to report the matter to the President of India. Thus the functions of the Governor in terms of Article 356 comes in only when he sends a report to this effect to the President.[32]

Normally, the first and foremost requirement of any action under Article 356 is the said report of the Governor. This practice is democratic, and of significance since it has transferred the responsibility back to the Governor from the President.

The Indian Constitution, which envisages the parliamentary system of government, makes it obligatory on the part of the Governor to exercise all his powers and functions in accordance with the advice of the Council of ministers. The Constitution does not say that sending of the report by the Governor in this connection is a function to be exercised in his discretion. Nevertheless, it is obvious that the Governor has to act on his own judgment in sending his report to the President on the breakdown of the constitutional machinery of the state concerned. This position is justified by the Governor's Committee Report thus:

> "Occasion may arise when the Governor may find that in order to be faithful to the Constitution and the law and his oath of office, he has to take a particular decision independently"[33]

Eminent constitutional authorities like D.D. Basu and H.M. Seervai seem to share this observation. "The reason is that" Basu justified, "as a result of such a report, if adverse, the state Government itself would be suspended, so that the Governor's Council of ministers cannot be expected to sign their own death warrant".[34]

H.M. Seervai is of the view that the Governor will be justified in making such a report to the President even contrary to the advice of his ministry as such a report might show that the ministry itself was responsible for the breakdown of constitutional machinery in the state.[35] This position is further endorsed by the Supreme Court in the following words:

> "Under Article 356, the Governor exercises real rather than formal powers, relating to the breakdown of the constitutional machinery in a state. When he makes a report in this regard, he has obviously to act in his discretion. The Chief Minister who is to be affected by this report, cannot be expected to advise the Governor to recommend his own dismissal to the President".[36]

All these observations clearly indicate the fact that the Governor can do it in his discretion. By the very nature of the function, it cannot be exercised on the advice of his ministry for it may very often happen that the report itself may be a condemnation of the Council of Ministers that the government run by the Council of ministers is no longer capable of being conducted in accordance with the Constitution. However, these discretionary powers do not affect the normal position that like the President of India, the Governor must act on the advice of the Council of ministers.

However, the Article does not mention specifically whether the report should be a "speaking one" or "non-speaking one". It is obvious that such report should be a speaking one, furnishing facts clear and specific and not vague so as to satisfy the President whether or not a situation contemplated in the Article has arisen. It should essentially contain the material facts and circumstances which are relevant to assess the situation and leading to a particular satisfaction. As the Sarkaria

Commission rightly observes:

> "We should emphasize that such a report of the Governor should be a speaking document containing a precise and clear statement of all material facts and the ground on the basis of which the President may satisfy himself as to the existence or otherwise of the situation contemplated in Article 356".[37]

In 'Remeswar Prasad and others v. Union of India', the Supreme Court observed that in the absence of relevant material much less due verification, the report of the Governor has to be treated as the personal *ipse dixit* of Governor. The drastic and extreme action under Article 356, the Court said, can not be justified on mere *ipse dixit*, suspicion, whims and fancies of the Governor.[38] The court demanded the Union government to verify such report by the Governor before accepting it as a gospel truth. It is now a well settled principle that no satisfaction can reasonably be formed by an authority on vague facts or report. In his report, the Governor should act truthfully with a high degree of constitutional responsibility in terms of oath and inform the President that the government of the state cannot be carried on in accordance with the constitutional provisions. When challenged in the constitutional Court, it gives an insight into the satisfaction reached by the President. The Governor, therefore, owes constitutional duty and responsibility in sending the report with necessary factual details.[39] If the report is non-speaking one, it would amount to satisfaction of the Governor and not that of the President regarding the existence of a situation in a state. Therefore, the Governor should be very cautious in making the report. He is supposed to act fairly and honestly consistent with his oath. It is for this reason that Article 356 places such implicit faith in his report. If, however, in a given case, his report is vitiated by legal *mala fides*, it is bound to vitiate the President's action as well. Therefore, the underlying assumption of the Constitution is that the incumbent of the office of the Governor must not only be imbued with qualities of perception, judgment, fact and initiative, but also be objective and fair in making his report on the point whether President's Rule should or should not be imposed.[40] What is important to remember is that the Governor should be an impartial constitutional authority and his acts and decisions should be seen from the constitutional point of view.

The intention, farsightedness and constitutional insight of the founding fathers of the Constitution to have insisted on the report of the Governor of the state concerned for its dismissal on the plea of it being on the brink of a constitutional breakdown cannot but be admired. Rendering the dismissal of the state government contingent upon the Governor's report, the founding fathers have provided for a prophylaxis against the misuse of the provision by the powers that be. The Sarkaria Commission rightly observes:

> Normally, President's rule in a state should be proclaimed on the basis of the Governor's report under Article 356(1). The practice will operate not only as a check against arbitrary or hasty exercise of this extraordinary power but also save the Union-government from embarrassment in case of an error. It will also protect them against an unwarranted accusation of malicious dismissal or suspension of the state government. The Union government is accountable for its action to the parliament. If the proclamation of the President's Rule is questioned on the ground of its being *mala fide* or otherwise, the union government can dispel that charge on the ground that it has acted in good faith on the basis of the Governor's report.[41]

This shows that the power of the Governor under Article 356 assumes great significance. Being a man on the spot, he possesses direct and first hand knowledge of the functioning of the government. In this regard, he emerges from his ceremonial shell and reports to the President with great authority as the agent of the Union government. As mentioned in the judgment of Bommai case, the Governor is like a person wearing two hats, with one hat, he is the head of the state government and with the other, he is a representative of the President.[42]

Rajeev Dhavan, a distinguished constitutional expert, writes: "The Governor's power to recommend and the President's power to impose central rule when there is the failure of the constitutional machinery of the state must simply be abolished. It is not necessary except as a tool of oppression by the centre".[43] But there are many instances of the Governors acting more as agents of political parties, with whom they have close connections, than as the constitutional head of the state.[44] Political parties ruling at the centre have often tried to extort a report in favour of a state government's dismissal from the Governor by using the 'carrot and stick policy' to gain political mileage. The recommendation of the Kerala Governor to dismiss EMS ministry in 1959, Governor Sampuranand's high-handedness in not allowing an opposition ministry in Rajasthan in 1967, the report of Governor Venkatasubhayya to dismantle the Bommai ministry in Karnataka 1989, Governor S.S. Bandari's action in engineering Rabari Devi's downfall in Bihar in 1999 and in more recently in 2005 Governor Butasingh's refusal to allow a NDA government in Bihar are only a few examples which bear testimony to the statement referred to above. The gubernatorial post often being a gift from the ruling party at the centre to its loyal servants, many Governors find themselves under pressure to act as stooges of the centre to keep it in good humour and ensure their political survival.

There are instances to show that if any Governor wills not to yield to undue pressure by the Centre and prepares his report objectively his report is rejected indiscriminately and he is either transferred from states to states or removed from office.[45] For instance, the Kashmir Governor B.K. Nehru who did not dare to play second fiddle to subvert Farooq Abdulla was transferred to Gujarath. The Tamil Nadu Governor Surjeet Singh Burnala was transferred to Bihar for not sending a report for dismissing Chief minister M. Karunanidhi. (It was alleged that, not without substance, the then ruling parties - Congress and AIADMK- felt that Burnala was not suited during President's Rule following his refusal to send a favourable report for the dismissal.) Burnala submitted his resignation because he did not want to become a tool for another possible

President's Rule in Bihar also. On the very same day, Bihar Governor Yunus Saleem was removed from his position because he had earned displeasure of the centre for criticising the imposition of President's Rule in Tamil Nadu in an address to the joint session of the Bihar Legislative Assembly and Council.[46] (He, however, later disclosed that he was asked by Prime minister Chandra Sekhar and certain other central ministers to send a favourable report for the dismissal of the Chief minister Lalu Prasad Yadav). The Nagaland Governor M.M. Thomas was recalled because he had dissolved the Legislative Assembly on the recommendation of the Chief minister without Delhi's green signal. (The Governor defended his action on the ground that 'when a Chief minister of a majority government recommends dissolution of the House, the Governor is bound to approve it'. 'The Centre', he said, 'was manipulating the state on its own whims which might create serious problems'). Like wise, Goa Governor Bhanu-Prathap Singh was unseated from office in 1994 when he dismissed the Congress Chief Minister and recommended imposition of President's rule when the Congress party faced a leadership crisis. Thus Dharmavira, the former Bengal Governor, was right when he said 'Governors generally had functioned objectively, but they have been guided by the wishes of the powers that be at the centre'. 'How', he asked, 'can Governor act independently when he hold office at the pleasure of the majority in power at the Centre'?[47]

In the light of the above study one cannot but agree that no institution or constitutional office has suffered greater erosion or degradation than the office of the Governor.[48] What makes this constitutional position controversial is not the provision contained in the Constitution but the man who interpret those provision to suit his own political, personal and selfish interests. This practice has undermined the value of the institution, accepted parliamentary norms and democratic processes. Actually, this is not a problem of Centre-State relations only. It is a vital political question between the Centre and the Governor on the one side and the states with elected representatives and responsible ministries and people on the other. What is nullified here is the democratic process in the states, the growth of healthy conventions and the principles of federalism.

The changing political scenario has largely contributed to this state of affairs. During the fifties and early sixties, Indian democracy could keep the pristine purity of the Governorship intact. What made it possible might have been the single party rule that prevailed at the Centre and in the states. However, the fourth general elections which were to inspire many significant changes, signalled the very end of one party domination both at the Centre and in many States. The deterioration and misuse of this power vested in the Governors began from this period. The frequent rise and fall of coalition governments, the split in the Congress party and the assumption of power by Indira Gandhi, all these accelerated the process of disintegration which had set in.[49]

The potentialities of a constitutional office, whether found good or bad in the process of its operation, in the changing situation, have to be sought not only in the changing situations but also very often, more significantly, in the genesis of the office and in the ideology and intention of those who created the office. The founding fathers of the Constitution undoubtedly envisaged a very strong centre and they preferred to call the newly independent Indian states as the Indian Union. That is why they thought that the new states should have only a semi-federal structure. Neither the Congress nor any other party or combination of parties which has come to power either in the union or in the states has so far envisaged for India a full fledged federal structure or a loose federation or a confederation with the rights for the federating units to secede from the union. Naturally, the framers or parties referred to above (when they were in power) would like to control the state governments as and when necessary, if in their opinion, the government of the state goes against the constitutional provisions. They had reason to believe that this is possible in a constitutional way only by providing a constitutional and thus a legitimate functionary as the agent of the centre. Formally, such an agent should be a constitutional head of the state appointed by the Centre, continuing in office on the pleasure of the Centre, primarily and ultimately responsible to the Centre and constitutionally not responsible to the States. The ingenuity and foresightedness of the founding fathers of the Constitution and the fool proof way in which they have provided for such an office can not but be admired. They have also provided for not questioning the action of the Governor in any court of law. Politics means power and any political party in power in the Union is likely to be influenced by its political interest and this will reflect in the actions of Governors. Only this much has happened in India before and after 1967. After 1967, the party in power at the Centre found itself in such a situation that if it wanted to remain in power in various states, constitutional provisions with regard to the office and functions of the Governor should be interpreted so as to suit them. Here, of course the political party doing it may lose its image or political legitimacy. But in a political situation, where there is no strong opposition to challenge the ruling party in the union, the arbitrariness of the interpretation of the constitutional provision would became absolutely undemocratic and the craze for power may ultimately lead to disintegration of that party.

Since 1980, however, there took place a different course to this trend. Whenever the Centre tried to dismiss the State governments for political prejudice and political gain, the opposition state governments offered strong resistance. Continued political struggle put forward by the opposition led to some restraint and even corrected the wrong decisions of the Governors also. Infact, the reinstatement of N.T. Rama Rao in A.P in 1984 and Wilfred Desuza in Goa in 1998 were the result of this continued struggle. Now, it becomes quite clear that though the Centre has sweeping powers, it has to act with restraint and caution. Opposition to the wrong decisions of the centre and its agents at the states would lead to political struggles and legal clashes. But still the Governors continue to act as the spade of the Centre, often blocking the state governments' functioning. Therefore, it is time to review the situation with a view to making it more harmonious. It is also clear that the Governor should not work against a state government, as he is only a nominee and the government is elected by the people. So if he stands against the wishes of the ministry, he is working against the people and it becomes undemocratic. This situation in which the head of the state becoming anti-democratic warrants a rethinking about his position and role. This rethinking should concentrate on his appointment, security of tenure and post retirement inducement that might prejudice the Governor's behaviour.

The first requirement in this direction is that the appointment to this independent constitutional office must be insulated against political prejudices. The Sarkaria Commission rightly observes:

> "In all the evidence before us, a common threat is that much of the criticisms against the Governors could have been avoided if their selection had been made on correct principles to ensure appointment of right type of persons as Governors. Even the most critical of the witnesses agree that if proper persons are chosen, there will be little cause of complaints".[50]

The cardinal fact is that Governorship has more political than legal dimensions, and as such, those who have clear political inclination should not be appointed as Governors [51] More important, the practice of appointing defeated, aged and tired politicians (as Governors) should stop. 'If political federalism is to survive', writes Rajeev Dhavan, 'there is need for the appointment of good statesmen as Governors'[52] There are many recommendations, and suggestions concerning the appointment of Governors. In this context, the Sarkaria Report has given ambitious suggestions. While discussing the criteria to be followed in the selection of the Governors, the Commission suggested that it is 'desirable' that a politician belonging to the ruling party at the centre is not appointed as Governor of a state run by some other party or parties. Another commendable recommendation by the Commission is that to ensure effective consultation with the state Chief ministers in the selection of the Governor the consultation procedure should be prescribed in the Constitution itself by suitably amending Article 155. Another suggestion of the commission is that the Vice-President of India and the Speaker of Lok Sabha may be consulted by the Prime-minister, in selecting a Governor. The Commission emphasis that such consultation should be confidential and formal and should not be a matter of constitutional obligation.[53] These suggestions even if adhered to, may not introduce any qualitative difference and as such of very little value. The Prime minister's Political interests are not likely to be challenged by the Vice-president and the Speaker equally when the former is strong and popular.

The independence of the office is equally nullified by the uncertainties surrounding the tenure as Krishna Iyer. J. pointed out: 'The ever present apprehension of the tenure being terminated at any time creates insecurity, impairment of capacity to withstand pressure and emergence of boneless wonders ready to carry out at the behest of the centre.'[54] H.M. Seervai believes that the exercise of the power to remove or transfer a Governor must cause grave disquiet in the public mind.[55] L.P.Singh is of the view that functioning with the apprehension of dismissal or transfer ... without willing consent' may make it difficult for the Governor to function with complete impartiality as an independent constitutional authority'[56] If the Governors are not allowed to exercise independence in their actions democracy cannot take its taproot in India.

The Sarkaria Commission's suggestions regarding the tenure of the office of the Governor are also realistic. The Governor's term of five years in a state, say the Commission, 'should not be' disturbed except very rarely and that too, some extremely compelling reasons. In case of termination, the Commission demands, the Governor should be informally apprised of the situation and the explanation of the Governor, if any, should be obtained by the president and examined by an advisory group consisting of the Vice President of India and the Speaker of Lok Sabha or retired Chief Justice of India. The President may take his decision after receiving their recommendation. Further, when a Governor resigns or is transferred or has his tenure terminated before the expiry of five years, the Union government may lay a statement before both Houses of the Parliament explaining the issue. The statement may include the explanation of the Governor when he was given an opportunity to show cause against the premature termination of his tenure.[57] The recommendation of the Commission on the tenure of office of the Governor will be a guarantee against premature termination, and frequent transfer of Governors. Moreover, the statement laid before the Parliament makes the Union government answerable and accountable to the legislature and this will prevent hasty action for party interests. Thus these recommendations on the whole are pragmatic, imaginative and democratic in spirit. In the final analysis, it can be stated that Governors hold office during the pleasure of the President and, therefore, they should not be transferred or removed for political reasons. They can be recalled only if they found guilty of violating the constitutional provisions.

Further, post retirement inducements induced the Governors to act as lackeys of the Centre, responsible only to the Centre. It has increased the possibility of Governors aspiring for post retirement enticement. A dispassionate revisit is needed to debar the Governors from accepting an office of profit and returning to active politics after retirement. Regarding post retirement inducement the Sarkaria's observation is equally valid and fair. The Commission rightly observe:

> The Governor, on demitting his office, should not be eligible as a matter of convention for any other appointment except for a second term as Governor or election as Vice President of India and he shall not return to active politics.[58]

The views of the Commission on the eligibility of further offices of a Governor have to be followed strictly to hold the dignity of the office. These recommendations have been concurred by the NCRWC in its report submitted to the Government of India. These suggestions, if accepted and practised, will go a long way against the Governor becoming a tool in the hands of the Union government and, there fore, it is necessary that they are seriously debated nationwide with a sense of urgency. However, a second term as Governor or election as Vice President or President is really tempting. Needless to say, Governor as a dignified constitutional functionary who has to act as a balance wheel in the discharge of his multifarious duties, has to be kept away from post retirement inducement.

What is important to remember is that recourse to Article 356 should be the last resort for the Governor to seek'.[59] According to the Sarkaria Commission, it is necessary for the Governor to explore all possibilities to have a government which enjoys majority in the Assembly. If this is not possible and fresh elections can be held without avoidable delay, he should ask the outgoing ministry to continue as 'caretaker' government, provided the ministry was defeated solely on a major policy issue, and not on any allegations of maladministration or corruption and is agreeable to continue. The Governor should then dissolve the Assembly, leaving the resolution of the constitutional crisis to the electorate. In the absence of this important ingredient, it would not be proper for the Governor to dissolve the Assembly and install a caretaker government. The Governor should recommend President's Rule without dissolving the Assembly.[60]

The Governor should not only be neutral but also seem to be neutral.[61] He must be an acceptable person with an active habits and sympathetic view, as K.V Rao observed. Much depends upon the political integrity of the Governor He should not allow himself to be misled by the vested interests. "A Governor can do a great deal of good if he is a good Governor and he can do a great deal of mischief if he is a bad Governor, in spite of the very little power given to him under the Constitution.[62] The discretionary powers of the Governor should not lead to the butchering of duly elected governments, as it would hasten the death of democracy.[63]

Clause, 'or otherwise' in Article 356

Article 356 provides that the satisfaction of the President may derive either from the report of the Governor 'or otherwise'. The words or otherwise' has given rise to an idea that the President can even form his satisfaction in all cases without the report of the Governor also.[64] This is justified in view of the obligation of Centre under Article 355. In view of the ultimate responsibility of the state, the framing fathers of the Constitution thought that it was proper not to restrict and confine the action of the Centre merely to Governor's report. Sometimes the Governor might not make a report. The President can act even without the Governor's report, if he is satisfied that such events call for the exercise of special responsibility placed upon the Centre to maintain the state under the Constitution, have occurred in a state.

The provision of the clause, however, makes even the report of the Governor unessential. The satisfaction of the President can be arrived at otherwise. It suggests that the President may get information from other sources or agencies as well. It is an extra precaution. However, it seems that the report of the Governor is almost binding and 'or otherwise' clause is subject to some specific contingencies making the Governor fail in his duty.

The words "or otherwise" can be interpreted in two ways:[65] First, it may mean that even if the President does not receive a report from the Governor, he is competent enough to assess the situation himself. Secondly, it may also be interpreted to mean that even on receipt of a report from the Governor, the President is free to accept or reject the recommendations to promulgate the President's Rule. In other words, the President may act 'otherwise' than the report of the Governor, in either of the two ways. Thus theoretically, the word otherwise shifts the whole burden of responsibility from the Governor's shoulders to those of the President and the Governor's role appears to pale into insignificance.

It is politically and constitutionally significant to note that as the provision was originally drafted at the time of the framing of the Constitution, the Article merely provided that the President would act on the report made by the Governor. The words 'or otherwise' were not there. Subsequently, Ambedkar moved an amendment according to which, under Article 278, as the Article was then numbered, the President could, if he felt that his intervention was necessary, act even when there was no report for this purpose made by the Governor. It might be salutary to reproduce the words of Ambedkar here:

> Now, it is felt in view of the fact that Article 227-A (now Article 355) imposes, a duty and an obligation upon the centre, it would not be proper to restrict and confine the actions of the President, which would undoubtedly be taken in the fulfilment of his duty, to the report of the Governor of the province. It may be that the Governor does not make a report...I think, as a necessary consequence to the introduction of Article 277-A, we must give liberty to the President to act even where there is no report by the Governor and when the President has got certain facts within his knowledge, on which he thinks he ought to act in the fulfilment of his duty. The width of the power is very wide. The satisfaction of the President must be based on relevant material.[66]

When this amendment was placed in the Constituent Assembly, there ensued a long and heated debate. H. V Kamath and others took a serious objection since, in their opinion, this would undermine the position of the Governor and also give the President wide powers. When he described the action of the President even without the report of the Governor as criminal, another member asked what was the crime there in. He there upon replied 'it is a constitutional crime to empower the President to interfere not merely on the report of the Governor or ruler of a state, but other wise'. He also condemned it as mischievous and diabolic. In his own words:

> "Otherwise is a mischievous word. It is a diabolic word in this context and I pray to God that this will be deleted from this Article. If God does not intervene today, I am sure that at no distant date He will intervene when things take a more serious turn and the eye of every one of us are more awake than they are today.[67] He warned that:"

We are laying ourselves upon to snare and traps in our path wherein we shall be caught beyond any rescue.[68]

Saxena was of the view that the words 'or otherwise' must be taken away because there was no justification for the President to interfere with a state until at least the Governor, who was his own nominee, had reported to him. Such a power according to him, 'would reduce provincial autonomy of the state to a farce'. P.S. Deshmukh was another member who did not agree to the conferment of power on the President to interfere in the administration of a state without the report of the Governor of that state. Such a provision, according to him, was not in conformity with federation, nor was it likely to be administratively beneficial or even practicable.[69]

Strong views were also expressed in favour of its inclusion. For instance, Thakur Das Bhargava observed that the clause 'or otherwise' denoted the affairs in which the Governor might not be doing his duties, or might give a wrong report. "If that premise is correct", he asked, "whatever manner the President may come to know, it is the duty of the Centre to interfere".[70] Arming the President with such power was, according to B.H Zaidi, necessary in the light of our historic past and in the light of fissiparous tendencies on the part of units to break away from the Centre. He, therefore, insisted that instead of being critical and putting the most unwarranted suspicion at the door of our would be Presidents of the future, we should take the historical tendencies into consideration.[71] Raj Bahadur was also in favour of granting liberty to the President to interfere in the affairs of the state without a report from the Governor, if there was breakdown of constitutional machinery in the state. He was of the view that there was no reason for us to distrust our Presidents, who were to be elected by us and were empowered to act under Article 278. Such power, according to him, was necessary to safeguard democracy and freedom.[72] In the same way, Alladi Krishna Swami Iyer could not find any justification in taking exception to the use of the words 'or otherwise' in Article 278.

Even in the case of the report from the Governor, the President acts on the advice of the cabinet. So the words 'or otherwise' have been inserted to include any situation where the Governor does not send a report, whatever may be the reasons, and the Centre may yet feel its intervention has become necessary.[73] In this regard, "the Constitution makers have made the duty and obligation of the Centre to maintain the Constitution unequivocal". by foreseeing the possibility of a conflict of the Governor, though a nominee of the Centre, with the Centre. This is the sweeping and wide connotation and scope attributed to the word otherwise in Article 356. They were not unaware of the situation in which the Centre being in conflict with the Governor or if the centre is satisfied to take emergent and inevitable action where waiting for the report of the Governor could be irretrievably late. The result of the introduction of these words, no doubt, in substance, leaves the door open for the Central government to gather its information as to the condition in regard to the government of the state from any source as it pleases.

What are the sources from which the President, receives information of the failure of the constitutional machinery in a state apart from the report of the Governor? Possibly, this 'or otherwise' may be Union agencies, such as the report of some union ministers or advice of the Union Council of Ministers or the Prime Minister himself. Central intelligence, members of the central legislature belonging to the states concerned, disgruntled politicians of the state with some kind of vested interests, and even the antagonistic party in power at the centre may also belong to this group in the practical sense.

Whether Courts can recommend President's Rule

A vital question arose: whether the constitutional court can direct the President of India a recourse to Article 356 under the 'otherwise' clause when the court came to the conclusion that there has been a breakdown of constitutional machinery in the state. The High court of Kerala was called upon to consider this question touching upon judicial control of President's Rule in the states. In this case the petitioner prayed the court to issue a writ of *mandamus* to the President for the imposition of President's Rule in the state of Kerala. Dismissing the petition the bench consisting of Malimath C.J. and Baskaran-Nambiar J. said that 'an Emergency was a matter on which the President of India had to be satisfied under Article 356 of the

Constitution'. The court also added that 'no case had made out for the issue of direction to the union of India and the Prime-minister to consider whether there was a breakdown of constitution in the exercise of its jurisdiction under Article 226'.[74]

In 1987, the Andhra Pradesh High court had to deal with a similar situation. A writ petition containing serious allegations against Chief Minister N.T. Raman Rao, and alleging a breakdown of the constitutional machinery was filed. The Court was called upon to decide whether Article 356 should be invoked. The full bench observed that 'for the purpose of Article 356(1) of the Constitution the satisfaction regarding the existence of the situation in the state is that of the President of India and this court cannot encroach upon the constitutional functions of the President of India'. The court said that the imposition of President's Rule was a matter entirely within the jurisdiction of the President and in the result mandamus was refused.[75] The Court observed;

> The question concerning the imposition of President's Rule is a matter entirely within the jurisdiction of the President of India, who may act upon the advice tendered to him by the Union government. There are no grounds to think that the Union government is unaware of what has been happening in the state or that the Union government failed to take any action even though it is satisfied that conditions existing in the state justifies the imposition of President's Rule. While we refuse to give any directions to the Central government in the terms prayed for by the petitioner, we have no doubt that the representation filed by the petitioner as well as the details set out in this judgment will receive consideration of the Central government and an appropriate decision will be taken.[76]

A Major break through in this regard came in the Samyukt Nagrik Samiti case in 1999. In this case the Patna High court held that the High courts are competent to give advice to the President for the declaration of President's Rule by virtue of 'Otherwise' clause in the Article 356 of the Constitution. The court in its observation in this case opined that various irregularities committed in the employment programme under Jawaharlal Rozgar Yojna in Sahabganj district of Bihar, as opined by the comptroller and Auditor General of India, made it appear that the state of affairs was ripe for the President to invoke Article 356 of the constitution and dismiss the state government on the ground of breakdown of constitutional machinery in the state. M. Lal CJ. and A.K. Sigh J. declared that recommendations of the Governor was inconclusive regarding invocation of the Article and the High Court was also competent to report to the President on the situations in the state. The Court went further and said that any constitutional authority including High court was competent to bring to the attention of the President the sordid state of affairs obtaining in a state [77]

The Supreme Court's observation in 2007 stirred another debate in this regard. The Court in an oral observation said that the Court would 'recommend to the President to dismiss the DMK Government in Tamil Nadu.' The Court made this observation as a response to the allegation of AIADMK Counsel that the Supreme Court restraining order on a bandh on the Sethusamundram issue in Tamil Nadu was not being 'obeyed in letter and spirit' by the DMK Government headed by M. Karunanidhi. During the Course of hearing on a special leave petition filed by the AIADMK challenging the Madras High court order declining to interfere with the bandh, Agarwal J. breezily observed: 'if what you say is true, then there is a complete breakdown of constitutional machinery in the state. We will recommend to the President to dismiss the DMK government in Tamil Nadu'.[78]

Now the question arises for consideration is: how far the observations of the courts are constitutional? At the outset, it is important note here that the law courts should neither recommend nor report the imposition of President's Rule in the state because such acts are neither expected from the judiciary nor within their jurisdiction. If the court recommends to the President to invoke Article 356 in a state it would amount to prejudging an issue. Further, it is also relevant to mention here that the law courts can sit in judgment over the legitimacy of the proclamations after the proclamations have been made and in this case the High Courts cannot hear the case because the judicial hearing is violative of the principle of '*nemojudex in resua*', one of the principles of natural justice. Further, if President's Rule is declared on the direction of the Courts where will the aggrieved party go?

A reading of Article 356 would show that 'failure of the constitutional machinery' is an inevitable condition for the imposition of President's Rule. In the cases under consideration, however, there was no evidence to show that the constitutional machinery in any of these states has broken down. The only reason given by the court was corruption in the case of Bihar and an allegation that Supreme Court's restraining order on bandh was not being obeyed in letter and spirit in the case of Tamil Nadu. Of course, corruption and bandh violate the rights of people and the intervention of the Courts in these cases can be regarded as a step in the direction of the fulfilment of the wishes and aspirations of the peoples. These charges, however, cannot be construed as breakdown of the constitutional machinery. How can the judiciary think of dismissing democratically elected Governments when there are no evidence of the failure of the constitutional machinery?

It is also to be noted that the observations of the courts amount to judicial overreach and shockingly unjust to the Bommai judgment which has laid down certain guidelines and standards for the constitutional exercise of the power under the Article. 'It is also constitutionally off-track, considering that there would be a flagrant conflict of interest between such pre-emptive, antidemocratic recommendation and the power of judicial review.[79] .Where it is laid down that the standards laid down by the court are not applicable to the court itself ?.

Again, what the Constitution provided has to be found out from the wordings of the provisions. Article 356 vests the power to recommend dismissal of a state government only in the Governor of the state concerned or in the union executive, by virtue of the 'or otherwise' clause. No where in the Constitution envisages any role for the judiciary in recommending the invocation of Article 356. Therefore it is submitted that, the court should not encroach upon the functions of the executive and thereby better refrain from being instrumental there to in any manner. 'The judges must know their limits and must not try to run the government'. If the judgment contains a recital of certain facts which the Union government would be interested to be acquainted with, a copy of the judgment may be forwarded to the government. There stops the role of courts.[80] Thus Alladi Kusppuswami was right when he observed that the courts were not justified in stating that it was competent to make a report to the President on the breakdown of the constitutional machinery in the states [81]

So far the President has acted independently of the Governor's report i.e., 'or otherwise' clause on four occasions. These acts were not only highly controversial but also against the spirit of parliamentary democracy and federalism. For the first time, President's Rule was imposed under this clause, without the report of the Governor in as many as nine states on 30 April 1977, when the Janata, the first non-Congress government, was in power at the Centre. Similarly, when Congress returned to power, President's Rule was imposed in nine states by taking shelter under this clause on 13 February 1980. This clause was invoked for the third time on 13 February 1991, when Karunanidhi's D.M.K. Government in Tamil Nadu was thrown out by the minority government of Chandra Sekhar.[82] Constitutionally, the President could relay on information 'or otherwise' than that furnished by the Governor and as such the imposition of President's Rule was not against the Constitution. Perhaps this was the first instance, except the mass dismissals', which constitutes a *suigeneris,* of imposition of President's Rule without Governor's report. While addressing the members of Lok Sabha Prime minister, Chandrasekher said that Governor's report was not necessary to invoke President's Rule because 'the Centre itself had certain information while the governor did not have' on the situation in Tamil Nadu. The Prime minister said that it was not law and order, but it was more serious. He obviously referred to LTTE activities in Tamil Nadu. Hence according to him Governor's report was not necessary but the Governor was fully informed of the fact at the disposal of the Centre before the President's Rule was invoked. He justified the dismissal by saying that the centre had taken the step after its plea to DMK Government to improve the situation in the state went unheeded. Nagaland was also placed under President's Rule in 1992 without the report of the Governor. This has already been referred to in the previous part of the discussion dealing with the report of the Governor. It is not necessary to engage in a further discussion of it here. But it is astoundingly paradoxical to note that no report from the UP Governor was the reason given by Narashimha Rao government for not dismissing Kalyansingh when the constitutional machinery was broken down in UP. !

Thus, we have seen that this clause "or otherwise" not only carries with it some inherent dangers but also certain constitutional inconsistencies. It fails to take into account the realities of power politics and the consequent perils. An unsavoury aspect of invoking this clause is that it neglects and ignores outright the office of Governor. It is constitutionally abnormal and unethical that the President while arriving at the satisfaction as to the fact that the government in a state cannot be carried on in accordance with the provisions of the Constitution ignores or overlooks, even by implication; the Governor of the state concerned, who is the constitutional head of the state and happens to be an agent of the President under the Constitution. Moreover, it is the Governor who would normally act as the President's agent during the President's rule, to perform the functions which otherwise would have been performed by the state government. It would not be constitutionally fair and just that the office of the Governor is bypassed while proclaiming the President's Rule in the states.[83]

In spite of the demand for the abrogation of the clause 'or otherwise' emanating from many quarters, nothing could be done since it necessitates a second look into Articles 355 and 356 of the Constitution. The constitutional relevance of the act lies in a situation wherein the Centre is in conflict with the Governor due to the fact that the Governor sends a wrong report or fails to make a report at all despite the Center's staunch conviction that an inevitable action under Article 356 is warranted. At this juncture, Bhagavati, J. conceded that the inclusion of the words 'or otherwise' in Article 356 gave the President a very drastic power which if misused and abused destroys the constitutional equilibrium between the Union and the states.[84]

The possibility of abuse of power is there. To ward off this possibility, our constitutional wisdom requires that the orbit of the operation of the clause be restricted. Its operation should be restricted to drastic breakdown of law and order or failure to maintain law and order and the state government shows no political will or administrative ability to cope with the situation. In this context, the Union government must place before the President full evidence and relevant papers revealing the circumstances which require action and he in turn should place them before the Parliament when the matter is being deliberated on in the House and if necessary, before the Courts. It is only by this reasonable and transparent process that the objectivity of the Central Government's decision could be established. In this regard, the latest decision given by the Supreme Court is a welcome development. The Court said:

> If the Union of India does not indicate or state that any other information/material was available to the President or the Union Council of Ministers other than the report of the Governor-much less disclose it, the Court must hold that there was no other information before the President except the report of the Governor and that the words 'and other information received by me' were put in the proclamation mechanically.[85]

Satisfaction of the President

Article 356 also stipulates that the President has to satisfy himself as to the existence of the situation contemplated in the Article. How can he be satisfied? That satisfaction of the President derives either from the report of the Governor 'or otherwise' or both ways. If the President's act is based on 'or otherwise' and not on the report of the Governor, the satisfaction is based on the disclosed facts in the Presidential proclamation. Whether he gets information from the Governor or otherwise, the President has to become satisfied that the situation contemplated by the Constitution has actually arisen. Therefore, he is not expected to act mechanically on the report of the Governor. He can call for further information, if necessary, from any other source. Thus, the existence of objective material showing that the government of the state cannot be carried on in accordance with the provisions of the Constitution is a condition precedent. Once such material is shown to exist, the satisfaction of the President based on the material is not open to question. "However, if there is a no objective material before the President, or the material before him cannot reasonably suggest that the government of the state cannot be carried on in accordance with the provisions of the Constitution, the proclamation issued is open to challenge".[86] This shows that the power so vested in the President is of widest amplitude.

The material before the President must be sufficient to indicate that unless a proclamation is issued, it is not possible to carry on the affairs of the state as per the provisions of the Constitution. It is not an ordinary situation arising in the state but a situation which shows that the Constitutional government has become an impossibility, which alone will entitle the President to issue the proclamation. It has to be further remembered that the Article requires that the President has to be satisfied that the situation in question has arisen. Hence, the material in question has to be such as would induce a reasonable man to come to the conclusion in question. The expression used in the article is "If the President is satisfied". The word 'satisfied' is understood in different contexts as:

> To furnish with sufficient proof or information; to set free from doubt or uncertainty; to convince; to answer sufficiently (an objection, question); to fulfil or comply with (a request); to solve (a doubt, difficulty); to answer the requirement of (a state of thing hypothesis etc.); to accord with (condition).[87]

In, State of Rajasthan v. Union of India, the Supreme Court observed:

> If the satisfaction is *mala fide* or is based on wholly extraneous or irrelevant ground, the Court would have jurisdiction to examine it because in that case there would be no satisfaction of the President in regard to the matter in which he is required to be satisfied.[88]

To understand true scope and ambit of the satisfaction of the President, a brief analysis of the powers and role of the President is highly essential. To begin with, the Constitution of India as it finally emerged, envisages a parliamentary government of the British model, wherein the President is the head of the state and the Prime-minister is the head of the government. Article 53 of the constitution vests the executive powers of the Union in the President who exercises it either directly or through officers subordinate to him in accordance with the Constitution. Thus all executive powers are vested in him. All executive actions are taken in his name. The Supreme command of the defence force is vested in him. Under Article 74(1) the President exercises almost all executive functions with the aid and advice of the Council of ministers with the proviso that the President may require the Council of ministers to re-consider such advice either generally or otherwise.

The Constitution had no such provision till 1978. The original Article 74(1) reads: 'There shall be a Council of ministers with the Prime-minister at the head to aid and advice the president. During emergency Prime-minister Indira Gandhi wanted to make the constitutional powers of the President vis-a-vis the cabinet very clear. She brought forth the 42nd constitutional amendment. The following was added to clause (1) of Article 74', 'who shall in the exercise of his functions, act in accordance with such advice'. The imperative 'shall' changed the whole perspective. The President became constitutionally bound to act according to the dictates of the Cabinet. Within two years the situation changed dramatically. The Janata government under Morarji Desai introduced a proviso to Article 74 through 44th amendment, empowering the President to ask the Cabinet to reconsider its 'advice'. The Article now reads:

> 'There shall be a Council of ministers with the Prime minister at the head to aid and advise the President who shall, in the exercise of such functions, act in accordance with such advice, provided that the President may require the Council of Ministers to reconsider such advice, either generally or otherwise, and the President shall act in accordance with the advice tendered after reconsideration.[89]

From the wording of the Article, it is very clear that the President has some discretion in responding to the advice of the Council of Ministers. Even in England, where the Monarch as the constitutional ruler retains with himself the right to be consulted, to encourage and to warn. That right of the constitutional head is incorporated in the Constitution of India by this amendment. However, any advice rendered by the cabinet after reconsideration, however, is binding on the President. The request for reconsideration, is a more powerful device than it might appear at first sight. It provides the president with a lever to call into question and direct public attention to a problematic piece of legislation or an executive action. The Supreme Court in Samshersingh v. State of Punjab observed:

> 'It does not necessarily mean immediate acceptance of the ministry's first thought. The President can state all the objections to any proposed action and ask his ministers- in -council, if necessary, to reconsider the matter. It is only in the last resort that he must accept their final advice.[90]

After the 44th amendment the Council of ministers was made to think twice before forwarding any subject of controversial nature for the assent of the President. 'This was in tune with the original intention of the framers of the Constitution, who gave the President, the status of a constitutional monarch, along with respect and dignity due to the high office. The 44th amendment not only elevated the office of the President but also made it an extremely purposeful one without making any radical change, unlike 42nd amendment which lowered the dignity of the office of the President'.[91]

Further, Article 75(3) lays down that the Council of Ministers shall be collectively responsible to the Lok Sabha . The thrust of the provisions in the constitution is that the Prime minister and Council of Ministers must enjoy the confidence of the Lok Sabha. There is no provision in the Constitution which makes the President answerable to the legislature. Hence, one may reasonably think that as the ministers are so answerable for the policy and administration of the Union, it is implied that they are recognised as possessing the authority to finally decide the affairs of the government. Therefore, the real ruler is the Council of Ministers and particularly the cabinet and not the President. Thus our Constitution embodies generally the parliamentary or the cabinet system of the Government of the British model. In this connection, the Supreme Court observed that 'the President has thus been made a formal or a constitutional head of the executive and the real executive powers are vested in the ministers or the cabinet.[92]

Thus the original Article 74(1), the authoritative dicta in the Constituent Assembly, the successive rulings of the Supreme Court and the opinions of the constitutional authorities established beyond doubt that our Constitution sought to establish the British parliamentary system in which the head of the state is bound by the advice of the Council of ministers subject to recognised exception. With this perspective the Supreme Court in Bommai case observed[93] :

> Whenever the Constitution requires the satisfaction of the President or the Governor of any power or function, the satisfaction required by the Constitution is not the personal satisfaction of the President or the Governor in the constitutional sense in the cabinet system of government, that is, satisfaction of his council of ministers on whose aid and advice the President or the Governor generally exercises all his powers and functions, the decision of any minister or officer under rules of business made under any of the two Article 77(3) and 166(3) is the decision of the President or the Governor respectively. These Article do not provide for any delegation. Therefore, the decision of the minister or any officer under the rules of business is the decision of the President or the Governor.

As things stand, the pertinent question which could be raised here is that: is it binding on the President to act strictly in accordance with the advice of the Union cabinet in this regard, or does the President have the power to act contrary to the advice of the government if he honestly feels that the situation does not warrant the imposition of President's Rule at all and the recommendation of the cabinet is patently unconstitutional?

Though under the scheme of our Constitution, the real powers are vested with the Council of Ministers and not with the President, the functions of the President under Article 356 stands on a different footing. While acting under Article 356, the President discharges a constitutional function and not an executive function. It cannot be constitutionally permissible that the President is rendered a formal authority. He has the power to ask the cabinet to reconsider its advice on imposing President's Rule in a state if he is not satisfied with it and thereby correct the wrong decision of the cabinet. If one were to follow the direction of the debate in the Constituent Assembly, it would become clear that the wisdom of the elected head of the state must be put to use if the recommendations of the cabinet are not to go completely of the rails. In the concluding debate of the Constituent Assembly on Article 356, Ambedkar made an apt quoted statement from the Chair, which indicated the federal role for the President personally. In his speech, he clearly pointed out that: "If at all they are brought into operation, I hope the President, who is endowed with these powers, will take proper precautions before actually suspending the administration of the provinces". This indicates the fact that the President should strike a balance between the party in power at the Centre and the claims of the party or parties in power in the states. The advice of the Council of Ministers, therefore, shall not be binding upon the President if it envisages the imposition rather than withdrawal of the Central rule in the states. The President considered to be above party politics, shall be given a freer hand to act as an impartial referee in Centre-State relations.[94] It is in this context, a valid and fair assessment of the constitutional position of the President is given by Krishna-Iyer J. He very pertinently states here:

> The President, like the king, has not merely been constitutionally romanticised but actually vested with a pervasive and persuasive role while he plays such a role, he is not a rival centre of power in any sense and must abide by and act on the advice rendered by his ministers except in a narrow territory which is sometimes slippery.[95]

A serious look-through of the above observation clearly points to the fact that the President has considerable discretionary powers under the scheme of our Constitution. However, it is quite clear that the President cannot exercise his powers under the Constitution as he thinks fit. He has to have facts, circumstances which can lead a person of his status to form an intelligent opinion requiring exercise of discretion of such a grave nature that the representatives of the people who are primarily entrusted with the duty of running the affairs of the state are removed with a stroke of the pen. His action must appear to be called fair and justifiable under the Constitution if challenged in a Court of law.[96] Thus, it must be pointed out that the exercise of discretion by the President is not his personal discretion or an absolute one. It never operates in vacuum. It should find it meaning by upholding sound constitutional principles and sanctity of democracy it cherishes.

In the light of above discussion, it is worthwhile to analyse the "constitutional activism" displayed by President K.R. Narayanan in the case of U.P. in 1997[97] and Bihar in 1998[98]. The context and grounds associated with the two 'dismissal' attempts, however, varied. If in U.P the issues were related to the majority legislature support' of the incumbent government and unruly behaviour of elected representatives in the Assembly when confidence motion was considered, in Bihar the reasons cited were corruption, maladministration, financial mismanagement and worsening of law and order situation. However, the President took the stand that the acts complainted of did not constitute the 'failure of constitutional machinery' in both cases so as to justify the imposition of the extraordinary power under Article 356. Therefore, he invoked the prerogative to return the advice for reconsideration by the respective cabinets and thereby blocked what was widely believed as a partisan act. President's action, however, did not cause any controversy on the relative power position of the president and the cabinet mainly because the cabinet accepted 'the return' instead of making an issue of it. In returning the Union cabinet's recommendation, President Narayan had gone by the provisions of the 44th amendment and the Supreme Court verdict in the Bommai case apart from the Constitutional Assembly Debates and there by he upheld the dignity of the office and defended the Constitution by refusing to be a rubber stamp. His decisions not to dismiss the governments bear the stamp of steel in him [99]

Though, the President was able to stall the undemocratic decisions of the Cabinets, but it cannot be regarded as constitutional activism in the true sense of the term. What made it possible for the President to stall this was the favourable political climate prevailing then. It is not Narayanan alone but two former Presidents also had expressed strong displeasure against the Cabinet decisions to impose President's Rule in the states. The first of its kind was in 1977 during the Janata regime.[100] Assuming power after emergency, the Desai Government decided to dismiss nine Congress ruled state governments on the ground that the state governments no longer represented the will of the people and accordingly, the Cabinet decided to advice the then acting President B.D. Jatti to dissolve the nine Assemblies. He refused. He told his secretary (K. Bal Chandran); "I want time to consider the recommendation". After another cabinet meeting Desai sent a strong letter to the President through Cabinet secretary N.K. Mukherji. It reminded Jatti of his duties and responsibilities as the constitutional head of the state. In the meantime, it was decided that Prime minister would take the people into confidence and make a broadcast to the nation in the evening paving the way for the dissolution of the Lok Sabha. The Law minister was asked to draft the address of the Prime minister to the Nation.[101] Following this, Jatti signed the order promulgating the Central rule in the nine states, bringing a twenty-four hour long constitutional crisis to an end with the

Cabinet having its own way. Now it is exactly the reverse, with the President having his own way. Similarly, it was reported (in the press) that President Shankar Dayal Sharma was reluctant to sign the proclamation under Article 356 with respect to the States of Madhya Pradesh, Rajasthan and Himachal Pradesh in 1992, in the aftermath of the demolition of the Babari Masjid.[102] He was right in expressing his disapproval. But it appears that he ultimately agreed to sign as he had no other option in the Constitution. What is to be derived from all these ? In the latest cases, the President was able to correct the wrong decision of the Cabinet because of the existence of the coalition Government in which the Prime Minister's position was rather weak. The Prime Minister of a coalition system cannot be treated at par with a Prime Minister in a single party majority rule. If they had been the leader of the single majority party as in the case of 1977 or 1980 they would not have accepted the instruction of the President to reconsider the decision. Further, there was no unanimity among the coalition partners and a few of them strongly recorded their displeasure against taking such a decision. Besides, the smooth relationship between the Prime Ministers and the President, on the one hand, and the Prime Ministers and their colleagues on the other, came to the help of K.R. Narayanan. Had that not been the case, the respective cabinets would perhaps have stuck to their decision, leaving no option for the President but to sign the proclamation.[103] Above all, many in the Cabinet realised the untenability of their earlier stand and were conscious of the probability of its reversal by the apex Court. Whatever may be the fact, Narayanan's decision constitutes a landmark and "could mark a decisive transformation of the much abused power of the Central government to end the rule of their political opponents in the states".[104]

The above analysis makes it very clear that political process is a crucible in which the constitutional process is melted in order to give a concrete shape to suit the political system. What Presidents like Rajendra Prasad, Zailsingh and S.D. Sharma could not do was accomplished by President Narayanan. He dared to do it not simply because of his constitutional position, personal equation, but because of the relevancy, the urgency, and the ramifications of the rising tides of new political orientation, phenomena formation and polarization in the absence of a political process propelled, controlled, led and managed by a single or two political parties headed by charismatic, capable and dynamic leaders commanding support bases throughout the length and breadth of the nation and in the emergence of a strong regional leadership. Thus this is a particular phase in the dynamic evolution of the political process of Indian society under the shadow of globalization and information technology. His action fell in the category of 'discretion' 'advice' and 'suggestion' as mentioned by Setalvad or opportunity for 'influencing decision' which president Prasad was keen the president have. Our country is on the threshold of a new era - an era of hung legislatures and coalitions and not exactly an era of political instability in the traditional sense both at the Centre and also at the state level under the condition of developing regional leaderships and power centres. This may lead to more decentralization, more federalism and more pluralism. Such a situation may invest the presidency with a pivotal role unknown in the past. The conventions and precedents established now may be crucial not only for the immediate situation but also for the future of Indian political system.

Failure of Constitutional Machinery

Failure of constitutional machinery was a clever political innovation of the British colonialists. It is an essential precondition for the exercise of power under Article 356, which is to be declared by the President when he is satisfied that a situation has arisen in which the government of the state cannot be carried on in accordance with the provisions of the Constitution. However, the Constitution does not specifically state what amounts to and what does not amount to such a failure. The ambiguity about the constitutional crisis is creating obstacles to an objective political approach. But we should also recognise the almost impossibility in defining constitutional crisis. The impossibility lies in the difficulty in defining the problems of a society which is in the process of evolution. It is by exploiting (misusing) the loopholes (ambiguity) in the constitutional provision that the Centre is exaggerating the smallest crises in states where the opposition reigns and simplifying even the gravest constitutional Crises in states where its own party is in power. Therefore, it has become a subject of perennial concern and is widely debated.

To understand the meaning of the expression and to comprehend the intentions of the founding fathers, we have to go through the debates in the Constituent Assembly. Needless to say, this phrase evoked strong criticism and arguments in the Assembly. The 'plurosignative' nature of the phrase became very clear when several members of the Constituent Assembly came up with divergent interpretations.[105] The extreme vagueness and uncertainty of the phràse was highlighted by the members of the Constituent Assembly itself. T.D. Bhargava described the question - what constitutes the failure of constitutioned machinery - as 'the question of questions'. Several members also stressed the necessity to lay down precisely the situations contemplated in the phrase.

The specific circumstances under which the Centre may be called upon to take over the administration of the states were detailed by Santhanam in the following terms:

> There may be physical breakdown of the government in the state owing to widespread internal disturbance or external aggression and for some reason or other, law and order cannot be maintained. Naturally, without the Centre's intervention there will be nothing but chaos. Then there may be a political breakdown. This is a point which requires careful analysis. A political breakdown can happen when no ministry can be formed or ministries that can be formed are so unstable that the government actually breaks down. Normally, according to the Constitution, when there is a great instability in government, the proper procedure will be to dissolve the lower House and re-constitute it. If after a dissolution also, the same factions are reproduced in the local legislature and they make a ministry impossible, it will then be inevitable for the Centre to step

> in.........Then there is a third contingency of economic breakdown. Suppose, for instance, in a state the ministry is all right, but it wants to make itself popular by reducing or canceling all taxes and running its administration on a bankrupt basis. Here again, the Centre will have to be very careful. But ultimately it will have to step in.[106]

Though Santhanam broadly analyses the circumstances in which the Article can come into operation, his categorization cannot be said to be comprehensive or exhaustive, given the fact that he could not bring within the ambit of his categorization those factors, which due to change of circumstances, later cropped up and which are likely to crop up in future. The fact is that years and decades bring with them changes, all of which can not be predicted and pin-pointed. The envisaged import of the phrase was clarified by Ambedkar when he was pressed by Hunzru to define it. He said:

> When we say that the Constitution must be maintained in accordance with the provisions contained in this Constitution, we practically mean what the American Constitution means, namely that the form of the Constitution prescribed in this Constitution must be maintained.[107]

This was an unfair and untenable comparison. The American Constitution does not envisage any suspension of a state government by the Federal Government at all. Nor can the Federal Government step in normally to protect a state unless the state itself makes an application to the Federal Government. Thus, his eloquence concealed more than it conceded and the Nehruvain ideas found rhetorical articulation in his diction.[108]

While speaking on this Article on another occasion, Ambedkar observed:

> It would take me very long to go into a detailed examination of the whole thing and referring to each Article, say this is the principle which is established in it and say, if any Government, any legislature of the province does not act

> in accordance with it, that would act as the failure of the machinery. The expression failure of the machinery, I find, has been used in the Government of India Act, 1935. Everybody must be quite familiar, therefore, with its de facto and de jure meaning. I do not think any further explanation is necessary.[109]

Further, he also stated that we would "reply only to those amendments which he thought had any substance and that he could not go on discussing every amendment that was moved".

The above statement of Ambedkar indicates that he himself was not fully convinced with his own answer. Significantly, he never replied to the objections. It is true that this expression has been borrowed from the Act of 1935, but it would be difficult to agree with him that the phrase has the same meaning in the present Constitution which it had in the Act since Article 356 is not the exact copy of section 93 of the Act. Further, one can also find difficulty in agreeing with him that "everybody must be quite familiar with its de facto and de jure meaning" and it does not need any further explanation. "It seems that", writes Siwach, "by not giving any explanation about the meaning of the phrase, Ambedkar intended to keep it vague".[110] Seervai also views "Ambedkar's answer are an evasion of the difficult questions raised by Kunzru".[111] The clarification made by Ambedkar could not lend any meaningful insight into the evasive provision and the dust still remained unsettled and the apprehensions and fears of the members were as hot as ever.

In sum, the Constituent Assembly has pin-pointed four circumstances responsible for the breakdown of the constitutional machinery. Even though these are not incorporated in the Constitution they are relevant and deserved to be considered. They are:

1. When there is a breakdown of Constitution due to internal violence.[112]
2. When there is a breakdown owing to majority party refusing to function at all.[113]
3. When the breakdown occurs due to the ministry in the

state refusing to follow the directions of the centre.[11]

4. The party alignment in the State is such that no stable government could be formed.[115]

However, the views of the framers do not explain fully the meaning of the expression "failure of constitutional machinery". Thus Naziruddin Ahamad was right when he said that the Article lacks clarity.

The expression and its implication have also been the subject of elaborate discussion in the report of Sarkaria Commission on Centre -State relations. The Commission report says that a failure of constitutional machinery may occur in a number of ways. It is difficult to give an exhaustive list of all such situations. Nevertheless, it discusses instances of what does and what does not constitute a constitutional failure under the following heads:

1. Political crisis
2. Internal subversion
3. Physical breakdown, and
4. Non-compliance with constitutional directions of the Union Executive.

A constitutional breakdown may be the outcome of a political crisis or deadlock. This may occur where: after a general election, no party or coalition of parties or groups is able to secure an absolute majority in the legislative assembly, and, despite exploration of all possible alternatives by the Governor, a situation emerges in which there is complete and demonstrated inability to form a government commanding confidence of the legislative assembly, or a ministry resigns or is dismissed on loss of its majority support in the assembly and no alternative government commanding the confidence of the assembly can be formed or the party having a majority in the legislature refuses to form or continue the ministry and all possible alternatives explored by the government to find a coalition ministry commanding a majority in the assembly have failed.

Internal subversion may occur where the government of a state, although carried on by a ministry enjoying majority support in the assembly, has been deliberately showing for a period of time, disregard of the Constitution and the law or where a government deliberately creates a deadlock or pursues a policy bringing the system of responsible government to a standstill or where the government in the guise of acting within constitutional arms flouts purposefully principles and conventions of responsible government to pursue dictatorship.

Physical breakdown occurs where a ministry although properly constituted, either refuses to discharge its responsib-ilities to deal with a situation of internal disturbance, or is unable to deal with such a situation that paralyses the administration and endangers the security of the state or where natural calamity such as an earthquake, cyclone, epidemic, flood etc., of unprecedented magnitude and severity completely paralyses the administration and endangers the security of the state and the government is unwilling or unable to exercise its governmental power to relieve it.

Where a direction issued by the Union in the exercise of its executive power under any provision of the constitution such as Articles 256,257 and 339(2) or, during the emergency under Article 353, is not complied with by the state government in spite of adequate warning and opportunity and the President there upon holds under Article 365 that a situation as contemplated under Article 356 has arisen. If public disorder of any magnitude endangering the security of the state has taken place, it is the duty of the state to keep the Union informed and if the state fails to do so, such failure will amount to impeding the exercise of the executive power of the Union and justify the latter giving appropriate directions under Article 257(1). If such a direction given by the Union to the state under Article 257(1) is not complied with in spite of adequate warning, the President may hold that a situation has arisen., which is contemplated under Article 356.[116]

Thus the Commission's categorization is comprehensive and quite illuminating. The discussion shows clearly that the failure of constitutional machinery may occur in a number of ways, contributing factors being determined by the dynamics of political process and the level of political development in the states concerned.

The heading of the Article 356 characterises it as a provision providing for the failure of constitutional machinery. Clause(1), however, does not use the words "failure of constitutional machinery" but the expression "a situation has arisen in which the government of the state cannot be carried on in accordance with the provisions of the Constitution".[117] Even so, the significance of the title of the section cannot be overlooked. It emphasises the level, the stage at which and the situation in which the power is to be exercised. Both the expressions are comparable with clause (1) of Article 352 of the Constitution, dealing with national emergency. It is evident that Article 356 does not speak of any kind of emergency. In fact, the word "Emergency" is not used anywhere in the Article. It is a proclamation intended either to safeguard against the failure of the constitutional machinery in a state or to repair the effect of the breakdown. As held in the Rajasthan case "it may be either preventive or curative action". The expression is of widest import and amplitude. If applied in the literal sense, it is capable of including the cases in which the government of the state has failed to respect or act in accordance with any provisions of the Constitution irrespective of their importance.

It is worthwhile to recall the interpretation and observation of Ambedkar on the point that the use of the Article should be confined to the sense of breakdown of constitutional machinery and that this was an exceptional provision which should be applied as the last resort.[118] Even excluding the marginal note to Article 356 and confining the interpretation to the words "in accordance with the provisions of the Constitution"[119] they should not mean to convey failure to comply with any particular provisions of the Constitution, which in relation to provincial part of the Constitution, means the form of responsible government, as Alladi Krishnaswamy Iyer explained. No doubt, the drastic nature of the consequences which flow from a proclamation under Article 356(1) amounting to the evaporation of executive and legislative authority of the state indicates that what is contemplated is something in the nature of complete breakdown of the constitutional machinery in the state, and not a mere failure to observe a particular provision. This would be so, particularly because the provision is to be found in part XVIII and follows the provisions as to grave emergency caused by a threat to security of the country contained in Article 352, even though it has no relation to emergency of any kind dealt in Article 352. This would lead to the conclusion that the situation contemplated in Article 356 is not one of mere irregularity or difficulty; but the one in the nature of emergency, breakdown of constitutional machinery which calls for an abnormal remedy. Further, the hope and expectation of Ambedkar that, "such Articles will never be called into operation and that they would remain a dead letter" signifies the fact that this provision would be used only in the rarest of the rare cases, that it would be virtually a sword which would never be taken out of its sheath, except in a flagrant case. In the light of the above discussion, the proper view would be that the power can be used only in an extreme difficult situation, viz., where there is actual or imminent breakdown of the constitutional machinery, as distinguished from the failure to observe a particular provision of the constitution or worsening of law and order situation. In order to justify the application of Article 356 of the Constitution, mere failure on the part of the state government to maintain public order cannot be a good ground for suspension of the government. To justify invoking of Article 356 of the Constitution public disorder must be of such an aggravated form as to result in failure of entire law and order machinery of the state.[120] Therefore what is necessary is to specify the conditions in articulate terms under which the Article should not be used rather than cataloguing the condition under which it can be exercised.

Machinery of a government does not ordinarily fail if this or that provision of the Constitution is violated. In the day to day administration of the state, its various functionaries in the discharge of their multifarious responsibilities take decisions which may not, in some particular case or other, be strictly in accord with all provisions of the Constitution. Every such breach or infraction of constitutional provisions, irrespective of its significance, extent and effect, should not be taken to constitute failure of the constitutional machinery within the contemplation of Article 356.[121] In this connection Jeevan Reddy, J. and Aggarwal, J., with whom Pandian J. expressly concurred on this point, observed : "It is not each and every non-compliance with a particular provision of the Constitution that calls for the exercise of power under Article 356(1)".[122] It is seen that, single or individual act or acts of the violation of the Constitution for good, bad or indifferent administration does not necessarily constitute failure of constitutional machinery unless and until the non-compliance shall be such as to give rise to such a situation where the government of the state is not carried on in accordance with the provisions of the Constitution. Chinnappa Reddy J. of AP High Court observed that,

> "There may be diverse and varied consideration. An outbreak of unprecedented violence which the government is unable to curb may be a consideration. A great natural calamity like severe earthquake or a flood creating a situation which the government of a state is unable to meet may be a consideration. A large epidemic leading to mass death may be another. In all these cases there may be such a failure of the government of the state as to amount to an abdication of its governmental powers. Any other causes which may paralyse the government of a state may be a consideration. The government of a state may enter into an alliance with foreign government and that may be a consideration".[123]

He also rejected the argument that if a party has an undisputed majority in the legislature to enable its leader to form a ministry, it can never be said that the situation has arisen where the government of the state cannot be carried on in accordance with the provisions of the Constitution.

It is pertinent in this regard to recall the opinions of a few leading constitutional commentators: "Failure of Constitutional Machinery" according to D.D. Basu, means such a breakdown which calls for immediate resort to Article 356, because a situation is such that it cannot be remedied by any other means.[124] "The failure in the constitutional machinery of the sate", says Rajeev Dhavan, "must be of a 'serious' nature—in other words, a paralysis is so severe that it is not possible for the state government to handle it in any way".[125] In the opinion of F.S. Nairman, failure of constitutional machinery means "really a complete breakdown or attempted secession of a state within the Union and does not apply to machinations of politicians and temporary political instability in states".[126] Justice V.R. Krishna Iyer has a different interpretation. "A situation has arisen means," he observed, "a critical situation, not a common dilemma or a minor imbroglio which, with tact, may well be sorted out".[127]

What standard does the Bommai case lays down for a proper determination that the constitutional machinery has broken down? The judgment of Sawant, J. and Kuldip Singh, J. suggested that "a situation of impasse" should have developed. There had to be a "legal inability as well as the physical impossibility" of governance according to the Constitution. "Hence a situation which can be remedied or does not create an impasse does not disable or interfere with the governance of the state according to the Constitution, would not merit the issuance of proclamation under the Article".[128] Thus the exercise of power under Article 356 is an extra ordinary one and needs to be used sparingly when the situation contemplated by Article 356 warrants to maintain democratic form of government and to prevent paralysing of the political process, as observed by Ramaswamy J. in the Bommai case[129] Thus the Bommai case sanctioned dismissal of a state government only under the most extreme circumstances.

A careful examination of the Constituent Assembly Debates, the relevant legal provisions, views and interpretations of authorities and Supreme Court rulings show that they all have one and the same thing to say. That is, the constitutional crisis in a state which appears to be an impasse which defies solution. This crisis will be such that could not be solved with all the resources at the disposal of the state or even with the assistance of the Centre. This view point by all concerned is a vindication to a certain extent for the weakness of the constitutional provision concerning "the Failure of the Constitutional Machinery in a state".[130]

It will be useful at this stage to illustrate the situations which may not amount to failure of constitutional machinery in the state inviting the Presidential power under Article 356 and where the use of the said power will be improper. Such situations are discussed by the Sarkaria Commission. They are [131]

1. A situation of maladministration in a state where a duly constituted ministry enjoying majority support in the Assembly is in office.
2. Where a ministry resigns or is dismissed on losing its majority support in the assembly and the Governor recommends imposition of President's Rule without exploring the possibility of installing an alternative government enjoying such support or ordering fresh election.
3. Where, despite the advice of the duly constituted ministry which has not been defeated on the floor of the House, the Governor declines to dissolve the Assembly and without giving the ministry an opportunity to demonstrate its majority support through the floor test, recommends its suppression and imposition of President's Rule merely on his subjective assessment that the ministry no longer commands the confidence of the assembly.
4. Where Article 356 is sought to be invoked for superseding the duly constituted ministry and dissolving the state Legislative Assembly on the sole ground that, in the general elections, to the Lok Sabha the ruling party in the state has suffered a massive defeat.
5. Where in a situation of 'internal disturbance' not amounting to or verging on abdication of its governmental powers by the state government, all possible measures to contain the situation by the Union in the discharge of its duty, under Article 355 have not been exhausted.
6. The use of the power under Article 356 will be improper if the President gives no prior warning or opportunity to the state government to correct itself. Such a warning

can be dispensed with only in cases of extreme urgency where failure on the part of the Union to take immediate action leads to disastrous consequences.

7. Where in response to the prior warning or notice or to an informal or formal direction under Article 256, 257 etc...the state government either applies the corrective and thus complies with the direction, or satisfies the Union executive that the warning or direction was based on incorrect fact, it shall not be proper for the President to impose Article 356.
8. The use of the power to sort out internal differences or intra-party problems of the ruling party would not be constitutionally correct.
9. This power cannot be legitimately exercised on the sole ground of stringent financial exigencies of the state.
10. This power cannot be invoked, merely on the ground that there are serious allegations of corruption against the ministry.
11. The exercise of this power, for a purpose extraneous or irrelevant to the one for which it has been conferred by the constitution, would be vitiated by legal mala fides.

Thus the Commission report covers almost all possible situations in which the power should not be resorted to. D.D. Basu also lists the situation which, he says, will not amount to a breakdown of constitutional machinery.[132] However, it is submitted that, both the Sarkaria Commission and Basu fails to add that a simultaneous presence of two or more of the conditions listed by them or a cumulative assessment of the situation by the President may definitely warrant the imposition of Article 356 in a state.

From the foregoing discussion, it is very clear that Article 356 itself is vague and gray in terms of the definition of the breakdown of the Constitutional machinery in a state. It is silent and has not provided any remedy. This constitutional lacuna was being exploited by the parties in power at the Centre.

A close reading and a careful analysis of the provisions under Article 355 and 356 of the Constitution of India clearly show that the two Articles together are intended to achieve a common purpose. The former stipulates the duty of the Union towards the states to protect them against "external aggression" and "internal disturbance" and to ensure that "the government of every state is carried on in accordance with the provisions of the Constitution". The latter empowers the President to fulfil the constitutional obligations imposed upon him by the former. Thus the power given under Article 356 is not the offshoot of a right, but a compliance with a duty. It is the performance of this duty which justifies the total invasion of the state's field. This shows that action under Article 356 is to be taken not out of liking, but out of compulsion when the circumstances are so grave as it cannot be dispensed with. Therefore, the orbit of operation of the powers of the President in this connection must be determined in the light of the provision of Article 355 and for all practical purposes, they have to be read together. When they are so read, it is amply clear that the power of the President under Article 356 of the Constitution "implies that the Union government has the obligation to do whatever in its power to help the states in its endeavour to conform to the Constitution. Only when the Union fails in its attempt or finds it impossible to do any thing, that it should think of the next step, namely action under Article 356".[133]

Article 365 of the Constitution of India

The above discussion on Article 356 will remain incomplete without a brief account of Article 365 of the Constitution of India which has a close connection with Article 356. Further, the Article is one such Article the authenticity of which has been put question time and again. There for it is useful to understand the real nature, scope and ambit of the Article in a disinterested perspective. The Article provides :

> Where any state has failed to comply with, or to give effect to, any direction given in the exercise of the executive power of the Union under any of the provisions of the Constitution, it shall be lawful for the President to hold that a situation has arisen in which the government of the

state cannot be carried on in accordance with the provisions of the Constitution.[134]

The meaning of the expression 'any direction' must be understood to mean that any direction issued under any of the provision of the Constitution in the exercise of the executive power of the Union as observed by K.P. Krishna Shetty.[135] A close perusal of the provision demands two conditions to be satisfied by the centre for the issuance of Article 356.[136]

1. There must be a direction given by the Union in the exercise of its executive power under any of the provisions of the Constitution; and
2. Such direction has not been complied with or given effect to by the state.

The idea of the Union giving directions to the states is not found in any true federations of the world. It is relevant to note here that it was not incorporated in the draft Constitution prepared by Rao and was also not found in the first draft prepared by the Drafting committee. However, on 3rd November 1949 while Ambedkar submitted the revised Constitution to Rajendra Prasad, he strongly explained the need and necessity for the inclusion of the punitive Article 365. He observed:

> 'In certain Articles of the Constitution such as article 256 (old 233), 257 (234 and 234A), 353 (276), 360 (280 A) and 371 (306 B) power has been given to the government of India to give directions to the states in various matters and in some of these articles it has been mentioned that the failure to give effect to those directions will be deemed to be a failure to carry on the government of the state in accordance with the provisions of the Constitution. We felt that this particular provision should be put in a separate article and hence we had proposed the insertion of this new article'.[137]

'In this connection it is to be noted that Article 365 is identified to section 126 of the Government of India Act of 1935.[138] However, the relevant section under the Act does not visualises that the non - compliance with the direction issued by the centre would be a ground for the invocation of Article 356. But the founding fathers of the Constitution has incorporated Article 365 so as to enable the centre to dismiss a state government in case of non compliance with the direction.

In order to get a proper focus and perspective to the Article, an understanding of the aspirations, expectations and apprehensions and caution of the framers of the Constitution become essential. When the Article was introduced in the Constituent Assembly views were expressed for and against the inclusion of the provision in the Constitution. The major opposition to the provision came from H.N. Kunzru. Strongly pleading for its deletion, he pointed out:

> The action of a provincial government is of such a character as to lead to misgovernment and to create the possibility of disturbances occurring in the state, it will be open to the President under Article 352 to issue proclamation of emergency or if the President himself feel that the Government of the State cannot be carried on in accordance with the provisions of the Constitution, the President will again be able to provide the necessary corrective under Article 356.[139]

Pt. Thakurdas Bhargava also shared the view of Kunzra and effectively exposed the adverse consequences of the Article in its true colours. He observed that such a provision will invest the central government with absolutely arbitrary powers should not be given to any person. Ministries and provincial government will have no security or stability and will change at the whim or caprice of the Prime - minister.[140]

On the other hand, many members strongly pleaded for the inclusion of the provision in the Constitution. The notable among them were Santhanam, Sidhwa and Brajeswar Prasad. They in one voice defended the article on the ground that the Centre should be strong enough and it should have strong control over provincial government to tide over the difficulties created by the fissiparous tendencies existing in the country. Strongly defending the Article, Ambedkar maintained that 'once there is power given to the union government to issue direction to the state ......, it seems to me that not to give the centre the power to take action when there is failure to carry out those direction is practically negating the direction which the constitution proposes to give to the Centre. Every right must be followed by a remedy. If there is no remedy then obviously the right is purely a paper right, a nugatory right which has no meaning, no sense and no substance'.[141]

The 'direction given in the exercise of the executive power of the Union under any of the provision of the constitution would naturally refers to Articles 256 and 257 among others'. Article 256 casts an obligation up on the state to exercise their executive power as to ensure compliance with laws made by the parliament and the existing laws. It further provides that it is open to the union to issue directions in exercise of its executive power to ensure that the state exercises its executive power in the aforesaid manner. In this context the Supreme Court in the Assembly dissolution case observed that this does not empower the Union government to interfere with any matter in the exclusive sphere of the State. The court went further and said that if the Prime-minister issues any directive to a state in the exclusive state sphere such directive shall not be binding up on the states:[142]

Article 257 (1) provides that the state executive power shall not impede the exercise of central executive power and 'the executive power of the Union shall extend to the giving of such direction to a state as may appear to the government of India to be necessary for the purpose. Clause (2) and (3) of the Article empower the union government to issue executive directions to states with respect to construction and maintenance of means of communication which are declared to be of national and military importance, and measures to be taken for the protection of railways within the states, Again in State of Rajasthan v. Union of India the Supreme Court held that under the Article, the union government can issue a direction to a state if only some actions of the State Government is likely to prejudice the exercise of the executive power of the union. It is debatable whether the union government can issue executive directions under any other provisions of the constitution. But one thing is beyond doubt the Union government cannot issue any executive direction to the States to comply with any state laws.

These Articles have been incorporated in the Constitution "for effective implementation of Union laws and national policies'.[143] If any of the state government disregards or flouts the direction given by the centre under the Articles 256 and 257 that would attract Article 365 which provides a ground for taking action under Article 356.

Till date, however, the Centre had never issued a direction under Article 256 and 257 and that no proclamation had been issued under Article 356 based on Article 365. However, at times, it seemed not improbable to take a state under President's Rule on account of the failure of state government to accede to the wishes of the Centre.[144]

However, the existence of this provision in the Constitution has been a subject of great controversy. On the one hand, it is argued that 'the Article is offensive to the very federal concept of federalism and need to be dispensed with'.[145] This demand has been specifically voiced by opposition-ruled state governments who felt agitated over the growing trend of centralization. In support of their demand they particularly refer to the observation of D.D. Basu that 'obviously the power conferred by the instant Article (365) is anti-federal.[146]' The Rajmannar Committee also recommended its deletion from the Constitution itself since it gives sweeping power to the Centre. 'If the Articles are to be retained', the committee demand, 'no direction contemplated in Article 256 and 257 should be issued except in consultation with the approval of the Inter State Council'.[147]

H.M. Seervai, on the other hand, strongly defended the existence of such an Article in the Constitution. He justified that 'a power essential for the existence of federal government can not be said to impair the federal principles',[148] On a closer examination, it seems that the provision should not be considered as contrary to federal principles.[149] For the smooth functioning of the federal system, it is essential that the Union should have the power to give necessary directions to the governments of its component parts as the executive authority of the former extends to the latter also. Further, this provision is also relevant in the light of fissiparous tendencies and the competitive nature of Indian polities with sub national loyalties which are current in many parts of India shaking the very foundation of the republic. If the centre does not have this power at its disposal, how can we face and overcome the threat and challenges from within?. We should also take in to account of the fact that the Union government has no separate federal agencies to carry out the union laws and policies. Consequently the union government is given the power under Article 365 to secure compliance with the union directions from the state governments.[150] Article 365 is also significant in the context of Article 355 which imposes an obligation upon the centre towards the states. Hence it is necessary for India's parliamentary democracy to have such an Article for the larger interest of the republic. If sufficient safeguards are fostered as convention against the political prejudice of the Centre, the Article can play a useful, vital and an inevitable role in the semi-federal constitutional scheme of India.

In this connection it is certainly needs to be mentioned that every non-compliance of the central directives irrespective of its significance, extent and effect can not be and should not be construed as a ground for action under Article 356. The non compliance with the provision of the constitution means substantial non compliance with the provision of the constitution applicable to the governance of the state and reasonably leads one to believe that the government of the non complaining state can not be carried on in accordance with the provisions of the Constitution. [151] The President should use the power in a reasonable manner with great care, caution and circumspection and in extreme cases only, and not mechanically. Any misuse or abuse of this important power would destroy the very autonomy of the states apart from generating stresses and strains in the working of Union- State relations. In this connection the Supreme Court in the Bommai case forcefully held that the direction given by the Union executive must be lawful and the state's failure to comply with them should give rise to a situation contemplated by Article 356.[152]

References

1. *The Constitution of India,* Article 355.
2. See *Report of the Centre – State Relations Inquiry Committee* (Government of Tamil Nadu, 1971) 188. See also Shiva Rao, *Framing of India's Constitution* – A Study (New Delhi : IIPA, 1968) 811-812.
3. Noorani, A.G., *Constitutional Questions in India* (New Delhi: OUP, 2000) 272.
4. Edwards Crown, *The Constitution and What it Means Today* (Princeton University Press, 1973) 216-217 and 149-150. For Australian position, See R.D. Lumb and K.W. Yan, *The Constitution of the Commonwealth of Australia-Annotated.* (London: Buttor-worths, 1974) 347.
5. See, *The Constitution of India,* Article 355.
6. *The Constitution of United States of America,* Article IV.
7. However, in America the Union government is not bound to wait for request from the state before intervening in the affairs of the latter. For e.g. in 1894, the Chicago Pullman strike was broken by President Cleveland of the United States over the protest of the Governor of Illinois. The Supreme Court upheld the action of the President *(Inre Debs* 1895). Similarly in 1941, President Roosevelt used the army to break up a strike in a California Aircraft Factory without any formal request from the Governor. (See Forguson and M.C. Henry, *The American Federal Government,* 4th ed. (New York, 1956) 78. In 1963, the Federal Government deployed national militia to deal with racial disturbances in Little Rock and to secure compliance with the decisions of the Supreme Court on racial integration, though much against the wishes of the state concerned. (See V.N. Shukla, *Constitution of India,* 9th ed. (Lucknow: Eastern Book Company, 1994) 863
8. *The Common Wealth of Australia Constitution Act,* Section 119
9. See, *The Federal Constitution of the Swiss Confed*eration, 1874
10. See, *The Weimar Constitution of Germany* (1919), Article 48
11. K.P. Krishna Shetty, *The Law of Union State Relations and Indian Federalism* (Madras: Sai Nag, 1981) 292-93.

12. It may be noted that "Internal Disturbance" which threatens the security of India or any part of India would normally be in the nature of "armed rebellion".
13. See K.P. Krishna Shetty, 292-93.
14. *Constituent Assembly Debates,* Vol. IX, 138.
15. *Ibid.,* 140-141.
16. *Ibid.,* 138.
17. P Gopala Krishnan, *The Constitutional Implications of President's Rule in Kerala, Supreme Court Journal* 22 (1959): 161-176.
18. 'Internal disturbance' should be distinguished from ordinary problems relating to law and order.... and cannot be equated with mere breaches of public peace. Internal disturbance is an aggravated form of public disorder which endangers the security of the state *(Sarkaria Commission Report on Centre-State Relation,* Part I, 197).
19. See, *Sunderlal Patwa v. Union of India, AIR 1993 MP 214.*
20. *Sarkaria Commission Report,* 170.
21. At the Inter-State Council's meeting in January 1999, Kerala had gone so far as to demand that the reference to 'internal disturbance' in Article 355 be deleted, describing it as "a relics of the colonial past" and that the state bear full responsibility for law and order (*"objectionable move"*, editorial, *EPW,* 1 July 2000).
22. For instance on 19 September 1968 the Union government deployed the Central Reserve Police to protect the Central government offices and installations as the Central government employees were going on strike. The State government objected that it should have been consulted by the Central government before doing so. The Central government took the opposite view and did not agree with it. It was argued by the Central government that the Central Reserve Police could be deployed in the state not only to protect central government's property and installations but also to make arrests or disperse unlawful assemblies if the state police did not perform these functions. The state was reminded of the responsibility of Article 355 placed on it to ensure of the administration of every state is carried on in accordance with the provisions of the Constitution. Similarly in December 1992 the Central government deployed the Central Reserve Police in Uttar Pradesh to protect the Babri masjid at Ayodhya. So there are many instances of deploying the Central force to the States without the latter's request (For detailed discussion, See also M.P Jain, *Constitutional Law,* 4th

ed. (Nagpur: Wadhwa and Co., 1994) 364.

23. *The Sarkaria Commission* Report, 197.
24. *Ibid*
25. *Ibid.*
26. *See Appendix III*
27. *See The Constitution of India,* Article 352
28. *CAD,* Vol. IX, P 175
29. See *The Constitution of India,* Article 360
30. It is important to note that these Articles have been repealed recently. However, for the purpose of the study they have been included.
31. See *The Constitution of India,* Article 356.
32. For more details see the *Administrative Reforms Commission Report (1969),* Vol. I, 226.
33. See the *Report of the Governor's Committee (1971).*
34. D.D. Basu, *Commentary on the Constitution of India,* 6th ed.. Vol. O (Calcutta: Kamal Law House, 1989) 15.
35. H.M. Seervai, *Constitutional Law of India,* 4th ed.. Vol. 2 (Bombay: N.M. Tripathi, 1993) 2065.
36. *S.R. Bommai v Union of India,* AIR 1994, SC 1918. See also *Samsher Singh v. Union of India,* AIR 1974, SC 2192.
37. *Sarkaria Commission Report,* 177.
38. *Rameshwar Prasad and others v. Union of India,* 2006, AIR SCW 494.
39. *AIR 1994, SC* 2013.
40. H.R. Khanna, *Article 356 and its Misuse-II, The Hindu,* 15 November 1997.
41. *Sarkaria Commission Report,* 177.
42. *AIR 1994 SC 1918.* However, the Governor *is not amenable to the directions of the Government of India, nor is he accountable to them for the manner in which he carried out his functions and duties. It is an independent constitutional office which is not subject to the control of the government of India. (Hargovind Pant v. Raghukul Tilak, AIR* 1979 SC 1113).
43. It may be news to many that on more than one occasion and in the case of more than one Governor, the report of the Governor which justified the invocation of Article 356 was actually written in the Union Home Ministry itself. (See S. Viswan, *Outcome of President's Initiative, The mainstream,* 21 June 1997:3).
44. See Soli Sorabjee, *The Governor: Sage or Saboteur,*(New Delhi : Roli Book, 1985) 88.
45. See *Is Governor the Lackey of the Centre* (Mal), editorial, *The Kerala Kaumudi,* 14 April 1992.

46. *Ibid.*
47. See Soli J. Sorabjee, *The Governor Sage or Saboteur* (New Delhi: Roli Books, 1985) 88.
48. *The Governor, Sage or Saboteur,* Soli Sorabjee writes: The public today generally regard the Governor as the employee of the central government, in some cases a spy of the Centre. This kind of perception on the role of Governor emanates from the misuse of the contentious Article 356. (See Soli Sorabjee 88).
49. K. Surya Prasad and VK. Ramjeev, *Pleasure of Governor and Life of the Ministry* (Mal.) *The Mathrubhumi Weekly,* 10 December 1995-6.
50. *The Sarkaria Commission Report,* 121.
51. A.G. Noorani recommended Panels of candidates chosen by a high level committee such as one composed of the Prime Minister, the Vice-President and the Chief Minister. He observed: Unless the Constitution is amended to ensure better appointments and greater independence, the office of the Governor will be damaged beyond repair. (A.G. Noorani, *Constitutional Questions in India* (New Delhi: OUP, 2000) 239.
52. Rajeev Dhavan, *A president demurs, the Hindu,* 28 Oct 1997
53. *The Sarkaria Commission Report,* 123-24
54. Krishna Iyer, V.R., *The Chemistry of Rajbhavan, The Hindu,* 24 and 25 April 1992
55. Seervai, H.M., *Constitutional Law of India,* Vol. 1 (Bombay: N.M. Tripathi, 1996) 1070.
56. Austin, Granville, *Working a Democratic Constitution,* 580.
57. See *the Sarkaria Commission Report,* 127
58. *Ibid.*
59. See *The Report of the Committee of Governors.* (1971)
60. See *Sarkaria Commission Report* 172 and 179.
61. The Governor should act as an umpire in an unpartisan manner with a detached view. He is an important functionary and is intended to act as the sheet-anchor of the federal-cum-parliamentary system and not intended to become a pawn and susceptible to manipulations for party ends of the ruling party at the Centre, S.C Arora, *President's Rule in Indian States* (New Delhi : Mittal, 1990) 24.
62. *CAD,* Vol. VIII, 436.
63. K. Surya Prasad and V.K. Ramjeev 9.
64. In case a Governor show the impertinence to withhold such a report, a rider has been added to Article 356—'otherwise'—it is this rider that came in handy for Mr. Morarji Desai to send nine

Congress Governments, Mrs. Indira Gandhi to send nine Janata Govenment and Mr. Chandra Sekhar to send Karunanidhi in to political wilderness.

65. Nalini Pant, *The Governor and Article 356: Problems and Challenges Journal of the Society for the Study of State Governments* 4 (1971): 296.
66. *CAD, Vol. IX*, 134.
67. H.V. Kamath, in the course of his speech, took strong objection to the incorporation of the words "otherwise" because it warranted the President assuming the power under the Article even without the report of the Governor. When Kamath described the act of the President in acting even without the report of the Governor as crime, another member asked what was the crime therein. Kamath there upon replied *"It is a Constitutional Crime"*
68. *CAD* 139-142.
69. *Ibid.* 146-147.
70. *Ibid.* 168.
71. *Ibid.* 145.
72. *Ibid.* 149.
73. Article 74(1) suggests that whether the President has or has not received a report from the Governor, the President can act under Article 356(1) only in accordance with the advice tendered by the Union Council of Ministers and if the latter so advice the President cannot but issue a proclamation under Article 356(1) in respect of the state concerned. (See *AIR 1977 SC 1361).*
74. *Kallada Sukumaran v. Union of India*, AIR 1987 ker.212
75. *Dhrona Maraju Satya Narayana v.N.T Rama Rao*, AIR 1988 AP 69.
76. *Ibid.*
77. *The Hindu*, 13 August 1997
78. *The Hindu*, 1 October 2007
79. *'Constitutionally off-track'*, editorial, *The Hindu*, 3 October 2007
80. David Aoussamy, *'Scanning of Article 356', Politics India*, 2.9 (1988) ;16
81. Alladi Kuppuswami, *'Was Patna High Court Right' The Hindu* 13th August 1997
82. See Sukhjinder Singh Tiwana, *Centre-State Relations in India : A Critique of Governor's Role, ISDA Journal 3* (1993):222-239.
83. Vilay V. Anjaria, *Clause 'or otherwise' in Article* 356, *AIR 1991 (J) 130.*
84. *State of Rajasthan* v. *Union of India*, AIR 1977 SC 1361.

85. *(1994) 3 SCC 278.*
86. See S.R. *Bommai v. Union of India,* AIR 1994 SC 1918.
87. *Shorter Oxford English Dictionary,* 3rd ed., 1972.
88. *AIR 1977 SC.* 1361.
89. See *The Constitution of India,* Article 74.
90. *AIR 1974 SC,* 2192.
91. Hande H.V, *Genesis of Presidential Activism, The Indian Express,* 14 June 2006.
92. *AIR 1974, SC 2192.*
93. *AIR 1994, SC* 1918.
94. Rajesh Pandey, *What Matters Most is the Constitution's Spirit, National Herald,* 28 November 1996
95. V.R. Krishna Iyer, *The Indian Presidency* (New Delhi : Dupord Dup, 1988) 62.
96. AIR *1994* SC 1966.
97. The United Front Ministry headed by I.K. Gujaral recommended to the President to impose Article 356 in U.P. This recommendation was made immediately after the B.J.P. Government led by Kalyan Singh secured a vote of confidence supported by 222 MLAs in a House of 425. President K.R. Narayanan, to whom the proclamation was sent for signature, asked the Central government to reconsider the decision and the same was accepted by the Union cabinet (See Rajesh Ramachandran, First *of its Kind, The Week,* 2 November 1997:35).
98. The B.J.P. led government recommended to the President that Bihar be brought under President's Rule. The President K.R. Narayanan sent back the recommendation for reconsideration and the Union cabinet decided that not to press any further.
99. Sachidanada Murthy, *Fairplay, The Week,* 2 Nov. 1997; 33
100. See Rajesh Ramachandran 35.
101. Shanti Bhushan, *What are the Indian President's Powers, The Hindu,* 6 June 2006.
102. T.K. Tope, *Dr. Amedbkar and President's Rule in a State: Some Reflections, Dr. Ambedkar and Empowerment: Constitutional Vicissitudes,* ed. Vibhute (Poona : University of Poona, 1993) 281.
103. Several factors and considerations have influenced the occupants of Rashtrapati Bhavan in the adoption of their own style and role. Personality factor, equation with the Prime Minister of the day, Prime Minister's position within the government and the party, and the political situation certainly influence the functional style of the President (See H.M. Raja

Sekhara, *The Indian Presidency: Plea for a Second Look, Journal of Constitutional and Parliamentary Studies* 31 (1997):117.

104. President Narayanan had made it clear that he will function as the working President. Being the guardian of the Constitution, he has the responsibility to protect it and contribute to achieving its great ideals. The Head of state's refusal to function as a rubber stamp in the U.P. and Bihar instances and on some other matters has not been to the liking of some political quarters. President Narayan has set a new example and holds the high office with decorum and invested it with dignity (See V.K. Madhavan Kutty, *Behind the Leak, Frontline,* 12 February 1999:24).
105. H.V. Kamath was of the view that ministerial crisis or maladministration would not fall within its ambit. Raj Bahadur visualised various reasons other than breakdown on account of disturbance or chaos, like frequent change of ministry or a financial breakdown. He even moved an amendment to add the words 'a grave emergency has arisen which threatens the peace and tranquility of the state after the words 'is satisfied that' to give more content and meaning to the phrase. H.N. Kunzru envisaged situations of lack of good government in the provinces, apart from corruption and mismanagement. T.D. Bhargava pointed out that the phrase should cover situations of apprehended breakdown also, apart from actual breakdown. He was of the view that the situation contemplated was one where the entire machinery has failed and ordinary people could not enjoy even common liberties. The situation would cover an entire gamut of possibilities from internal disturbance to disturbance to peace and tranquility according to him (See *CAD*, Vol. IX 130-180).
106. *CAD* 154.
107. *Ibid.* 175-176.
108. R.L.M. Patil, *Article 356 of the Indian Constitution: Why deletion is no Solution, Vidya Bharathi,* 10 (1995): 64.
109. *CAD* 177.
110. J.R, Siwach, *Politics of President's Rule In India* (Shimla : Indian Institute of Advanced Study, 1979) 6-7.
111. H.M. Seervai, *Constitutional Law of India,* 4th. ed., Vol. 3 (Bombay: N.M. Tripathi, 1996) 3089.
112. *CAD* 125.
113. *Ibid.* 132.
114. *Ibid.* 157.
115. *Ibid.* 147.

116. *Sarkaria Commission Report,* 171-173.
117. The phrase *"a situation has arisen…Constitution"* appeared for the first time in the relation to an emergency provision in the Government of India Act of 1935. Later on in the Constituent Assembly when the draft emergency Article was formulated, this usage was altered considerably. However, in the provision that was finally adopted the phrase reappeared.
118. *CAD,* 177.
119. *Ibid.* 150. In the Bommai case Jeevan Reddy, J. observed: The words provisions of the Constitution mean what they say. The said words can not be limited or confined to a particular set of Articles. It is indeed difficult nor is it advisable to catalogue the various situations which may arise and which would be comprised within clause (i). It would be more appropriate to deal with concrete cases as and when they arise.
120. *Sunderlal Patwa v. Union of India, AIR* 1993 MP 214.
121. *Sarkaria Commission* Report 177.
122. *S.R. Bommai v Union of India* (1994) 3 SCC. 273.
123. *Inre Sreeramulu,* AIR 1974 A.P. 106.
124. See D.D. Basu, *Shorter Constitution of India,* 12th ed. (New Delhi: Prentice-Hall of India, 1990) 1101-1103.
125. Rajeev Dhavan, Interview, *Of President Rule and Trigger Politicians, Frontline,* 17 July 1998: 26-27.
126. FS. Nairman, Interview, *Strengthen the Institution of Governor,* Ibid: 27-28
127. V.R. Krishna Iyer, Interview, *Article 356 should be Abolished,* Ibid: 24-25.
128. (1994) 3 *SCC 103.*
129. *S.R. Bommai v. Union of India,* AIR 1994 SC 1914
130. K. Surya Prasad and C.R. Santhosh, *Article 356 of the Constitution of India* (Mal.) (Cover story) *Mathrubhumi Weekly,* 26 September 1999.
131. *Sarkaria Commission Report,* 173-74.
132. See D.D. Basu 1104-1105.
133. David Annoussamy, *Scanning of Article 356, Politics India,* 2.9 (1988):17.
134. *The Constitution of India,* Article 365.
135. Krishnashetty, K.P, *President's Power under Article 356 of the Costitution- Theory and Practice,* in Alice Jacob, *Constitutional Development since Independence* (Bombay: Tripathi, 1975) 342.
136. See Madhusudhana Rao. K. *The Scope of Article 365 of the Constitution,* (2004) 4 SCC (J)1.

137. Shiva Rao, B. *The Framing of India's Constitution,* (New Delhi: IIPA, 1969) 749.
138. Section 126 of the Government of India Act, 1935 empowered the Governor General to give direction to the provinces and if it appears to the Governor General that effect has not been given to any such directions he can in his discretion issue orders to the Governor who was to act in his discretion in the matter of carrying out the direction given by the Governor General.
139. *Constituent Assembly Debates,* Vol.XI, 518-519.
140. *Ibid.,* 512-513.
141. *Ibid.,* 507.
142. *State of Rajasthan v. Union of India, AIR 1977 SC.1361*
143. See *the Sarkaria Commission Report* 110.
144. For instance Central Government Employees threatened to go on a token strike on September 19, 1968. The Union government resorted to by promulgating an anti - strike ordinance. This ordinance could not get the support of some state governments, viz., West Bengal and Kerala. The Kerala Chief Minister, Namboodiripad, even publicly announced that his government cannot follow the central government's directives to take necessary measures against strikers, such as arrest, prosecution, etc. The Kerala Government, by refusing to centre its co-operation had really constituted a breach of trust. Disobedience to central laws could have led to lawlessness and anarchy, Whether or not the president could have declared a state of emergency at that time is a matter of speculation (see. Nalinipant, *The Governor and Article 356, Journal of the society for the study of State Governments*", V.4 (1971):307-08)
145. Basu ,D D .*Commentary on the Constitution of India,* 6th ed., Vol. 0 (Calcutta: Kamal Law House, 1989)
146. Basu, D.D. *Commentary on the Constitution of India,* 6th ed., Vol. O (calcutta : Kamal Law House, 1989) 129.
147. *Rajmanner Committee Report* (1971) 22-23.
148. Seervai, H.M. *Constitutional Law of India,* V.2 (Bombay N.M. Tripathi, 1986) 3091.
149. Akhtar Majeed *India's Federal Structure: Some Reflections,* in *Indian Federalism in the New Millennium* ed. by Dua, B.D and Singh M.P. (New Delhi: Manohar, 2003) 209.
150. Madhusudhana Rao, *The scope of Article 356 of the Constitution, (2000) 4.SCC* (J)1.

151. *National Commission to Review the working of the Constitution, A consultation paper on Article 356 of the Constitution* (2002) at http://lawmin.nic. nerwe/final report/v2b2-5httm.
152. *S.R. Bommai v. Union of India,* AIR 1994 SC 1918.

Chapter 4

The Steamroller in Operation: A Historical Survey

There have been a large number of occasions when the President of India has acted under Article 356 of the Constitution on the ground of the 'failure of the constitutional machinery in the states'. It would be useful to make a brief survey of them so that we may be able to assess the constitutional reality arising from the application of the Article. To make the survey more analytical and comparative, it would be very much expedient to classify the instances on the basis of the performance of the political parties which resorted to this extreme measure with or without adequate justification. Hence, a general categorization of the instances of the President's Rule under the headings Congress rule, Congress backed minority rule and the non-Congress rule can be made. The non-Congress minority regimes supported by the Congress party can actually be counted as a continuation of the Congress rule for all practical purposes. These regimes were propped up by the Congress party which was buying time to stage a comeback to power. The Congress party was obviously pulling the strings from behind. The very survival of these Prime Ministers depended on the mercy of the Congress party which used them as mere pawns in the political game of one-upmanship. This chapter confines itself to the historical survey of the imposition of Article 356, and does not attempt an analytical and critical evaluation which will be taken up in the next chapter.

I. IMPOSITION OF PRESIDENT'S RULE DURING CONGRESS RULE

The Indian National Congress was the dominant political party which ruled the country for almost forty-eight years. President's Rule under Article 356 has been imposed in many states during the reign of all the Congress Prime Ministers.

A. Imposition of President's Rule during Nehru-Shastri Period

1. Punjab (1951)

Punjab was the first state to witness the imposition of President's Rule since the inauguration of the Constitution. The facts of the case can be briefly summarised as follows. Punjab was ruled by Congress party which was deeply faction ridden. Although Gopichandra Bhargava was the Chief Minister and the leader of the Congress legislature party, there was within the party, a faction jointly led by Bhim Sen Sachhar and Pratap Singh Karion. The factionalism crossed its limit when thirty members of the Congress legislature party in a petition appealed to the Congress high command to permit it to pass a vote of non-confidence in Bhargava's leadership. The Congress party, in these circumstances decided that Bhargava should resign. An alternative leader was not immediately elected by the Congress party, though the party enjoyed absolute majority in the legislature. In this context President's Rule was imposed following the Chief Minister's resignation. The Assembly was kept in a state of suspended animation.[1]

2. PEPSU (1953) [2]

The Congress ministry headed by Regubir lost the confidence of the legislature as a result of defection. It was replaced by a coalition government with Gain Singh Rarewale as the Chief Minister. The coalition broke up because of defection and also because the court set aside the election of the Chief Minister, two other ministers and six MLAs. Rarewale approached the Central government with the request that he should be allowed to carry on for six months and expressed the hope that in the meanwhile he would get elected. But this was refused by the Central government. Then members of the United Front approached the Centre with a fresh proposal that they were prepared to elect another leader in the place of Rarewale. But this request was also rejected by the government and President's Rule was imposed with the dissolution of the Assembly.[3]

3. Andhra (1954)

T. Prakasam's ministry supported by the Congress fell when a non-confidence motion by the opposition was passed on the issue of prohibition. The opposition composed of forty Communists, eight Krishikar Lok Party members, seven Praja Socialist Party members, two dissident Congress men and ten independents. The opposition approached the Governor for a mandate to form a new ministry.[4] However, the Governor took the position that opposition consisting of heterogeneous elements was not capable of forming a stable government.[5] He then recommended President's Rule on the advice of the defeated Chief Minister, who refused to work as a caretaker government.

The Governor's action was attacked from many quarters on the ground that according to the principle of British parliamentary behaviour the Governor could have invited the leader of the opposition to form the Government, and that resort to Article 356 would have been legitimate only if the formation of an alternative Government was impossible.[6]

4. Travancore-Cochin (1956)

The Praja Socialist Party government formed by Pattom Thanupillai after the 1954 election resigned owing to the withdrawal of support by the Congress party. The successor ministry of the Congress under Govinda Menon also fell consequent on the resignation of six members from the Congress party because of the difference of opinion regarding the transfer of Tamil speaking districts to the Madras state. The opposition PSP, a party with fifteen members in the house, claimed to have the support of fifty seven members in a house of hundred and eighteen members. However, they were denied the chance to form a ministry because they were in a minority. The Raja Pramukh recommended the imposition of President's Rule which was acceped.[7]

Table 1
Details of President's Rule Under Various Prime Ministers (1950-2010)

Sl.No.	Prime Minister	Period	Total Tenure			Frequency			Justifiable Cases		
			Years	Months	Days	Number	National Average in a year	Average for the period	Number	National Percentage	Percentage for the period
1	Jawaharlal Nehru	26 Jan 1950 – 27 May 1964	14	4	1	7	1.85	0.5	3	37	43
2	Gulzari Lal Nanda (Two spells)	27 May 1964 – 9 June 1964 and 11 Jan 1966 – 24 Jan 1966	0	0	28	0					
3	Lal Bahadur Shastri	9 June 1964 – 11 Jan 1966	0	7	2	2	1.85	3.4	0	37	0
4	Indira Gandhi (Two spells)	24 Jan 1966 – 24 May 1977 and 14 Jan 1980 – 31 Oct 1984	15	11	19	48	1.85	3	18	37	37.5
5	Morarji Desai	24 March 1977 - 28 July 1979	2	4	6	12	1.85	5	2	37	16.7
6	Charan Singh	28 July 1979 – 11 Jan 1980	0	5	15	4	1.85	8.7	2	37	50
7	Rajiv Gandhi	31 Oct. 1984 – 1 Dec. 1989	5	1	1	6	1.85	1.2	1	37	16.7
8	Viswanath Pratap Singh	2 Dec. 1989 - 10 Nov. 1990	0	11	9	2	1.85	2.1	1	37	50

Sl.No.	Prime Minister	Period	Total Tenure			Frequency			Justifiable Cases		
			Years	Months	Days	Number	National Average in a year	Average for the period	Number	National Percentage	Percentage for the period
9	Chandrasekhar	10 Nov. 1990 – 21 June 1991	0	7	11	4	1.85	6.5	2	37	50
10	Narasimha Rao	21 June 1991 – 16 May 1996	4	10	25	11	1.85	2	4	37	36.3
11	H D Deva Gowda	1 June 1996 - 20 April 1998	0	10	20	2	1.85	2.3	0	37	0
12	Indrakumar Gujral	20 April 1997 – 18March 1998	0	10	27	0	1.85	0			
13	Adal Bihari Vajpayee (two spells)	16 May 1996 – 28 May 1996 and 19 March 1998 – 22 May 2004	6	2	16	4	1.85	0.65	3	37	75
14	Man Mohan Singh	22 May 2004 – till date	6	3	0	9	1.85	1.5	5	37	55

Source: Computed from the available secondary sources.

5. Kerala (1956)

Kerala state is the political continuation of the former Travancore-Cochin state and Malabar, which was part of the former Madras Presidency. President's Rule was in force in the Travancore-Cochin state on the eve of the formation of the new state of Kerala. So, a fresh proclamation was issued on 1 November 1956 to continue the President's Rule with reference to the new state which now also included Malabar, till the legislature was formed.[8]

6. Kerala (1959)

On 31 July 1959, a proclamation under Article 356 was issued in respect of the state of Kerala where the twenty eight month old Communist ministry headed by EMS Namboothiripad was in power, fully enjoying the confidence of the legislature. The Government was pulled, down on the basis of the report of the Governor calling for the imposition of President's Rule. The report stated that the spirit of give and take 'has been crushed' and the government cannot function 'normal way'. Justifying the presidential intervention the Governor also stated that: 'I am convinced that the government has lost the support of the majority of people..... securing ... a majority of seats in the legislature cannot be pleaded as conferring the continuing right to claim the confidence of the majority. The report concluded that 'the only solution' is to exercise the power under Article 356.[9] This proclamation was criticised very severely not only by the communists but also by a number of independents in the House of People. The Prime Minister justified the dismissal on the ground that maladministration by the Communists had evoked a "liberation struggle" in the nature of a civil war which was beyond the power of the state to control.[10] It was further stated that the struggle against the ministry had taken a communal shape by reason of certain measures adopted by the ministry against the Christian community. The other focal point of the controversy was that the Communist party was directly interfering in the administration at different levels and that the so called Communist movements which were developing in. the urban trade union sector and agricultural co-operative.[1] were being given police protection. It was also alleged that the police was asked not to interfere with the unlawful and violent activities of Communist feeder organisations.[11] There was another side of the picture. The communists had created a viable government which was slowly finding its feet and also managed to mobilise a fair bit of cross sectional support. It was true that some of its decisions and deeds were controversial and undermined the statusquo of vested interests.[12]

There are two important Constitutional issues involved in the imposition of President's Rule in Kerala. The Namboodiripadu Government still enjoyed a majority in the state legislature. Law and order is the special responsibility of the state and all possibilities of evolving a working arrangement through political and official negotiations were not exhausted before the intervention by the Centre.[13] This implied that the Union Government could interfere if it felt that a certain matter which was within the exclusive competence of the states was not being dealt within what the Union Government considered to be a correct manner. The imposition of President's Rule in Kerala further proved that the whole amplitude of Article 356 was very wide and that the Congress party would not hesitate to interpret and implement Article 356 in its own controversial way.

7. Orissa (1961)

The elections to the Orissa legislative Assembly in 1957 did not give a clear mandate to any party to rule the state, though the Congress emerged as the single largest party. The coalition ministry between the Congress and the Gana Tantra Parished under the Chief Minister Ship of Hare Krishna Mahatab (Congress) came to an end owing to difference of opinion between the coalition partners accompanied by floor crossing by the members of the legislature. President's Rule was imposed as no one came forward to form an alternative ministry after the resignation of the incumbent ministry during the budget session.[14]

8. Kerala (1964)

A mid-term election took place in February 1960. A three party alliance comprising the Congress, the PSP and the Muslim

League was returned to power with Pattom A Thanupillai as the Chief Minister. When Pattom was appointed as the Governor of Punjab R. Shankar (Congress), the Deputy Chief Minister, was sworn in as the Chief Minister. Though the Congress continued to be the ruling party, it was deeply faction-ridden. P.T. Chacko, the home minister, who had differences with Shankar, made allegations against the Chief Minister but Nehru who looked into it rejected them as baseless. In this background, on 8 September 1964 a no confidence motion was passed against the ministry. After exploring possibilities of forming an alternative government, the Governor recommended President's Rule.[15]

9. Kerala (1965)

The March 1965 elections in Kerala produced an inconclusive result as it gave no clear majority to any party. It is significant to note that the Communists had won forty seats in the House of 103 and had emerged as the single largest party. The other major parties had Congress (36), K.M. George Congress (23) and SSP (13). The minor parties and independents had 21 seats. The Congress was not prepared to form a government. The CPI (M) was however, prepared to form a ministry but the SSP, while not opposed to their forming a ministry, was not prepared to join it. The Governor, A.P. Jain, after a brief discussion with party leaders regarding the formation of a ministry, reported to the President that 'It will be impossible for a representative government to come into existence ... because the communist party cannot 'command a working majority'.[16] Consequently, the legislature was dissolved and President's Rule imposed. Here, the points involved were: Could state legislature be dissolved without meeting at all ? Could a proclamation under Article 356 be issued when the concerned state was already under President's Rule ? Was it necessary to have a sitting Legislative Assembly at the time of proclamation ? All these were answered by Kerala High Court which upheld the actions of the President and the Governor.[17]

The Nehru era witnessed seven instances of President's Rule, (i.e., .5 times a year). This low frequency was mainly because of the political stability (domination of the Congress party in the Parliament, as well as in the State legislatures) and the charismatic and towering personality of Nehru in particular and other Congress leaders in general. However, five out of seven of his decisions were not free from controversies. The imposition of President's Rule in Punjab, Pepsu, Andhra, Travancore-Cochin and Kerala revealed the shape of things to come. In this context, Rajeev Dhavan writes:

> Nehru manipulated President's Rule in Punjab, Pepsu, Andhra to benefit Congress. The case of Kerala, where the Congress used breakdown of law and order (mostly created by the Congress) as an excuse to remove a popularly elected state government, was particularly ugly. It tainted Nehru's record permanently and expanded the scope of the abuse of this draconian provision.[18]

The Nehru era also provided convincing proof that Article 356 was not seen as a weapon of last resort to be used only in extreme situations. It was during his reign that an incipient and embryonic pattern had evolved which suggested that the use of Article 356 was politically negotiable at the instance of the Union government and the Congress party[19] It might be true that Nehru actually opposed the evolution of this new pattern in Kerala. However, since he was the Prime Minister then, he must be regarded as giving covert, if not overt, support to the evolution of such kinds of interpretation of Article 356.[20] 'if it could benefit the Congress organization. In this process, the Congress party scarified the federal rules of the game for the purpose of maintaining hegemony. The net result of this was that no non-congress Chief minister lasted his full term of office in the Nehru era' [21] The fact is that Article 356 was resorted to even during Nehru period to thwart the formation of non-Congress ministries or to resolve an internal crisis in the ruling party It became a trendsetter for the post-Nehruvian period as well.[22]

Lal Bahudur Shastri continued the same tradition as existed in the Nehru era. During his tenure there were only two cases where President's Rule was imposed. These instances cannot be justified by a dispassionate observer. The dissolution of the Kerala legislature before meeting even once in 1965 showed that he was also not prepared to encourage parties other than the ruling party at the Centre to form governments in the states.

B. President's Rule during Indira Gandhi's Prime Minister Ship

1. Punjab (1966)

Following the decision in June 1966 to divide Punjab into Punjab and Haryana, there was a split in the ruling Congress party. There was mounting agitation for and against the division of Punjab. On the instruction of the home minister and against the advice of the Governor, Ujjan Singh, the Chief Minister Ramkishan resigned. The attempt to form an alternative ministry failed. In the meanwhile, the Governor was transferred to Tamil Nadu and Dharma Vira was made the Governor on whose advice President's Rule was imposed on 6 July 1966. The legislature was suspended but not dissolved. The purpose of doing so was that in accordance with Article 4 of the Constitution, the State Legislature had to express its opinion on the Bill to reorganise the state. Unless that is done Parliament could not have enacted the Bill. It was also thought prudent that after the new set up, the legislature of the composite state of Punjab could be broken into two parts so as to constitute the legislatures of Punjab and Haryana which might function till the new legislatures of the respective states were created.[23] The circumstances under which the Congress party and the Centre intervened are difficult to explain in formal terms.[24]

2. Rajasthan (1967)

A peculiar situation arose in Rajasthan in 1967. After the election, no party got a majority in the legislature. The Congress was the single largest party in the Assembly. Against this, there was a coalition of non-Congress parties which claimed enjoying a viable majority.[25] They were not given a chance for the formation of a ministry as some of the legislators who had broken away from Congress and joined Janata party after the elections, were not recognised as belonging to that party. Instead, the Governor invited Mohanlal Sukhadia of the Congress party to form government. It raised a controversy whether it was Congress mandate from the Centre to invite sukhadia or the verdict of the people of the state. Sukhadia ultimately declined to take responsibility of forming a government due to the agitation of the opposition. The situation became so tense that it was thought advisable to postpone the formation of a ministry for a few days and to take over the state under Article 356.[26] The assembly was kept suspended.

3. Haryana (1967)

A week after the formation of the ministry, the official congress nominee for speakership was defeated. Rao Birendra Singh (Congress) supported by the opposition along with twelve other Congressmen who had also voted against the nominee resigned. As a result of this, the Congress ministry fell in March to be replaced by the Samyukt Vidhyak Dal (SVD) coalition headedby Rao Birendra Singh. Soon after the formation of the ministry, floor crossing started and continued on a massive scale. To stall this, Singh offered ministerial portfolios to the defectors.In the Assembly with an effective strength of 79, some 30 members had defected not once but three or four times. Singh's strategy, however, inviting defectors to join his ministry paid and he managed to preserve his majority. In such situation, when defections had become a style in Haryana politics, the Governor felt that defection made a mockery of theConstitution, bringing democracy to ridicule[27] On this ground the Governor dismissed the ministry and recommended to the President to declare Emergency. Was his action constitutional? The Governor justified his action on the ground that daily defection and transfer of loyalties had created a situation amounting to the failure of the constitutional machinery as it was impossible to find out whether the will of the majority in the Legislature represented the will of the people.[28]

4. Wcst Bengal (1968)

In west Bengal the Ajoy Mukherjee's ministry was dismissed in 1967 when P.C. Ghosh and 16 other MLAs defected and the support of the Chief minister was reduced to 136 MLAs in a

House of 280. Ghosh formed Progressive Democratic Front (PDF) and indicated his readiness for a PDF - Congress coalition.[29] The Congress demanded immediate resignation of the ministry. The Governor asked to Chief minister on 6 November 1967 to convene an early session of the Assembly to prove his majority. The Chief minister told the Governor that the Assembly would be convened on 18 December and that some of the defectors had returned to the United Front. Then the Governor asked Mukherjee to convene the Assembly not later than 23 November. This suggestion was also turned down by the Chief minister Again the Governor requested the Chief minister to call the Assembly earlier than December 18, but the Chief minister again declined to accede to the request and repeated his early stand. The ministry was dismissed on the ground that it had lost its majority and P.C Ghosh was invited to form the ministry.

P.C Ghosh sworn in as the Chief Minister with the support of the Congress party. He advised the Governor to summon the session of the Assembly to prove his majority. When the session of the Assembly began, the Speaker, B.K. Banerjee, adjourned the Assembly indefinitely and declared that the dismissal of Ajoy Mukherjee, the installation of a new ministry headed by Ghosh and the summoning of the Assembly were unconstitutional. He threatened to adjourn the House every time the Assembly was called in to session to give Ghosh a chance to prove his majority. In these circumstances, the Governor in his report to the President said that the Speaker's ruling had made the functioning of the Assembly and thereby all constitutional process, impossible. Consequently the President took over the administration of the state and the Assembly was placed in a state of suspended animation[30] despite the fact that the Calcutta High Court had in the meantime upheld the Governor's decision to appoint P.C. Ghosh.

5. Uttar Pradesh (1968)

In U.P. after the resignation of C.B. Gupta (Congress), Charan Singh (SVD) was invited by the Governor to form the ministry. Defection from the SVD to ongress and vice-versa became an every day affair after the formation of the ministry.

Under these circumstances, Charan Singh tendered his resignation to the Governor in spite of the fact that he still continued to be the leader of the SVD and also commanded the confidence of the House. At the same time he advised the Governor "to invite the new leader of the SVD for forming the government. In case the Governor did not consider it advisable to do so, or if the SVD failed to elect its leader, he might dissolve the legislature and hold a mid-term election". Notwithstanding this, the Governor recommended President's Rule. The Assembly which earlier kept suspended, was dissolved subsequently.[31]

6. Bihar (1968)

After the 1967 elections no party had a clear majority. Defections, communal troubles and disagreements on the status of Urdu as the second language of the state led to a succession of ministries. The SVD (non-Congress) coalition ministry resigned after a defeat in the Assembly on 25 January 1968 This was followed by Soshit Dal ministry, led by B.P. Mandal (1-2-68 to 18-03-68) to be replaced by the Samyukta Dal ministry under B.P. Sastri, leader of the new Lok Tantrik Congress Dal (22-03-68 to 25-06-68). Against the background of failure of three successive ministries of different parties in the legislature within a short period of time, the Governor did not agree to give four more days to Mahesh Prasad Sinha (Congress, which was numerically the largest group) and one more chance to the just defeated Chief Minister to form a ministry. Moreover, the appropriation bill had to be passed before 30 June 1968.[32] So he recommended President's Rule.

7. Punjab (1968)

When Assembly elections were held in 1967, no single party obtained a majority in Punjab. Though Congress emerged as the largest single party, it refused to form a government. In this circumstances, Gurnam Singh, the leader of the United People's Party was sworn in as the Chief Minister. Upon the breaking up to the ministry, Sardar Lachman Singh Gill formed a ministry with the support of defectors from Akali Dal and a few independents. The Congress legislature party, which initially supported the Gill ministry split into two factions. In this situation, Gill as well as the leaders of the People's United Front and the Congress legislature party advised the Governor to recommend President's Rule. As no party or combination of parties could provide a stable government, President's Rule was proclaimed.[33]

8. Bihar (1969)

The coalition ministry in Bihar headed by Bhola Paswan Shastri (Lok Tantrik Dal) submitted its resignation on 1 July 1969 after having been in office' for only nine days. Between 1967 and 1969 six ministries were formed in Bihar. Out of this only the first ministry of Mahamaya Prasad Sinha could cling to office for about nine months and the rest held office for a period ranging from four to hundred and fourteen days. In this circumstance, the Governor did not recognise the claim of the opposition (Congress) as their numerical strength included "unpredictables".[34] So President's Rule was imposed and the Assembly was kept suspended.

9. West Bengal (1970)

Following the resignation of Ajoy Mukherjee (U.F. Bangala Congress), Joyti Basu [CPI(M)] asked for time to explore the possibility of forming a ministry. However, he refused to disclose the names of his supporters on the plea that his party had rejected the Governor's request for revealing such names. Meanwhile, ten parties wrote to the Governor stating that they were totally opposed to any government led by CPI(M) and that it would be wrong, immoral and illegal on the part of the Governor to invite CPI(M) to form the government. The Congress also did not attempt to form a ministry because of the problem of the influx of Bangladesh refugees. Taking into account these factors and the deteriorating law and order situation, President's Rule was proclaimed.[35] The Assembly which was kept in the cold storage was subsequently dissolved.

10. Kerala (1970)

On the advice of Chief Minister C. Achutha Menon (CPI-led UF government) the Governor dissolved the Assembly on 6 June 1970. He was requested to continue till the formation of a new ministry. But, suddenly on 4 August 1970, while arrangements for fresh election were in progress, Menon preferred to resign, declaring that he had done so in view of criticism that the continuance of his ministry would have hindered free and fair election in the state. The Governor obliged and recommended President's Rule.[36]

11. Uttar Pradesh (1970)

The Congress withdrew its support to the coalition government headed by Charan Singh. But as soon as the Congress withdrew its support, the leaders of the opposition parties wrote to the Governor that they had decided to support Charan Singh and that they commanded a majority. Shortly after the formation of the BKD-Congress ministry headed by Charan Singh, serious differences arose among the coalition partners. The Chief Minister requested the Governor to remove thirteen out of 26 Congress ministers from the ministry. However, the Governor sought the opinion of the Attorney General and on whose advice the Governor asked the Chief-Minister to resign because he was heading a coalition in which the major partner was Congress (R). But Charan Singh refused to resign and informed the Governor on 29th September that he still had a majority in the Assembly because other parties had extended their support to him and asked for permission to face the Assembly on the 30th of September or on 6th October or even within 24 hours. But the Governor did not accept the proposal and recommended the imposition of President's Rule. as no party in his opinion was able to form a stable ministry. The Assembly was put in a state of suspended animation.[37]

In support of his action, Governor Gopala Reddy propounded a new philosophy relating to the functioning of the coalition governments.[38] He held that the Chief minister of a coalition government can not be treated at par with a Chief-Minister of a single party majority government in the matter of removal of ministers or reconstitution of Council of ministers, which involves a fundamental change in the complexion of the government. On such occasions, he argued, the Chief minister should first resign and then reconstitute the government. Regarding the question whether the Chief minister had lost the confidence of the legislature, the governor held that after the withdrawal of the support of the coalition partners, Charan Singh's ministry was reduced to a minority. The question arises for consideration is, whether Governor's action was justified, especially when the Assembly was to meet on October 6, only 4 days ahead?

12. Orissa (1971) (11/1/1971)

Consequent upon the withdrawal of support by the Jana Congress the coalition ministry headed by R.N. Singh Deo (Swatantra party) lost its majority in the Assembly. The Chief Minister submitted his resignation. Since no party was capable of forming the government, the Governor recommended President's Rule. The Assembly was kept suspended.[39]

13. Orissa (1971) (23/1/1971)

On 20 January 1971, the Governor reported that no party had come up with the proposal to form an alternative ministry. The earlier proclamation on 11 January 1971 was revoked and a fresh proclamation was issued on 23 January 1971 dissolving the legislative Assembly[40]

14. Orissa (1971) (23/3/1971)

Following elections, while the state was under President's Rule, no single party emerged with an absolute majority. The Congress (R), which obtained the largest number of seats claimed a majority with support from Utkal Congress, Swatantra Party and a few independents. The Utkal Congress had not made any announcement supporting Congress(R) nor had the Governor any final list from Mahatab who was the leader of the Congress party till 22 March 1971. President's Rule was proclaimed with suspension of Assembly after revoking the earlier proclamation, even though Mahatab had issued a statement that Governor should ask him to form a government.[41]

15. Mysore (1971)[42]

The ministry of Veerendra Patil (Cong. (O)), was reduced to a minority owing to defection from Congress (O) to Congress (R) in the wake of the landslide victory of Congress

(R) in the Parliamentary elections. On 18 March 1971, the Chief Minister submitted his resignation. The Governor accepted the resignation and after exploring the possibilities of forming an alternative ministry recommended the imposition of President's Rule. Moreover, the budget had to be passed before 1 April, 1971[43]

16. Gujarat (1971)

Immediately after the landslide victory of Congress (R) in the Lok Sabha elections, the Congress (O) ministry headed by Hitendra Desai was reduced to a minority due to defection. The council of ministers held an emergency meeting which decided to submit the resignation of the ministry and to recommend the dissolution of the Assembly. The Assembly had passed a vote on account for expenditure for only four months of the financial year 1971-72 and the budget for the remaining part of the year had to be passed before 31 July 1971. In view of this fluid situation and difficulties in holding election before the deadline, President's Rule was imposed.[44]

17. Punjab (1971)

The withdrawal of support by Jan Sangh to Prakash Singh Badal (Akali Dal) on the question of affiliation of the colleges of the Jullandhar district with Gurunanak Dev University led to instability. The government, however, could defeat a no-confidence motion taken up in July 1970, but its strength was adversely affected by further defection. When one of the ministers resigned, he demanded an enquiry into charges of corruption against some ministers. In this situation, the Chief Minister recommended dissolution of the Assembly, which was accepted by the Governor. The government had obtained a vote on account for only three months up to June 1971 and the budget had to be passed. This situation necessitated President's Rule and the Assembly was dissolved.[45]

18. West Bengal (1971)

Elections to the Assembly in 1971 did not produce a clear majority in the House having 280 seats. The coalition ministry . formed by Ajoy Mukherjee (Congress) was forced to resign because of defection. Budget had to be passed by the end of

June and there was an abnormal situation owing to the influx of refugees from East Pakistan.[46] The Chief Minister requested that the legislature be dissolved for obtaining a larger majority and subsequently tendered the resignation of his council of ministers. President's Rule was imposed to deal with this situation and also to face law and order problem arising out of the refugee problem.

19. Bihar (1972)

The coalition ministry under Bhola paswan Shastri including the Congress, CPI, PSP, the Jharkhand party and Soshit Dal was in power for one year and resigned three days before the beginning of the session of the Assembly, when a no-confidence motion was given against the ministry. This was the ninth fall of the state ministry since 1967 and the fifth fall since the mid-term poll in 1969. Shastri himself headed the government three times during this period. The Chief Minister recommended dissolution of the Assembly which was accepted by the Governor and later on President's Rule was imposed on 9 January 1972.[47] The presidential proclamation in Bihar revealed the amazing extent to which political instability dominated the politics of Bihar. Bihar politics gradually drifted from non-congress coalitions, to Congress coalitions to a Congress majority. It is possible that this political process would not have taken place in the absence of Article 356 in the Constitution.

20. Bihar (1972) (9/3/1972)

The proclamation of 9 January 1972 remained in force for two months after which it ceased to operate for want of Parliamentary ratification. A fresh proclamation was issued by the President on 9 March 1972.[48]

21. Manipur (1972)

Manipur was under President's rule since 16 October 1969 under the Government of Union Territories Act, 1963. It had become a full-fledged state on 21 January 1972 by virtue of the provisions of the North Eastern Area (Re-organisation Act), 1971. A fresh proclamation was issued under Article 356 on that date for the continuance of President's Rule till the formation of a new legislature.[49]

22. Tripura (1972)

It was under the direct administration of the President by virtue of an order dated 1 November 1971 under section 51 of the Union Territories Act. The new state of Tripura came into existence on 21 January 1972 when North Eastern Areas (Reorganization) Act of 1971 was passed. Till the elections were held to the Legislative assembly of this new state and a popular government assumed office, it was not possible to carry on the administration of the state in accordance with the provisions of the Constitution. President's Rule was, therefore, introduced in the state on 21 January 1972.[50]

23. Andhra (1973)

The Congress Chief Minister P.V. Narasimha Rao was asked to resign by the Congress High Command in the wake of Mulki Rules[51] agitation and on the question of separation of Andhra and Telungana regions of the state, though the Congress legislature party enjoyed an absolute majority in the legislature. President's rule was declared following the resignation of Rao since an alternative leader was not immediately elected. The Assembly was placed in a state of suspended animation.

24. Orissa (1973)

Nandini Satpathy ministry (Congress) was reduced to a minority following the differences between Congress and Utkal Congress, a major partner, on the issue of the absorption of the Utkal Congress MLAs into Congress. The Chief Minister tendered her resignation on 1 March 1973 and advised the Governor to dissolve the Assembly, On the very same day Biju Patnaik, the leader of the Orissa Pragati Legislature Party, met the Governor, and staked claim to form a ministry. He claimed the strength of 72 MLAs out of a total of 139 members in the Assembly. The Governor recommended the imposition of President's Rule along with the dissolution of the Assembly on the ground that a combination of differing political ideologies would not be able to form a stable government.[52]

25. Manipur (1973)

The coalition ministry of Mohammed Alimuddin, the leader of the United Legislature Party, faced rough weather as a result of defection by nine of its supporters including two cabinet ministers. When a no-confidence motion was debated in the Assembly, the Chief Minister resigned and recommended the dissolution of the Assembly. Immediately after the resignation of the ministry, A. Diaho, the leader of the Progressive Democratic Alliance which also included Congress staked his claim for the formation of a new ministry. The Governor did not invite the opposition because the budget had to be passed before 31 March 1973 and the President's Rule was declared.[53]

26. Uttar Pradesh (1973)

The serious situations stemming from the grave indiscipline found among a sizeable section of the Provincial Armed Constabulary (PAC), severe drought and scarcity conditions, shortage of power and the widespread unrest forced the Congress high command to ask for the resignation of the Congress Chief Minister Kamalapati Tripathy. It was thought that direct involvement of the Central government was necessary for restoring peace and safeguarding the security of the state. Consequently, the Chief Minister resigned even though he enjoyed the confidence of the legislature. Hence the President's Rule was clamped and the Assembly was kept suspended.[54]

27. Gujarat (1974)

G. Oza, the Congress Chief Minister since 1972 was replaced by Chimanbhai Patel in 1973. The anti price-rise agitation coupled with the student unrest made the political situation worse. The agitators demanded the resignation of the ministry and dissolution of the Assembly. Patel resigned at the instance of the Congress High Command and President's Rule was imposed in February. The legislature was merely suspended. Meanwhile, the opposition legislators began to resign. The centre sought to remedy this by asking Patel to resign from theParliamentary party. This did not work, Patel resigned from the Congress itself. On 11 March 1974, Morarji Desai went on an indefinite fast demanding the dissolution of the Assembly, which was conceded on 15 March 1974.[55]

28. Nagaland (1975)

The Naga National Organization ministry by John Bose Jasokie plunged into crisis when as many as ten legislators decided to defect to the UDF. S.C. Jamer, UDF leader, met the Governor and submitted a list of 33 of his supporters. The Governor, however, told him to prove his claim on the floor of the House, which was then having the budget session.[56] The Speaker adjourned the House on 20 March 1975 after a heated discussion. President's Rule was imposed with suspended Assembly but subsequently dissolved on 20 May 1975.

29. Uttar Pradesh (1975)

H.N. Bahuguna's Congress ministry was plunged into crisis because of the emergence of a dissident group within his party. The then Prime Minister and party President Indira Gandhi asked him to quit, and he tendered the resignation of his ministry. Thereupon the Governor, M. Chenna Reddy, recommended President's Rule as the Congress party had not elected its new leader in place of Bahuguna. On 30 November 1975 the state was placed under President's Rule, but the Assembly was merely put under suspension.[57]

30.Tamil Nadu (1976)

In Tamil Nadu, the DMK had been in power for almost eight years. Less than two months before the expiry of the term of the Tamil Nadu legislature, Governor K.K. Shah, recommended President's Rule on the ground of maladministration, corruption and misuse of power for achieving partisan ends. It was also recommended to appoint an investigative Commission to enquire in to the alleged malpractices of the public corporations in the state. The imposition of President's Rule was treated with great suspicion since the Assembly's term was about to expire and the DMK ministry had majority in the legislature and there was no breakdown of the constitutional machinery of the state.[58]

31. Gujarat (1976)

The Janata Front ministry by Babubhai Patel was defeated on the floor of the House in February 1976 when the demands for grant of Foods and Civil Supplies department came up for voting in the Assembly. The coalition also had inevitable problems and after its defeat on vital budget proposals, the Chief Minister resigned. Since the Congress was not ready to form the government and in view of the urgency of passing the budget, the Governor recommended the imposition of President's Rule while keeping the Assembly suspended.[59]

32. Orissa (1976)

The smooth functioning of the Congress ministry led by Nandini Satpathy was hindered by the rise and growth of factionalism within the Congress party. The Council of ministers had lost faith in the leadership of the Chief Minister.[60] Sharp division within the cabinet created political uncertainty which had its repercussions on the administration and law and order situation. Above all, serious charges of corruption and misuse of emergency powers were leveled against the Chief Minister. Then, on the advice of the Prime Minister, she resigned and President's Rule was imposed on 9 December 1976 along with the suspension of the Assembly.[61]

33-41. The mass dismissal (1980)

When the Congress (I) party gained a thumping majority in the Lok Sabha elections in 1980, President's Rule was imposed in the non-congress ruled states of Punjab, Rajasthan, Orissa, Madhya Pradesh, Uttar Pradesh, Maharashtra, Bihar, Gujarat and Tamil Nadu on the ground that the governments of these state were no longer represented the wishes and aspiration of the electorate.

42. Manipur (1981)

Rishang Keishing's (Congress (I)) ministry fell when ten members of the ruling party, including one Minister, crossed the floor and thus reduced the strength of the ministry to 29 in a House of 60. The Governor did not consider the claim of the opposition leader. He declined to believe that the opposition had the requisite majority to form a stable government. Moreover the Governor believed that the mounting insurgency necessitated central intervention. As a result, President's Rule was declared and the Assembly was kept suspended.[62]

43. Assam (1981)

Upon the resignation of the Congress (I) ministry of Anwara Taimur, opposition parties staked the claim for forming a government with their combined strength and support of other groups. The Communist Party of India and the Socialist Party did not support the formation of any ministry because of the law and order problem created by the Assam agitation. Some political parties appeared to be in favour of President's rule without dissolving the Assembly. The large number of defections among the members of the Assembly after 1978 election reflected the extent of political instability. Considering the changes in party loyalties and multiplicity of parties wherein no party had adequate majority to ensure a stable ministry with a coherent policy, the Governor recommended President's Rule which was proclaimed on 30 June 1981 with the suspension of the Assembly.[63]

44. Kerala (1981)

The Left Democratic Front ministry under the CPI (M) leader E.K. Nayanar lost majority support in the Assembly consequent upon the withdrawal of support by two of its coalition partners, namely Congress (S) and the Kerala Congress (M). President's Rule was imposed but the legislature was kept suspended on the plea that "a viable alternative ministry is not immediately possible".[64]

45. Kerala (1982)

The United Democratic Front ministry led by K. Karunakaran resigned when Lonappan Nambadan, a Kerala Congress (M) member, withdrew his support to the ministry which was being run by casting vote of the Speaker. The request of the opposition parties to form an alternative ministry was turned down. The Assembly was dissolved and President's Rule was declared.[65]

46. Assam (1982)

The Congress (I) ministry headed by Gogoi bowed out of office as the Assembly met on 18 March 1982 to discuss a no-confidence motion. While resigning, the Chief Minister advised the Governor to dissolve the Assembly. With a history of large-scale defections during the past four years and four ministers having bowed out of office in a short period, the Governor recommended President's rule with the dissolution of the Assembly as he did not see any possibility of forming a ministry.[66]

47. Punjab (1983)

The Chief Minister informed the Central government in his letter of resignation that the development in the state (the Akali agitation) had acquired a severe dimension not confined to the state alone but with serious implication for the whole country. He therefore suggested direct intervention of the Centre for the temporary period even though he continued to have an absolute majority in the Assembly. The recommendation was accepted and President's Rule imposed. The Assembly was initially suspended but dissolved subsequently.[67]

48. Sikkim (1984)

The continuation of the Congress (I) ministry headed by Gurung was in jeopardy with "frequent shifts in loyalties of legislators due to various tactics including intimidation; kidnaping, blackmail and monetary inducement".[68] Though Bhandari, the leader of the Sikkim Sangram Parishad, claimed the majority—16 members in the House of 32—the Governor recommended President's Rule on the ground of possibilities of defection and that the life of the Assembly was also due to expire within a few months.

Thus, during Indira Gandhi's Prime Minister ship i.e. from 1966-1977 and from 1980-1984, President's Rule was imposed forty-eight (32+16) times in various states. It shows an average of three times each year. This is really high figure when compared with the imposition of President's Rule on seven occasions in the Nehru era of more than fourteen years. Unlike her predecessors, she used the novel device of suspending rather than dissolving state legislature where there was some hope for her own party to reconstitute the government. It seems that the selective use of presidential suspensions was clearly along partisan lines.[69] During Indira's period, President's Rule was used as a device to manage the transitional problems and a short spell of this was usually effective in restoring stability in the states.[70] In the late 60's, many states came to be ruled by coalitions opposed to the Congress, which accelerated the frequency of the declaration of President's Rule in the states. Indira Gandhi's rule also witnessed consolidation and strengthening of Central authority and the concentration of power in the Prime Minister. During this period there were many cases in which President's rule was imposed without exploring the possibilities for forming an alternative ministry or even allowing Chief Ministers having doubtful majority to prove their strength on the floor of the House. An important feature of her regime was that this provision was invoked even to settle the internal problems of the Congress party. "It was quite unfortunate that Article 356 was used as a solution to end group rivalry within a political party". During the second tenure, she in fact became independent of the party bosses and the party she represented since she was both the leader of the Parliamentary party and the President of the Congress party. The way in which Karunanidhi of Tamil Nadu was ousted in 1976 on the allegation of corruption and maladministration a few weeks before the expiry of the state assembly indicated that the provision could be used for almost any purpose. But the most unfortunate subversion of democratic values took place in 1980 when nine non-Congress state governments were dismissed on the ground that those governments did not enjoy the confidence of the people in their respective states. No greater proof is required to establish the fact that the Article was being misused by the Prime Minister to further the Congress party's objectives. In many cases this arbitrary application led to considerable debate, political acrimony, hunger strike, widespread agitations and even constitutional controversies.

C. President's Rule during the Prime-Minister Ship of Rajiv Gandhi

1. Jammu and Kashmir (1986)

When the Congress (I) withdrew support to the twenty month old G.M. Shaw ministry (National Conference dissident group), the ministry fell. As no alternative government was feasible, the Governor's rule was proclaimed under section 92 of the Jammu and Kashmir Constitution on 7 March 1986. However, the Assembly was put under suspended animation. All the opposition parties repeatedly demanded that Assembly be dissolved so that fresh election could be held for installing a popular government. Farooq Abdulla, the National Conference leader, even went to the extent of threatening that thirty four members of his party in the legislature would resign if the Assembly was not dissolved. Under section 92, the proclamation was operative only up to 6 September 1986. The Governor reported to the President that the security of the state was under threat and that the composition and strength of political parties and groups in the state Assembly were such that political instability would continue. On the basis of this report, President's Rule was proclaimed on 7 September 1986 but the Assembly was kept suspended.[71]

2. Punjab (1987)

After the Rajiv-Longowal agreement, elections were held in Punjab and an Akali Dal government was formed under Surjit Singh Barnala. "The violence and terrorism that plagued Punjab did not abate but escalated and there was complete breakdown of law and order. In his report to the President, the Governor stated that the law and order situation had deteriorated seriously and that the situation was further aggravated by the fact that the ministers had close links with terrorists and extremists. Hence President's Rule was imposed but the legislature was kept under suspended animation in the hope that a popular government could be revived if the situation improved.[82]

3. Tamil Nadu (1988)

After the death of M.G. Ramachandran, the Governor called upon his wife Janaki Ramachandran to form a government on the condition that she must secure a vote of confidence within three weeks. The trial of strength took place on 28 January 1988. On that day the legislators indulged in violence and the police had to be called in to restore order. In this situation the

Governor reported to the President that Janaki Ramachandran was leading a minority government. The Governor's report was also critical of the Speaker's role in adjourning the House on frivolous grounds. The report also underlined that horse-trading had taken place before the actual consideration of the confidence motion[73]

4. Nagaland (1988)

The eight month old Congress (I) ministry under Kokisha Sema plunged into crisis following the resignation of thirteen legislators, including four ministers, from the party, who formed a separate group known as Naga Regional Congress (NRC). The 13 dissidents along with eighteen Naga National Democratic Party formed a joint legislature party in an attempt to form an alternative ministry. Vamuzo, the leader of the dissident group was unanimously elected as the leader of the joint group. He claimed the strength of 35 members in the sixty member Assembly. The Chief Minister submitted his resignation to the Governor and recommended the imposition of President's Rule. President's Rule was clamped and the Assembly dissolved.[74] In the case of Nagaland v. Union of India,[75] a division Bench of the Guwahati High Court found the report of the Governor to the President on 6 August 1988 recommending the imposition of President's Rule under Article 356 and dissolution of the Assembly unacceptable. The two judges were divided as to whether the material placed for the union cabinet's advice to the president leading to the proclamation of President's Rule was protected from judicial scrutiny under Article 74 (2). The Chief Justice (one of the two judges of the Bench) held it was not. Here the most significant point is that the opposition (of course including the defectors from the Congress), even though it commanded a majority, was not allowed to form an alternative ministry. There are examples when the congress party which formed the opposition was allowed to form alternative ministry even though its majority was due to defection from non-congress parties.

5. Mizoram (1988)

The Mizo National Front ministry of Laldenga had to face crisis when eight members of the ruling party formed a separate group, Mizo National Front (I), reducing the strength of the ruling party to sixteen in the Forty member House. The Congress (I) chief Lanthanwala staked his claim to form a coalition government with the help of the break away group. However, the Speaker created constitutional crisis by suspending eight of these members during the pendency of proceedings for their disqualification. These developments paved the way for President's Rule in the state.[76]

6. Karnataka (1989)

The eight month old Janata Dal ministry headed by S.R. Bommai was put into constitutional crisis when Kalyan Rao Molankery, a dissident leader met the Governor and presented nineteen letters purported to have been signed by seventeen Janata Dal MLAs, one associate independent MLA and one BJP member withdrawing their support to the government. However, the Chief Minister reported to the Governor that he still had majority and was prepared to prove his majority on the floor of the legislature. But the Governor did not agree. He sent a report which was considered by a section of the press as biased and acting on that report, the ministry was dismissed and legislative assembly was dissolved.[77] In this report the Governor said: 'horse trading is going on and atmosphere is getting vitiated'. He reiterated his opinion that Chief Minister Bommai had lost the confidence of majority in the State Assembly and requested action being taken on his previous letters. In his proclamation the President stated that 'the said action was taken on the basis of the report of the Governor of the state of Karnataka and other information received.[78]

The validity of the proclamation was challenged by the ousted Chief Minister Bommai and other members of the Council of ministers by way of writ petition in the Karnataka High Court. The Court dismissed the petition holding that the facts stated in the Governor's report could not be held to be irrelevant. Governor's bonafides were not questioned and his satisfaction was based up on reasonable assessment of facts, the court observed. The court also ruled that recourse to floor test was neither compulsory nor obligatory and was not a prerequisite to the sending of the report to the President.[79] The Supreme Court, however, held that the question of the lack of majority support for the ministry was not tested on the floor of the House. The court observed that a duly constituted ministry was dismissed on the *ipse dixit* of the Governor who made no effort to install in office an alternative ministry. The Governors report thus was faulty and clearly smacked of *mala fide*. The proclamation based on such a report also suffered from *mala fide* and was liable to be struck down.[80]

The Rajiv administration (1984-1989) promulgated Article 356 six times, i.e. 1.2 times a year. The occasions of President's Rule during his era were few in comparison with the frequency with which Article 356 was invoked during the time of Indira Gandhi and the Janata regime. The situation stabilised to some extent during his era when the ruling party at the Centre realised the political futility of the use of this coercive power in the opposition ruled states as a matter of policy[81] This healthy trend was mainly due to the adoption of anti-defection law in 1984. This reduced or minimised the possibilities of defection, which was one of the main reasons for the lowest number of recommendations for President's Rule during the Rajiv era. But it is important to note that on all occasions except one, in Punjab in 1987, it was not only highly controversial but also subversive of Parliamentary democracy. The way in which the Bommai ministry in Karnataka (1989) was dismissed revealed the fact that Rajiv Gandhi continued the same personalised and centralised style of governance of his mother. By arbitrarily dismissing Bommai he had added one more dubious feather to his crown.

D. President's Rule under Narasimha Rao's Administration

1. Meghalaya (1991)

In Meghalaya, B.B. Lyngdoh's ministry, which was enjoying the majority support was dismissed, in complete disregard of the Supreme Court order.[82] The fact of the case is as follows. The Assembly was summoned on 7 August 1991 to discuss a vote of confidence in the ministry. On the motion, thirty members voted for it and twenty seven against. Before announcing the result, the Speaker, however, declared that five members who had voted for the motion, had forfeited their right to vote for having attracted disqualification under the anti-defection Law. The Supreme Court had ordered that the support of four independent members, who were declared disqualified by the speaker, should be counted. The Speaker allowed the four MLAs to vote, but did not count their votes for the motion, and exercising his casting vote, he declared the motion lost. In this circumstances, the Governor directed the Chief Minister to resign. When the Chief Minister did not comply with the direction he dismissed the government and made a recommendation to the President to take action under Article 356 with suspended Assembly.

2. Manipur (1992)

The six party United Legislature Front headed by R.K. Ranbir Singh was reduced to minority after 7 legislators, including two ministers, withdrew support thereby reducing the strength of ULF to 24 in the 60 member Assembly. However, the Speaker created a constitutional crisis by disqualifying the opposition members (defectors) whenever a no-confidence vote against Ranbir Singh government came up in the Assembly. The Supreme Court set aside such disqualifications, but the Speaker, for collateral and *mala fide* reasons did not allow them to vote. This drama led to President's Rule.[83] The Assembly was kept suspended.

3. Nagaland (1992)

The 21 months old Nagaland government of Mr. Vamuzo fell when 12 members of the Nagaland People's Council withdrew support accusing him of mismanaging funds. The Chief Minister recommended the dissolution of the Assembly which was accepted. The Governor had done so in exercise of his power under Article 174 (2) b without consulting the centre before taking such a decision. The centre did not approve of this action of the Governor. Accordingly the centre imposed President's Rule in the state and dismissed the Governor thereafter. The centre's justification for taking the action was that the chief minister. had already lost his majority in the Legislature when he advised the Governor to dissolve the

House. The opposition parties in Parliament described the centre's action as an attack on the federal character of the constitution.[84]

4. Uttar Pradesh (1992)

On 6 December 1992, President's rule was imposed in UP . because the U.P Government headed by Kalyan Singh failed to perform its constitutional responsibilities and was a silent witness to the anarchy and disorder unleashed in Ayodhya which led to the demolition of the 430 year old Babri Masjid which was a place of worship of the Muslims.[85] The state government could not maintain law and order and totally failed to fulfil the assurances given to the Supreme court and the nation that it would never be allowed the kersevaks to demolish the Babri Masjid. The belligent and rampaging kersevaks had the run to the place around the mosque sending shock waves across the nation and inviting the Prime-minister to declare an open war against the Machiavellian tactics of the BJP - VHP combine to grab power, whipping up a communal frenzy to undermine the secular fabric of the nation. The Chief Minister of U.P., however, asserted that he had resigned.

5-7. M.P., H.P. and Rajasthan (1992)

On 15 December 1992 president's Rule was imposed in the three BJP ruled states of Madhya Pradesh, Rajasthan and Himachal Pradesh and their Assemblies were dissolved on the plea that these states were not sincerely implementing the ban imposed by the Centre up on certain organizations.

Consequent on the demolition of the Babari masjid on 6 December 1992, the communal organizations like the RSS, VHP, ISS, Bujrang Dal and Jamait-e-Islami were banned and the demand for the dismissal of the three BJP Governments within the Congress gathered momentum especially after the Congress working committee on 14 December 1992 which decided in principle that the three Governments should be dismissed.[86] The CPI, CPI (M) and the National Front also demanded the dismissal of the three BJP state governments.[87] The three Governors had also submitted more or less identical report in 24 hours.

The Governor of Himachal Pradesh in his report to the President has pointed out that the Chief Minister himself had admitted that he was a member of R.S.S. He also observed that one ruling party MLA had publicaly admitted that he had participated in the demolition of the disputed structure at Ayodhya. The report said : "The people of the State felt that the Chief minister himself being an RSS member, he will not be able to carry out the instructions of the centre regarding the ban on communal organizations'. The Governor had stated in his report that in order to carry on the administration of the state in accordance with the provisions of the Constitutions, he had no other alternative but to recommend the dismissal of the Government led by Shanta Kumar and dissolution of the Assembly in the public interest.[88]

The Rajasthan Governor in his report pointed out that one member of the State ministry had actually participated in the Karseva at Ayodhya. The other charges levelled against the government by were: non-implimentation of the ordinance, worsening of law and order situation and anti-minority bias. The Governor concluded that the 'administration cannot function effectively under the present setup'. Hence, he recommended to the dismissal of the Government and the dissolution of the Assembly.[89]

In the case of Madhya Pradesh, the President had three reports from the Governor within six days which pointed to fast deteriorating law and order situation. The Governor was highly critical of the state government and recommended "President's Rule" in the state as an inevitable course of action.[90]

The mass dismissals of the three BJP governments in general and M.P in particular have emerged significant both politically and constitutionally because of the case Sundarlal Patwa v. Union of India and others before the M.P. High Court and decision thereof. The petitioner challenged the imposition of President's Rule on the ground that it was a colourable exercise of power by the Centre and thus a gross misuse for political vendetta. The majority judgment held that from the matter placed before it, no inference could be drawn that the state government had disrespected or disobeyed any Central directives nor was there any specification of alleged deeds or misdeeds in meeting the law and order situation. The Bench held that the union government had not been able to support the imposition of President's Rule only in the BJP ruled states and ordered the revival of the state ministry and the legislature.[91]

8. Tripura (1993)

President's Rule was imposed in Tripura when the term of the Tripura Assembly had expired and the election could not be held because it was postponed by the Election Commission on the ground that the state government had failed to ensure proper atmosphere for holding free and fair elections. The Chief Minister had resigned before the expiry of the term of the Tripura Assembly in wake of 'political uncertainty' in the state. President's Rule was imposed on the recommendation of the Governor.[92]

9. Manipur (1993)

The coalition ministry headed by the Congress (I) leader R.K. Dorendra Singh could not combat the law and order problem effectively. In the wake of continued Naga-Kuki clashes, resulting in about 1000 deaths, President's Rule was imposed in the state.[93] The Assembly was placed in a state of suspended animation.

10. Bihar (1995)

President's Rule was imposed in the state of Bihar to enable the Parliament to fulfil a constitutional obligation of approving the expenditure for the state beyond 31 March 1995 as the term of the Assembly expired on 15 March and the new House could not be constituted before the expiry date.[94] The Governor recommended imposition of President's Rule to enable the Parliament to pass the Vote-On-Account.

11. Uttar Pradesh (1995)

The BJP-BSP government under the Chief Minister ship of Mayawati fell when BJP withdrew its support to the Government. The claim of BJP to form a fresh government was neither considered nor allowed. On the basis of the report of the Governor that no viable ministry was possible the President of India declared the imposition of Article 356 in the state. The state assembly was, however, not dissolved but kept under suspended animation. Later, the Assembly was dissolved.[95]

During the five years of Rao's Prime-minister ship, Article 356 was invoked eleven times, i.e., two President's Rules in a year. The frequency during his era was less in comparison with the frequency with which Article 356 was invoked during the second decade of Independence. This was mainly on account of the emergence of strong opposition which adopted a tough stand that involved political struggles and legal tussles. However, the majority of these proclamations do not fall within the purview of what is called the failure of the constitutional machinery. The dismissal of the three BJP governments in 1992 in the aftermath of Ayodhya incident revealed that opposition parties would not be allowed to continue in office on one pretext or another. Likewise, the invocation of the provision in U.P. in 1995 and Nagaland in 1992 indicated the bare fact that opposition parties were also not allowed as far as possible to form ministries after the defeat of a ruling government. Imposition of Presidents Rule in Nagaland in 1992 and sacking of Governor, M.M. Thomas, for accepting the advice of his non-congress Chief-minister, without prior consultation with the Centre, to dissolve the state legislative Assembly testifies the fact that he had no regard for political fair play and constitutional morality. It was an open secret that the Congress(I) was basically trying to destabilise the Nagaland People's Council government headed by vamuzo and capture power by engineering defection as Dua observes.[96] So, it can be concluded that Rao followed the same pattern started by Nehru and followed by Indira Gandhi and continued by Rajiv Gandhi.

President's Rule Under Manmohan Singh

1. Bihar (2005)

The General election held in 2005 to the Bihar Legislative Assembly produced a fractured verdict which in turn witnessed a political deadlock and constitutional impasse. The two leading alliances – (R.J.D - Congress and BJP - JD (U)) could not obtained 122 seats (the magic number necessary for the formation of a government). Further, the formation of a government was made difficult by the stiff stand taken by the 29 member LJP. The party Chief Ramvilas Paswan had already informed the Governor about unwillingness of his party to support any government formed with the help of either the RJD or the BJP. Since no party was in a position to form the Government, Governor, Buta Singh, reported to the President that in his opinion no political party was in a position to command a majority and President's Rule was only option. Acting on the report of the Governor President's Rule was imposed in March 2005 and the Assembly was kept in suspended animation with a view to explore the possibilities of forming a government later.[97]

However, while discussion on the formation of a Government was going on, the Governor sent another report on 27 April 2005 stating that the various newspaper reports and other reports, including intelligence report gathered indicated a trend to gain over the elected representatives of people through various allurements like money, caste, posts etc... which was a disturbing feature. According to the said report a situation was fast approaching a scenario wherein if the trend is not arrested immediately the consequent political instability will further give rise to horse trading being practised by various political groups trying to allure elected MLAs. That it would not be possible to contain the situation without giving the people another opportunity to give their mandate through fresh poll and, he recommended the dissolution of the Assembly. Therefore, the still born Assembly, which had placed under suspended animation was dissolved. However, it was alleged that this was done with a view to provide an advantage to the UPA by aborting the JD (U) BJP ministry, when the alliance was closer for getting a majority and the situation has reached where claim may be staked to form a government.[98]

2. Goa (2005)

The elections to Goa Assembly in 2005 was not conclusive. However, BJP managed to form a coalition Government with the support of smaller parties including independents. The government was put in to crisis because of a routine change of portfolio of a minister which resulted in the resignation of four MLAs supporting the ministry. It was alleged that these resignations were induced by Congress party with an eye on the formation of Congress ministry in the state. Faced with loss of majority, the BJP sought to disqualify an independent MLA who had declared his support for the Congress on the ground that he had joined the BJP earlier. In this circumstances, Governor S.C. Jamir asked Chief minister Parikar to demonstrate his confidence on the floor of the House. Yet the floor test turned out to be an exercise tainted by the Speaker's partisan act of keeping an independent MLA (who failed to appear before him for an enquiry in their disqualification) out of the House for disorderly conduct in an attempt to manage a majority for the Parrikar Government. The Speaker also counted an opposition Maharashtra wadhi Gomantak party MLA as a ruling camp supporter before declaring that the Government had the support of 18 members in a House of 36, down from 40 after the resignation of four BJP MLAs.[99] Governor S.C. Jamir dismissed the Government even before Speaker could send his report on the out-come of the confidence motion and a Congress coalition headed by Pratap Singh Rane was hurriedly installed without specifying a date for him to prove his majority. In a bid to tilt the number in its favour, the Congress persuaded a BJP MLA to resign from the Assembly. However, the Speaker disqualified a Congress supporter and he resigned along with deputy Speaker to strengthen the BJP camp and weaken the Congress camp. It was in this situation that the proterm speaker prevented a MLA (United Goans Democratic Party) who was in the BJP camp, from voting. The BJP members recorded their protest and said that the proterm Speaker had no power to restrain a member from casting his vote. Ignoring their protest the proterm speaker asked Rane to table the motion. Those in favour of and against was 16 each, as the Speaker ignored the vote of UGDP MLA who stood up against the motion. Declaring that there was a tie the proterm Speaker, Sardina cast his deciding vote and declared the motion passed by 17 to 16. The Union Government after a cabinet meeting imposed President's Rule. Later the home-minister in a press conference said 'what happened in the legislative Assembly of Goa is not acceptable to the Government.[100]

3. Karnataka (2007) (9/10/2007)

On 9 October 2007, the Union Government decided to impose President's Rule in Karnataka and keep the Legislative Assembly in suspended animation following the resignation of Janata Dal (S) Chief minister H.D. Kumaraswami; whose government had lost its majority following withdrawal of support by its coalition partner, B.J.P.[101] The Janata Dal(S) refused to honour its 20:20 power sharing agreement with BJP, leading to BJP to withdraw support, and resignation by the Kumaraswami Government. The two parties formed an alliance in January 2006 under which the Janata Dal(S) was to head the government for the first 20 months and the BJP the remaining 20 months of the term of the Assembly. Every thing was fine till the end of the tenure of Kumaraswami as the Chief Minister of the State. Consequently, the BJP was to take over the Chief Minister ship on 3rd October 2007. But the Janata Dal(S) declined to handover power, leading to the two parties snapping their ties. It became clear that no stable government could be formed in the state with the Congress (64) showing no inclination to tie up with JD(S) (58) and the BJP (79). In this circumstances the Governor, left with no option, recommended President's Rule to bring to an end the impasse and the State was placed under President's Rule with suspended Assembly.

4 Karnataka (2007) (20 -10- 2007)

During President's Rule, the BJP and the JD (U) again agreed to come together and the BJP leader B.S. Yeddurappa was Sworn in on 12 November as the Chief minister. However, the first BJP ministry did not last long since its coalition partner JD (S) decided to vote against the government's confidence motion on the floor of the Assembly[102] on the contention that BJP was trying to convert the state in to a Hindutva laboratory. The trouble between the coalition partners surfaced when the

JD (S) wanted the BJP to sign a twelve point power sharing agreement drafted by JD (S) and the refusal of the BJP. The Chief minister resigned before the Assembly could vote on the trust motion. With all the three major political parties in the state demanding President's Rule and the holding of fresh elections, Governor Remeshwar Thakur probably believed that he had no option but to recommend President's Rule. The Cabinet considered the Governor's report and accepted his recommendations. The centre's decision brought to an end the political drama that was witnessed in the state on the issue of transfer of power between the coalition partners. The assembly initially suspended was dissolved later.

5 Nagaland (2008)

Nagaland came under President's Rule on 2 January 2008 following a controversial ruling by the Assembly Speaker on the opposition sponsored non- confidence motion. The Assembly was placed under suspended animation.[103]

The political Crisis began on 13 December 2007 when the Assembly met for a day's session to take up the non- confidence motion moved by Congress led Nagaland Progressive Alliance (NPA) against the Democratic alliance of Nagaland (DAN) government led by Chief Minister Nephiu Rio. Rio survived the non- confidence motion in the Assembly. The motion was defeated 23-19 in the 60 Member House after the Speaker barred three independents from taking part in the voting on the ground that they had earlier supported the DAN and then wanted to support the NPA and also held that the vote of nine dissidents were invalid as they went against party whip. The Speaker ruled that the motion against the coalition government had failed. The opposition Congress questioned the decision and claimed that 31 legislators had voted in favour of the motion and 23 legislators voted against it and maintained that the Rio government had been voted out of power. The party legislators had demanded the Governor to dismiss the government, alleging constitutional impropriety on the part of the Speaker. They also rushed to New Delhi and called on the President demanding the invocation of President's Rule under Article 356. A Union Cabinet meeting was convened at a short notice to discuss the fluid political situation in Nagaland which had decided to recommend President's Rule with suspended animation of the Assembly.

6. Jammu and Kashmir (2008)

President's Rule was imposed in the state of Jammu and Kashmir in July 2008 after the Congress (I) - P.D.P. coalition Government fell over the controversial Government order of transferring 800 kanals (40 hectares) of land to Shri Amarnath Shrine Board (SASB) headed by the Governor of the state and then by its revocation. Before the Government order the SASB had no land with it. All arrangement of the pilgrimage to the shrine were made by the departments of Government and local Muslims. The government order for the transfer of forest land to the SASB was for a temporary period to provide shelter for pilgrims. But the Kashmiri separatist leaders had interpreted it as a part of a plan to settle Hindus from outside to change the demography of the state, reducing its Muslim majority into minority.[104] This sparked days of rioting in Muslim dominated region resulting in the death of 6 people apart from injuries sustained by hundreds. Instead of leaving the controversy to be handled by his government, the Governor offered a defence of the land transfer which made the problems worse.

The PDP minister also joined the popular protest, even though two of them holding the forest and law portfolios (who were directly responsible for the land transfer order), and other members in the cabinet were parties to the government's unanimous decision. However, swimming with the popular wave, the PDP gave notice to the Chief minister Gulam Nabi Azad, to withdraw the order, if not, it would quit the coalition government. In the face of unending protest from the Muslims, the state Government withdrew its decision as desired by the PDP by June 30. But the PDP withdrew its support a day earlier by reducing the government into a minority. As he had no other alternatives the Chief Minister submitted resignation of his ministry. The new Governor, N.N. Vora there upon dissolved the Assembly and sought the concurrence of the President of India for issuance of a proclamation to enforce Governor's Rule in Jammu and Kashmir. Kashmir came under New Delhi's direct rule on 13 July 2008.[105]

7. Jharkhand, (2009)

Jharkhand was placed on 19 January 2009 under Article 356 of the Constitution in order to end the political uncertainty in the State in the wake of Chief minister Shibu Soren losing a by- election which forced him to resign.[106] An unscheduled meeting of the union cabinet accepted the recommendation of Governor Syed Sibta Razi to impose President's rule as none of the political parties came forward to form government in the State after the resignation of the Chief minister following his defeat in the Tamar by - poll. The Cabinet's recommendation had been sent to the President who approved it and sent it to the home-ministry.

The report of the Governor, the recommendation of the cabinet and the consequent decision of the President came as a relief. 'The union government appeared to have opted for the inevitable after it became clear that there was no agreement on a successor to Soren following his shock defeat'[107] at the hands of a rebel Jharkhand party candidate, Gopala Krishna Patar Alias Raja peter. The state has been thrown into political and ministerial instability by six governments within a period of eight years speaks volume of the unprincipled and unethical power politics played by all parties. The Union government has done the right thing since the predicament stems not from any over reach by the Centre but from the unique circumstances arising from the defeat of an incumbent Chief minister. The situation was complicated by Mr. Soren's preposterous attempt to appoint the J.M.M legislator, Champai Soren as his successor. This attempt was viewed as a stop-gap arrangement to enable him to try and win from another constituency and reclaim the Chief Minister post.[108]

8. Meghalaya (2009)

The nearly one year old Meghalaya Progressive Alliance Ministry headed by Donkupar Ray was put into constitutional crisis when five members withdrew support to the Government. The Speaker had suspended these MLAs under the Anti-defection law ignoring the Governor's directive to maintain statuesquo on the voting right of members.[109] However, the Shillong bench of the Guwahati High Court stayed the impugned interim orders suspending both Lyngdoh and Sangma. It held that each of the political parties forming the MPA appeared to have contested the election separately as a separate political party. Therefore *prima facie* finding of the respondent that a *prima facie* case of disqualification of the petitioner under Tenth Schedule made out was 'nothing but perversity'. The order gave the respondents the liberty to apply for modification or cancellation there of. The four out of the five members were present during the trust vote and voted during division. However, the speaker announced that their votes were invalid owing to their suspension.[110]

The Government, however, survived the trust vote on 17 March with the Speaker casting his vote in favour of the Government to break the tie of 27:27 in the 60 member House, during division. However, the state was placed under President's Rule and the Assembly was kept under suspended animation after Union Cabinet took the decision following the recommendation made by the Governor Ranjit Sekhar - Mooshahary in his report. The report said that Meghalaya was undergoing a spell of political uncertainty and instability and the constitutional machinery had broken down'.[111] The decision to impose President's Rule triggered large scale protest across the political horizon of the state. Political leaders of the state, cutting across party lines, unanimously described the government's decision as unconstitutional and unethical. They even termed the development as something tantamount to defacing the Constitution.

9. Jharkhand (2010)

Jharkhand was placed under President's Rule on 1 June 2010 with President Prathibha Patil accepting a recommendation of the Union Cabinet after the two key players - Congress and BJP - gave up an effort to form an alternative government following the resignation of Chief Minister Soren[112]. The Assembly, however, was kept in a state of suspended animation as per the mandate of the Bommai Judgement. The recommendation of the Union Cabinet was based on the report of the Governor, Farooq, in which he strongly recommended clamping of President's Rule. The Governor, in an attempt to form an alternative government, held discussion with leaders of different parties which had representation in the legislature. However, the BJP and the Congress both indicated their inability to form a viable alternative government[113].

The December 2009 Assembly elections delivered a fragmented Assembly. In an attempt to keep the Congress out of power, the BJP with 18 MLAs and JD(U) with two MLAs rushed with an alliance with JMM of Shibu Soren. However, the marriage of convenience did not last long because the BJP withdrew support to the coalition government a day after Soren, a member of the Parliament, went with the ruling progressive alliance in Loksabha by voting against opposition sponsored cut motions. The five month old Soren government reduced in to a minority on 24 May 2010 and he resigned ahead of a trust vote in the Assembly that he was guaranteed to loss[114].

II. PRESIDENT'S RULE UNDER NON-CONGRESS MINORITY REGIMES SUPPORTED BY THE CONGRESS PARTY[115]

A. President's Rule during the Prime-Ministership of Charan Singh

1. Sikkim (1976)

The Chief Minister resigned because the life of the Assembly ended. The Governor dissolved the Assembly on the advice of the Chief Minister on 13 August 1979. Thereafter, the Chief Minister tendered his resignation which was accepted on 17 August 1979. On 18 August the state was placed under President's Rule.[116]

2. Manipur (1979)

The Janata ministry headed by Shaiza was dismissed by the Centre for corruption and demoralised administration. The government's ineptness in dealing with the growing extremist violence was also given as a cause for the dismissal. The Governor L.P. Singh, had already recommended the dissolution of the state Assembly and imposition of President's Rule in the states. The Governor in his report has also pointed out to the deteriorating law and order situation in Manipur and said that the administration has been rendered increasingly ineffective in dealing with the activities of extremists because of maladministration corruption favouritism and Nepotism.[117] The Governor in his report stated:

I have never known a government which, according to my own best judgement has been so corrupt, devoid of integrity and unprincipled, and which is given functioning so continuously without any regard to the laws or considerations of justice and fair play.[118]

3. Kerala (1979)

Mohammed Koya, the Muslim league leader, was sworn in as the Chief Minister on 12 October 1979 with the support of the congress(I). However, the four member ministry could continue in office only for a short time due to the withdrawal of support by the Congress faction led by A.K. Antony. The Chief Minister advised the Governor to dissolve the Assembly and hold fresh elections "in order to end the political uncertainty in the state". The opposition claimed a majority enabling it to form a ministry and opposed the dissolution of the Assembly. After discussion with various political parties, the Governor concluded that even if the Left Democratic Front was allowed to form a government, it was unlikely to be stable. In these circumstances, he dissolved the Assembly and later on, President's Rule was imposed.[119]

4. Assam (1979)

The Assam Janata Vidhayani Dal coalition government lost support when Congress (U) and the Communist Party of India withdrew their support. The leaders of almost all political parties were of the view that the state should be placed under President's Rule for a brief period so that they might consult one another about a proposal to form a viable government.[120] The Governor, therefore recommended imposition of President's rule with the suspension of the Assembly. In his report, the Governor stated: "A brief spell of President's Rule would help to stabilise the political situation and also revamp the administration which had been affected by the agitation over the issue of inclusion of the 'foreigners' in the electoral roll".

B. President's Rule under Chandra Sekhar

1. Assam (1990)

In Assam, President's Rule was imposed on 29 November 1990 on the ground that free and fair election was not possible due to the deteriorating law and order situation arising out of activities of United Liberation Front of Assam (ULF).[121] The Assembly was put under suspended animation. The tenure of the Assembly was about to expire on 8 January 1991. The Government took the decision on the report of the Governor in which he referred to the worsening law and order situation in the state. ULFA, the report said, had been indulging in secessionist activities and crime like murders and kidnapping. It was running training camps to train from abroad and also snatched arms from state authorities.[122]

It was alleged that despite strong advice by the Central government, the Assam government had refused to declare eight district in upper Assam as disturbed areas. It was also charge sheeted that the terrorist had link with some members of government.

2. Goa (1990)

President's Rule was imposed on 14 December 1990 and the Legislative Assembly was kept under suspended animation after a series of political developments that resulted in a situation in which no group was able to establish a majority in the Assembly. The Governor Khurshid Alam Khan in his report had recommended that the state should be placed under Central rule and the state was put under President's Rule.[123]

3. Tamil Nadu (1991)

Tamil Nadu was placed under President's Rule on the ground of breakdown of law and order situation as well as failure of constitutional machinery in the state. Reportedly, the state government was charged with encouraging the violent activities of Liberation Tigers of Tamil Elam (LTTE), and the United Liberation Front of Assam (ULFA). For quite sometime, the AIADMK and the Congress (I) were demanding the dismissal of the Karunanidhi government. It must be noted that the Governor S.S. Barnala had not report to the President about the failure of constitutional machinery in the state. The Governor made a public statement to that effect.[124] However, Prime Minister Chandrasekhar justified his decision while addressing members of Loksabha on 6th February 1991, he said that Governor's report was not necessary to invoke President's Rule because the 'Centre itself had certain information while the Governor's did not have' on the situation in Tamil Nadu. The Prime Minister said that it was not land order, but it was more serious.[125] It was reported in the press that Jayalalitha and Rajiv Gandhi wanted the Karunanidhi government to be dismissed. Hence, Chandra Sekhar advised the President accordingly.

4. Haryana (1991)

Om Prakash Chautala ministry (Janata Dal-S) was reduced to a minority following the disqualification of three legislators, including a newly inducted minister of state by the Speaker under the Anti-Defection Law. The Chief Minister recommended the dissolution of the Assembly. However, the Governor called upon Chautala to prove his majority in the Assembly on or before 3 April. Chautala challenged the right of the Governor to ask the Chief Minister to prove his majority after he had recommended the dissolution of the Assembly.[126] The seven day old stalemate in the Haryana politics ended on 2 April 1991 when the Governor recommended the imposition of Article 356 of the Constitution.

During the brief spell of Chandra Sekhar, President's Rule was imposed in five states. So, great has been the extent of misuse that it is indeed difficult even for a dispassionate observer to justify the dismissals. If anybody has any doubt, it would be dispelled by the manner in which the DMK government in Tamil Nadu was dismissed at Rajiv Gandhi's bidding on the ground that its continuance in office threatened national unity. In fact, "naked abuse of power under Article 356 by the government of India was once again exhibited in 1990".[127] The dismissal of Mahanta ministry in Assam in 1990 is another glaring misuse of the provision for mere power politics. Here, it is significant to note that Chandra Sekhar headed a minority government with only 56 members of his party in the Lok Sabha and his government could continue in office only with the support of the Congress and other factions. The question also arises whether a minority government which does not enjoy a majority in the Parliament can recommend imposition of President's Rule in a state [128]

The Congress party which had propped up the Charan Singh and Chandra Sekhar governments wanted to use them as proxy governments without burning its fingers on many controversial issues. Chandra Sekhar and Charan Singh or their splinter groups could never have got mandate in an election to run the Central government. The aspiration to become the Prime Minister for at least some days and thereby get into the pages of history usually motivates lighter weights among the politicians to attempt any sort of alliances and compromises. Any major political party vying to return to power usually uses such an opportunity to get its things done through such proxies because what they then enjoy is power without accountability. This explains why the misuse of Article 356 during this period was so blatant.

III. PRESIDENT'S RULE UNDER NON-CONGRESS GOVERNMENTS

A. President's Rule during Morarji Desai's Period

1-9. Mass dismissals (1977)

In the 1977 Lok Sabha elections, the ruling Congress party suffered massive defeat, securing only 153 seats as against 350 in the 1971 elections. The people rejected the Congress so convincingly that it could win only one seat in the whole of north India. On 24 March 1977 the Janata party formed a new government with an overwhelming majority. At that time, the Congress governments were in power in the nine states of Haryana, Punjab, Himachal Pradesh, Uttar Pradesh, Bihar, Orissa, Madhya Pradesh, West Bengal and Rajasthan. The Union Home Minister, Charan Singh, wrote a letter (on April 18) to the Chief Ministers of these nine states suggesting that they should seek fresh mandate from the people as the rout of the Congress party indicated that they had lost people's support. On April 1977, in an interview the Union minister of Law said that 'a clear case has been made out for the dissolution of the Assemblies in nine Congress ruled states and holding of fresh elections' since a serious doubt has been caste on their enjoying the people's confidence, their party having been rejected in the recent Lok Sabha polls'. Another contention of the centre was that the term of most of these nine state Assemblies were completed. They had already completed five years of their term but since the 42nd constitutional amendment extended the life of the Assemblies to six years, they were on lease period.[129]

Six of the nine states filed suits under Article 131 of the constitution in the Supreme Court praying for a declaration that the letter of the Home minister was illegal, ultra vires to the Constitution and prayed for an interim injunction restraining the Union Government from taking any step to dissolve their Assemblies before the expiry of their term fixed by the Constitution. Three members of the Punjab Assembly also filed a writ petition in the Supreme Court impugning the same matter and praying substantially for the same relief.

The three preliminary objections raised by the union were: (a) the suit was not maintainable. under Article 131; (b) that the question which arise for gauging the existence of a situation calling for action under article 356 are, by their very nature, non-justifiable and they are also expressly made non-justifiable by clause (5) of the Article; (c) that the suit and the writ petitions were pre-mature as the process which was being challenged might or might not actually produce the apprehended result or action.[130]

The Supreme Court held that the question was beyond the range of judicial review because it was of a political nature. The Court also held that President's satisfaction would be opened to judicial review if it is manifest or is based on wholly extraneous or irrelevant grounds. The Court was of the view that the case did not fall within this exception. However, the following observation made by the court was significant. The court observed:

Merely because the ruling party in a state suffers defeat in the elections to the Lok Sabha .... by itself can be no ground for saying that the government of the state can not be carried on in accordance with the provisions of the constitution. The federal structure under our constitution clearly postulates that there may be one party in power in the state and another at the centre.[131]

In the end, however, the court held that the letters neither constituted a thread nor were unconstitutional and therefore dismissed the suit. President's Rule was thereafter declared in these nine states on 30 April 1977.

10. Manipur (1977)

The Congress ministry run by Dorendra Singh was put into trouble because as many as 26 Congress legislators defected from it and joined the Janata party. This reduced the government to a minority in the Assembly and it resigned on 13 May 1977. The Governor in his report to the acting President B.D. Jatty reported that "the political situation in the state was fluid and no alternative ministry was possible for the present and the situation needed to stabilise". President's Rule was declared but the Legislative Assembly was kept suspended even though the Chief Minister had recommended its dissolution.[132]

11. Tripura (1977)

The Janata—CPI (M) coalition ministry under the Chief Ministership of Radhika Ranjan Gupta fell due to the withdrawal of support by the latter. Since there was no possibility of an alternative government, the Governor recommended imposition of President's Rule and dissolution of the Assembly which was complied with.[133]

12. Karnataka (1977)

The Congress party had absolute majority in the Karnataka Assembly. Owing to internal dissension, some members of the Congress party publicly announced in December 1977 their decision to withdraw support from the Devaraj Urs ministry.

However, the Chief Minister claimed a majority and was prepared to face the Assembly. Since the Assembly was to meet on 3 January 1978, the Governor and the Central government were of the view that Urs should be given an opportunity to test his strength on the floor of the house. However, for the reason best known to him, the Governor reversed his decision and submitted a report to the President on 31 December, in which he recommended the proclamation of Article 356 of the Constitution.[134] The Governor in his report stated that: 'it is abundantly clear from signed memoranda, verified letters and physical presentation of the members of the Assembly before me fully understanding the position that 109 MLAs have expressed their lack of confidence in the present ministry. The ministry has, therefore, lost the support of the majority of the members of the Assembly'.[135] On the basis of the report of the Governor the Urs Ministry was dismissed along with the dissolution of the Assembly on 31 December 1977. In this context J.R. Siwach, a notable political scientist, writes: 'the dismissal of Urs ministry was not proper and the Janata government followed the same policy in this respect which was followed by the former Congress government. The real ground for dismissing the ministry was that there was a fear in the mind of the central government that Urs might prove his majority in the Assembly and that case he would remain as a caretaker Chief minister during the following elections. For this eventuality the Janata Government was not ready particularly in Karnataka where it base seems to be very weak.[136]

There were twelve instances of President's Rule when the Janata party [137] was in office under Morarji Desai (1977-1979). i.e., an average of five times a year. With Janata Party coming into power new hopes were raised about a genuine re-structuring of Centre-State relations, because many regional parties which had been raising such demands were either part of Janata party or were supporting it. However, instead of restoring the lost credibility and essence of the federal provisions, the new ruling party indulged in new practices and used the power under Article 356 for pure political reasons rather than under administrative compulsions. in order to reap the benefits of Janata electoral momentum. It was a clear case of the partisan use of presidential rule, the Janata argument that the assemblies had 'lost the confidence of the people' notwithstanding.[138] The extensive use of the Article, very much contrary to the expectations of the people, in dissolving nine Congress ruled state governments at a stroke within a few days of its coming into power became a convention later. This incident reinforced the view that the power under Article 356 could be used for almost any purpose by any government. Political vengeance, which became the characteristic of the new regime led to its downfall two years later. Thus, the non-Congress rule for the first time lasted only for a short period leading to the return of the Congress party in power.

Howsoever, much we condemn and critcise the Janata party and its government, the fact remains that from the point of view of party politics the mass dismissals were inevitable Constitutions are not worked by God and Angels, but by people organised into political parties which form the government. The new government believed that the upper hand secured by the Congress party in the country's politics through blatant misuse of constitutional provisions, that too for about twenty seven years (1950-1977), could be undone easily through a policy of "tit for tat". So it was quite natural for any non-Congress party or alliances which came to power to try to overstep the predecessor government's footsteps. So what the Janata government actually did about Article 356 simply revealed the fact that in a plural democracy where governments are formed alternatively by different opposing parties, only those sets of policies and political situations will be allowed to remain in force which are conducive to the prospects of the new ruling party or group. The new government naturally was suspicious of the remaining Congress led state governments. The fear psychosis that by using the vast resources of these state governments the Congress would re-emerge in the national political scene also led to their dismissals. Again, it was the very same factors which made the successive Congress ministry to order the dismissal of the Janata led state governments in the year 1980. This kind of political reaction is natural to a polity like that of India. So, the problem to be addressed is how best we can plug the loopholes in the emergency provisions of the Constitution.

B. President's Rule during V.P Singh Era

1. Jammu and Kashmir (1990)

Governor's rule was imposed under section 92 of the Jammu and Kashmir Constitution in July 1990 after the resignation of the National Conference—Congress (I) coalition government headed by Farooq Abdulla, in protest against the appointment of Jag Mohan as the Governor of the state.[139] Under the Jammu and Kashmir Constitution, Governor's rule cannot be extended beyond six months. The Governor had recommended to the President that the state be placed under President's Rule on the expiry of Governor's Rule on account of widespread terrorists activities which deteriorated security and political situation in the state.

2. Karnataka (1990)

President's rule was imposed in the state of Karnataka in peculiar circumstances in the wake of a crisis in the ruling Congress party. The political crisis arose out of Congress(I) President, Rajiv Gandhi's public announcement that Veerendra Patil, the Chief Minister, had been asked to step down in view of his bad health and his incapacity to deal with the communal situation, which was worsening.[140] Patil refused to abide by the party chief's directive and said there was no question of his quitting. The Congress legislature party met and elected a new leader. But the Governor sided with the Chief Minister and said that he would ignore the decision of the Congress Parliamentary party as it would be illegal and against the party's Constitution. He told that under the party's Constitution, only the leader could convene the meeting after giving seven days' notice. The out going Chief Minister did not attend the CLP meeting and claimed that he had majority support and recommended the dissolution of the Assembly. However, the Governor recommended the imposition of President's Rule for a "short period" keeping the Assembly in suspended animation.[141] In his report, the Governor referred to the 'utter confusion' prevailing in the state at the political and administrative level and said that the spirit of joint responsibility of the cabinet had been 'totally shattered. He also referred to the communal violence in the state, which had claimed a number of lives and resulted in the loss of property worth crores of rupees. The Governor said that he had come to the conclusion that a situation had arisen in which the government of Karnataka could not be carried on in accordance with the provisions of the constitution. Acting on the report, the President issued a proclamation under Article 356 of the constitution.

During his tenure as Prime Minister for eleven months, V.P Singh declared President's Rule in the States of Jammu and Kashmir and Karnataka i.e. two instances of President's Rule in a year. In Kashmir the President's Rule was necessitated by an impasse as contemplated by the founding fathers of the Constitution whereas the Karnataka episode tells the story of the misuse of the provision.

C. Deva Gowda Government and President's Rule

1. Gujarat (1996)

On 18 September 1996, the eighteen month old BJP government headed by Suresh Mehta was dismissed and President's Rule imposed but the legislature was kept suspended. The controversy centred around the vote of confidence "won" by the BJP ministry with ninety-two votes to nil. The voting was preceded by unprecedented bedlam and violent scenes, during which opposition members, including some independents, were evicted from the house. In his report, the Governor had expressed doubts about the Chief Minister's claim of majority support in the Assembly.[142]

2. Uttar Pradesh (1996)

President's Rule was imposed in UP with the suspension of the Assembly on 17 October on the ground that no party or group was in a position to form a stable government. In a House of 425 members, the single largest party, BJP, and its allies had a strength of 179 and it staked the claim for the formation of ministry. However, the Governor Ramesh Bhandari felt that: (i) BJP did not have majority support, (ii) it was not clear about where from it could get the necessary support, and (III), the Congress, the Bahujan Samaj Party and the United Front did not extent support to BJP. The Congress BSP combine also lacked the strength and as such no alternative coalition could emerge due to the adamant attitude of the major parties.[143]

President's Rule under Vajpayee's Period

1. Goa (1999)

On 10th February 1999, Goa was placed under Article 356. The Assembly was also dissolved by the President. The decision was taken by the President on the basis of the recommendation of the Governor and the assessment of the Union Cabinet that no party was in a position to form a government. The state plunged into a fresh spell of political crisis when two legislators withdrew support to the Congress(I) government headed by Luizin-ho Faleiro. All the major parties, including the Goa Rajiv Congress, the major opposition, and the majority of MLAs in the state had demanded Central rule and holding of fresh election.[144]

2. Bihar (1999)

The R.J.D. government headed by Rabri Devi was dismissed by the President on 12 February 1999 on the ground of the failure of the civil administration to maintain law and order situation in Bihar. The Assembly was also placed in a state of suspended animation.[145] The decision was taken by the President on the basis of the report of the Governor S.S. Bhandari and the recommendation of the Union Cabinet in the wake of the macabre cruelty exhibited by the Ranbir sena, slaying over a dozen dalits including women and children. But the proclamation was revoked since the government knew that it could not be passed in the Rajya Sabha where they were in a minority.

3. Manipur (2001)

The barely three months old Samata party led People's Front ministry headed by Radhabinod Koijam collapsed after the ministry lost confidence vote in the 60 member Legislative

Assembly.[146] The Governor Ved Marwah consulted almost all political parties which had representation in the legislature in an attempt to form an alternative ministry. Government formation, however, was made difficult with the high commands of B.J.P and Samata Party (they together had nearly two - third majority) jointly deciding not to participate in or support any government formation exercise. But the Speaker of the Assembly Sapam Dhananjoy staked a claim and submitted a list of 34 MLAs in the House of 60 members. Mean while M. Hemanta of MSCP (C) who had also staked his claim had sought Dhananjoy's disqualification for staking claim without quitting speakership. The Speaker's claim could not sustain after the Governor asked him, as a matter of propriety, to step down from the Speaker's office before putting forth his claim.[147] As the speaker had formally withdrawn his claim and Hemanta did not have enough support, the Governor recommended the imposition President's Rule. Almost all parties except the BJP and the Samata Party had demanded imposition of President's Rule. The cabinet accepted the Governor's report that it was not possible to form a government in the state.

The imposition of President's Rule in Manipur was an 'inevitable step' as it had 'a substantive element of inevitability'. Shifting of loyalties by MLAs has indeed been the rule rather than the exception in the region over the years. And parties cutting across the spectrum have encouraged this in the past to their own advantage.[148] The imposition of President's Rule is a sad reflection of the same.

4. Uttar Pradesh (2002)

A hung Assembly situation developed in Uttar Pradesh following the 2002 Assembly elections in which no political party or combination of parties secured an absolute majority in the Legislature. The Samajvadi party under Mulayamsingh Yadav emerged as the largest single party with 145 seats in the 403 member House. The situation was such that no two parties that were in a position to allay and form the government were willing to do so.[149] However, Yadav staked claim for the formation of a government (even though he lacked sufficient numbers in the legislature). But he failed to submit a list of supporters to prove his majority as demanded by the Governor. Instead, he insisted that he should be allowed to prove his majority on the floor of the House within a month which was not acceptable to the Governor. The Governor after a brief discussion with different party leaders regarding the formation of a ministry reported to the President that in his opinion no political party was in a position to command a majority and the President's Rule was the only option.[150] On receipt of the report the state was placed under President's Rule with the Assembly under suspended animation.

However, after a few days the BJP and the BSP came to an understanding and submitted a letter to the Governor to support each other in the Legislative Assembly. The Governor of U.P thereafter invited the BJP-BSP combination to form the ministry with the BSP leader Mayawati as Chief minister and the President's Rule was revoked.

About Article 356, it can be said that the BJP's performance was not much different from those of the other non-Congress parties. During the first few months in office, the government showed some good sense in resisting pressures from within the coalition to invoke Article 356 against targeted state governments. The phase of restraint ended when the Vajpayee government recommended President's Rule in Bihar in September 1998. Unexpectedly, the President sent back the recommendation for re-consideration much to the political embarrassment of the Vajpayee Government. However, the Cabinet reiterated its decision in February 1999 and thereby closed all options before the president except approving it. A careful examination of the political events which led to the proclamation leaves little room for doubt that the power under Article 356 has not been used by the BJP government with the responsibility which its exercise necessarily involves. The government has laid itself open to the justifiable comment that it has acted hastily in assuming to itself power under Article 356. This was done not in the interest of the country but in the interest of the BJP and its alliance partner, the Samata party. However, the imposition of President's Rule in Goa (1999), Manipur (2001) and Uttar Pradesh (2002) were not controversial declarations.

Table 2
Table showing Presidential Proclamations Under Various Political Regimes - A Comparison

Party	Total Tenure in Years	Frequency	Yearly average	Justifiable Cases	
				Number	Percentage
Congress	48	83	1.72	30	36.1
Non Congress minority party with Congress backing	1.1	8	8	4	50
Non Congress	11	20	1.81	6	30
Total	60	111	1.85	40	36

Source: Computed from available secondary sources

In the case of Chandra Sekhar government, it was the majority party which blackmailed a minority government. In the case of BJP government it was a case of minor regional parties in the coalition government trying to blackmail the major party with the threat of withdrawal of support, unless the Central government connived with their political ambition in their states. The fragile majority of the Vajpayee government forced it to succumb to such demands and pressures. Only a strong, capable and principled leadership could have withstood this.

From a comparative analysis of the frequency with which both the Congress and the various non-Congress governments invoked the provision, it becomes evident that the average frequency was greater during the non-Congress era. The Table 2 shows that the non-Congress governments invoked this provision twenty times during a shorter spell of eleven years (i.e. 1.81 times a year), while the various Congress regimes took recourse to this provision eight-three times during a longer period of forty- eight years (i.e. 1.72 times in a year) and the non- Congress minority rule supported by the Congress had proclaimed it eight times during thirteen months of its existence [i.e. 8 times in a year).

As regards the justifiability[151] of the proclamation too, the record of the non-Congress governments is worse than those of the Congress governments. This is borne out by the fact that while the Congress governments had to their credit thirty justifiable instances out of eighty-three proclamations (i.e. 36.1%), the non-Congress rule could be credited with only six such instances out of the total of twenty proclamations (i.e.30%). The record of Congress backed non-Congress minority regimes, shows four justifiable instance out of the total eight proclamations made (i.e. 50%).

Figure 1
Pie-Diagram showing justifiable and non-justifiable cases of President's Rule under various political regimes : A comparison

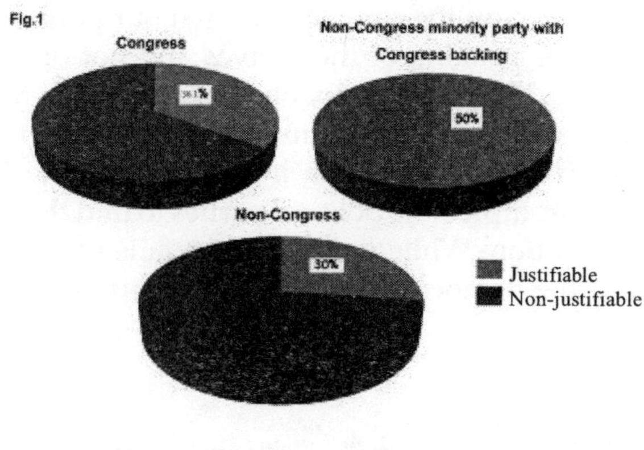

However, when we take into account both the length of power and the frequency with which it had proclaimed the President's Rule, the two Congress backed minority rulers, namely Charan Singh and Chandra Sekhar stand in the forefront, i.e. Charan Singh declared President's Rule four times during a brief spell of five and half months (i.e. 8.7 times a year) and Chandra Sekhar also proclaimed it four times during a short period of seven months and eleven days. (i.e. 6.5 times a year) as against the national average of 1.8 times a year.

From the above historical survey, one can say with candour that all political parties are culpable of using or misusing Article

356 whenever they were in power or were supporting those in power. This amply illustrates the saying that "whoever goes to Lanka becomes Ravana". It is an irony that while most political parties criticise what they perceive as the 'misuse' of the Article when they are out of power, they never resist the temptation to 'misuse' it when they get an opportunity to do so solely for settling political scores and to achieve their objectives.[152] Soli. J. Sorabjee is perfectly justified in stating:

> 'It is my considered opinion that it is the most abused provision of the constitution and there is no single party which can take exclusive credit for it or blame for it. No party at the centre has escaped or overcome the strong temptation to use this article against the powers in the states.[153]

This substantiates the simple truth that our political parties and leaders are thinking of themselves and not of the nation and the people. They have probably forgotten what transpired during the debates in the constituent assembly on the use of Article 356. The way politics in independent India has been shaped itself prompted the political parties to find the loopholes in the Constitution. While doing so they failed to understand the spirit of the democratic federal Constitution.

References

1 S C Arora, *President's Rule in Indian States* (New Delhi: Mittal 1990) 71-89

2. Pepsu was merged into Punjab on the Reorganisation of States

3. For detailed facts, see C A Alexandro Wiez , *Constitutional Development in India* (Delhi: OUP, 1957) 163

4 *Ibid,* the Governor's action was attacked from many quarters on the ground that according to the principles of British Parliamentary Behaviour the Governor could have invited the leader of the opposition to form the government, and that resort to Article 356 would have been legitimate only if the formation of an alternate government was impossible.

5. B P Pandya, The *Role of Governor, Journal of Constitutional and Parliamentary Studies, 30 (1996): 153*

6. Nalini Pant, *The Governor and Article 356, Journal of the Society for Study of State Governments*, Vol. IV, (1971): 299.
7. See Meera Srivastava, *Constitutional Crisis in the States in India* (New Delhi : Concept Publishing, 1979) 50-51.
8. *Ibid*
9. See *Austin, Granville, Working of a Democratic Constitution*, (New Delhi,: Oxford, 1999) 162.
10. M.C. Setalvad, *Grave Emergency and Emergency arising out of the Failure of the Constitutional Machinery in a State* (Madras : University of Madras, 1966) 23.
11. Rajeev Dhavan, *President's Rule in the State* (Bombay : N.M. Tripathi, 1979) 73.
12. Rajeev Dhavan, *President's Rule in the States*, 74.
13. *Ibid.*
14. See Shriram Maheswari, *President's Rule in India* (New Delhi: Macmillan, 1979) 43.
15. K. Suryaprasad, President's Rule in Kerala : *A Historical Overview, Journal of Kerala Studies*, 15 (1988) : 116-117. The proclamation was defended by the Union government and supported by almost all political parties inside and outside the Parliament. The political reason for this unanimity might be that both the governments at the Centre and the state were of the same party. Naturally, the opposition parties were happy over the development.
16. *The Stateman*, 25 March 1965
17. *Ibid.*: 117-118. See also Nalini Pant, *The Governor and Article 356: Problems and Challenges, The Journal of the Society for the Study ofState Governments*, 4(1971) : 305.
18. Rajeev Dhavan, *BJP or the Constitution, The Hindu*, 24 September 1998.
19. Rajeev Dhavan, *President's Rule in the States 75.*
20. It has been alleged by Morarji Desai that Nehru was against the imposition of President's Rule and that Indira Gandhi, at that time President of the Congress, was responsible for the imposition of President's Rule, See, *Ibid. 74.*
21. Dua B.D., *Prime Minister and the Federal System of India* in *Indian, Federalism in the new Millennium*, ed. by Dua, B.D and singh, M.P. (New Delhi: Manohar, 2003) 136.
22 .K. Chatterjee, *How to Safeguard Article 356 from Abuse or Misuse, The Hindu*, 19 November 1996.
23 Nalini Pant 308.
24 Rajeev Dhavan, *President's Rule in the States 79.*

25 See Nalini Pant 300.

26 Nalinipant, 301.

27 *Sarkaria Commission Report,* Part I, 186. The Governor's Report said : What Haryana badly needs now is a clean and efficient administration. Fresh elections may be arranged as soon as possible, after the administration has been toned up by a brief spell of the President's Rule. (See *Rao Birinder Singh v. Union of India AIR 1968,* Punj 442).

28 See Nalinipant, *The Governor and Article 356. Problem and Challenges, Journal of Society for the Study of State Governments,* Vol .IV, No.3 and 4 (1971), 300.

29 For a comprehensive account See Shriram Maheswari, *President's Rule in India,* pp 60-65. See also J.R. Siwach, *Politics of Presidents Rule in India,* 398-404

30 For a detailed political account, see J.R. Siwach, *Politics of President's Rule in India* (Shimla : Indian Institute of Advanced Study, 1979) 398-404. Chief Minister Ajoy Mukherjee urged the President to take the Supreme Court's advice under Article 143 on the Governor's discretionary power, but the President refused. Later the Calcutta High Court upheld the validity of Governor's action.

31 Harbirsing Kathuria, *President's Rule in India* (New Delhi : Uppal, 1990) 100-105.

32 *Sarkaria Commission Report,* 188.

33 S.C. Arora 93-119.

34 *Sarkaria Commission Report,* 187.

35 *Ibid.*

36. Lok Sabha Secretariat, *President's Rule in the State and Union Territories* (New Delhi, 1996) 30.

37. For detailed facts, see P.L. Mathur, *Role of Governor in Non-Congress States* (Jaipur : Rawat, 1988) 99-100. The Attorney General also advised the Governor to demand Chief Minister's resignation. The Advocate General of UP was not of this opinion. Should a Governor, in such controversial situations, seek the advice of the Attorney General ? This is an open question (See Nalini Pant 302).

38. Shriram Maheswari, *President's Rule in India,* 79-80

39. Siwach 240-243.

40. *Sarkaria Commission Report,* 188.

41. *Ibid.*

42. The name of the State of Mysore was changed to Kamataka with effect from 1 November 1973.

43. For facts, see Harbir Singh Kathuria, 157-60.
44. For detailed facts, see J.R. Siwach, 140-142.
45. See S.C Arora, 160-195.
46. *Sarkaria Commission Report,* 189.
47. For details, see J.R. Siwach, 126-130.
48. Lok Sabha Secretariat, 8-9.
49. *Sarkaria Commission Report,* 188.
50. *Ibid.*
51. Native rules 1919 framed by the then Nizam (Ruler). Government posts and admission to educational institutions in Hyderabad were reserved for persons who had born in the princely state or had been permanently residing there for 15 years (for facts, see Lok Sabha Secretariat 2).
52. Siwach 245-52.
53. *Sarkaria Commission Report,* 189.
54. See Lok Sabha Secretariat 68.
55. See Rajeev Dhavan, *President's Rule in the States* 80.
56. J.R. Siwach 230-231.
57. *Ibid.* 369-370.
58. For a detailed political account, see Harbir Singh Kathuria, 199-203.
59. See *Sarkaria Commission Report* 189.
60. *Ibid.* 187.
61. Siwach 253.
62. *Sarkaria Commission Report* 186, See also Harbir Singh Kathuria, 272-74.
63. *Sarkaria Commission Report* 1988.
64. For facts see, K. Suryaprasad 123-124.
65. *Ibid.*
66. *Sarkaria Commission Report* 89.
67. For comprehensive political events, see SC Arora 203-209.
68. *Sarkaria Commission Report* 189.
69. Dua B.D., *Prime Minister and the Federal System in India,* 130
70. Jain, *Article 356 and Centre-State Relation, Mainstream,* 2 April 1993 : 5.
71. *Sarkaria Commission Report,* 188.
72. R. Venkata Raman, *My Presidential Years* (New Delhi : Harper-Collins, 1944) 141.
73. Janaki survived the confidence motion by 99 votes in the crucial session of the Assembly but could not secure the required majority support of 112 members in a House with an effective strength of 223 members. A question arose whether the vote of

confidence needed a majority of the total membership of the House or a majority of members present in the House and voting on the motion. The language of Article 189 (1) is clear. A resolution seeking a vote of confidence would require only a majority of the members present and voting. The Constitution had not provided for a special majority for a vote of confidence (T.K. Tope) For a comprehensive analysis sec O.P. Verma and ML Sharma, *Failure of Constitutional Machinery in Tamil Nadu, Journal of Constitutional and Parliamentary Studies,* 22 (1988 : 184-191).

74. *AIR 1994 SC* 2101-2103.
75. (1988) 2 Gau.LJ 468
76. See Venkata Raman 203.
77. T.K. Tope, *Constitutional Law of India,* 2nd ed. (Lucknow : Eastern, 1992) 853.
78. For more details see Harbirsing Kathuria *President's Rule in India,* pp.243-245.
79. *S.R. Bommai v. Union of India,* AIR 1989, Kart 5.
80. *S.R. Bommai v.Union of India, AIR 1994 SC 1918.*
81. S.K. Chatterjee, *How to Safeguard Article 356 from Abuse and Misuse, The Hindu,* 19 Nov. 1996.
82. *AIR 1994 SC* 2099-2101.
83. *Ibid.* 123.
84. Jain, M.P. *Indian Constitutional Law* (Nagpur: Wadhwa and Co.), p.808
85. For a detailed facts see Sunil Deshta, *President's Rule in the States: Constitutional Provisions and Practices:* (New Delhi : Deep and Deep, 1993) 124-25
86 See *The Times of India,* 16 December 1992.
87 *Ibid.*
88 *Ibid.,* 17 December 2002.
89 *Ibid.*
90 See *Sunderlal Patwa v: Union of India, AIR* 1993, MP 214.
91 *See Sunderlal Patwa v. Union of India, AIR 1993, MP 214.*
92 *Lok Sabha Secretariat* 66.
93 *Ibid* 40
94. *The Hindu,* 29 March 1995.
95. Ibid. 19 September 1995.
96. Dua B.D. *Prime Minister and Federal System,* p.150
97. See *The Hindu,* 7 March 2005.
98. For more insights into the topic See Purnimas. Tripathi, *A Dissolution at Midnight, Frontline,* 17 June 2005 and See also the

author's another article *A Role for the Governor, Frontline* 20 May 2005.

99. See *A Farcical vote of Confidence, The Hindu* 4 Feb. 2005.
100. See *The Hindu* 5 March 2005. See also *A Race to bottom'* editorial, *The Hindu*, 5 March 2005.
101. See *The Hindu*, 10 Oct. 2007
102. *The New Indian Express*. 21 November 2007.
103. See *The Times of India*, 3 Jan. 2008
104. For more insights see Balaraj Puri, *Jammu and Kashmir: the Issues of Regional Autonomy, EPW*, 23 Aug. 2008
105. *Ibid.*
106. *A Dream Gone Sour*, Editorial, *The Hindu*, 20 January 2009.
107. *The Times of India*, 20 January 2009
108. *Ibid.*
109. *The Hindu*, 19 March, 2009.
110. *The Hindu*, 21 March, 2009.
111. *The Hindu*, 20 March 2009.
112. *The Hindu*, 2 June 2010
113. *Ibid*
114. *Jharkhand's predicament, Editorial, The Hindu*, 4 June 2010
115. Though the United Front Governments led by Deva Gowda and Gujral had the support of Congress (I), it could not be included in this category, since these Governments had been formed after fresh mandates form the people notwithstanding the shortage of the requisite majority. They had the outside support of the Congress (I) because of political compulsions on the Congress party and as such the Gowda and Gujral governments retained their independence. Hence for all practical purposes, these governments can be included in the III category, *i.e.*, Non-Congress governments.
116. *Lok Sabha Secretariat* 60.
117. Harbirsingh Kathuria, *Presidents Rule in India*, p.248.
118. *Ibid.* 40.
119. Surya Prasad 120-21.
120. *Lok Sabha Secretariat* 4.
121. J.N. Pandey 615.
122. Sunil Deshta, *Presidents Rule in the State* (New Delhi: Deep and Deep, 1993).
123. *Sunil Deshta* 119.
124. T.K. Tope 856.
125. *Sunil Deshta* 119.
126. R. Venkata Raman 386 and 496.

127. T.K. Tope 858.
128. See Rathna Swamy, *Political Question and Article 356* (New Delhi : Manas, 1998) 40.
129. *The Sarkaria Commission Report*, 174.
130. *Ibid.* 174-175.
131. *AIR 1977, SC 1361*
132. *The Sarkaria Commission Report*,189
133. *Ibid*
134. For detailed facts see, J.R. Siwach 221-226.
135. *The Indian Express*, 2 January 1977.
136. Siwach J.R. *Politics of President's Rule*, 226.
137. The party which came to power in the aftermath of emergency. It was formed by the merger of different political parties of divergent ideologies for the common cause of fighting the authoritarianism of the emergency regime.
138. Dua, B.D, *Prime-Minister and the Federal System*, 141.
139. Suni Deshta 115.
140. *Ibid.* 116.
141. In his report, the Governor referred to the utter confusion prevailing in the state at the political and administrative level and said that the spirit of joint responsibility of the Cabinet had been totally shattered. He also referred to the communal violence in the state which had claimed a number of lives and resulted in the loss of property worth crores of rupees. (For facts, see Venkata Raman 419).
142. For facts see Shyama Nand Singh, *Imposition and Revocation of President's Rule, Mainstream*, 16 November 1996 : 13-17.
143. See *The UNI Back Grounder*, 22.18 (1997) : 2-5.
144. *The Hindu*, 10 February 1999.
145. *Ibid*,. 13 February 1999.
146. *The Hindu*, 3 June 2001.
147. *An Inevitable Step*, editorial, *The Hindu*, 6 June 2001.
148. *Manipur conundrum*, editorial, *The Hindu* 30 May 2001.
149. Purnimas. Tripathi, *In suspended animation, Frontline*, 29 March, 2002.
150. See *The Hindu*, 6 March 2002; See also *Central Rule in U.P.*, editorial, *The Hindu*, 8 March 2002.
151. The relevant Constitutional provisions, the Constituent Assembly Debates, recommendation of various Commissions and Committees and the ruling of the Courts are relied upon in identifying the case which are justifiable (See the next chapter).

152. For instance, the Congress(I), which had the largest number of instances of the use of the provision to its credit, criticised the Deva Gowda government when the Suresh Mehta ministry in Gujarat was dismissed or when the Gujral government recommended the dismissal of Kalyan Singh in UP in 1997 or when the Rabri Devi in Bihar was dismissed by the BJP government. In the same way, Gujral who took the decision to recommend the dismissal of Kalyan Singh ministry found fault with the BJP's recommendation to dismiss the Rabri Devi government. Similar is the case of the Left parties also. The CPI(M) which has always staunchly opposed the exercise of these powers by the Congress regimes and had in fact been demanding the repeal of this Article, extended support to the use of this provision when the Article was imposed against the BJP led state governments. Likewise the BJP which praised the President for rejecting the Gujral government's recommendation to impose President's Rule in Uttar Pradesh in 1997 did exactly the same thing in Bihar (1998). Again, it is on the basis of the difficulties the government will have to face in invoking Article 356 that the Vajpayee government has turned down the demand from its allies like the AIADMK, the Trinamool Congress and the Biju Janata Dal. (See *Precept and Practice,* editorial, *The Indian Express,* 27 February 1999).

153. See Alladi Aruna, *unfederal features of Indian Constitution,* 295.

Chapter 5

The Steamroller in Operation: The Emerging Model

An attempt has been made in this chapter to analytically and theoretically understand the emerging model of Article 356, keeping in view the federal nature of the Constitution and the actual political process which motivated the application of the Article.

The misuse of Article 356 began as early as in 1951.[1] The very first occasion of its use in Punjab for resolving an internal crisis in the ruling party contained in it the seed of the coming crescendo of its misuse. During the sixty years since the inauguration of the Constitution in 1950 the Article was invoked one hundred and eleven times for various reasons. That amounts to an average of 1.85 times each year. Uttar Pradesh, Bihar, Kerala, and Punjab have been the States where the largest number of President's Rule has been imposed. This was quite contrary to the assurances and expectation of Ambedkar that "such Article will never be called into operation and that they would remain a dead letter"[2]. It would not be far from the truth to say that a majority of the imposition has been ordered for partisan ends, to further the interest of the party in power at the Centre, and not for the reasons contemplated by the founding fathers of the Constitution.[3] It is corroborated by the views expressed in the judgment in S.R. Bommai v. Union of India. The judgment said:

> Dr. Ambedkar's hope that in the rarest of the rare cases only there will be an occasion to invoke the emergency provisions was soon belied as we were told by the bar that the provision of Article 356 of the Constitution have had to be invoked over ninety times by now. What was, therefore, expected to be a dead letter has in fact become an oft-invoked provision[4].

In the initial years, since the promulgation of the Constitution, the instances of its use were not many. But with the passing of years this Article has been invoked with increasing frequency. This is evident from the table below.

Table 3
Chronological Table Showing the Imposition of President's Rule from 1950-2010 Arranged Chronologically Taking Five Years as One Unit

Sl. No.	Period	Frequency	Remark	Percentage
1.	1950-54	3		2.7
2	1955-59	3		2.7
3.	1960-64	2		1.8
4	1965-69	9	4 cases in 1968	8.1
5.	1970-74	19	7 cases in 1971	17.1
6.	1975-79	21	12 cases in 1977	18.9
7.	1980-84	16	9 cases in 1980	14.4
8.	1985-89	6		5.4
9.	1990-94	15	4 cases in 1990 and 6 cases in 1992	13.5
10.	1995-99	6		5.4
11.	2000-04	2		1.8
12.	2004-09	8		7.2
13.	2010-	1		
Total	60 years	111		100

Source: Computed from available secondary sources.

An analysis of President's Rule in chronological order shows that it was in the year 1977 that maximum number of imposition

(12) was made followed by 1980 (9). It was due to nearly total defeat of the ruling parties in a large number of states during the Lok Sabha elections in 1977 and 1980. There were only sixteen years during 1950-2010 when President's Rule was not proclaimed[5]. The figures reveal a sharp rise in the incidence of President's Rule from 1967 onwards. Hundred instances out of hundred and eleven have taken place since the year 1967 i.e. an average of 2.6 cases of President's Rule per year. There were various reasons for this: like the eclipse of one party (Congress) dominant system both at the Centre and in the states and the emergence of coalition politics with all its attendant evils, the rise of sub-national trends, the rise of regional parties[6] and above all the spine-chilling power politics ridden political process in various states due to caste and religious rivalries. All these factors in their systemic totality could better explain what has actually happened. Some of these factors point to the shape of things to come in future. The situation stabilised to some extent during 1985-89 partly because of the introduction of the Anti-defection Act and partly because the ruling party at the Centre realised the political futility of the use of this draconian provision in all the opposition ruled States as a matter of policy. Further, whenever the Centre, tried to decapitate the States, the opposition State Governments offered strong political resistance which had the effect of restraining the Centre. Combined political actions of the opposition ministries at the State level prevented the Union Government from taking wrong decisions. In fact, the reinstatement of Rama Rao ministry in Andhra Pradesh (1984), Wilfred De Sueza in Goa (1995), Kalyan Singh in Uttar Pradesh (1998) and Rabri Devi in Bihar (1999) were the results of this combined struggle. The scope of misuse of this power was substantially reduced after the Supreme Court verdict in the Bommai and Rameswar Prasad cases. Now the Court has established the fact that the Presidential proclamation under Article 356 is judicially reviewable and in the case of excesses, the Court has ruled that, it would even revive the dissolved Legislative Assembly and reinstate the dismissed ministry. Above all, the constitutional activism displayed by the former President K.R.

Narayanan is a warning to the Centre to be extremely cautious in imposing President's Rule. Now it becomes quite clear that though the Centre has sweeping powers, it has to act with restraint and caution.

Figure 2

Graphical Representation of President's Rule showing variations in the incidence over the years

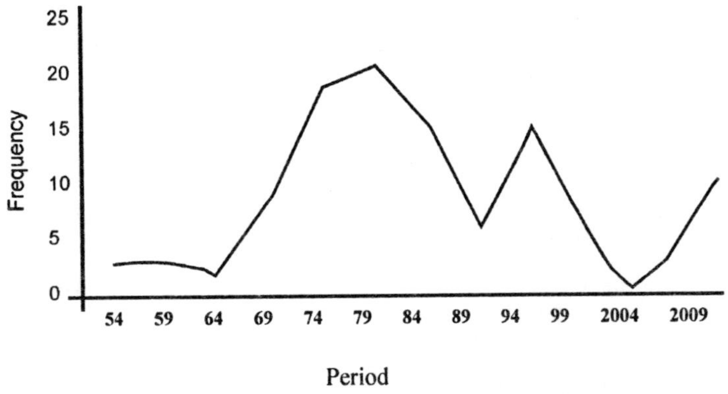

An in depth and careful analysis of the application of Article 356 brings to light that the provision has not been used very much for the purpose for which it was incorporated. The wishes of the patriarchs of the Constitution during the debates in the Constituent Assembly have also not been understood well while invoking the Article. It has been used as an instrument of political management in favour of the ruling party at the Centre and not as a Constitutional tool to protect any State against external aggression or internal disturbances and to ensure that the government of the State is carried on in accordance with the provisions of the Constitution. In this process, even the limited federal features of the Constitution are sacrificed for power politics.

After analysing the circumstances which led to Central intervention in various States at different times, it can be deduced that situation resulting in the imposition of President's rule could be put under the following twelve broad categories. Many of these situations are not Constitutionally correct, but that is how the system has evolved.

Table 4
Table Showing Classification of Situations under which President's Rule has been Imposed

Sl. No.	Category of President's Rule	Number	Percentage	Justifiable	
				Number	Percentage
1	Mass dismissals	21	19	0	0
2	Hung assemblies	6	5.4	1	10.6
3	Corruption and Maladministration	2	1.8	0	0
4	Breakdown of law and order	8	7.2	4	50
5	Party wranglings	8	7.2	0	0
6	Paralysis of Parliamentary process	9	8	0	0
7	Delay in electoral process	3	2.7	3	100
8	In the context of Re-organisation of States	3	2.7	3	100
9	Failure to honour the assurance to the Nation and the Court	1	0.9	1	100
10	Violence within the precincts of the Assembly	1	0.9	0	0
11	To get the interim budget of the State passed in the Parliament	7	6.3	7	100
12	Political instability	42	37.8	21	50
	Total	111	100	40	36

Source: Prepared from a historical survey on the basis of available secondary sources.

Figure 3
Pie-Diagram showing percentage contribution of different causes of President's Rule

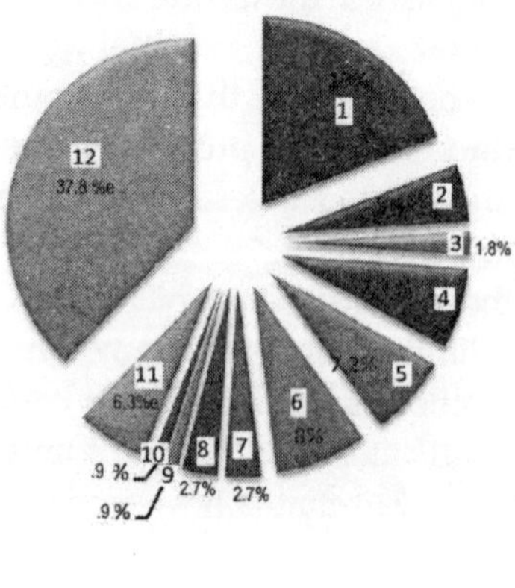

1. Mass dismissals
2. Hung Assemblies
3. Corruption and maladministration
4. Breakdown of law and order
5. Party wranglings
6. Paralysis of parliamentary process
7. Delay in electoral process
8. In the context of Re-organisation of States
9. Failure to honour the assurance to the Nation and the Court
10. Violence within the precincts of the Assembly
11. To get the interim budget of the State passed in the Parliament
12. Political instability

I- Mass Dismissals

Under mass dismissals are discussed the proclamation of President's Rule by the Janata government in 1977 in nine States and those by the Congress (I) government in 1980 in the same number of States and the three proclamations by the Narasimha Rao government in the State of Madhya Pradesh, Himachal Pradesh and Rajasthan in the aftermath of the Ayodhya incident in 1992. The first two (nine each) instances may be placed under one category while the latter three under a different one. The first category was based on the defeat of the ruling party in the concerned States during the ensuing Parliamentary elections of 1977 and 1980 and on the plea that the State Governments no longer represented the will of the people. The second category was based on the satisfaction of the President that the central ordinances banning communal organizations such as Rashtriya Swayam Sevaksangh (R.S.S), Viswa Hindu Parishad (V.H.P) and Bajirang Dal etc. were not effectively, expeditiously and whole-heartedly implemented by the concerned B.J.P governments in the States of M.P, H.P and Rajasthan.

Category A. Imposition of Article 356 on the ground that the State Governments no longer represented the will of the people.

To quote the Sarkaria Commission, "here is an instance of wholesale misuse of Article 356.... for political purpose, extraneous to one for which the power has been conferred by the Constitution"[7]. Here the dismissals on both the occasions were made on the ground that the change of government at the Centre, supported by a massive mandate, warranted fresh elections in such States which were ruled by the opposition because they had, evidently, lost the popular support. The law minister himself pointed out that 'democracy was the most important element of the Constitution's basic structure and if state governments continued in power after having lost the confidence of the people, they would be undemocratic governments.[8] However, there is no Constitutional ground to justify the dismissal of these popularly elected and legally constituted governments. A pertinent question raised here for deliberation is: whether the same criteria should not hold good when the party in power at the Centre is routed in the election to the Assemblies of majority of States.

In a federal system, it must be pointed out that, the scenario of one party wielding power at the Centre and others ruling in the States is a common phenomenon and, being democratically elected and having secured a mandate of the people both sets of governments have an equal *locus standi* to remain in power. 'The mosaic of variegated pattern of political life is potentially inherent in a pluralist multiparty democracy like ours'. First of all, it must be remembered that the issues in the election to the State Assembly and to the Parliament are different. In elections to the state legislatures the issues involved are primarily of local interest while all India consideration and party strength act in an election to the Parliament. Parties have to evolve different programmes for the Parliamentary elections and the Assembly elections. Further, People do not necessarily vote the same way in the Assembly and Lok Sabha elections; they may vote for a certain party in the State and elect another to the Parliament. The pattern is evident when subsequent elections to the state legislatures follow LokSabha elections. For instance, in West Bengal in 1977 while the Janata Party captured a majority of seats in the Lok Sabha elections, in the election to the State Assembly, the CPI(M) was returned with an overwhelming majority. Similarly, in 1980 in Tamil Nadu, people gave a clear mandate to the DMK-Congress alliance in the Lok Sabha elections, while they preferred AIADMK in the Legislative Assembly Elections. Therefore, the defeat of the candidates of a Party power in the State in the elections to Lok Sabha should not automatically mean a vote of no-confidence of the people in the ruling party in the State. Moreover, there is no provision in the Constitution that a government (State or Union) should command the confidence of the people. Our Constitution simply provides that the Council of Ministers shall be collectively responsible to the House of the People. In view of it, the dismissal of opposition ruled State Governments, on both occasions, were against federal principles, undemocratic and completely at variance with the spirit of the Constitution.

In a writ petition filed against the mass dismissals in the state of Rajasthan v. Union of India in 1977, the Supreme Court took a view which is more political than in conformity with the ethos of the Constitution. What Bhagawati J. said in the case is significant which provides an interesting persctive. In a leading judgment he observed that satisfaction of the President under Article 356 is subjective satisfaction and hence, it is not a subject matter for the judiciary. He further observed that the Home minister's letter was an advice, not a directive and therefore cannot be unconstitutional; and where there has been a total rout of ruling party candidates 'it is a proof of complete alienation between government and people'.[9] It was also held that:

> The extent of federalism is largely watered down by the need of progress and development of a country which has to be nationally integrated, politically and economically co-ordinated, and socially, intellectually and spiritually uplifted. In such a system, the State cannot stand in the way of legitimate and comprehensive planned development of the country in the manner directed by the Central government. The question of legitimacy of particular actions of the Central government taking us in particular directions can often be treated and determined by the verdict of the people at appropriate times[10].

The view seems to be debatable because the Constitution itself has conferred on the Central government the power to issue directions to the State governments for the purpose of achieving co-ordination, and contemplates the dissolution of the latter on other grounds including the non-compliance of the directives so issued. Since the *raison d'etre* of party system is competitive politics whereby different political parties seek to obtain the mandate on the policies, which are often mutually exclusive and different from each other, to permit and legalise dissolution of State Governments simply for the reason that it was ruled by a different party, cuts at the root of democracy and federalism. The Constitution does not permit the Central government to take action against a State on a mere surmise and suspicion that, belonging to a different party, it would not extend necessary co-operation to the Centre. If the ground, which was invoked to validate the dissolution, is considered in a broader perspective the whole Constitution will crumble down like an edifice built on sand[11].

However, in S.R. Bommai v. Union of India the Supreme Court rejected the philosophy invoked in deciding the Rajasthan case. In a leading judgment Ahamadi J. held:

> Having noticed the nature of the federal structure under the Constitution, the possibility of different parties ruling at the Centre and one or more States cannot be ruled out. The Constitution clearly permits it. Therefore, the mere defeat of the ruling party at the Centre cannot by itself without any thing more, entitle the newly elected party which comes to power at the Centre to advise the President to dissolve the Assemblies of those States where the party in power is other than the one in power at the Centre. Merely because a different party is elected to power at the Centre, even with a thumping majority, there is no ground to hold that "a situation has arisen in which the government of the State cannot be carried on in accordance with the provisions of the Constitution". Such action betrays intolerance of the Central government clearly basing the exercise of power under Article 356 (I) on consideration extraneous to the said provision and therefore, legally *mala fide*[12]

A similar view has been expressed by the Sarkaria Commission[13]. The Commission very pertinently stated that an overwhelming majority of those interviewed by them were unanimous in expressing the view that the use of Article 356 in 1977 by Janata government and the dissolution of Assemblies in nine states and the repetition of the same experiment on the same ground by the successor government in 1980 'were clearly improper'[14]. Therefore it can be concluded that the defeat of the party in power in the state in the election to Lok Sabha – however complete the defeat may be- cannot be a ground or sound logic to dissolve the state assemblies of the opposition ruled states. Unfortunately, the Janata government in 1977 and the Congress (I) government in 1980 committed this outrage to curb the growing influence of the respective opposition parties which hold the reins to power in the states. To use Shakespeare's words: the dismissals were 'the most unkindest cut of all'

CategoryB: Imposition of Article 356 on the plea that the State Government run by a political party failed to effectively implement the central ordinances banning certain communal organizations.

It is an acknowledged fact that the dismissal of the three BJP governments consequent upon the demolition of the Babri Masjid on 6 December 1992 was a *mala fide* exercise of power by the Centre for its own political advantage rather than to fulfil Constitutional obligation and hence it is not justified. The Central government banned certain communal organizations like R.S.S., I.S.S., V.H.P. and Bajrang Dal in the aftermath of the Ayodhya incident. The governments (M.P., H.P., Rajasthan) were decapitated on the plea that with the existence of these governments the ban could not be effectively implemented. The bigger question for serious consideration is: whether the dismissals were in consonance with the spirit of the Constitution?

The fact that the Chief Minister who heads a government in a BJP ruled State belongs to a banned organization cannot by itself lead to the inference of the failure of the Constitutional machinery i.e. the ban could not be effectively implemented.

Our Constitution does not permit pre-emptive action for imposing President's Rule. On the other hand, Article 356 permits President's Rule upon the occurrence, and not in anticipation of events, namely ".... a situation has arisen in which the government of the State cannot be carried on in accordance with the provisions of the Constitution". As has been stated in the previous part of the discussion, if the government fails to comply with or give effect to the directions given by the Centre, Article 365 provides an effective remedy. Further, there was no material to show that any of these State Governments, at any time by act of commission or omission refused to enforce the ban. Indeed, the Chief Minister of Himachal Pradesh, in so many words, told the Governor on 13 December, 1992 that he desired to implement the ban imposed upon the organizations[15]. The fact that the Chief Minister of one of these States had criticised the ban would not necessarily show that he would not implement the ban. Mere suspicion or doubt that there will not be an effective or total implementation of the ordinance surely cannot be a permissible ground for dissolving the State Legislatures.[16] Indeed, that would make the life of the State Governments depend upon the whims and fancies of the Centre. The drastic action of imposing President's Rule must be founded on cogent and objective material. There has been no breach of any undertaking or commitment by the governments in the States in which the President's Rule has been imposed.

If the capacity or incapacity of the State Government to control the situation was to be advanced as justification, then the intensity and dimension of the communal flare-up in the aftermath of the demolition was much greater in Maharashtra and Gujarat, compared with the three States in question.[17] The actual situation in these states seems to have been quite different. It was reported that the law and order situation particularly in Rajasthan and Himachal Pradesh was quite satisfactory. The communal situation in the Congress ruled states like, Maharasthra, Karnataka and Gujarath conversely was very bad.[18] So, the only criterion applied was that these two States had Congress governments, while in the other three States there were BJP governments[19]. Among the three dismissed State Governments, Himachal Pradesh had the rare distinction of being one in which not a single incident of communal violence took place subsequent to the demolition. The fact that these states were also ruled by a party which was responsible for Ayodhya incident could not be a sound reason for dismissing these governments. Both situations were different and demanded and deserved separate treatment. Here is a situation where political considerations have driven constitutional requirement to a back seat

One of these State Governments, Madhya Pradesh challenged the imposition of President's Rule in the High Court on the ground that it was a colourable exercise of power by the Centre and it was gross misuse of the Article for political vendetta. The majority judgment held that from the matter placed before it, no inference could be drawn that the state government had disrespected or disobeyed any central directive nor was there any specification of alleged deeds or misdeeds in meeting the law and order situation. Mere worsening of the law and order situation due to the sudden outbreak of violence did not call for the extreme step,[20], the court pointed out. The majority judgment held that the Union Government failed to come up with valid argument for the imposition of President's Rule in the BJP ruled States and ordered the revival of the dissolved State Legislature and reinstatement of the dismissed ministry[21]. However, on appeal, the Supreme Court upheld the validity of the imposition of President's Rule and the dissolution of Assemblies by upholding secularism as a basic feature of the Constitution and observed that the three dismissed governments had been acting against secularism by their various acts[22]. Upholding of President's Rule in the three states can hardly be supported. President's Rule in UP can be justified as rule of law and secularism received set back which constitute the basic structure of the Constitution. But, it was not so in the case of the three states in question where no danger posed threat to secularism to dismiss the government lock, stock and barrel.[23] Nani Palkhivala vehemently criticised the Supreme Court for invoking secularism as justification for the dismissal of popularly elected and legally constituted ministries. What he said is worth remembering in this context:

> 'They had done no harm. Their only fault was that they belonged to the BJP government'. He asked, 'who is to decide who is secular and non-secular ..... the party ruling at the centre?'[24]

Palkhivala's observation is sound and logic. It has to be borne in mind that the Court was concerned only with the constitutional validity of the act and not with the ethical and moral aspects of the question. What ever the clarifications and justifications offered, the fact remains that the unseating of the BJP government was a *malafide* exercise of power to restore lost credibility and improve political fortune of the Congress party which found itself in a defenceless position because they could not protect the masjid as was assured. They believed that the dismissals would enable them to hide their own omissions and short comings and there by retreive the feelings and sentiments of minorities. Thus it would be seen that the imposition of Article 356 in the three states was nothing but a game in the direction of power politics.

II. Imposition of Article 356 on the Plea of Hung Assemblies

A reason suggested casually to impose President's Rule was that the election results to the State legislative assemblies were not conclusive viz., no party or pre-existing coalition of parties wins a majority of seats in the Assembly. Thus President's Rule was imposed in Kerala in 1965, in Rajasthan in 1967, in Orissa in 1971, in Uttar Pradesh in 1996 and again in 2002 and in Bihar 2005 Virtually, each case except UP (2002) is controversial. Each imposition points to the culmination of political opportunism and power politics. Even the semblance of constitutional discipline is sadly missing in the above cases. In Kerala and Bihar the Assemblies were dissolved simultaneously whereas Assemblies were put in cold storage in the other four cases. Does the Constitution permit the imposition of Article 356 on this ground? This calls for greater analysis, for this will help to streamline various conventions and standards to be adopted as and when hung legislatures emerge in future.

Coming to the Kerala case, the newly elected Assembly was dissolved without the members taking the oath. It is politically significant to note that the CPI(M) emerged as the largest single party in the Assembly. The opposition parties under the CPI(M) stood for the convening of the newly elected Assembly, where the parties could explore the possibilities of electing a leader and forming a ministry. If no alignment or coalition was able to do this then the Assembly could be dissolved. This procedure was not accepted and emergency was declared. The political situation in the state became thick with suspicion. Allegations of partisanship, constitutional immorality and violation of ordinary decency were made against the Governor. The same situation was repeated in Bihar 2005. The Bihar episode demands deeper analysis and closer scrutiny since it has generated much heat, anguish and grievance.

The midnight dissolution of the still born Bihar Assembly in 2005 was an unexpected one in terms of analysis made by independent observers in general and NDA leadership in particular. The initial suspension of the Assembly, however, did not create any controversy since no two parties that were in a position to form the government were willing to do so. Further, President's Rule was perhaps inevitable as there was no possibility of a new government being formed before the financial year so that budget could be passed by the Assembly. If the state is under President's Rule, the Parliament is empowered to pass the budget. But what is worrying is the recommendation of Governor Bhutasingh to dissolve the Assembly when it appeared that the NDA leader Nitish Kumar was on the verge of forming the government with the support of some MLAs belonging to L J P of Ramvilas Paswan.[25]

An impartial political observer with an unbiased opinion could see that the Assembly which had been placed under suspended animation was dissolved to scuttle the possibility of government formation by NDA leader Nithish Kumar. Let us examine the Governor's charge that he had credible evidence about 'an atmosphere of horse trading of the worst kind prevailing in the State'. However, there was no relevant material with the Governor to assume that there was illegitimate realignment of political parties and there was blatant distortion of democracy by induced defection through 'unfair, illegal, unethical and unconstitutional' means. Further, the Assembly was kept suspended only to facilitate the realignment of political groups and explore the possibility for' formation of a government. In the context of hung Assembly situation and coalition politics, alliances and re-alliances are inevitable and quite common. He could have, therefore, waited to see if the NDA or the RJD could muster enough support If the Governor had any suspicion that Kumar was indulging in horse trading he should have waited for a while until Kumar staked claim. Instead of following this prudent course of action, he straight away recommended the dissolution of the Assembly. By doing so, Governor Singh virtually violated all canons and conventions of parliamentary democracy and has definitely exposed himself to the charge of functioning as 'hatchet man' of the parties in power at the Centre as charged by the NDA leadership. It is not clear what conventions and precedents in the democratic set-up had been exemplified by the act of the Governor. The tradition of parliamentary democracy was unmistakably on the side of NDA and Kumar. Therefore, he should have been given an opportunity to form the government. However, it seems that what was constitutionally appropriate was not politically acceptable to the Governor. Consequently, an irreparable damage was done by the Governor in recommending dissolution when the political deadlock was about to be broken and possibilities for the formation of a government became real. Unfortunately, priority was given to his political ambitions over and above constitutional propriety. Here the Governor had reduced himself from the position of the guardian of the Constitution to the level of a spy of the Centre or even a mere power broker. Had it not been the case, he would not have recommended to the President to dissolve the Assembly when the NDA was within a striking distance of forming a government. All these clearly point to the fact that the Governor's action carried the stamp of 'command job' with the deliberate purpose of scuttling the possibility of forming a government by the NDA leader. Had the Centre taken the decision to dissolve the House soon after it became evident that no party would form a government, it would have been justified to a certain extent.[26]

In the decision taken by the Centre, there is valid objection on some count. The Prime-minister's justification that 'an atmosphere of horse trading of the worst kind prevailed' is difficult to digest. Granted, the Centre had no option, but what cannot be overlooked is the haste with which the decision was taken when the President was out of the country.[27]. The speed with which the development took place shows the desperation of the UPA government to prevent the NDA from forming a government with the support of some MLAs belonging to the LJP. This found its expression in the observation of the Supreme Court that the move was unconstitutional and the decision was motivated to prevent Mr. Kumar from taking office.[28]. It seems that the Assembly was kept suspended with the intention of evolving a favourable climate for the RJD led UPA coalition to come to power and the UPA waited three months anticipating the formation of a government by a group acceptable to it. Finding the trend favourable to the BJP led NDA, it opted for dissolution. It was not only an insult but also a plain and simple short - circuiting of the democratic process which no amount of tub-thumping can conceal [29]

In this connection it may be stated that under our system of Parliamentary democracy, the people elect a Legislature acting in effect as an electoral college, choose the executive government through votes of confidence or, more commonly, through rejecting the motion of no-confidence. The people do not directly elect the executive. So the general election process is not really complete until the House has determined in whom it has confidence. If the House were to be dissolved before it had the opportunity to consider in whom it has confidence, the supreme act of popular sovereignty would be prematurely aborted. Virtually, all notable commentators agree that a dissolution should not be ordered if the House has not yet met, and unless it proves impossible to form a viable alternative government. The rationale for this argument is that the electoral verdict must not be thwarted by premature dissolution. As Eugene forsey expressed it, with characteristic eloquence:

> "Of course, the new House may not be capable of functioning, but it must be allowed to meet, and try". If Parliamentary government is to mean anything, a newly elected Legislature must be allowed to meet and see whether it can transact business. To dissolve it before it can so decide would be not only an affront to common sense (on which, after all, all Constitutional conventions ultimately rest) and an expensive insult to the electors, but subversive of Parliamentary government[30].

In both the incidents referred to above the concerned Governors misunderstood or conveniently forgot the relevant criterion for appointing chief ministers. Their task was simply to appoint, a person as Chief Minister capable of forming a government enjoying the confidence of the House. Instead, the Governors recommended the imposition of Article 356 of the Constitution of India. Considerable damage was done by the Governors when they recommended the President to dissolve the Assembly even before the newly elected members taking the Oath. In this context M.C. Setalvad (in the case of Kerala) observed:

> "It is not surprising that the action of the central government should have been considered as an unjustified use of Article 356 in order to keep out of power the ministry of a party other than the Congress party. This inference was strengthened in the public mind by the fact that a large number of members of the Legislature of the State were preventively detained under the Defence of India Rules"[31].

The right of the people to govern themselves through their elected representatives is fundamental to democracy. It is only rational to try the utmost to form and run a representative Government and not to allow a nominated Governor to assume power. K.V. Rao is right when he says that 'the provincial political machinery should be left to be shaped by the electors of the units alone and the Centre step in as a last resort.[32] This argument was upheld by the Supreme Court in the Bommai case. Therefore, it is suggested that legislation should be made to forbid dissolution of Assembly until the House has actually met and proved itself unworkable, for instance, because of the inability to elect a Speaker.

The U.P. (1996) incident is also similar to the Kerala episode. The only difference was that, here, the Assembly was not straightaway dissolved but kept in a state of suspended animation. The B.J.P., the largest single party in the Assembly, staked the claim for forming a government. So what was now constitutionally appropriate and permissible was not politically feasible or acceptable to the party heading the Central government[33]. By denying opportunity to the largest political party in the legislature, the bright light of democratic empowerment turned dim.

Rajasthan and Orissa cases also look similar. In both the cases, while there were no clear majority after the elections, the Congress party emerged as the largest single party on both occasions. The United Fronts in both cases claimed support for viable ministries and requested the respective Governors to give them an opportunity to form governments. Moreover, the Governors were assured in writing by the opposition parties together that they were willing to work together to form a government. However, the opposition was denied their right and, instead, President's Rule was imposed and the Assemblies were kept in abeyance until Congress party could muster the necessary majority to form governments. This shows the scant respect the Central government and the party had for the Constituion and the rules of natural justice.

The imposition of Article 356 in Uttar Pradesh in 2002, however, is an instance of failure of the constitutional machinery since it was not possible to form a viable government after fresh elections because of fractured mandate of the people. Governor, Vishnu Kant Shastri, was left with no option other than to recommend that the State be placed under Central rule. The fractured mandate and inability of the key players in the political game had foreclosed all the possibilities for the formation of a ministry. In an attempt to form a viable ministry, the Governor consulted all the major key players including S.P, BSP, BJP, Cong (I) and even Rashtriya Lok Dal of Ajith

Singh, which had won only 14 seats. Mulayam Singh Yadav's claim that he be invited on the strength of being the leader of the single largest party was indeed 'not sustainable'.[34] He was not in a position to convince that he had the support of the magic number (202) to enable him to form the government as per the insistence of the Governor. Further, formation of any government by any party was made impossible by the bizarre stands adopted by the key players: the BJP had announced its intention to sit in the opposition; the BSP had declared that it would not support a Government by the S.P, and the Congress was unwilling to give an undertaking that it would support Mulayam.[35] Thus, the argument that 'his claims were based on the possibility of managing a majority by way of engineering split in the BSP as well as some other smaller parties assumed much significance. This certainly could not have served the cause of democracy in Uttar Pradesh'[36]. Considering the political crisis and confusion and also the unethical and undemocratic practices, it would appear that President's Rule was inevitable. The imposition of President's Rule in this case did not cause much controversy since the Governor's recommendation and the President's declaration were in accordance with the spirit of the Bommai judgement. It is pertinent in this regard to recall the judgment. The court said:

> 'After the general election is held, if no political party or combination of parties or group is able to secure absolute majority in the Legislative Assembly and despite the Governor's exploring alternatives, a situation has arisen in which no political party is able to form a stable government commanding the confidence of the majority of the legislature, it would be a case of failure of constitutional machinery'[37]

Viewed strictly from a non-partisan angle and in terms of the spirit of the Constitution, there were no impasse or Constitutional crisis as such in all these cases except UP (2002). The Governors should have discharged their Constitutional obligation of choosing the Chief Ministers by appointing persons who appeared really capable of commanding the support in the respective Houses.[38] However, it cannot be forgotten that there are no, concrete rules about government formation in the background of a hung Assembly[39]. According to Jennings "where no party obtains a majority at general elections there are two possibilities only, the formation of a coalition government or the formation of a minority government with opposition support; for another dissolution is not practicable"[40]. The committee of Governors' also recommended that the leader of the largest single party in the Legislative Assembly may be invited to head a government if he is able to satisfy the Governor that, in combination with other parties or with the support of other parties in the Assembly, he is in a position to command a majority in the Legislature. He has, however, no absolute right as the leader of the largest single party or group to claim that he should be entrusted with the task of forming government to the exclusion of others. The relevant test is not the size of the party but its ability to command the support of the majority in the Legislature[41].

In the absence of any party or combination of parties which commands a majority in the Assembly, the Sarkaria Commission evolved a set of guidelines for Governors tackling vague mandate. The commission listed the course of action to be taken in the order of preference given below:[42]

1. Pre-electoral alliance of parties;
2. The largest single party staking claim to form the government with the support of others, including independents;
3. A post electoral coalition of parties with all parties in the coalition joining the government; and
4. A post electoral coalition of parties with some of the parties in the alliance forming a government and the remaining parties, including "independents" supporting the government from outside

The Commission give only some typical situation. These categories could usually cover different possibilities, but not always. Further, no Commission or expert may be able to give an exhaustive list of situations since the prevailing politics is ever changing and fluid. The Commission's suggestions and recommendations, however, are the result of a comprehensive and deep study of the exercise of the discretionary powers of the Governor in the past. However, one doubts whether it is necessary or even always feasible to assess the relative merits in clear terms of each claimant or group of claimants in a matter like this. In some situations, the leader of the post-electoral coalition of parties may be having a better chance of providing a stable government than the largest single party with the support of independents. Similarly, in some other situations the largest party staking claim to form the Government with the support of independents may be in a stronger position to provide a stable government than an alliance of parties formed prior to the election.[43]. However, if the recommendations of the Sarkaria Commission are accepted and followed strictly and judiciously and not without political partisanship, healthy parliamentary convention could be developed and adhered to. However, it may not be forgotten that constitutional provisions may be interpreted not according to the letter of the provision so as to meet the challenges of the dynamics of time and the voting behaviour of the electorate.

The subject is also discussed by the National Commission to Review the working of the Constitution. The Commission would not allow any scope for the Governor's discretion or judgment. The well considered recommendation of the Commission is that:

> 'In a situation where no single political party or pre-poll alliance of parties succeeds in securing a clear majority in the Lok-Sabha after elections, the rules of procedure and conduct of business in the Lok Sabha may provide for the election of the leader of the house by the Lok Sabha along with the election of the Speaker in a like manner. The leader may be appointed as the Prime minister. The same procedure may be followed for the office of the Chief Minister in the State concerned.[44]

This suggestion deserves attention and consideration since its basis is the assumption of the impartiality of the constitutional head and it facilitates formation of a government. It is also democratic in the sense that in a parliamentary system of government, the obligation to choose the executive is one of the important responsibilities that directly falls upon the elected representatives. In this sense, Parliament will be really doing what Harold Laski called a selective function. The most important merit of following this procedure is that it not only insulates the office of the constitutional heads from unnecessary controversies in the exercise of discretion but also reduces unhealthy claims of various groupings in the House. The Sarkaria Commission, however, rejected this proposal of direct election by the House.[45] But Geoffrey Marshall says, 'It seems safe to predict, however, that such novel and adventurous expedient will not in fact be adopted' But when this constitutional expedient is balanced against the stark reality of the huge expenditure involved in conducting elections again, it would be safe to plump for the former. The adoption of new norms or constitutional expedient to meet extraordinary circumstances is the hall mark of the Constitution as it is an organic instrument[46]

In the light of above observations, it would be seen that it was the regime's interests that have triumphed over constitutional sensibilities in the above instances under study. President's Rule was declared in Rajasthan and Orissa with the deliberate purpose of enabling the Congress party to form its own governments later by indulging in horse trading. In the same way, Article 356 was imposed in Kerala (1965), in Uttar Pradesh (1996) and in Bihar (2005) with the ulterior intention of keeping away the CPI(M), the BJP and the NDA respectively from power. It is quite unfortunate, politically puerile and absolutely indefensible to treat a party with maximum support of people as untouchable and keep it out of power[47]. In this connection, it must be pointed out that there is nothing unusual in any party or combination of parties not getting absolute majority in the elections. There were several instances in the past when after fresh elections, it was not found possible to form a ministry. Thus minority governments, in principle are inevitable in India. "What is necessary is that the government should enjoy the confidence of the House. This aspect does not appear to have been kept in mind by the Governors. This is not a matter within his subjective satisfaction. It is an objective fact capable of being established on the floor of the House"[48]. The right to self government cannot be hijacked by politicians and justification sought in distorted constitutional interpretations[49].

In view of these observations and varying precedents obtaining in other countries where parliamentary democracy exists, we have to come to the conclusion that a more democratic and flexible approach consistent with Article 164(2) of the Constitution has to be adopted in our search for a solution to deal with hung legislatures. Therefore, it is submitted that the party with the largest number of seats must be invited only after exploring whether there exists an alternative post-electoral combination of parties which results from the realization of ground realities and is more likely to win the confidence of the legislature [50]. The logic behind giving the post-poll coalition of parties a chance to form the government is to give maximum scope for the formation of a democratically elected government[51]. If the post poll alliance is not able to demonstrate a majority in advance on the basis of verified letters of support or does not obtain the confidence vote the proper course for the Governor is to invite the single largest party by insisting on written support from all parties combining to form the Government. Again if the single largest party is unable to produce written assurances from the supporting parties and if the Governor is not satisfied with the claim of the single largest party about an absolute majority in the House, he will invite the next largest party for discussion. The Governor may continue this course of action till he finds a person able to command the confidence of the House. This procedure would go a long way to ensure that, the inevitable uncertainty arising from a hung Assembly would be resolved as quickly as possible, and in accordance with the wishes of the people's elected representatives. On the other hand, if democratic rule are to be suspended under emergency provision simply because election results and other, political mechanisms do not yield absolute support for the party in power, a large part of India may be under emergency rule on a constant basis. The States cannot be treated as possessing a lesser or requiring a higher form of Parliamentary democracy than the Union simply because President's Rule can be imposed on a State but not on the Union. For securing confidence vote, the ruling party should be permitted only a reasonable time. This procedure should be followed as a matter of convention. In this context, in a latest article R. Venkataraman, the former President of India, observed:

> 'By calling parties according to the strength in the House and allowing the House to decide is positively a more democratic way of choosing the Prime minister than the President trying to find out which party in his opinion has greater support in the House.[52]

Any doubt regarding the majority should be tested on the floor of the House as observed by the Supreme court in the famous Bommai case. This should be the norm in a democracy unless the constitutional head is assured in writing by the other parties together constituting a majority that they are willing to work together to form a government. Any other decision by the President or the Governor without such assurance is speculative and subjective and capable of being misused. This procedure would go a long way to ensure that the inevitable uncertainty arising from a hung legislature would be resolved as quickly as possible and in accordance with the wishes of the people's elected representatives.

In this connection, it may be pointed out that the Governor should refuse to invite a person to form the government unless he agrees to produce the written proof of his majority in the House and to summon the legislature to prove his confidence of the house with least possible delay. It is in this context the following considered observation of Rodney Brazier, a foreign constitutional authority, is worth remembering. He observed:

> Before she (Queen) would consider taking any action proof would have to be made public that a coalition government would be viable. There would have to be a copper-

> bottomed agreement between the proposed coalition parties, including the name of the proposed Prime-minister, disposition of cabinet offices, an agreed Queen's speech and a guarantee that the coalition would not seek dissolution within a stated minimum time.[53]

This has assumed added importance since we can not underestimate the aspect of power politics. In the world of power polities, it is an indisputable fact that incumbency is the key factor which decides the outcome of floor tests. Further, this procedure may help the President or Governors to decide whether the party or Front staking claim commands, *prima facie*, a working majority. However constitutional experts like H.M. Seervai and Rajeev Dhavan are of the view that it is wrong for the President or the Governor to ask the Chief Minister or the Prime-Minister to obtain a confidence vote within the stipulated time. In support of their arguments, they argue that there is no provision in the Constitution or even rule of procedure for a confidence motion. For instance, Rajeev Dhavan holds that 'A confidence motion is a second invitation to instability. It should not be insisted on unless a minority government asks for it.[54] The Patna High court, however, in Supra Jayakar Motilal C.R. Das v. Union of India held that the Governor can impose the condition for confidence motion in his discretion where there is doubt about the majority support enjoyed by the government in the House. The principle of collective responsibility means that the government must enjoy majority support in the House and how that majority support is to be ascertained is a matter left to the discretion of the Governor.

No doubt, the individual judgment of the head of the state is an important factor. However, it is expected from the President and Governors that they would keep themselves away from party politics and act as true trustees of the people. They have to satisfy essentially that the person whom they invite to form the government, commands majority support. In Sham Sher singh case Krishna Iyer.J. wisely counselled:

> 'The paramount consideration is that a future Prime minister should command a majority in the House'.[55]

For making a wise and thorough assessment, the Governor may initiate discussion with different party leaders who have representation in the Legislature to discover whether a coalition government could be formed. He may also hold discussion with constitutional experts and political scientists, if he thinks such a course is useful. Armed with all these information, the Governor has to reach a decision which should bear a stamp of statesmanship. This procedure, however, was not followed in the cases under study except U.P. (2002). In this regard the following observation of notable jurist Nani Palkhiwala becomes quite relevant. He very pertinently states:

> The President (Governor) has to make a value based decision that democracy may survive in India beyond our time... The President has to make decisions at critical moments in a totally non-partisan spirit... Decency in public life is the only solution, if we are to preserve the true spirit of democracy... We are faced with the stark alternations of either dharma in public life or the twilight of Indian Democracy.[56]

The choice of the Chief minister is a simple problem. It is made complicated not only by the party system, but also by the party politics of the Union government, which appoints the Governor. For checks against power politics, the political system should have constitutional safeguards and healthy democratic conventions. Therefore, it is suggested that the Constitution should be amended to clarify what ought to occur if an election produces hung legislature' which is bound to repeat in future so long as the political process of our country remains the same. The existing political process will continue to be so, as long as the electorate exhibit strong political division that reflects the national and regional pulls determined by the forces of ideology and national consciousness.

III. Imposition of Article 356 on Charges of Corruption and Maladministration

Corruption and maladministration have often been cited by the Centre as sufficient reasons to dislodge a State

Government from power. Two cases, that of Tamil Nadu in 1976 and Manipur in 1979 are placed under this category. The Tamil Nadu government headed by M. Karunanidhi was dismissed on the basis of the report of the Governor that the DMK government indulged in serious acts of mal - administration, corruption and misuse of power for partisan ends, setting at naught all canons of justice and equity[57]. It is to be noted that the normal term of the State Assembly was to expire on 21 March, 1976, but it was dissolved fifty days earlier than its scheduled term.

If the grounds as mentioned in the Governor's report are critically analysed, then it will be found that there was no justification for the imposition of President's Rule in this case. Let us examine the Governor's charge 'that the allegations made against the DMK government are substantially true'. It raises a legitimate question of the constitutional responsibility of the Governor with regard to the administration of the State since these allegations were leveled in 1973, and for nearly three years no action was taken on that account. The question arises whether the Governor was waiting for the people and parties to level these charges. It was the Governor who has taken oath to "preserve, protect and defend the Constitution". But if the allegations were true, it could mean that he bypassed this responsibility for three long years and was guilty of not acting according to the oath of his office[58].

If charges of corruption had been made as a basis for dismissing a government and dissolving its Assembly, the ministries of Pratap Singh Kairon in Punjab in 1963, Devaraj Urs in Karnataka in 1977, Bansilal in Haryana in 1972 and A.R. Antulay in Maharashtra in 1983 should have been dismissed since there were very serious charges of corruption against them.[59] However, the Congress government at the Centre ignored these serious charges. In addition to what is stated above, the Sarkaria Commission of Enquiry found that many allegations of corruption - several of which dated 1972 - could not be proved beyond reasonable doubt. It is in this background the allegation that 'the DMK ministry was dismissed only on the ground that it refused to extend its support to the proclamation of emergency under Article 352 declared by the government of Mrs. Indira Gandhi becomes relevant[60]. Keeping in view this aspect, it may be stated that the dismissal of the DMK government was not in consonance with the letter and spirit of Article 356 and hence malafide, improper and fraud.

The dismissal of Yangamasha Shaiza's (Janata) ministry in Manipur in 1979 was also based on the report of Governor L.P. Singh that he had never known "such a corrupt ministry"[61]. However, a close inquiry into the available facts and circumstances that led to the dismissal brings to light the fact that the proclamation was surcharged with political motive as in the case of the dismissal of the DMK ministry in Tamil Nadu.

The question now arises as to how far the imposition of President's Rule on the allegation of corruption is justified. At the outset, it may be stated that the theory and practice of Parliamentary democracy does not confer this right on the Union Government. It was made very clear by the Constitution framers that this power was not meant to be exercised for the purpose of securing good government[62]. Dr. Ambedkar was emphatically of the view that the Centre could intervene only when the government is not carried on in consonance with the provisions laid down for the constitutional government of the provinces. Whether there is good government or not in the province is not for the Centre to determine'.[63] Moreover, the Supreme Court forcefully held that the extraordinary emergency power of recommending dissolution of legislative Assembly is not a matter to be resorted to for good governance or cleaning of politics'[64] when a duly constituted ministry, enjoys majority support is in office. The Sarkaria commission, over and above, has also expressed similar view. The Commission make it very clear that: "this power cannot be invoked merely on the ground that there are serious allegations of corruption against the ministry"[65]. All these clearly converge on the fact that President's Rule cannot be imposed on the ground of maladministration in a State when a duly constituted ministry, enjoying majority support, is in office.

It is now almost agreed on all counts that certainly the Constitution of India does not give such a right to the Union

Government because such a right will be fatal to the working of democracy in the States. If the Centre could get the majority supported State Governments dismissed because of the allegation of corruption and maladministration, then our Parliamentary system would collapse like a house of cards. If, indeed, this was to be the reason for bringing a state under President's regime, many states, not just Tamil Nadu or Manipur, should qualify for the application of the provision. The remedy for corruption or similar social ills and evils lies elsewhere and not in Article 356(1). No doubt, corruption is all- pervasive and engulfed the entire Indian Society and is one of the major factors that has eaten into the very vitals of national income and made the life of common man miserable. The disease has assumed monstrous proportions and has to be chopped off as patch work would not do. The malady should be treated appropriately with simplification of rules and procedure, empowerment of people, and speedy and effective punishment of the guilty apart from fool proof laws. However, the most unfortunate aspect is that our legal safeguards against corruption are sleeping in the archives. It is high time that public spirited people including intellectuals should mould public opinion against corruption and they demand necessary reforms to discourage it, if not rootout altogether. However, what is stated above is not a green signal for a State Government to pursue corruption. What is stated is that maladministration may not be a single cause. When the ministry is absolutely corrupt and misusing the machinery of the government for dishonest purposes or arbitrarily exercising its power in a manner not permitted by the Constitution itself, then certainly the situation warrants intervention under Article 356. It is pertinent in this regard to recall the dissenting judgement of Ramaswamy J. in the Bommai case., he significantly observed that when corruption or abuse of power is rampant in a state, President's Rule could be imposed. However, this was not the situations and conditions in the cases under study. As the system has evolved over decades, now we are in a position wherein any State Government which is not liked by the party in power at the Centre is not safe from President's Rule irrespective of its majority in the Legislature.

IV. Imposition of Article 356 Due to the Alleged Breakdown of Law and Order

There are many instances to point out that the State Governments were dismissed on the basis of the alleged failure of law and order. It was to become a favourite excuse for imposing President's Rule, and was used liberally in Kerala (1959), in Assam (1990), in Tamil Nadu (1991) in Punjab (1983 and 1987), in Jammu and Kashmir (1990) in Manipur (1993) and in Bihar (1999). It was also cited as supportive or supplementary reason in Pepsu (1953), in West Bengal (1968, 70 and 71), in Andhra Pradesh (1973), in Uttar Pradesh (1973), in Gujarat (1974) in Manipur (1979), and in HP, M.P and Rajasthan (1992). The question is whether deteriorating law and order situation and disturbed peace and tranquillity in a State come within the four walls of the definition of the 'breakdown of the Constitutional machinery'.

The most well known example of this is the dismissal of the Kerala government headed by E.M.S Namboodhiripadu in 1959. The reason advanced was the inability of the Kerala Government to maintain law and order. Here, it must be pointed out that, the liberation struggle against the Communist ministry was actually not a question of law and order and it has never been so from a holistic perspective.[66] The dismissal of the ministry was a neatly worked out secret plot as Krishna Iyer J. observed. The Communist rule has introduced structural/radical innovations in the socio-economic system of the State that included land reforms, banning eviction of tenants, providing legal aid to the poor, granting amnesty to political prisoners, and reserving 35 percent of places in educational institutions and Civil Services for the backward classes apart from the Kerala Education Bill.[67] This disturbed the powerful vested interests of the dominant economic, caste and religious groups. All the adversely affected groups came together and launched the 'liberation struggle', (Vimochana Samaram) to pull down democratically elected EMS ministry.

It was alleged that the breakdown of law and order was engineered by the leaders of liberation struggle and their agents who deliberately created tension points in various parts of the State so as to make the entire administration of the State unworkable[68]. The Congress party in the State and at the Centre could not but support the struggle because opposition to it would have undermined the socio-economic basis of the structure of the congress party and its politics. Further, the Congress leadership had reason to convince that if CPI(M) was in power any longer, the image and the political fortune of the Congress party would suffer a lot. So it was inevitable from a political, if not Constitutional, point of view for the Congress at the State and national levels to support the liberation struggle and ultimately to dismiss the first elected Communist government in the country and to dissolve the Assembly even though it enjoyed a majority in the Legislature.

The Kerala episode unequivocally proved that President's Rule is also imposed when radical governmental reforms disturb and challenge the dominant economic, caste and communal interests which decisively shape the political process of the State in favour of the ruling party at the Centre. Hence, in the opinion of the author, the constitutional process is conditioned by the socio-economic system. Therefore, students of constitutional law or researchers on the use of Article 356 should do their exercise in the light not only of the formal constitutional provisions but also of the socio-cultural and economic roots of the political process. Constitutionalism is the reflection of the political process and there is no denial of the fact that Constitution would and can influence the political process also. This aspect has been studied in detail by R.K. Suresh Kumar and P. Suresh Kumar in their classic work Development, politics and society.[69] Over and above, the 1959 dismissal also gave a warning to all radical or revolutionary political movements that the scale would be tipped against them. Here, T K Tope is perfectly justified in observing that: "invocation of Article 356 in Kerala in 1959 was an instance of abuse of power conferred by the Article on the government of India"[70]. Now, almost all impartial political observers, media analysts, constitutional commentators and even educationists unanimously hold the view that the imposition of President's Rule in this case is a politically motivated, malafide act to further the nefarious aims of the Congress party.

An impartial analysis and a closer scrutiny of the events leading to the dismissal of the Tamilnadu Cheif minister M. Karunanidi in 1991 and the very cause behind such events reveal that this emergency provision was used as a tool to gain the support for the Chandra Sekhar's minority government from Jayalalitha, who threatened to withdraw her party's support unless Karunanidhi was sacked. The main charge put forward to dismantle the government was that it allowed 'the LTTE to freely conduct its operations from the state leading to the breakdown of law and order. Also, allegations were made that the LTTE had links with the militant ULFA of Assam and was passing on secret government information, to the latter'.[71]

It is true that violence raised its ugly face in some pockets of the State and Chandra Sekhar, the then Prime Minister hinted at a possible collusion between the DMK and the LTTE. But little was heard on the subject since then. In fact, the Prime Minister expressed on several occasions in the intervening period his satisfaction with the way the government was coping with the LTTE threat and he assured that he would "think a thousand times" before imposing President's Rule in Tamil Nadu. Moreover, Karunanidhi sought the assistance of Central security forces for the purpose, which the Union Government readily provided. In spite of this, in order to placate the AIADMK on whose support the Chandra Sekher government continued, the DMK government was dismissed.

In this connection, two pertinent points should be taken up for consideration. In the normal course of things, a State Government is dismissed under Article 356 on the receipt of the report of the Governor recommending the imposition of President's Rule. Here the action was taken without the report of the Governor to the President for the Central takeover. The Governor Burnala refused to submit a written or oral report to the President confirming unhappy state of law and order as alleged by the Prime Minister, the Congress (1) Chief and the

AIADMK leader. He told in a press conference that he had made no 'adverse comments' in his report to the President.[72]. On the contrary, the Governor, in his opening address during the budget session (only a few days back) in the State Assembly emphatically exonerated the government from the charges leveled against it. Barnala told the Assembly "law and order was under control, and the Tamil militants had been rounded up"[73]. Not only this, in a valid warning to the Centre, he advised against the dismissal of a democratically elected government until there was solid evidence to substantiate the charges. If there is any truth in the report, obviously the Governor gave clean chit to the government, and reportedly he gave the same report to the President too. Despite the disagreement of the Governor, President's Rule was imposed from above on the pretext of the breakdown of law and order and the two year old government was dismissed in spite of its 2/3 majority in the legislature. It was alleged that the material for the politically immature act was provided by tainted sources. The sources were Jayalalitha, Rajiv Gandhi and Chandra Sekhar[74]. For the furtherance of their personal and selfish objectives – the dream of Chandra Sekhar to continue as Prime Minister, the desire of Rajive Gandhi to make an electoral alliance with Jayalalitha and Jaya's intention to escape from the corruption cases involving hundreds of crores of rupees – the DMK government was dismissed. This conviction has been strengthened by the gushing expression of gratitude that the AIADMK and the Congress spokesman used in welcoming the dismissal. It leaves no one in doubt about the partisan nature of the decision. Moreover, the AIADMK leaders' trip after trip to New Delhi, the recurrent meetings with the PrimeMinister, and the Congress (I) chief, the ensuing dismissal of Karunanidhi etc. enhance the suspicion of foul play. Thus it appears from the above analysis that the original concept, real meaning and true spirit of the Article 356 were not observed in its application in Tamil Nadu[75]. As long as political parties look upon power as the matter of life and death, unmindful of democratic values, the Constitution carries little or no significance.

Equally unfortunate and shameful misuse of power was the dismissal of Mohanta government in Assam in 1990 on the alleged ground of the incapacity of the State Government to combat the worsening of law and order situation in the State. It was alleged that United Liberation Front of Assam (ULFA) had been indulging in criminal and secessionist activities. However, a close observation of the available facts indicates that it was not a law and order problem but the Chief Minister's close allegiance with former PrimeMinister, VP. Singh which threatened Chandra Sekher[76]. Thus the motive behind Central intervention was political and not constitutional. It is submitted that the action of the Chandra Sekher government cannot be justified at any cost. It only exhibited the intolerance of the Union Government towards a State ministry controlled by another political party. While doing this unconstitutional act they conveniently forgot that they had trampled upon the principles of popular sovereignty and federalism.

The dismissal of the Rashtriya Janata Dal (R.J.D.) government headed by Rabri Devi (1999) under Article 356 on the ground of failure of law and order clearly showed the willingness of the BJP government to subvert the constitutional principles of governance for the sake of political convenience. That the dismissal of the government was high on the agenda of the BJP-Samata combine and they were willing to go to any extent to achieve this was evident to all[77]. The accusation of deterioration of law and order situation may be true to a great extent. But the question that now comes up for consideration is whether the situation had reached to a point which attracted the provision under Article 356. According to the Constitution, President's Rule can be imposed in a State in case of "failure of Constitutional machinery". The 'Jehana Killings' can be described as an "administrative failure" of the popularly elected government of Bihar, but it was surely not the case of failure of Constitutional machinery. Further, if law and order is projected as a prime reason to dismiss the Bihar government, the BJP led coalition cannot absolve itself of the charge of using the provision in a selective manner. Had it not been so, it would certainly have counted the rising number of murders, rapes and incidence of atrocities against Dalits and Christians and would have asked for the dismissal of ShivSena-BJP government in Maharashtra and the BJP government in Gujarat.[78] Further, the law and order in Bihar had not shown any improvement even after the imposition of President's Rule and the massacre of the innocent people continued unabated even under President's Rule and the situation remains as such even now. More over, if this is taken as a reason for imposing President's Rule, the state would find itself under President's Rule throughout. Considering all these things, it can be safely concluded that the declaration of President's Rule in Bihar was totally unjustified and undemocratic.

It should be kept in mind that breakdown of law and order is totally different from failure of Constitutional machinery. The former is the failure or inability of the Home department to resolve a law and order problem, but the latter is a collapse of the entire administration of the State in all spheres[79]. Further, problems of law and order arise in every State. Law and order is the special responsibility of the State and it is open to the State Government to seek the help and co-operation of the Union if the problem of law and order is so grave. Simple law and order problems and even the violent situation in the wake of emerging political culture in India cannot be interpreted as Constitutional breakdown. If the situation continues to be anarchic and uncontrollable either on account of incapacity of the State Government or on account of its unwillingness, and if the State Government itself is encouraging disorder and fails to take appropriate action then only the security and integrity of the country demands action. There could be extraordinary circumstances as in some of our border States, where swift action is required for the dismissal of a State Government when the unity, integrity and security of the country is threatened owing to serious rebellion, secession, mass upsurge etc. The situation of breakdown of Constitutional machinery is explained by the Madhya Pradesh High Court thus:

> Mere worsening of law and order situation in a State due to sudden outbreak of violence does not attract extreme step of imposition of President's Rule unless the President

> is satisfied that law and order situation in the State, due to sudden disturbances,, has made or is likely to make the functioning of the State Government impossible in the State[80].

This situation is further clarified by F.S. Nariman, a senior Supreme Court lawyer and eminent constitutional authority, in the following words:

> There is a lot of difference between the failure of law and order and internal disturbance. Unless the State Government is not in a position to cope with law and order problems, you cannot conclude that its Constitutional machinery has broken down. Only if the Constitutional organs of a State refuses to co-operate, if the State Government is unable to manage its day to day affairs, if the police go on strike, if the industries are unable to work and if the entire economy is paralysed or unable to move, then the Constitutional machinery can be said to have failed[81].

All the above observations clearly point to the conclusion that deterioration of law order situation cannot constitutionally justify the imposition of Article 356. On the basis of this standard, four instances in this regard, two times in Punjab (1983 and 1987) and one each in Kashmir (1990) and in Manipur (1993) can be justified for the obvious reason that situation in these cases reached such a flash point that the governance could not be carried on in accordance with the spirit of the Constitution. In the case of Kashmir the subversive activities came to such alarming proportion that they threatened the very existence of the State and therefore, the Union Government had no alternative but to impose Article 356. Whereas in Punjab, the entire administrative machinery seemed to be on the brink of a collapse and the ministry was unable to combat the fundamentalist movements and the terrorist and the extremist forces within the State with all the powers in its hand. Further, the gravity of the situation (1983) can be gauged from the fact that the Chief Minister himself requested the Centre to intervene and impose President's Rule in the State for a temporary period. Further, it was alleged that (1987) some of the ministers entertained extreme views and had links with the terrorists. Under such circumstances the only way out for the President was to assume all the powers and functions of the government of the State[82]. Similar was the situation in Manipur (1993). The intensity of the Naga-Kuki clashes was alarming and uncontrolable notwithstanding the best effort of the state administration. It was not a mere question of violence alone but some thing grave which was much beyond the capacity and reasources of the state to tackle. The state was in a benighted situation, with organised violence becoming an order of the day and hundreds and thousands of death occurring within a short span of time which signalled the complete break down of the constitutional machinery of the state.

V. Imposition of Article 356 on the Ground of Party Wranglings

It is also seen that in certain cases President's Rule was imposed primarily to enable the Legislature party of the ruling party to tide over the crisis of internal dissensions which might even take the form of dislike of the ruling Chief Minister by the party high command.[83] This indeed is a "disturbing precedent" as it definitely amounted to the violation of the spirit of the Constitution. This was done in Punjab (1951 and 1966), in U.P (1973 and 1975), in A.P. (1973), in Gujarat (1974), in Orissa (1976)[84] and in Karnataka (1990). In all these cases the surprising aspect was that there were Congress ministries with majorities in the Legislatures which were temporarily put to sleep whenever its factional fight crossed the reasonable limit of party discipline and revived after political differences were resolved under the threat of the continuance of the President's Rule. This created the precedent for the ruling parties in crisis to use the President's Rule provision to resolve party crisis and march into power' as Rajeev Dhavan observes.[85]

Imposition of President's Rule in Punjab in 1951 amply illustrated the facts mentioned above. An impartial political analysis of the events, facts and circumstances in this case reveals that the main cause that led to the proclamation was not the breakdown of the constitutional machinery but the factional quarrels between two congress groups led by Nehru's loyalists under Bhim Sen Sachar and the supporters of Sardar Patel led by Bhargava which had done enough damage to the prospects of the party.[86] Actually, the situation did not warrant the exercise of power under Article 356 and the imposition of President's Rule in this case was a bad constitutional precedent. President Rajendraprasad was unhappy with the situation. This was evident from his letter to Prime-minister Nehru in which he wrote: 'I consider it wholly wrong to permit a non constitutional body (Congress parliamentary Board) to interfere with the normal working of the Constitution by producing an artificial emergency. My feeling is that we have created a very bad and a wrong precedent (and) acted against the spirit of the Constitution[87]. Thus the imposition of President's Rule in this case was a far cry from the Constituent Assembly's intentions. The Congress leadership at the centre had blended its interest with questionable national needs to take over a state government. In this process, he observed, the office of the Governor had been mangled between the Congress party and the Constitution to the detriment of even limited federalism and of representative democracy. It was widely acknowledged that Nehru had set the country a bad example.[88]

Equally indefensible was the imposition of President's Rule in the very same State in 1966. The circumstances under which the Congress party and the Centre intervened are difficult to explain. The reason suggested for the imposition was the division of the State. But this was not the real reason. It was true that there was a lot of agitation in the State. It was also suggested that President's Rule made the division smoother. However, 'the resignation of the Chief Minister as demanded by the Centre and against the advice of the Governor, keeping the Legislature suspended and transferring the Governor who advised the Chief Minister not to resign and appointing another Governor on whose report President's Rule was declared were not above suspicion'. Further, if the reason given by the Centre is true, does the Constitution permit to place the Parliamentary democracy at risk to facilitate the division of a State? In Punjab, there was actually no breakdown of Constitutional machinery of the State as envisaged by Article 356 and the Congress party had a clear majority in the State Legislature. Therefore, "the imposition of President's Rule in Punjab on the ground of division of Punjab was considered contrary to the ground contemplated in Article 356 as Nakede observes. Here also Article 356 was made the instrumentality for stabilising the state Congress party against the threat of dysfunctional diversities.

This exercise was also repeated in Andhra Pradesh when the Chief Minister Narasimha Rao was asked to resign at the instance of the Congress party at the Centre. The resignation was ostensibly effected to stabilise the Congress party in A.P which apart from factional quarrels, was in a very bad condition because of the Telungana agitation. Thus, President's Rule in this case is a more revealing example which requires even greater analysis, for interference by the ruling party at the Centre. The Assembly was merely suspended until December 1973 when J.V. Rao was elected Congress leader. There was criticism against imposing President's Rule on a stable state government headed by Narasimha Rao so that the situation arising out of public agitation for the creation of a separate state of Telengana could be adequately handled. One possible and plausible explanation is that the Congress needed time to replace Narasimha Rao. The actual imposition of President's Rule and the political bribe that it would be replaced when the state Congress party would sort itself out, proved to be a useful combination of political devices to enable the Congress party at the Centre to make necessary adjustments as required by the Centre.[89] As far as the Congress party was concerned, this has worked and political stability was restored. But the question to be considered is whether Article 356 could be justifiably used for such a purpose

In U.P., in 1973 President's Rule was imposed so that the Chief Minister KamalapatiTripathi could resign and Bahuguna could take over as Chief Minister. The ostensible reason for the President's Rule was the need for help from the Centre to deal with constabulary indiscipline. However, a close scrutiny of the circumstances that lead to the proclamation of President's Rule bring to light that Article 356 was declared not because of the revolt and the consequent failure of law and order but because of the internal fighting within the party. There is no doubt that the administration had failed when the Provincial Armed Constabulary (PAC) rose in revolt. Central take over at that time could have been justified. But Centre took action only when elections to the State Legislature approached. It was alleged that the Prime Minister wanted not only a man of her own choice as the Chief Minister but also a man who could win the forthcoming election as she feared that the divided Congress party under the leadership of Tripathy might not fare well and hence President's Rule was imposed[90]. President's Rule continued till June 1975. The Congress returned to power after the ensuing elections. Here again, President's Rule became a political tool or a magic stick in the hands of the Centre to stabilize the Congress party in the state. The same events were repeated once again in U.P. in 1976. In this case also the Centre had no convincing reason to give for replacing Bahuguna with N.D. Tiwari. Bahuguna reportedly resigned because of Sanjay Gandhi's opposition to him. President's Rule lasted only enough for the Congress legislature party to elect a new leader. But this change could have been achieved without the suspension of the State Legislature.

The Gujarat example merits even a greater analysis. It has been claimed that President's Rule was proclaimed in the State to face the critical situation created by the student unrest and the anti-price rise agitation. But the motivating factor behind this was that Chief Minister ChimanBhai Patel had earned the displeasure of the Congress high command and the Centre desired to replace him with an acceptable leader. It was for the furtherance of this objective that the Centre accelerated a food crisis in the state to get rid of the 'out of line' Chief minister Chimanbhai patel. Here also the power was made an instrumentality for stabilising the state Congress party.[91] It was observed that 'the reasons advanced by the governments were hardly convincing. These plainly looked like a dilatory tactic on the part of the ruling party and appeared to be an illustration of how constitutional duties were, on occasion, getting subordinated to political considerations'.[92]

Similarly, imposition of President's Rule in Orissa in 1976 did not have any justification. In the present case the State was placed under Article 356 on the pretext of an artificial failure of Constitutional machinary by asking Chief Minister Nandini Satpathy to resign with a view to solving the internal crisis in the party.[93] In this connection it is to be noted that Satpathy did not formally face a defeat in the state legislature. She had to bow out of power on the ground of New Delhi's displeasure with her. Satpathy had been weakened by factionalism in the state and was unpopular with the Gandhis'. Sanjay thought her as a Communist[94].

The Karnataka incident in 1990 amply proved the fact that Chief minister, Veerendra Patel had been forced to quit office not on the ground of his bad health and his failure to curb communal violence but because of the desire of Congress (I) chief Rajiv Gandhi to change the Chief Minister and the refusal of the Chief Minister to resign[95]. However, it has been said that conditions were engineered to ensure his ouster because he was found to be too independent of the party's central high command and hence too risky[96]. In this context S.R. Bommai very pertinently observed that the Centre's decision to impose President's Rule was 'invited and forced by Mr. Gandhi by his unilateral, arbitrary, unethical and forced inhuman act of declaring like a Mughal at Bangalore airport that Mr. Patel will step down and the new leader will be elected'[97]. It was also alleged that 'many Chief ministers have been unseated between elections because Rajiv Gandhi was suspicious of strong state level leaders'.

In all the cases examined above, the Congress ministers had majorities in the respective legislatures. The Assemblies were merely kept in suspension so that the Congress formed ministries under a new leader after some time. The failure complained in all cases was law and order problem which is the constitutional responsibility of the state concerned. It seems ironic that after a self confessed failure to discharge the responsibilities of a very important portfolio, the Congress was permitted to return to power with new Chief Ministers. The Congress and the Centre have obviously used Article 356 to consolidate their hold on the concerned states at a time when there was considerable political uneasiness in the air [98].

These instances bring out the fact that the width of the power under Article 356 cannot be cut down, clipped or crabbed. It has not been uncommon for the political party in power to use Article 356 for dealing with party squabbling and cases of indiscipline in their State units. But these changes could have been effected straightaway without placing Parliamentary democracy in peril especially as there was no question of the ruling party's majority in the Assembly being in question. This is not a sound logic to order the imposition of President's Rule[99] because even without the imposition of President's Rule the process of electing a new leader could have been completed. It is despicable that this Constitutional provision which was proposed to be applied in the rarest of the rare cases to prevent the breakdown of Constitutional machinery in a State has been used "as a solution to end group rivalry within a political party[100]. A survey of the discussion in the constituent Assembly and deliberation by the Sarkaria Commission would affirm that the use of the power under 356 to sort out internal differences or intra-party problems of the ruling party would not be constitutionally correct. This kind of matters should be settled through other extra constitutional means available. Hence, it may be stated that the imposition of President's Rule in all these cases were certainly uncalled for.

VI. Imposition of Article 356 on the Allegation of the Paralysis of Parliamentary Process

A detailed study of the application of Article 356 shows that on nine occasions the Speakers of the respective Assemblies created deadlock[101]. The power was used to resolve the deadlock. This has added a new dimension to the imposition of President's Rule in the States. One of the methods used by the Speakers is to adjourn the House every time it is convened and thereby prevent the House from functioning. This can be best illustrated from the survey of President's Rule in West Bengal (1968) and Nagaland (1975). In Tamilnadu (1988) also, the Speaker was loyal to the government and adjourned the Assembly thrice in a day to help Janaki Ramachandran, who was heading a minority government[102]. The respective speakers made it clear that they would continue to repeat their earlier decision of abruptly adjourning the Legislature unless President's Rule was imposed. These Speakers were acting at the behest of ruling party and the Constitutional crisis was .created with the deliberate intention of preventing the opposition party which formed the government from proving confidence (Bengal 1967), blocking the opposition from forming government (Nagaland 1975) and giving more time to the ruling faction to muster support (Tamil Nadu 1988).

The controversial ruling in deciding disqualification of the members of the Assembly under the Anti-defection law also culminated in the imposition of Article 356. This was what happened in Mizoram (1988) Meghalaya (1991 and 2009), Manipur (1992) Goa (2002) and Nagaland (2008). In all these cases, the highly desirable, democratic and the constitutionally mandated process of of floor test was turned into a farce, with supposedly impartial and fair constitutional functionaries changing the rule of the game and manipulating the outcome. Even in Meghalaya and Manipur, the speakers concerned have issued arbitrary, whimsical and *mala fide* orders of disqualifying members of the respective Assemblies in defiance of the Supreme Court. The Supreme court in the Bommai case observed that the dismissal of Meghalaya government (1991) on the basis of such manipulated voting was clearly unconstitutional. The court, therefore, quashed the proclamation and stingingly observed:

> 'It is a matter of deep regret that the Governor of Meghalaya did not think it is his constitutional duty to give effect to the orders of this court, not even after a specific direction to that effect. He could not have been unaware of the obligation created by Article 144 viz, the duty of an authority, civil and judicial in the territory of India to act in aid of Supreme Court and its orders.[103]

By any standard, such actions of the Speakers, like abrupt adjournment of the House and arbitrary decisions relating to disqualification of the members are not proper and justifiable.[104] Here, the Speakers as in the case of Governors have reduced themselves from the position of the impartial Constitutional functionaries to the level of ordinary party workers, or even mere power brokers of their respective parties to which they owe allegiance. These happenings proved that the people who hold constitutional posts have not got out of partymen's mind set despite elevation on to the impartial constitutional offices. Many of them are looking for an opportunity to grab power even violating the basic principles of democracy and parliamentary conventions. It is unfortunate that the quasi judicial powers vested in the office of the Speaker have been 'abused' without any regard to the constitutional institution of the office. The question as to disqualification of the members has to be exercised on the basis of sound constitutional principles to uphold the highest tradition of partliamentay democracy and not on whim or caprice or without application of mind. In this connection it must be stated that we may have certain institutional arrangement at the top to ensure that everything is done as per the spirit of the constitution. It is also time to take note of whether the power to disqualify legislators on the ground of defection may be conferred on the Election Commission or the Judiciary and not on the presiding officers of legislatures.

The fundamental question to be debated is whether the Constitutional deadlock created by the Speaker amounted to the failure of the Constitutional machinery. It is submitted that Article 356 is not a proper solution to this problem. In fact, as long as there is a ministry in office which is ready to face the Assembly, and if it is performing its functions in accordance with the provisions of the Constitution, it cannot be said that a situation has arisen which warrants the use of Article 356. The proper remedy is that, in such a situation the Governor should summon the Assembly and nominate a member to preside over its meeting which could pass a vote of no-confidence against the Speaker and elect a new Speaker and allow the House to function. In Punjab v. Satpal Dange, (1969) the Supreme court held that even if the Speaker adjourned the Assembly, the Governor could summon it and direct the Assembly to transact only one specific business.[105] This shows that the Speakers do not enjoy absolute power to adjourn the legislatures and their decisions in this regard can be called in to question on the ground of want of good faith and constitutional propriety. On the other hand, "if President's rule is imposed to face such a situation it is like killing a patient simply because the doctor was unable to diagnose the disease"[106].

VII. Imposition of Article 356 to Deal with the Delay in Electoral Process

A recourse to Article 356 is taken to deal with the delay in the electoral process also. There are cases where President's Rule was imposed in some States where new Legislatures could not be constituted even after the expiry of the 'concerned State Legislatures. This happened in Sikkim (1979), in Tripura (1993) and in Bihar(1995) [107]. In Bihar, though the elections were held even before the expiry of the Legislature, the electoral process was not completed before the expiry of the term of the Legislature because of the stiff stand of the Election Commission. In the other two States under study, election did not take place because of different reasons. Since there were no Legislatures to pass the budget before the beginning of the financial year, the Parliament had to fulfil the Constitutional obligation of approving the expenditure for the State. Therefore, those Presidential proclamations can be justified to a certain extent, for the Union Government was obliged to pass the budget for the State in the absence of State Legislatures and to avoid Constitutional crisis.

VIII. Imposition of Article 356 as a Result of the Reorganization of States

We also have examples of non-controversial imposition of President's Rule as an interim measure, which can be perfectly justified. Three instances in three different States in same situations may be grouped under this category. For instance, when the new State of Kerala was created by uniting parts of

Travancore-Cochin and Malabar districts of the Madras State, Travancore-Cochin was already under President's Rule. Therefore, a fresh Presidential proclamation was issued on 1 November 1956 to continue the President's Rule with reference to the new State, till its Legislature was constituted. Similarly, when Manipur and Tripura were created as separate political entities in 1972, there had been no election to the respective Legislatures President's Rule was imposed for approximately two months to enable elections to be held[108].

IX. Imposition of Article 356 on Account of Failure to Honour the Assurance given by the Chief Minister which led to the Demolition of Babri Masjid in U.P.

The dismissal of the U.P. government of Kalyan Singh and dissolution of the Assembly in 1992 were justified by many on the ground that law and order situation in the State deteriorated considerably and that the U.P. government failed to give protection to the Babri Masjid as was assured by the Chief Minister to the Courts, the nation and the people[109].

The imposition of President's Rule in this case is also unique in several respects. The Centre's action was quite natural and was absolutely inevitable. The State Government could not maintain law and order and totally failed to fulfil the assurance to the U.P. High Court, the Supreme Court and the nation that it would never allow the karsevaks to demolish the 'disputed' structure. It was for the first time in India's history that a State Government failed to fulfil its assurances to the Supreme Court and the nation and conveniently remained a mute spectator to this despicable act. Had the Centre dislodged the U.P. government earlier as demanded by the opposition parties, the disputed structure would have been protected and there by the biggest and the most shameless violation of secular democracy would have been avoided. What made the Centre delay in dismissing Kalyan Singh government and simultaneously air lifting commandos to Ayodhya to stop the demolition is quite dubious. In this context, it may be observed that there was a peculiar confluence of inadequately explained intricacies in the unprecedented situation which ultimately led to the demolition of the mosque, the resignation of the Chief Minister and the proclamation of President's Rule. In spite of the repeated warnings and demand by the different political parties and leaders including those in the Congress that the UP government should be dismissed, the Centre waited and waited and even the armed forces of the Centre which were stationed not quite away from the mosque were not ordered to stop the tearing down of the mosque. This delay created a situation that was avoidable, unfortunate and extremely awkward. The karsevaks were unarmed and they could have been driven away if the administration wanted it. This has not happened, why? Nothing more is needed to demonstrate the governmental inertia to discharge its primary constitutional duties to the nation. Both the Constitution and secularism were put into the melting pot with a view to winning the battle of politics and power politics. The entire episode was both a short and long shot in the game of politics and power politics in favour of the Centre and against the BJP and the left opposition. Surely, the demolition and the resultant communal violence in different parts of the country changed the very fabric of Indian society.

X. Imposition of Article 356 Due to Violence within the Precincts of the Assembly when the Confidence Motion was Taken up for Voting

Article 356 is also imposed to deal with the supposedly unruly behaviour of the elected representatives inside the House when the confidence motion is being voted upon. The case of Gujarat in 1996 is the one and only example of this kind of glaring abuse. In this case the BJP ministry headed by Suresh Mehta won a confidence vote in the floor test amidst violence in the Assembly and after ejecting the opposition including the rebel BJP MLAs from the floor of the House. Next day, the BJP government was dismissed and the Assembly was put in suspended animation. The constitutional question for serious examination is: Can a scene of violence and disorder deliberately stage-managed on the floor of the House invalidate the demonstration of majority by the Chief Minister? Is it adequate to satisfy the President that the Constitutional machinery of the State has failed? It is important to note here that there is no gainsaying that the pernicious behaviour of elected representatives will surely undermine the Parliamentary system. But this by itself cannot be a reason to invoke Article 356[110]. For instance, Soli J. Sorabjee pointed out that 'the violence within the Assembly cannot be treated as an instance of failure of the constitutional machinery; it would otherwise become very easy for malicious legislators to dissolve a duly elected legislative body by creating pandemonium in the Assembly and thereby prompting improper invocation of Article 356'.[111] Further, Jeevan Reddy and Agarwal J.J, in the Bommai case wisely counselled that it is not each and every non-compliance with particular provisions of the Constitution that calls for the exercise of power under Article 356.[112] Thus, Bommai sanctioned dismissal of a state government only under most extreme circumstances. Clearly, by this test, the unruly behaviour of elected representatives inside the Assembly, however offensive they might have been, does not lead to the inference of the failure of the constitutional machinery even though such a behaviour tend to impair the functioning of the parliamentary democracy. This malady of the political body, however, has to be treated appropriately. The correct procedure to be followed in such a situation is to disqualify the guilty Legislators instead of adopting the strange practice of imposing President's Rule. But what happened here was that a State Government was dismissed under Article 356 although there was no "all pervasive violence or other extraordinary reasons" in the State and hence this imposition of President's Rule cannot be justified on the ground that has been given for it. It was an unwarranted act destroying a democratically constituted government in the State[113].

The rules are very clear on the issue of pernicious behaviour of elected representatives inside the law making bodies. Para 43(4) of the Handbook for the Members of Lok Sabha categorically states that 'members should not interrupt any member while speaking' and 48(8) says that 'members should not obstruct proceedings'. Further, the presiding officers are clothed with sufficient powers to discharge their duties to the nation. Rule 373 of the rules of procedure and conduct of the business in the Lok Sabha allows the Speaker to direct any member whose conduct is 'grossly disorderly to withdraw immediately from the house'. Rule 374 permit him to name a member who disregard the authority of the chair or abuses the rule of the house'. Again there is another rule that whenever the Speaker rises, he shall be heard in silence and any member who is then speaking or offering to speak shall immediately resume his seat. It is also provided that any abuse of the procedure and wilful persistent disregard or defiance of the authority of the Speaker are considered grave offence of breach of privileges and contempt of the House. Members violating the rule should be dealt with severely without any fear or favour. They should be asked to leave the House for the day and if they refuse, they should be suspended for the session. A second suspension should entail disqualification and termination of membership and the members should be debarred from contesting elections for a specific period. In this circumstances, the following observation of C.K. Jain seems to be valid and fair. He observed:

> 'It is for serious consideration whether the Constitution or the R.P. Act may be amended to provide for vacation of seats and disqualification from any election in the event of members having suffered the punishment of serious withdrawals and suspension from the service of the House. This will act as a real deterrent and restore the prestige and dignity of Parliament and state legislatures facing serious erosion for quite some time[114].

Associated with what is stated above, tough measures should be resorted to, against those who found guilty of unruly behaviour in the Legislatures. They must be brought to book for the offence of criminal intimidation and physical assault. To achieve this political parties should rise above parochial considerations and come forward with requisite courage to bring in fundamental changes in the privileges of the members inside the Houses. Some may think that the suggestion is rather stringent, but to take care of a maıady which eats into the very vitals of democratic process, strong panacca is to be administered to save the patient.

XI. Imposition of Article 356 in order to Get the Interim Budget of the State Passed in the Parliament

A thorough study of the imposition of President's Rule also indicated that Article 356 was invoked several times to facilitate the passing of the budget[115] in the States where it could not be passed because of the existing political and ministerial instability resulting from the rise and fall of ministries due to defections and shifts in alliances. In this circumstance it was not possible for the state legislatures to pass its' budget within the stipulated time and that only the Parliament can fulfil the financial obligation of the State and this could not be done without placing the State under the direct control of the President. Therefore, President's Rule in all these cases becomes sine qua non and its application can be vindicated on the ground of Centre's obligation to see that the budget is passed before the next financial year begins. Hence, all such instances of imposition of President's Rule—in Bihar (1968), Mysore (1971), Gujarat (1971), Punjab (1971), West Bengal (1971), Manipur (1973) and Gujarat (1976)—are justifiable.

XII. Imposition of Article 356 due to Political Instability as a Result of Party Splits, Defection etc.

A bewildering and structurally kaleidoscopic variety of political and constitutional combination has emerged out of the interaction in the coalition politics in India since 1967 and the imposition of Article 356. This, in turn, has opened up a new vista in State/Sub-national politics, comparative government and dynamics of federalism. Further, the coalition syndrome has firmly established the intimate and inevitable nexus between the intricate political process and the working of the Constitution with reference to the application of Article 356.

In 1967, a major change occurred in the Indian political scene which in its evolutionary process, passed from essentially transitional phase of the politics of one party dominance to another phase of the politics of polarization or political coalitions[116]. When the Indian political scene was marked by one party dominant system, the imposition of Presidents' rule was less frequent. By and large, the' ruling party at the Centre and in the States was the same (Congress) and this ensured that the tensions, conflicts, controversy and instability arising between both the levels of government could very often be resolved through the mechanism of the party set-up. But Indian political scene since 1967, as has been mentioned above, witnessed a period of turmoil and uncertainty.

The fourth General election in 1967 brought an end to the monopoly of the Congress party and the party was thrown out of power in many States where non-Congress governments rose to power. No party was able to command absolute majority in the non-Congress ruled States and this resulted in the formation of hotchpotch of coalitions. The emergence of coalition politics expanded the scope for the misuse of Article 356. In some States as many as a dozen parties entered into electoral/post-electoral alliances to seize power. The drama of splits and counter splits, alignments and realignments, and defections and counter defections became common. In some cases when certain persons and parties lent their support to a particular Chief Minister, others withdrew their support to him. Chronic ministerial and political instability was the result. Many States witnessed this instability more than any other time. This uncertainty prevailing in some of the States gave the Centre, through its agent (Governor), occasion and opportunities to use Article 356. In about a decade from 1967 to 1976, the Central takeover under Article 356 took place in thirteen States as many as 26 times[117]. The 'safety valve' under Article 356 was increasingly and unscrupulously used as a weapon of political management and as an effective tool of power politics.

An attempt has been made here to examine the cases of coalition politics and defection. These two types of cases cannot be separated. Ministerial instability due to party split, defection or withdrawal of support was made a ground for imposing President's Rule in A.P. (1954), in Assam (1979,1981 and 1982), in Bihar (1969 and two times in 1972), in Goa (1990, 1999), in

Haryana (1967, 1991), in Jammu and Kashmir (1986), in Karnataka (1977,1989), in Kerala (1956,1964,1970,1979,1981 and 1982), in Manipur (1977, 1981, 1992), in Nagaland (1988), in Orissa (1961,1971,1971 and 1973), in Punjab (1953,1968), in Sikkim (1984), in Tripura (1977), in Uttar Pradesh (1968, 1970 and 1995) in West Bengal (1970)[118], in Manipur (2001), in Karnataka (2007 Oct. and 2007 Nov.) in Jammu and Kashmir (2008) and in Jharkhand (2008 and 2010).

A detailed study of all these cases brings to light the fact that political uncertainty which prevailed in these States due to the emergence of multiparty system and the absence of any strong party and the presence of the evil game of defection and counter defection led to the Presidential take over. In majority of these cases, the ruling party at the Centre maneuvered crisis for its own benefits. It is also seen that there were many occasions when Governors recommended President's Rule in their respective States without using the constitutional opportunities to form a stable government when political instability prevailed. But political instability can never be a sufficient reason because it is the inherent attribute of Parliamentary system. Even England, the mother of Parliamentary democracy, is not an exception to this situation. Therefore the emergency proclamation under Article 356 should not be made to remedy the malady caused by defection, political instability, ministerial crisis etc. This can be gathered from the proceedings of the Constituent Assembly. While participating in the debate on Article 356 H.V. Kamath observed:

> I am sure that this Article is not intended for resolving any ministerial crisis that might arise in a particular State. For that remedy lies elsewhere; the remedy lies in the dissolution of Legislature by the Governor and a reference to the electorate.... a mere crisis or vote of no-confidence in the ministry by the Legislature, even a repeated vote, does not, cannot empower the President of the Union Government to intervene and proclaim an emergency[119].

The Supreme Court in Bommai case also ruled that the political instability does not constitute sufficient and valid reason to dismiss State Government and declare President's Rule[120]. Thus, if a ministry is defeated or resigns due to ministerial instability, President's Rule should not be made a reasonable course of action. Since Article 356 was conceived to be the last remedy, Governors should take Parliamentary remedies first before calling Article 356 into operation. That is to say, the Governor is expected to take all the steps to have a Council of Ministers to advise him, and to install as Chief Minister a person, who appears to him to be in a better position to command the support of the stable majority in the House. If ministry after ministry is voted out of power, and the Governor comes to the conclusion that the Assembly has to be dissolved, he can do so, if the last ministry has tendered an advice that the outgoing ministry may be allowed to continue as a care taker government, and order fresh election at the earliest, thereby allowing the people of the State to settle the matter among themselves. Thus it is for the Governor to handle the situation as per the traditions of Parliamentary democracy without placing the State under President's Rule.

Here we see that most of the Governors straightaway opted for the extraordinary remedy under Article 356. In many cases the possibilities of alternative ministries had not been fully explored by the Governors concerned. In some other cases the demand for the alternative ministry by the opposition was turned down by citing political instability as reason. This speaks volumes about charge sheet that Governers went out of their way to perpetute the political ambitions of the union government. Things as they are, it should be inserted in the Constitution that in case of ministerial instability taking place, before taking resort to the extraordinary provision of Article 356, the Governor shall make use of all Parliamentary remedies to diffuse the crisis[121]

To conclude, it may be pointed out that the political system is the subsystem of the socio-economic systems and hence is very much influenced by it. At the same time it is also equally true that the political system could change and transform the socio-economic system. They are interactive. Political process, whether stable or unstable has to take place. Complexities could never be avoided. When the political process changes , the political behaviour of parties changes, new expectations of the people are brought to the forefront and naturally we need new consitituional process.

References

1. Though there had been misuse of this Article from the very beginning, the blatant misuse was made by the Janata Party, the first non Congress party, when it dismissed nine Congress ruled state governments en masse without any Constitutional problem of one kind or the other and thereby added a new dimension to the use of the provision. Drawing inspiration from this, subsequently the Congress Prime Ministers like Indira Gandhi and Narasimha Rao misused this provision for partisan end. A common phenomenon running through all these is that when a particular party which is opposed to the ruling party at the centre gains ground in a state, the Centre could do anything including invoking Article 356.
2. *CAD,* Vol. IX, 177.
3. Over the years, President's Rule became extremely controversial because it was thought often used to serve Central Government's convenience or political party interests, not to protect Constitutional governance and sound administration. Deplored as coercion, the device came to erode the sense of unity rather than confirming it. (Austin, Granville *Working a Democratic Constitution—The Indian Experience* (New Delhi: OUP, 1999) 157.
4. *AIR 1994 SC 1994.*
5. The years were 1952, '55, '57, '58, '60, -62, '63, 78, '85, '94, '97, '98 and 2000, 2003, 2004, 2006.
6. K. Surya Prasad, *President's Rule in Kerala : A Historical Overview, Journal of Kerala Studies* 15 (1988) : 112.
7. *Sarkaria Commission Report,* Part I, 175.
8. Shantibushan (law minister)'s interview on All India Radio. See Austin, Granville, *Working a Democratic Constitution,* (New Delhi: OUP, 1999) 443-44
9. *AIR 1977 SC* 1361.
10. *Ibid.* 1362.

11. B.P. Pandya, *The Role of Governor, The Journal of Constitutional and Parliamentary Studies,* 31 (1996): 162
12. *S.R. Bommai v. Union of India,* AIR 1994 SC.1952-53
13. *Sarkaria Commission Report* 175.
14. *Ibid*
15. H.R. Khanna, *Dismissal of the BJP Governments, The Hindu,* 1 June 1994.
16. Soli J. Sorabji, *"Outrageous onslaught on Constitution", The Hindu,*
17. The official ground for imposing President's Rule in the three states was the actual or feared breakdown of law and order resulting from the Mosque's destruction. The actual situation in these states seems to have been quite different. Law and order situation particularly in Rajasthan and Himachal Pradesh was quite satisfactory. The communal situation in the Congress governed states of Maharashtra, Karnataka and Gujarat conversely was 'very bad'. The Chief Ministers of the BJP governed states all were members of RSS, and, because the central government had banned the RSS, they were subject to the provisions of Unlawful Activities Prevention Act, 1997. No action was taken against them under this law. (See Austin 613.)
18. See Austin, Granville *'Working a Democratic Constitution,* 613
19. H.R. Khanna, *Dismissal of the BJP Governments, The Hindu,* 1 June 1994.
20. *Sunderlal Patwa v. Union of India, AIR 1993* MP 214
21. *Sunderlal Patwa v. Union of India, AIR 1993* MP 214.
22. *S.R. Bommai v. Union of India,* (1994) 3 SCC 236.
23. Sura Reddy, *Judicial Review vis-a-vis Article 356, Supreme Court journal,* Vol 2 (1994) :14
24. *Ibid.*
25. For a comprehensive analysis of the role of the Governor see Purnima.S. Tripathi, *A Role for the Governor, Frontline,* 20 May 2005.
26. See *Unavoidable for a While,* editorial, *The Hindu,* 9 March 2005.
27. See Purnima .S. Tripathi, *A Dissolution at Midnight, Frontline,* 17 June 2005.
28. *AIR SCW* 494.
29. *Short - Circuiting the Democratic Process,* editorial *Mainstream,* 27 May 2005.
30. George Winterton, *Tasmania's Hung Parliament, 1989, Public Law* (1991): 439.

31. M.C. Setalvad, *Grave Emergency and Emergency Arising out of the Failure of the Constitutional Machinery in a State* (Madras: University of Madras, 1966) 25.
32. Rao K.V. *Centre State Relations in Theory and Practice, The Indian Journal of Political Science*, Vol.14:352.
33. Rajeev Dhavan, *A Requiem for Democracy, Mainstream*, 2 June 1996: 9.
34. *Central Rule in UP*, editorial, *The Hindu*, 8 March 2002.
35. *The Hindu*, 6 March 2002.
36. *Central Rule in UP*, editorial, *The Hindu*, 8 March, 2002.
37. *AIR 1994 SC 1918*
38. In 1967 the Home minister, Y.B. Chavan, sought the opinion of three former Chief Justices of India, Justices M.C. Mahajen, A.K. Sarkar and P.B. Gajendragadkar, former Attorney General M.C. Setalvad, and the then Advocate General of Maharashtra, H-M. Seervai on the subject. The matter was also discussed with the leaders of the opposition parties in March 1968. The consensus that emerged was: 1. The Assembly should have an opportunity to express its confidence in a new government without delay; and there should not be an interval of more than a fortnight between the swearing-in of ministry and the commencement of the new session of the legislature. 2. The alignment of independents should not be ignored while assessing who is likely to command a majority in the Assembly. 3. The Governor should invite the person who has been found by him, as a result of his soundings, to be the most likely to command a stable majority in the legislature to form the government. (For a detailed discussion (See. A.G. Noorani, *Constitutional Questions in India* (New Delhi: OUP, 2000) 70-71).
39. For more insight, see Rodney Brazier, *Constitutional Practice*, 2nd ed. (Oxford: Clarenden Press, 1944) 25-47.
40. Ivor Jennings, *Cabinet Government*, 3rd ed. (Bombay: OUP, 1953) 30-31.
41. *Report of the Committee of Governors* (1971) 29.
42. *Sarkaria Commission Report* 128.
43. Alexander, P.G. *India in the New Millennium* (New Delhi: Somariya, 2001), 2007.
44. *http:/law min.nk/ncrwc/final report.htm.*
45. See the *Sarkaria Commission Report* V.I, 128.
46. See Krishna Shetty, K.P,. *Hung Parliament and Volatile Government - A Constitutional Riddle, The Hindu*, 4 June 1996.

47. Subhash C Kashyap, *President's Rule Illegal, The Indian Express,* 18 October 1996.
48. *S.R. Bommai v. Union of India,* AIR 1994 SC 2097.
49. Rajesh Pandey, *What Matter Most is the Constitution's Spirit, National Herald,* 28 November 1996
50. In this context Subash C. Kashyap observed that in a representative democracy, we select our rulers through a system of election. The system adopted by us is that of first-past-the-post system *i.e.* one who gets the largest number of votes is assumed to have received the mandate of the people and is declared elected even though-as most often happens-he may have received nothing like a majority of votes cast. Applying the same principle and the Constitution does not ordain any other to the post-poll scenario and the selection of person to be appointed by the Governor as Chief Minister, it is pretty clear that the party with the largest number of seats in the Assembly should be regarded as the one having received the best mandate of the people-even if it is not absolute-and as such its leader should be invited to form the government. (Subash C. Kashyap, *President's Rule Illegal, The Indian Express,* 18 October 1996). S.A. De Smith says that when no parry has an overall majority in the House the Queen will have to decide who has a reasonable prospect' of maintaining himself in office. That person will normally, but not invariably, be the leader of the largest party in the House of Commons (S.A.De Smith, *Constitutional and Administration law,* 4th ed. (1981) 176. See also 173)
51. The noted constitutional expert A.G. Noorani observed that' the president ought to insist on clear agreement on the coalition leaders, besides a common minimum programme plus an accord to work in coalition, both of which should be in writing and made public (Noorani, A.G, *Constitutional Questions in India* (New Delhi: OUP, 2000) 136).
52. Venkata Raman R, *President's Function, The Hindu,*12 May 2005
53. Brazier, Rodney, *Constitutional Reforms* (2nd ed) (New Delhi: OUP, 1998) 136.
54. Seervai H.M. *Constitutional Law of India,* Vol.II (3rd ed) (Bombay, N.M. Tripathi 1986), p.2718. See also Rajeev Dhavan, *choosing a Prime Minister, The Hindu,* 13 May 2004
55. *Shamsher Singh* v. *State of Punjab,* AIR 1974 SC 2192.
56. Referred to in by Rao UNR, *Tamil Nadu Governor's Action, The Hindu,* 29 May 2001

57. The Sarkaria Commission found that many allegations of corruption several of which dated to 1972—could not be proved without a reasonable doubt; found evidence to substantiate the allegation that he had abused his official position when awarding a contract; and found 'with a preponderance of probability' that the Chief Minister had received large amount of cash in matter of sugar supplies for the State. (Granville-Austin 609).
58. See J.R. Siwach, *Politics of President's Rule in India* (Shimla: Indian Institute of Advanced Study, 1979) 309.
59. Although Karunanidhi was accused of corruption and misuse of power for achieving partisan ends, closer to reality was the Governor's charge that ministry was guilty of deliberate attempt to thwart national policy and disregard of instructions of the Central Government in relation to emergency. In other words, according to the officials in Madras and New Delhi at the time, this was a 'Coup' against Karunanidhi because he was not implementing Sanjay Gandhi's and V.C. Shukla's telephonic instructions (Austin 609).
60. See Alladi Aruna, '*Unfederal features of Indian Constitution* (Chennai: Muthivan Publications, 2001) 277.
61. Lok Sabha Secretariat, *President's Rule in the State and Union Territories,* (New Delhi, 1996) 40.
62. In the Constituent Assembly when a question was asked whether Article 356 was intended to enable the Centre to intervene for the sake of "good administration" in the state or not, it was made clear by Ambedkar that: "No, no. The Centre is not given that authority" (See *CAD. IX, 176)*. This shows that Article 356 is not meant to ensure good governance. That is the job of the political parties and the political system. If the people elect a party which governs badly, the final Court is the people again. Article 356 is only an emergency measure to safeguard national unity and the democratic political system when they come under threat.
63. *C.A.D*, Vol.IX, 176.
64. *Rameshewar Prasad v. Union of India, AIR SCW* 494.
65. *Sarkaria Commission Report* 173.
66. In this context C.P. Bhambhri stated that if political movements are the basis of judging the shift in public opinion and dismissing the ministry, the Punjab ministry should have been dismissed because there were mass movements against its language policy (Akali and Hindi agitations). Why was the

Punjab ministry not dismissed ? When these movements were going on in Punjab, it seemed that the majority of people were against the government. There was great communal tension in the state. Hindus and Sikhs were becoming very hostile to one another. The state of Punjab was facing great linguistic and communal tensions, and peaceful life was always threatened, why was the President's Rule not proclaimed in Punjab. It is also alleged that situation had arisen in many states similar to the situation in Kerala, but different standards were applied to different states because of party consideration. (C.P. Bhambhri, *The Governor in Theory and Practice,Mainstream,* 4 May 1996:3).

67. Austin, Granville, *Working a Democratic Constitution*, 159.
68. Rajeev Dhavan, *President's Rule in the States* (N.M. Tripathi: Bombay, 1979) 73
69. Suresh Kumar, R.K and Suresh Kumar P, *Development, Politics and Society* (New Delhi: APH, 2009)
70. T.K. Tope, *Constitutional Law of India,* 2nd ed. (Lucknow: Eastern, 1992) 858.
71. See Saumyajit Ray, *Politics of Blackmail, Mainstream,* 23 February 1991: 4.
72. See Guhan, S., *Constitutional Collapse: In Tamil Nadu or in Delhi, Frontline,* 16 February 1991: 110.
73. *The Times of India,* 1 February 1991.
74. See *The Indian Express, 3rd februaly 1991.*
75. Sudama Singh, *Changing Concept of Article 356: The Tamil Nadu Experiment, U.P. journal of Political Science,* 2 (1990): 52.
76. See Sunil Deshta, *President's Rule in the States: Constitutional Provisions and Practices* (New Delhi: Deep and Deep, 1993) 118.
77. *President's Rule in Bihar,* editorial. *The Hindu,* 15 February 1999.
78. In Maharashtra the very apparatus of the state was responsible for the killing of innocent dalits at Ramabhai Nagar of Mumbai in July 1988. The state government was under the total control of Bal Thackarey whose role in inciting violence is not merely well known but has even been recorded by the Srikrishna Commission that investigated one of the worst communal carnages that independent India had witnessed. The several incidents of violence perpetrated by the Shiv Sena cadre such as vandalising cinema halls and attacking artists were in fact actively supported by leading players in the state government. Similarly the situation in Gujarat was grave as the Patel Government failed to provide effective protection to the Christians who were attacked by Hindu outfits. Though

violence in Gujarat did not lead to any massacre of the kind witnessed in Bihar, the fact that the Chief minister and other members of his Cabinet identified with the VHP and other such groups is clearly a case of partisan use of official machinery. But in both the cases, the parties have not shown the same urgency as they showed in Bihar. (See *The Hindu*, 24 September 1998).

79. Alladi Aruna, *The Use of Article 356, The Hindu*. 25 June 1998. For more details see. Sudama Singh, 48-49.
80. *Sunderlal Patwa v. Union of India*, AIR. 1993 MP. 214.
81. F.S. Nariman, Interview, *Strengthen the Institution of Governor, Frontline*, 17 July 1998.
82. There had been an alarming deterioration in the law and order situation in Punjab. The daily killing of innocent men and women in market places, buses and trains was mounting. Policemen themselves were mortally afraid of terrorists and looked the other way when it came to saving the lives of their kin. In other words, the police force was totally demoralised. The .subordinate judiciary was threatened with dire consequences if they convicted any accused militants. The-government was unable to protect the lives of those who had actually ventured to depose against the militants. In short, an effective civil administration had ceased to function in Punjab. (See R. Venkata Raman, *My Presidential Years*. (New Delhi: Harper collins, 1994) 142-43).
83. Since 1980, many Congress Chief Ministers have been unseated between elections because Indira and Rajiv Gandhi were suspicious of strong state-level leaders and had the power to oust them when factional fighting (which the Gandhi often fomented) became too intense. (James Manor, *India's Chiefministers and the problem of Governability* referred to in by Granville Austin 605).
84. See Giri Lal Jain, *The Centre State Relations: No Foolproof Solution*, referred to in The *Times of India*, 13 October 1983.
85. Rajeev Dhavan, See *The Hindu*, 3 July 1998.
86. President's Rule was imposed when Bhim Sen Sachar group failed to dislodge Bhargava's group from power, and when Bhargava refused to form the ministry selected by the Congress High Command, which particularly annoyed Nehru. Hence, in order to restore unity in the Congress before the elections, Bhargava was asked to resign. But at the same time, the Assembly was suspended with the intention that if the unity of

the Congress was restored in due course, and if a broad-based ministry acceptable to the High Command would be formed, the ministry would be reinstalled. In this case President's Rule was imposed by creating an artificial failure of the Constitutional machinery by asking the Chief Minister to resign with a view to solve the internal conflicts of the party (J.R. Siwach 279).

87. Austin, Granville, P158
88. Austin 607. President Rajendra Prasad was not happy with the imposition of President's Rule in Punjab in 1951. This is evident from what he had written to Prime Minister Nehru. He wrote: "I intensely dislike suspending the normal working of the Constitution in the Punjab and assuming to myself the functions of the state Government". No emergency had arisen in the state and the Chief Minister said he had resigned, "in obedience to a directive of the Congress Parliamentary Board". Not because he has lost the confidence of the legislature. "I consider it wholly wrong", Prasad continued, to permit a non-Constitutional body (the CPB) to interfere with the normal working of the Constitution by producing an artificial emergency. (Rajendra Prasad's letter to Jawaharlal Nehru dated 19 June 1951. Referred to in by Granville Austin 158).
89. Rajeev Dhavan *President's Rule in the States* 180
90. See JR Siwach 46
91. See Rajeev Dhavan, *President's Rule in the States,* 80-81
92. Rajeev Dhavan, *President's Rule in the State,* 80
93. See Austin 608
94. *Ibid*
95. In this case the ruling party at the Centre and in the States were different. The Centre had acted on the report of the Governor who was totally responsible for the Presidential take over.
96. See Sunil Deshta 166-17.
97. *The Tribune,* 11 October 1990. A Survey of the discussion in the constituent Assembly would affirm that Article 356 was never intended for political clean up operations of this kind. This kind of matters should be settled through other extra constitutional means available.
98. Rajeev Dhavan, *President's Rule in the States,* 81
99. On the imposition of Article 356 in Kamataka in 1990, President Venkataraman wrote: I was reluctant as there was nothing to show that a situation has arisen in which the government of the state cannot be carried on in accordance with the provisions

of the constitution as required by Article 356. There was a government under Veerendra Patel and it had not been defeated in the House. The governor need not concern himself with internal dispute within the ruling party but could leave it to them to fight it out. (See Venkataraman 419).

100. Chandrapal, *State Autonomy in Indian Federalism* (New Delhi: Deep and Deep, 1984) 181.
101. See the previous chapter on historical survey.
102. O.P Verma and M.L. Sharma, *Failure of the Constitutional Machinery in Tamilnadu, Journal of Constitutional and Parliamentary Studies,* 25 (1990): 188-89.
103. *S.R. Bommai v. Union of India,* AIR 1994 SC 1948.
104. The issue of Speaker V. Legislature has also added a new dimension to imposition of President's Rule in a state. The Constitution, the rules of procedure of the legislature, rulings of the Supreme Court and certain conventions evolved over the years govern the relationship between Legislature, Speaker and Governor. In the legislature, the House is the master of its own proceedings as Article 212(1) of the Constitution clearly states. Normally, it is the Speaker's prerogative to draw up the agenda and conduct the business of the Assembly. The Speaker is to preside at the sittings of the House and to ensure that it functions in an orderly manner in accordance with the Constitution and convention. He should regulate the proceedings in accordance with the wishes of the House. While the House is the master of its procedure, the Speaker is only a servant of the House. He cannot shut the House against itself and make it dysfunctional nor can he substitute his own judgement for that of the House.
105. *AIR 1969, S.C. 903.*
106. JR. Siwach 404. See also Madhu Karrao Choudhari, *Four Decades of Indian Democracy, Journal of Constitutional and Parliamentary Studies,* 27 (1993): 61.
107. Computed on the basis of the available sources.
108. See the *Sarkaria Commission Report* 188.
109. Kalyan Singh gave the assurance that: *Pending a final solution; the government of U.P. will hold itself fully responsible for the protection of Rama Janma Bhumi-Babri Masjeed structure.* (See *The Hindu,* 7 December 1992).
110. *Frontline,* 14 November 1997 : 18.
111. Soli J. Sorabjee, *Constitutional morality violated in Gujarat, The Indian Express,* 21 September 1996.

112. *S.R. Bommai v. Union of India,* AIR 1994, SC.1918.
113. Nagindas Sanghavi, *President's Rule – Temporary Quiet, Economic and Political Weekly,* 31 (1996) : 2588.
114. Jain, C.K., *Crime on the Floor, JCPS,* Vol.33 (1999) : 36-37
115. V.N. Narayanan, *An Article of Bad Faith, News Week,* 27 September 1998.
116. Iqbal Narain, *Twilight or Dawn: The Political Clange in India 967-71* (Agra: I.S.L. Aggarwall, 1972) 73
117. H.R. Khanna, *Article 356 and its use and misuse, The Hindu,* 14 November 1997.
118. Computed on the basis of the available secondary sources.
119. *CAD,* Vol. IX 141.
120. *AIR 1994* SC 1918.
121. Applying this procedure it could be argued that the declaration of President's Rule in Assam (1979, '81 and '82), in Goa (1990, '99), in Haryana (1991), in Kerala (1964, 70 and '81), in Manipur (1977), in Orissa (1961, '71 two times), in Punjab (1968), in Sikkim (1984) and, in Tripura (1977), Karnataka (2007 Oct and 2007 Nov), Jammu and Kashmir (2008) Jharkhand 2009 and 2010 were in order.

Chapter 6

The Emerging Model: An Evaluation

In a federal polity, where it is difficult to bring in political stability under mature political parties due to the peculiar nature of multi-party system and the resultant governmental instability, the ruling parties at the Centre in order to create a stable situation which may be temporary, but convenient for the present, use the Constitution as a pliable instrument even if it is unjustifiable. There are several instances to show that Article 356 has been frequently used by the party in power at the Centre as an effective instrument of political management to regulate, adjust, promote and stabilise the political process preferably in favour of the ruling party at the Centre and to create inconveniences' for the opposition parties to continue in power. It seems that the power has been employed as a suitable pretext to get rid of inconvenient state governments, recalcitrant Chief ministers or to deal with minor matters not amounting to the failure of the constitutional machinery in the states as envisaged by the founding fathers of the constitution. Thus M. Karunanidhi is justified in stating:

> "Article 356 hangs above the head of the state governments, like the 'Sword of Domocle's there by the central government threatens to avenge the state for not falling in line"[1].

This becomes quite evident to any scholar who peruses the history of the implementation of this provision in the light of accompanying circumstances. That is whenever there occurred political chaos or confusion in the States run by opposition parties, it was treated as a matter of great concern on the specious plea that the State's constitutional machinery had broken down and President's Rule was immediately declared without making any effort to restore normal condition. One can very well point out the situations in Kerala (1959), Assam (1990), Tamil Nadu (1991) and Bihar (1999) on the eve of the declaration of President's Rule in this context. On the contrary, if the same situation occurred in a State where the ruling party at the Centre was in power, different yardsticks were applied to assess the crisis. Maharashtra (1982 and 1992) and Gujarat (2002) are examples [2]. All these depended on the political complexion of the State Government. But there have been exceptions where the Centre had clamped emergency to replace its own Chief Minister for 'refusing to toe the party line'.

The Union Government has also deliberately kept the Assemblies of certain States suspended or dissolved keeping in view the interest of the ruling party at the Centre. Whenever the State ministries other than the ministries of the party at the Centre resigned or fell because of defection or in anticipation of defeat, split or withdrawal of support, the Assembly was ordinarily suspended if the ruling party had a chance to form an alternative ministry later.[3] A few illustrations may be given to substantiate the point. The Meghalaya MUPP ministry led by B.B. Lyngdoh was dismissed and the Assembly suspended on 11 October 1999. The suspension was revoked after D.D. Lapang of the Congress (I) formed the government on 5 February 1992. The Manipur ULP ministry led by R.K Ranbir was removed and the assembly suspended on 7 January 1992. The suspension was revoked when Congress (I) coalition ministry led by Dorendra Singh was formed on 8 April 1992.[4] The Table 5 gives an idea about Assemblies placed under suspended animation and the resultant political change.

Table 5
Table Showing Details of Assemblies Placed under Suspended Animation and the Political Fallout

Sl. No.	State	Year	Ruling Party (Centre)	Ruling Party State	Resultant Political Change
1	Punjab	1951	Congress	Congress	Congress formed a new Ministry
2	Punjab	1966	Congress	Congress	Congress formed a new ministry.
3	Rajasthan	1967	Congress	Opp.coalition claimed a majority	Congress formed a ministry.
4	U.P	1968	Congress	Opp. coalition	Subsequently dissolved.
5	Bihar	1969	Congress	Opp. coalition	Congress formed a ministry.
6	West Bengal	1970	Congress	Opp. coalition	Subsequently dissolved.
7	U.P	1970	Congress	Opp. coalition	Opposition formed a new government.
8	Orissa	1971	Congress	Opp. coalition	A fresh proclamation wasissued which dissolved the Assembly
9	Orissa	1971	Congress	Opp.coalition emerged as the largest group	Congress formed a ministry
10	Mysore	1971	Congress(R)	Congress(O)	Subsequently dissolved.
11	A.P.	1973	Congress	Congress	Congress formed a new ministry.
12	U.P	1973	Congress	Congress	Congress formed a new ministry.
13	Gujarat	1974	Congress	Congress	Subsequently dissolved.
14	Nagaland	1975	Congress	N.N.O.	Subsequently dissolved.
15	U.P	1975	Congress	Congress	Congress formed a new ministry.
16	Gujarat	1976	Congress	Non congress coalition	Congress formed a ministry
17	Orissa	1976	Congress	Congress	Congress formed a new ministry.
18	Manipur	1977	Janata	Congress	Janata party formed a ministry.
19	Assam	1979	Janata	Assam J.D.	Congress formed a ministry.
20	Manipur	1981	Congress	Congress	Congress formed a new ministry
21	Assam	1981	Congress	Congress	Congress formed a new ministry.
22	Kerala	1981	Congress	CPI(M) coalition	Congress formed a coalition ministry.

Contd...

23	Punjab	1983	Congress	Congress	Subsequently dissolved.
24	Punjab	1987	Congress	Akalidal	Subsequently dissolved.
25	J and K.	1986	Congress	N.C. (Shaw)	N.C (Farooq) formed a ministry with Congress support.
26	Karnataka	1990	J.D.	Congress	Congress formed a new ministry.
27	Goa	1990	J.D(S)	PDF	MGP splinter group formed a new government
28	Meghalaya	1991	Congress	Opp. coalition	Congress led United Meghalaya Front formed a government.
29	Manipur	1992	Congress	U.L.F. Opp. coalition	Congress formed a coalition ministry
30	Manipur	1993	Congress	Opp. coalition	Congress party formed a new ministry
31	U.P	1995	Congress	BSP	Subsequently dissolved.
32	Gujarat	1996	U.F	BJP	BJP rebels formed a government with U.F. support.
33	U.P	1996	U.F	BJP emerged as the largest party.	BSP formed a ministry with BJP's support.
34	Bihar	1999	BJP	RJD	Presidential proclamation was revoked
35	Manipur	2001	BJP	Samata – BJP coalition	Secular Progressive Front coalition formed a government
36	UP	2002	BJP	Hung Assembly	BSP – BJP formed a coalition government
37	Goa	2005	Congress	BJP coalition	Congress formed a government
38	Bihar	2005	Congress	Hung Assembly	Subsequently dissolved
39	Karnataka	2007	Congress	JD(S) – BJP coalition	BJP –JD(S) formed a coalition government
40	Karnataka	2007	Congress	BJP – JD(S) coalition	Subsequently dissolved
41	Nagaland	2008	Congress	Democratic Alliance of Nagaland	Subsequently dissolved
42	Jammu & Kashmir	2008		Congress	Congress – PDP Alliance Governor dissolved the Assembly
43	Jharkhand	2008	Congress	JMM coalition	Subsequently dissolved
44	Meghalaya	2009	Congress	Meghalaya Progressive Alliance	Congress formed a government with NCP support
45	Jharkhand	2010	Congress	JMM - BJP	BJP formed a ministry with JMM support

Source: Computed from available primary and secondary sources.

When we subject the instances of suspension of Assemblies to an objective scrutiny, it becomes quite clear that this device has often been relied on by the ruling party to gain advantage. As long as the Assembly was suspended, no election could be held. Equally, there was no responsible government in the State answerable to the Legislature. The claim that these Legislatures were suspended in order to give all parties a fair chance to form a government is wholly untenable in each one of these cases. It is to be noted from the table that Assemblies were suspended in forty- five instances; of these on eight occasions, the ministries enjoyed the confidence of the respective Houses. These are the instances where the provision was invoked to deal with intra-party problems of the then ruling Congress party or for considerations not relevant for the purpose of the Article. To conceal the charges of inefficiency or corruption against the State Governments, Assemblies were put under suspension for the time being to facilitate the easing out of the involved Chief Ministers. This process helped the party to effect a smooth change in the leadership and provided the new government with a chance to have a fresh start. When the government was formed in thirty cases, it was the government of the same party at the Centre in twenty two cases and the opposition was found to be benefited only in eight cases. In the remaining fifteen cases Assemblies were subsequently dissolved in fourteen cases and in one case (Bihar 1999) the Presidential proclamation was revoked.

Contrary to this, Assemblies were straightaway dissolved and President's Rule imposed whenever a State Government headed by the ruling party at the Centre or a coalition ministry led by it or a coalition ministry in which it is a major partner or a ministry supported by it from outside lost the confidence of the State Legislature and if the party had less or no chance at all of assuming power again. For instance, in Andhra Pradesh in 1954, the CPI was denied an opportunity to form a government after the defeat of the Congress led Prakasam ministry. Again in the erstwhile Travancore-Cochin, the PSP leader, Pattom Thanupillai was not given a chance to form an alternative government after the resignation of the Congress government in 1956. Similarly Assemblies were dissolved in Kerala (1965, and again in 1982), in West Bengal (1970), in Uttar Pradesh (1968, 1995 and 1996), in Orissa (1971 and 1973), in Assam (1982), in Sikkim (1984), in Nagaland (1988) in Karnataka (1989) and in Bihar(2005). Thus the dissolution and suspension of legislative assemblies under Article 356 have invariably been politically motivated in order to perpetuate the interests of the ruling party at the Centre[5]. This is evident from the Table 6.

Table 6
Table Showing Details of Cases in which Opposition Parties were not Allowed to Form Alternative Governments

Sl.No.	State	Year	Ruling Party (Centre)	Parties which were not Allowed to form Government
1.	Pepsu	1953	Congress	United Party
2.	Andhra Pradesh	1954	Congress	[PSP and CPI)
3.	Travancore-Cochin		1956	Congress PSP
4.	Kerala	1965	Congress	CPI(M)
5.	Rajasthan	1967	Congress	U.F. (opp. coalition)
6.	Uttar Pradesh	1968	Congress	SVD (opp. coalition)
7.	Bihar	1969	Congress	U.F. (opp. coalition)
8.	West Bengal	1970	Congress	CPI(M)
9.	Orissa	1971	Congress	U.F. (opp. coalition)
10.	Orissa	1973	Congress	U.F. (opp. coalition)
11.	Manipur	1981	Congress	U.F. (opp. coalition)
12.	Kerala	1982	Congress	LDF (oppo. coalition)
13.	Nagaland	1988	Congress	N.N.P
14.	Uttar Pradesh	1995	Congress	BJP
15.	Uttar Pradesh	1996	United Front	BJP
16.	Bihar	2005	Congress	BJP - Samata coalition

Source: Computed from available secondary sources.

In short, whenever the opposition ministries fell or resigned, the ruling party at the Centre, if it was not able to form an alternative ministry immediately, placed the Legislature in a suspended state so as to enable it to form a ministry later. The second approach consisted in rejecting the request of the opposition to form an alternative ministry if a State Government led or supported by the ruling party at the Centre fell or resigned. Hence, one could see the violation of democratic norms and Constitutional and Parliamentary conventions. 'So it was to be either the Congress ministry (ruling party) or no ministry at all'[6].

Likewise, a recommendation for dissolution of Legislative Assembly made by a Chief Minister not belonging to the ruling party at the Centre under Article 174(2) (b), was rejected and dissolution was generally made under Article 356. This betrays the fact that it was so done to give time to the ruling party at the Centre to improve its position during the spell of President's Rule and then at an appropriate time, to make a bid for power. For instance, in Gujarat, Chief minister, Hitendra Desai resigned on account of defection and advised the Governor to dissolve the Assembly. The Governor, however, did not accept the advice but recommended President's Rule. In Mysore also, after the resignation of the Virendra Patil ministry, the recommendation of the Chief minister for the dissolution of the House was not conceded but the state was taken under Article 356 of the Constitution. The recommendations of Gurnam Singh in Punjab (1968), Charan Singh in UP (1968), Karpoori Thakur in Bihar (1971) etc. were not conceded because of this political interest. As against this, in certain cases the recommendations of the Chief Ministers with doubtful majority or even defeated Chief Ministers were accepted under Article 174(2) when there was absolutely no ground for the dissolution of the concerned Assemblies. For example in Kerala in 1979 the advice of Chief Minister Muhammed Koya (IUML Chief Minister with the support of Congress) for dissolution of the Assembly was allowed. It is interesting to note that Koya had not proved his majority on the floor of the house since the Assembly was not convened during the forty days of its existence. The Constitutional question which could be pertinently raised here is whether the Governor was bound to accept the advice of the Chief Minister heading a government in which the Chief Minister's party had only thirteen members in the 140 member Assembly The government found itself in a precarious position with the withdrawal of support by some parties in the ruling coalition. When the opposition parties staked their claim for a new government, it was rejected by the Governor. The reason was purely political and not Constitutional. This kind of situation again arose in Kerala in 1982 when Karunakaran, the Congress Chief Minister, resigned for want of majority. Here also the request for dissolution was accepted even though his government had depended on the casting vote of the Speaker and the opposition parties were ready to form a government[8]. Similar exercises of power have also been seen in AP (1951), Bihar (1972), Gujarat (1972), and in Nagaland (1988).

In several cases, President's Rule was imposed even though the respective Assemblies were dissolved by the Governor under Article 174(2)(b) and elections were ordered. The Chief Ministers of these States were not allowed to continue as heads of the care-taker governments which was the proper course of action. If we analyse the facts of these cases critically from a Constitutional perspective, we will find that all these cases could not be denounced as what is called the misuse of the power. A close examination of the available facts reveals that the Kerala instance in 1970 is justifiable since the care-taker Chief Minister himself had submitted his resignation in the wake of allegations. Similar is the case of Sikkim (1979). In these circumstances, the Governor had no alternative but to recommend President's Rule. Similarly, President's Rule in Punjab (1971) and West Bengal (1971) were necessitated in order to enable the Parliament to pass the budget for the State before the commencement of the forthcoming financial year. Likewise, the Jammu and Kashmir instance in 1990 was made on account of widespread terrorist activities which almost paralysed normal life in the State. However, the imposition of President's Rule in Nagaland (1992) was widely criticised as a politically immature act and a clear case of the violation of the constitutional provision for partisan interest. 'The Centre, it appears, was upset because the Governor's action to accept the recommendation of the Chief minister to dissolve the Assembly stopped the Congress (I) gameplan'.[9] This found its expression in an editorial of The Hindu Newspaper. In the editorial the Hindu categorically stated that 'it was an open secret that the Congress (I) was basically trying to destabilize the Nagaland people's council government headed by Vamuzo and capture power by engineering defection'.[10] And the Statesman weekly went a step further and commented that 'a most disturbing aspect of this matter was that the Prime Minister himself was involved.'[11]. Thus by all indications, it needs to be pointed out that, this was an example of short-circuiting of the democratic process in pursuit of political ambition of the Centre.

Table 7
Table Containing the Details of Cases where no Caretaker Ministry was Allowed

Sl.No.	State	Year	Ruling Party (Centre)	Party which was not allowed to functioned as caretaker govts.	Reasons given
1.	Haryana	1969	Congress	SVD	Defection
2.	Kerala	1970	Congress	CPI coalition	Chief Minister tendered resignation
3.	Punjab	1971	Congress	Akali Dal	Budget had to be passed.
4.	West Bengal	1971	Congress	Congress	Budget had to be passed.
5.	Bihar	1972	Congress	Opp. coalition	Ministerial instability
6.	Sikkim	1979	Lok Dal	Janatha	Chief Minister tendered resignation
7.	Kerala	1979	Lok Dal	Muslim League coalition in which Congress was a major partner	Ministerial instability
8.	Jammu and Kashmir	1990	Janata Dal	It was Governor's Rule in J and K at that time.	Breakdown of law and order.
9.	Nagaland	1992	Congress	Naga National Organisation.	Law and order.

Source: Computed from available secondary sources.

The question arises whether it was expedient to resort to Article 356, when the dissolution of the Assembly had been ordered under Article 174(2) (b). Article 174(2) (b) envisages dissolution and not abrogation[12]. It might be true that sometimes the ministry might have misused its authority to gain advantage in the elections. But in most of the cases there was no evidence to show that this was true. If at all there is any truth in this argument, then to prevent the misuse of governmental machinery and funds, a convention may be established that no funds will be spent and that no major decisions will be taken before an election[13] unless it can be publicly justified as necessary in national interest. In the same way, efforts must be made to make the election free, fair and peaceful. If there are any apprehensions about partisan officials in the state or arm-twisting by the party in power, the Election Commission of India should take up the challenge. Resort to President's Rule will be tantamount to expressing lack of confidence in the Election Commission's impartiality, ability and commitment. Instead of imposing President's Rule, the Centre must get ready to back the Commission wholeheartedly with all the resources it needs including the police forces.[14] On the other hand imposition of Article 356 in such a situation is like using a steam-roller to crack a nut. Further, it was also wrong on the part of the Governor, first to dissolve the Assembly under Article 174(2) (b) and then to recommend the imposition of President's Rule, because in that situation the President had absolutely no option but to accept the recommendation of the Governor. Under Article 356 of the Constitution, the President is supposed to apply his mind for which there was absolutely no possibility in this case[15]. In this background the Sarkaria Commission recommended that:

> The Governor should explore all possibilities to have a government with a majority in the Assembly. If this is not possible and if fresh elections can be held without avoidable delay, he should ask the outgoing Chief Minister to head the caretaker government, provided the ministry was defeated solely on a major policy issue, unconnected with any allegations of maladministration or corruption and is agreeable to continue. But if the outgoing ministry was responsible for serious allegations of maladministration and corruption, it would not be proper for the Governor to install such a ministry as care-taker government. Then

the Governor should recommend President's Rule without dissolving the Assembly[16].

The Commission makes strong recommendation in line with the representative form of government wherein the people are the ultimate repositories of political power. Thus if a ministry is dismissed or has resigned for want of confidence of the House, the introduction of President's Rule is not a normal course of action. In such cases, the ministry may be allowed to work as a caretaker government till a new ministry is formed. This aspect will be discussed later in this chapter.

The allegation that opposition parties were not allowed to prove their strength on the floor of the House is also corroborated by facts. In some cases the Governors, in their subjective satisfaction, even in a situation when the Assembly was under summons or the concerned Chief Ministers were very much willing to face the Assembly at an early date, had taken the view that they had lost majority support and recommended the imposition of Article 356. This hypothesis is very much strengthened by the dismissals of Rarewala ministry in pepsu (1953), the Rao Birendra Singh ministry in Haryana (1967), the Charan Singh ministry in U.P (1970), the Devaraj Urs ministry in Karnataka (1977), and the Bommai ministry again in Karnataka (1989). In U.P, the Chief Minister was not allowed to prove his majority on the floor of the House amidst confusion in the house. Governor Gopala Reddy virtually dismissed Chief Minister, Charan Singh and recommended President's Rule when the legislature was to meet within a few days and when the Chief Minister has taken initiative even for an early session of the Assembly to demonstrate his majority. In West Bengal, the Governor actually sacked the Chief Minister. All that he wanted was a little time, permitted by the Constitution itself, to consolidate his political position. The dismissal of Bommai ministry in Karnataka, before the issue was decided on the floor of the Assembly in spite of request, generated much heat and anguish which in turn prompted critics to comment that it was an improper exercise of an important discretion. A close scrutiny of facts and circumstances that led to the President's Rule in all these cases bring out the fact that the Governors often stretch discritionary powers for partisan inerests. No doubt, the Governors have used the sword of discritionary powers in a manner not permitted by the Constitution. In short, there is total disregard of chief ministers' requests to demonstrate their majoority. V.R. Krishna Iyer. J. Sees this as 'Central puppetry' and writes that 'the Governors are acting like marionettes.'

Table 8
The Table Showing Instances in which Floor Test was Not Allowed in Spite of the Request of the Concerned Chief Ministers

Sl. No.	State	Year	Ruling party at the Centre	The party which was not allowed to test its strength
1	Pepsu	1953	Congress	UDF (opp. coalition)
2	Haryana	1967	Congress	SVD (opp. Coalition)
3	Uttar Pradesh	1970	Congress	BKD (opp. Coalition)
4	Karnataka	1977	Janata	Congress (opp.)
5	Karnataka	1989	Congress	Janata Dal (opp.)

Source: Computed from available secondary sources.

These incidents raise a host of pertinent constitutional and political issues for deliberation pertaining to the functioning of Parliamentary democracy in a federal setup. Can a Governor acts on his own pleasure even when the government claims to enjoy the confidence of the House? What is the basis of "Governor's pleasure"? Why did the Governor not allow the floor test, particularly when the Assembly was in session or about to meet or when there was a request by the Chief Minister for summoning of the House? Even if the government had lost the confidence of the House, was it proper to impose President's Rule? An answer to these and allied questions is so vital for the continuance of a federal polity.

Article 164 of the Constitution of India says that the Chief Minister of the State shall be appointed by the Governor. Other ministers who are appointed by him on the advice of the Chief Minister are subject to being removed by him on the advice of the Chief Minister[17]. The Constitution, therefore, says that these ministers hold office during the pleasure of the Governor. However, there is a categorical provision saying that the Council of Ministers as such is collectively responsible only to the Legislative Assembly *i.e.* not to the Governor. Once the Council of Ministers is in position, therefore, whether it stays or goes is entirely a matter between the House and the Council of Ministers. If the Council of Ministers does not command the confidence of the House, there are necessary provisions for introducing the motion of no-confidence, financial control of the House etc. Therefore, the Sarkaria Commission suggested that "the Governor should not dismiss a Council of Ministers, unless the legislative assembly has expressed on the floor of the house its want of confidence in it". This position is supported by Sawant and Kuldip Singh J.J. in the Bommai case which reads' In all cases where the support of the ministry is claimed to have been withdrawn by some legislators the proper course for testing the strength of the ministry is holding the test on the floor of the House.' Jeevan Reddy and Agarwal, J.J., however, permitted the Governor to bypass the requirement of a floor test only in the event of all pervasive violence or other factors ensuing that the government of the state cannot be carried on in accordance with the provision of the Constitution.[18] In fact, a NCRWC consultation paper sensibly recommended that Article 356 should be amended to ensure, among other things, that 'whether the ministry in the state has lost the confidence of the legislative Assembly or not should be decided only on the floor of the Assembly and no where else and that only where the Chief Minister refuses to resign after his ministry is defeated on motion of non-confidence should the Governor dismiss the state government'.[19] Similarly, before dismissing or recommending President's Rule, the Governor should also verify the claims of the rivals on the floor of the House since it is the right forum to vindicate the doubts. This is the Parliamentary convention. This procedure will be not only fair but also seem to be fair. It will definitely save the Governor from embarrassment consequent upn any error of judgement on his part as Sarkaria observed.

Closely allied with the questions posed above is the vital question of whether loss of majority or defeat of a ministry on the floor of the Assembly amounts to the breakdown of constitutional machinery?. Constitutionally speaking, such situations do not fall within the scope and ambit of Article 356. It is a question of losing or not having a majority in the legislature. To face the situation we may workout some other constitutional conventions and clearcut guidelines that the Governor can follow. Imposition of President's Rule to face such a situation is against the very spirit of the Constitution and democracy it cherishes. Article 356 clearly envisages real breakdown of constitutional machinery in a state and by these tests ministerial defeats on the floor of the House does not fall within its four walls. If opposition party or parties which is in power in states, loses its majority in the Assembly, it is always interpreted as an indication of the failure of the constitutional machinery enabling the President to assume the functions of the state governments through a proclamation under Article 356. In this connection, it may be noted that at the Centre there is no constitutional provision for imposing President's Rule. If a government is reduced to a minority, it continues in power until an alternative government is formed, Alternatively, the outgoing ministry remains in office as a caretaker ministry until fresh elections are held, following the dissolution of Lok Sabha by the President.[20]. The caretaker ministries of Charan Singh in 1977, Chandrasekher in 1991 and Vajpayee in 1999 may be referred to in this connection. Unfortunately Indian democracy has failed to build similar convention in the states. It is important to mention here that we have adopted a parliamentary system of government both for the Centre and the States. Therefore, it is required to be ensured that what is acceptable at the union level should be made so in the case of states as well unless some complications arise. This is not to say that resort to Article 356 should be avoided at any cost. Sometimes there may arise certain circumstances where by it becomes imperative to dismiss a ministry under Article 356 of the constitution irrespective of its confidence of the Legislature. Such a situation presents itself when the ministry either disregards the Constitution and law or infringes the very essence of democratic and parliamentary norms and conventions or pooh-poohs the direction given by the Centre.

Many cases can also be cited to prove that the President's Rule was extended indefinitely and beyond the prescribed time limit with a view to evolving a favourable climate for the ruling party at the Centre to come to power in the States. That is if sufficient time was required to consolidate the strength and position of its party in the State it was extended for a longer period. This is what happened in Nagaland (1975), in Tamil Nadu (1976), in West Bengal (1968), and in Kerala (1964). It is only when Morarji Desai went on fast unto death, the Union government announced to revoke President's Rule and hold elections in Gujarat. However, the extension of President's Rule in Punjab in 1983 and 1987 and in Jammu and Kashmir in 1990 were on unavoidable grounds and therefore justifiable. What is worrying is that even if the original imposition was justified, there was no reason for delaying elections after the first six months period. Therefore, it is submitted that in such cases fresh elections must be held immediately[21]. There is no justification whatsoever for continuing President's Rule beyond the time necessary to organise elections unless there are very compelling and convincing reasons.

On the other hand, even short spells of President's Rule were sometimes politically motivated. In Rajasthan (1976), in U.P. (1970), in Orissa (1976), in Manipur (1977), in Kerala (1979), dissolution of nine States in (1977 and 1980), in Karnataka (1990) and in Bihar (1999) President's Rule was revoked even before the expiry of the two months period when Parliamentary approval for the proclamation is required.

Gujarat Imbroglio - Failure of Constitutional Machinery at the Centre?

We have seen that the power under Article 356 has been frequently used by the Union government wrongly more on political reasons rather than administrative compulsion. However, here is an instance of the failure of the Union government to invoke the Article when there was a real breakdown of the constitutional machinery occurred in Gujarat, calling for action under Article 356. In this context, it is relevant to make a brief analysis of the issues and events involved in the problem.

The religion - fuelled violence in Gujarat following 'the horrific Godhra train massacre' on 27 February 2002 where sixty karsevaks travelling from Ayodhya were burnt alive by religious fundamentalists and the subsequent communal riots resulted in real breakdown of constitutional machinery in the state. What happened in Gujarat in the aftermath of Godhra was 'reprehensive', 'shameful', 'barbaric' and 'uncivilized' as described by even Prime minister Vajpayee and Home minister Advani.[22] As a reaction or revenge, fundamentalists 'killed innocent people including women and children, looted and plundered properties owned by a particular section, desiccated and destroyed places of worship. Not fewer than 600 people have died across the state, thousands rendered homeless and many a thousands of people abandoned their homes.[23] This unending violence which continued over eighty days was targeted against a particular community. This showed that the government was either unable or unwilling to face the situation unleashed by the post Godhra massacre. Thus the vital questions to be seriously debated in this direction are: whether the post Godhra massacre of the minorities was orchestrated by the Majority or was it just the inefficiency or apathy of the Chief minister to quell the riots during the initial period which gave a long rope to the fundamentalists and antisocial elements to take advantage of the situation.[24]

Unfolding of the available facts and events points to the deliberate inaction on the part of the Gujarat administration. The dismal action is evident from the damning record of administrative failure, first in preventing the violence and then in providing relief. Undoubtedly, the massacre of karsevaks shocked the national consciousness and agitated the V.H.P. As a confidence building measure it was essential that the criminals behind the dastardly act be swiftly identified, arrested and punished. It was also essential that the administration should have anticipated the reaction of the incident and taken precaution on the very same day that the karsavaks were burnt alive in the light of Ahamadabad's bad history of communal violence.[25] Had the government taken preventive measures and precaution, there would not have been intensification of such a ghastly violence to this magnitude. Presuming that the violence was abrupt, spontaneous and widespread, it would still have been controlled if the administration wanted it.[26] In this connection we have before us the example and experience of the Delhi riots that followed in the aftermath of Indira Gandhi's assassination. It was brought under control when police were ordered to shot at the mob. This did not happen in Gujarath. Why did the government not take hard measures to prevent retaliatory attacks? Is it not the government's duty to ensure the safety of its citizens? There is no rationale for the deliberate inaction on the part of the Gujarat government.

There is also much criticism over the delay in calling for the army's help. It was alleged, not without substance, that 'the state government's inordinate delay in calling in the army established beyond doubt that the ant-minority pogrom was being carried on with the involvement of not only the politicians but the state machinery as well'.[27] Tragically, the army was not called in until more than eighty people have lost their precious lives in the clashes. What explains the governmental inertia? This inactive and passive attitude of the Chief Minister has been exploited thoroughly by opportunists, fundamentalists and anti-social elements among others and the situation had gone out of administrative control. Had it asked the central assistance in time much of the unfortunate incidents would have been averted. This kind of partisan approach to critical issues of governance like maintaining peace and ensuring right to life and property of citizens would seriously undermine the very legitimacy of an administration which is bound to protect and defend the Constitution and uphold the rule of law and democracy.

The inert and prejudicial attitude of the Chief Minister is also obvious from his insensitive and provocative statements during the course of the carnage. His remarks such as 'the angur of people over the Godhra is understandable' and 'policemen were possibly biased in their reaction to communal bias because they are members of the community and would be affected by public sentiments'[28]etc. have thrown much light on his inept and irresponsible attitude. Further, though the electronic media tellingly brought out the involvement of the VHP volunteers in the carnage, the Chief Minister claimed that no specific complaints had been received against them. All these provocative and irresponsible statements clearly indicate that the widespread carnage took place with the connivance of the state government.

What was shocking and worrying was the police personnels' failure to prevent such attacks taking place in front of them, as vividly telecasted by channels. It was reported in the press that the police did not even register complaints that named ruling party and V.H.P. leaders.[29] It was also alleged that the police had become passive spectators at many places in Ahamadabad. It was also accused that the police personnels' were party to the carnage. They either looked in the other way round or collaborated with the massacre. The Gujarat Chand committee, a body of Islamic preachers, petitioned that the state government had virtually directed the police not to take action against mobs attacking Muslims. The admission of the police commissioner, P.C. Pandey that the police force is not immune to the vicious communal sentiments[30] sweeping civil society was stating the obvious. The biased, prejudicial and apathetic attitude of the police, especially its rank and file reminded us of the role of police in the Mumbai riots of 1993-94. Further, Defence Minister, George Fernandez, has also reportedly stated that lack of support from the Government and the police led to the loss of many lives that could have other wise been saved. All these testify the police culpability and after weeks, a still rising graph of arson and killings points to the dismal failure of the state administration.[31]

Thus the Chief minister's insensitive and provocative remarks, the unpardonable failure of the law and order enforcing agencies, the inexplicable delay in calling the army and seeking central assistance which claimed hundreds of lives and destruction of properties clearly send out the message that the state administration was reluctant to discharge its primary and fundamental responsibilities towards the citizens. It was a clear case of breakdown of the constitutional machinery in a state which necessitated immediate action under Article 356. The communal riots were not a mere law and order problem. They were challenges to our entire secular fabric. There was break down of law and order in a frightening scale. There was political corruption in government activity, secularism has been tarnished. Communalism ruled through terror.[32] Thus the issues at stake were of critical importance, affecting the very foundation on which the constitutional edifice stands. Further, the gravity of the situation can be gauged from the fact that it lasted not for days or even weeks but continued through out three long months and shocked the constitutional conscience of every body in India and abroad.[33] Considering seriousness of the situations, the centre should have immediately dismissed the government and impose President's Rule not only on grounds of constitutional propriety but also for the very preservation of country's unity and integrity and above all secularism as enshrined in the Constitution. In this connection the Supreme Court's observation in the Bommai case seems relevant. The Court said:

> Secularism is a part of the basic structure of the Constitution. The acts of state govenements which are calculated to subvert or sabotage secularism as enshrined in our Constitution can lawfully be deemed to rise to a situtaiton in which the government of the state cannot be carried on inaccordance with the provisions of the Constitution.

Almost all political parties including those in the ruling coalition recorded and registered their strong and deep concern over the escalating violence targeted against a particular community and urged the central government to 'intervene effectively in the restoration of law and order and provide relief and rehabilitation to the victims. Instead of handling the issue in a responsible manner, the centre, however, remained a mute spectator and did not take any effective and expeditious action to reassure the basic human rights of citizens. On the contrary, the central government allowed Chief minister Narendra Modi to continue on the plea that 'the Chief minister had done a splendid job of controlling the riots' and also on the ground that law and order is a state subject that brook no external interference.[34] It is deplorable that the central govenement too had failed or unwilling to realise the enormity of the situation that existed in the state. This provoked F.S. Nariman who while participating in the Rajya Sabha debates said:

> 'Vital statistics tells us that there are more than 100000 persons in refugee camp and more than 30,000 people have been charge sheeted. Are these figures not enough to compel the government to take action under Article 355 and 356'.[35]

Nariman's argument is thought provoking and a genuine concern over the unpardonable omissions of the administration. He rightly reminded the government of its primary responsibility to uphold rule of law and Constitution by focusing on the untold agonies of a particular section of the population. In this connection it may be noted that the NDA government invoked and attempted to invoke, Article 355 and 356 even in less serious situations. This is conspicuous from the 'fact finding teams' sent by home minister, Advani, to various states to investigate constitutional breakdown. The Home minister justified his actions on the ground that it was the duty of the centre to protect the state against internal disturbances. The centre sent such teams against Jyothi Basu in West Bengal, Rabri Devi in Bihar and Jayalalitha in Tamil Nadu.[36] Again, the union government dismissed the Bihar government under Rabari Devi when twelve dalits were murdered by Ranbir Sena. But when the real breakdown as envisaged by Article 356 took place in Gujarath, the Union government was silent and failed to discharge its basic constitutional responsibilities. The centre refused to invoke Article 356 or even sack Modi when there was irrefutable evidence of organized mass - killings and destruction of properties that took place with the connivance of the State Government. No democratic government responsible to the people can allow a tense situation to persist in a state without effective intervention. Instead of defending Modi, the Centre should have acted with vision and wisdom in time under the constitutional mandate to protect the life and properties of people, and uphold the rule of law.

The obvious question to be debated is what prompted the Centre to remain a mute spectator despite demands from various quarters? The reason was purely political and not constitutional. It is obvious from the available facts that the Centre's hesistance to act on time was intended to gather present and future electoral dividends. Perhaps, the BJP leadership had reason to believe that prospect of victory in the elections that followed the carnage would be enhanced by supporting communalism associated with Modi's various acts of omissions and commissions. Thus the desire for political power might be the reason that had tempted them to afford to ignore the magnitude of the problem. Had it not been the cause the Centre would have at least unseated Modi from Chief Ministership and thereby retrieved the feelings and sentiments of the affected sections. The central government felt that Modi was indispensable to lead the state in the elections that ensued. This has been amply demonstrated by the premature dissolution of the Assembly and the subsequent victory of the BJP in the successive elections in Gujarath.

The communal politics practiced by the leaders of all parties to build and enrich vote banks is pushing the country to anarchy and widening the differences among different communities at the expense of national unity and development and other higher values of life. Hyperactive, Power hungry, and opportunistic politicians are not concerned with loss of innocent lives and destruction of properties in communal clashes. We have to strike at the very root of the problem for which a committed comprehensive approach is necessary. It is the bounden duty of both the central and State governments to crush the communal violence with an iron hand without the fear of losing votes. Therefore what is obvious and is perhaps laking, is a strong political will coupled with a free hand to the law and order enforcing machinery to nip in the bud itself all forms of communal disharmony. Associated with this task, it is also essential that religious slander and instigation must be made a federal crime. If the existing legislations are inadequate, it is necessary to enact fool proof laws so that communal violence might be deftly handled. Inaddition to what is stated above, we need a trained central professional agency dedicated to fight against this kind of war like situation without any fear or favour. Over and above, we require a sagacious and vivacious political leadership committed to national unity and integrity, secularism and other higher values of life rather than clinging to power some how or other. Democracy is at stake in a country where citizens live under the shadow of violence and fear. Any type of religious fundamentalism should be resisted tooth and nail as it cut at the very root of secularism, democracy and rule of law.

Any discussion on the emerging model will be completed only with a brief analysis of the working of Article 356 in the age of coalition politics and the resultant developing regional leadership and the emergence of power centres in different part of the country apart from New Delhi which provides an interesting and relevant perspective on the whole question of use and misuse of the Article.

Article 356 in the Age of Coalitions

A remarkable feature of recent elections to the Parliament and various states Legislatures is the rise of regional parties particularly smaller parties and the relegation of national mainstream parties. The trend which set in a few states as in Kerala, Tamil Nadu, Andhra Pradesh, Punjab, Assam and Jammu and Kashmir during the past has now got confirmed. What is noteworthy is that even the two major national parties - INC and BJP- are forced to fight the election battle in alliance with regional parties. This clearly sends out the message that multiparty coalition governments have now become an indispensable reality of Indian polities. Therefore, governance at the Centre is not possible without the active participation of important regional parties and this development has been described by C.P. Bhambhri as 'political refederalization of India without changing the Constitution.[37] This would necessitate according greater priority to the demand of various state governments run by regional parties.

The growth of regional parties and the emergence of regional leaderships and power centres in various parts of India have helped to transform and strengthen India's federal structure. This trend towards regionalism in party politics is viewed as an indication that India is now less centralised and more federal, as Douglas V.Verney observes. Some of these parties play a vital role in the determination of national polices and how they are implemented. However, it is true that in some ways the states are still subordinate to the centre, but they are less subordinate than they were. The Union government may still replace a recalcitrant Chief minister of its own party. But it is less likely to remove an opposition government through Article 356.[38] Truth of this statement is testified by the reinstatement of Kalyan Singh Government in Uttar Pradesh in 1998, Rabridevi Government in Bihar in 1999 and the aborted attempt of the first Man Mohan Singh government to dismiss Mulayam Singh government again in Uttar Pradesh in 2007. Of these, the latest episode warrants a deeper analysis and closer scrutiny as it carries with it new lessons for parties and leaders who arbitrarily exercise powers in an increasingly fragmented polity.

A dispassionate look at the crisis suggests that there was no failure of constitutional machinery in U.P. as envisages by Article 356. All that happened was that a constitutional bench of the Supreme Court disqualified thirteen MLAs who originally belonged to the BSP and extended support to Mulayam government (they later formed Loktantrik Bahujan Dal with Twenty four other MLAs of the BSP). The judgement stirred up hornet's nest which in turn put a question mark on the legitimacy of the government. Taking advantage of this situation opposition political parties including the ruling Congress launched a partisan political campaign for the dismissal of Yadav government on the ground that his government was 'unconstitutional', 'illegitimate', illegally conceived' and 'illegally born'. In justification of the demand, they put forward the argument that the thirteen MLAs have been disqualified with retrospective effect and this rendered the very formation of the Mulayam government unconstitutional. The Congress party with its associates in the Union government had prepared the ground for invoking Article 356 in U.P. However, the 'Outs Mulayam Operation' was defeated by the frontal opposition of the CPI(M) which was reluctant to becomes a partner in the political game. The attempt was further weakened by the Election Commissions's announcement of the poll for the state. Also, there were reports that President Abdul Kalam was hesitant to order the dismissal. The central question that confronts one is whether the attempt of the Union government to dismiss the U.P government was constitutional? For this a detailed analysis of the issues involved in the developments becomes necessary.

First of all, it may be argued that a government that is duly constituted, administered the oath of office and obtained the confidence of the House can not become illegal on a later finding. It is to be noted that the Chief minister had 37 plus majority at the time of the formation of the government. Significantly, one year prior to the court's decision, Mulayam repeatedly demonstrated his government's majority on the floor of the House.[39] It is also important to note here that the Supreme Court's verdict disqualifying the MLAs made no reference to the unconstitutionality of the government.

Further, what ever the arguments and counter arguments put forward, the facts remain that the issues thrown up by the development have to be examined in the light of successive Supreme Court verdicts. The court wisely counselled that the floor of the house is the only constitutionally permitted arena to determine the majority or otherwise of a government. A detailed discussion of the Court's ruling will be taken up later. This view point is also echoed in the report of the NCRWC.[41]

Besides, the attempt to dismiss the government when elections to the Legislative Assembly were round the corner would be a violation of the well established convention that even a minority government which lost a vote of confidence should continue as a caretaker government if elections are due soon. In this context, Rajeev Dhavan, a distinguished constitutional authority, observed that 'it would be wrong not to apply the conventions to the state while accepting legitimacy of central government functioning as caretaker after they lost their majority in 1977, 1991 or 1998'.[41]

More over, if the intention of the dismissal was to ensure free and fair elections without being influenced by Mulayam or his party, the government must seek other remedies including close and rigorous scrutiny of the electoral process through the Election Commission rather than imposing President's Rule. Further, it may be noted that this kind of apprehension has been voiced against many state governments of different political orientation on various occassions. This is a political judgment and can not be a sole basis for invoking a constitutional bramastra.[42] Constitutionally speaking, President's Rule is not a guarantee for free and fair election because for all practical purposes it is the government of the party in power at the centre that counts. In case the state is placed under the governance of the Governor, who is invariably an agent of the Centre, and consequently those parties at the helm in Delhi shall be deriving an unfair advantage.

Over and above, under Article 356, the President can dismiss a state government and impose President's Rule only when he is satisfied that the government of the state is not carried on in accordance with the provisions laid down for the constitutional governance of the State. In the instant case, however, there was no evidence to show that the constitutional machinery collapsed in any way. A fraudulent use of the Article 'which has a vital bearing on the parliamentary form of government and autonomy of states' in matters like this would have significantly eroded the federal principles and intensified tension in the polity.

In the final analysis, it may be stated that the Congress party and the central government should share a large part of blame for the unconstitutional intent to impose Presidents Rule in haste. It seems that the intention was not to ensure free and fair elections but the desire to control the state during election to achieve unfair advantages. It was alleged, not without substance, that a section of the Congress leadership was convinced that Mulayam would have and advantage, if he remained in power at the time of election. It was also alleged that the Congress move was motivated by dubious calculation pertaining to the election of the President of India. If U.P, with its 83824 votes, is excluded from the electoral college of 5,49,474 voles, there would be no need for the Congress to seek the SP's support for its own candidates'.[43]

Though the unconstitutional attempt of the Centre was defeated by coalition pressures, it can not be asserted that coalition politics led to a new federal consensus in governance. The experiences of our coalition politics for the past decade show that these regional parties are not reliable allies as they are ambitious about expanding their base within their states, marginalising the influence of mainstream parties. In a sense, regional political parties have proved to be an impediment to the stability and progress of the nation. The motive and agenda for these parties are generally limited to their personal interest or at the most to their region, group or caste they represent. They joined hands with the national parties in forming the Central government and always pressurises the government for fulfilling their narrow selfish interest which may not be in the interest of the nation. Flushed with success, many a time regional political parties as coalition partners have successfully vetoed national public policies for sectarian or partisan interests. For instance DMK party as a coalition partner in the UPA government successfully blocked the decision of the Centre to disinvest the shares of Neyveli Lignite Corporation and National Aluminium Company. More such demands may hamstring the working of the government which has to depend upon these smaller parties for its very survival.

When the NDA coalition government was in power at the Centre, the pulls and pressures from its voracious allies caused serious strains in the federal polity mainly because of their unconstitutional demands and threats. The Centre seemed incapable to grapple with the demand for the imposition of

President's Rule in a few states. In fact one of the allies of the NDA even demanded President's Rule to be imposed in a particular state as there was allegedly a pre- election understanding.

The question of using Article 356 as an instrument to settle political scores has once again come to the fore with the demand for some of the regional parties to use the provision against their political rivals as a pre-condition for extending support for the formation of a government at the centre. In the course of the last Lok Sabha elections campaign, Samajwadi Party chief Mulayam Singh Yadav declared that his party would support that coalition at the Centre which would agree to dismiss the government of Mayawathi in U.P. Similar pressure tactic was also employed by the AIADMK Supremo Jayalalitha. She had hinted that her support would lay with the government at the Centre that might dismiss Karunanidhi government in Tamil Nadu. Mamata Banerjee, the Trinamool Congress chief, has also been clamouring for the imposition of President's Rule in West Bengal in view of deteriorating law and order situation in the state.

As already mentioned, such demands have not been new. During NDA regime in India, other regional allies such as Samata Party in Bihar, Bijujanata Dal in Orissa and Jayalalitha in Tamil Nadu forcefully demanded the President's Rule in their respective states to oust their rivals under the threat of withdrawal of support. The Vajpayee, government, however, resisted the pressure of its regional allies presumably on the plea that dismissal of popularly elected government would back fire the federal structure of the nation. The demand for dismissal of democratically elected and legally constituted ministries had added a new chapter in the chronicle of President's Rule. Such unreasonable, unconstitutional and antidemocratic demands, sometimes lead to far-reaching consequences. What happened in 1999 during the NDA regime reminds us that it is not a mere apprehension but a reality. Jayalalitha's demand for the dismissal of Tamil Nadu Chief Minister Karunanidhi (unjustifiable by all means), Prime minister Vajpayee's stern decision not to accede to Jayalalitha's pressure, subsequent withdrawal of support to the Vajpayee government by Jayalalitha and the inevitable resignation of the Union ministry and the declaration of thirteenth Lok Sabha election may be referred to in this context. Vajpayee had to sacrifice his ministry at the Centre to keep the Karunanidhi ministry in Tamil Nadu going. In a sense it may be a revenge of history that an Article which has been a nightmare to the state governments for the last fifty years has turned out to be a death -knell of the Union government. As K. Raman Pillai, a leading political scientiest, unequivocally comments: 'coalition led to a politics of manipulation rather than purpose; a quest for power for its own sake'[44] The era of hung legislatures and the resultant coalition governments will continue in the foreseeable future, unless and until unforeseen remarkable political developments dramatically change the future of the Congress and the BJP. This may enable the regional parties to put more pressure on the Centre to increasingly use Article 356 to settle political scores with political opponents in future. The already fragile federal polity will further degenerate once and for all the tender regional parties and power seekers influence the trajectory of power.

It is even more unfortunate and ridiculous to think that a major party that lead the Central government would give an assurance to a particular party that Article 356 would be used against its rival if it extended it support for the formation of a government at the Centre. Dismissal of a government under Article 356 cannot be a matter of clandestine agreement between two parties or individuals. It is also a power coupled with a duty to follow the guide lines laid down by the Supreme Court and various Commissions including constitutional experts. At this juncture V.R. Krishna Iyer J. Observed;

> Demands made by regional or even national parties to overthrow state level democracy under Article 356 cannot be acceded to by the Centre. This is not a matter of political vendetta or hostility or estrangement. Constitutional values must regulate the President's conscience when exercising Article 356. Noises made by regional parties or others cannot affect the voice of the Constitution[45].

But the question to be considered in this connection is why these political leaders, who are expected to know better the constitutional and legal viability are making such unjustified and opportunistic demands?. The simple answer is that most of the regional parties are arbitrarily controlled by ambitious regional heads and volunteered increasingly by their families with least regard for constitutional propriety and political sagacity. Most of them find it hard to stay out of power even for a while because they had reason to believe that staying in power gives them comfort and other added advantages and allow them to commit irregularities and also to take revenge upon their political enemies through the misuse of state machinery as was happened on many occasions in Tamil Nadu. Thus it is the unending lust for power after power which is responsible for the degeneration of the sacred constitutional provisions and institutions.

No doubt, the tendency shown by myopic regional parties and regional leaders to demand what ever they want set a bad precedent to the future of India's democracy. It is imperative that in an era of political coalitions the major party that spearhead the coalition handle the situation with farsightedness and sagacity and should not allow such illegitimate demands. It is also essential that these regional parties must shed their personal and selfish mindset for the sake of general interest of the nation and its people. Therefore, a firm commitment by all political parties to stick to the intention of the constitutional principles is warranted. The founding fathers of the Constitution never forseen the danger of the coalition politics and , therefore no provision was incorporated in the constitution for dealing with coalition governments . Since the era of one party rule has become a thing of past and coalition government are the only possibility, the Constitution has to be amended to incorporate necessary provisions with regard to the formation of coalition governments and its functioning. Such an amendment ought to prescribe certain coalition norms and code of conduct for the coalition partners. This step would definitely go a long way to ensure political ethics and standards necessary for ministerial stability.

The preceding analytical study betrays the fact that all the apprehensions, caution and doubts expressed by our eminent constitution makers like H.V. Kamath, H.N. Hunzru and P.S. Deshmukh in the Constituent Assembly proved to be prophetic. The real essence of Article 356, as it has been understood and practiced in our polity is against the autonomy of the States and is anti-federal, and historically speaking, this conclusion has been corroborated by facts. Krishna Iyer calls this trend "Constitutional terrorism"[46]. Instead of remaining a 'dead letter' or a 'dormant provision' — to be used only in the last resort in any ailing State as a sort of "salvage operation" or "resume operation" in a politically sick State, it has been used almost as a non-emergency power on unconvincing political and administrative grounds[47].

Why does this flagrant violation of the spirit of the Constitution and Parliamentary democracy continue unabated despite the warnings, recommended standards and guidelines by constitutional experts, Courts and commissions? The first and foremost reason is the lack of commitment on the part of political parties—national as well as regional—to a restruct-uring of the provision or even a balanced approach within the existing framework. This is evident from the fact that every party that had opposed the abuse of Article 356 while in opposition abused the very same provision while in power. Moreover, the present coalition politics with its attendant evils like casteism, religious fundamentalism, party splits, defections, alignments and realignments along with regional and sub-national assertions makes it easy for the Central government to intervene in the States with partiality, even violating the federal principles and deep rooted traditions of Parliamentary democracy. Now the question to be considered is how the abuse of this power can be checked and prevented. In this connection two checks are available—legislative control and judicial activism.

Figure 4
Pie-Diagram showing justifiable and non-justifiable cases
of President's Rule in the States (1950-1999)

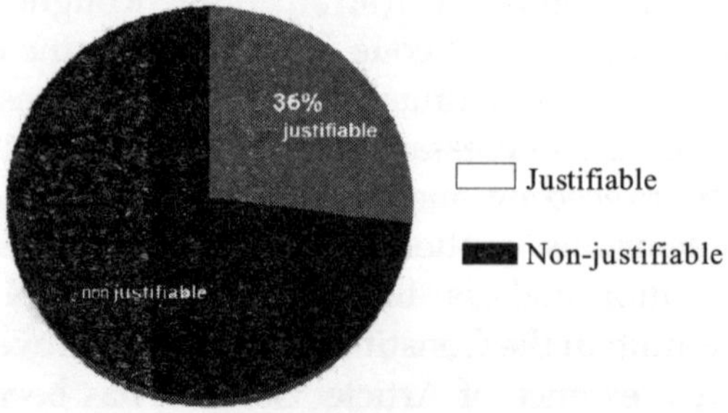

A close scrutiny of these checks are highly warranted for a clear perspective. Therefore, the next two chapters take up for discussion on how far the abuse of Article 356 can be checked and prevented by the Legislature and the Judiciary.

References

1. Alladi Aruna, *Unfederal Features of Indian Constitution,* (Chennai: Muthivan, 2001) 294.
2. The Center's partisan and discriminating approach to the exercise of this Article became glaringly exposed by its inaction in Maharashtra, although the Congress(I) government in the State deserved the boot no less promptly than the Kalyan Singh government in U.P. (See *Self-made Predicament, Economic and Political Weekly,* 28 (1993):601).
3. P.G. Mavalankar observed in the Lok Sabha : "*This whole business of keeping Assemblies in animated suspension, keeping them in a sort of refrigerators and bringing them up again when opportunity suit them does not behave well*" (See *LSD* Vol. XXXVI, Col. 358, 1974).
4. Dua B.D., *The Primemister and the Federal System in India,* in Indian federalism in the new millennium (New Delhi: Manohar, 2003) 175
5. For comprehensive analysis on this topic see J.R. Siwach, *President's Rule and Politics of Suspending and Dissolving State Assemblies, Journal of Constitutional and Parliamentary Studies,* 11 (1977): 45-52.
6. Surya Prasad, *President's Rule in Kerala: A Historical overview, Journal of Kerala studies 15 (1988):*.128.
7. *Ibid.* 121.
8. *Ibid.*
9. Dua B.D. *The Primeminister and the Federal System in India,* 150
10. *The Hindu,* 18 May 1992
11. *The Statesman,* 25 April 1992
12. There are two kinds of dissolution. A normal dissolution contemplated under Article 174 (2) (b) and a dissolution leading to emergency. Under the first, if the Governor is satisfied that no party or combination of parties is in a position to form a stable government, he dissolves the House and keeps the reigning ministry in power as a caretaker ministry till fresh elections are completed. Under the second, when the House is dissolved the

ministry quits and President's Rule is recommended. The first type of dissolution does not disrupt the democratic set up of the state, whereas the second type leads to Central supervision. K.V. Rao has very succinctly drawn a distinction between two types of dissolution; the first is dissolution and the second is abrogation (See K.V. Rao, *Dissolution of Assembly and Article 356,journal of Constitutional and Parliamentary Studies,* 4 (1970) See also *AIR 1977, SC 7367.*

13. K.V. Rao, *Guidelines for the Governors, Journal of the Society for the Study of State Governments.* 4 (1971): 379.
14. *Desist from Article 356 Fraud,* Editorial, *The Hindu,* 19 February 2007.
15. J.R. Siwach 292.
16. *Sarkaria Commission Report,* 180-81.
17. *The Constitution of India,* Article, 164.
18. *AIR 1994, SC* 2097.
19. *NCRWC,* A consultation paper on Article 356 of the Constitution (2002) *at http://law min nic.in/ncrwe/final report/v_2 b_2 - 5 htm*
20. See Venkatesan V., *Governor's Choice, Frontline,* 16 Nov. 2007:14
21. Rajeev Dhavan, *President's Rule: Recent Trends, Journal of the Indian Law Institute,* 31 (1989): 524
22. See *The Hindu,* 7 May 2002.
23. See *The Hindu,* Editorial
24. Tavleen Singh, *Pogram Politics, India Today,* 18 March 2002.
25. *Ibid.*
26. *Ibid.*
27. Roshni Sengupta: *Communal Violence in India, EPW,* 14 May 2005.
28. Tavleen Singh, *Pogrom Politics, India Today,* 18 March 2002.
29. See *The Hindu,* 24 March, 2002.
30. See, *The Hindu,* 24 March 2002.
31. *The Hindu,* 29 March 2002.
32. Rajeev Dhavan, *The Gujarat Imbroglio, The Hindu,* 19 April, 2002.
33. On I May 2002, the New York based Human Rights watch wrote a 76 page report stating that 'the attacks were planed in advance with extensive participation by police and the state government officials.
34. See *Stigma of Gujarat,* editorial, *The Times of India,* 1 May 2002.
35. *RSD 2/5/2002 at http://rajya sabha-nic.in/rs debate/ Synopsis* 195/so 2005 2002 htm.
36. Anjaly Mody, *When will the Centre intervenes?, The Hindu,* 26 April 2002..

37. C.P Bhambhri. *Central Government* in *the Age of Globalization,* in *Indian Federalism in the New Millennium,* ed. by Dua B.D. and Singh M.P. (New Delhi: Manohar, 2003) 322
38. Verney, Douglas V., *Has Proliferation of Parties Affected the Indian Federalism, in India's Living Constitution,* ed. by Zoya Hassan and others (New Delhi: Cambridge, 2000) 152.
39. Vidya Subramanyan, *Who is Guilty Party* in Uttar Pradesh, *The Hindu,* 21 February 2007
40. See *NCRWC, A Consultation paper on Article 356 of the Constitution (2002) at http://law.min.inncrwc*
41. *Frontline, Beyond the Obvious, http://www.praful.net/archieves/ 2007.0302ft.htm.*
42. *Ibid*
43. *Ibid*
44. See K. Raman Pillai, *Facets of Indian Politics* (New Delhi: Deep and Deep, 2010)
45. V.R. Krishna Iyer, interview, Article 356 should be *Abolished, Frontline,* 17 July 1998, 24-25
46. In the words of Krishna Iyer "To politicise Article 356, to terrorise state administrators and to achieve illegitimate ends through colourable means is now becoming a habitual constitutional delinquency of the party in power at the Centre". (See V.R. Krishna Iyer, *Indian Federalism Dialectics and Dynamics* (Gauhati: Ashok Publishing, 1992) 94)
47. See H.M. Raja Sekhara, *President's Rule in the Indian States, Indian Journal of Political Science,* 48 (1987): 622-23 see also the same author's article, *It is Time to Stop Misuse of Article 356, The Hindu,* 4 March 1997.

Chapter 7

Safeguards Against Abuse of Article 356: The Parliament

The proclamation of President's Rule under Article 356 is a very serious matter as it not only disturbs the federal equilibrium but also adversely affects the rights of the people, their elected representatives and responsible ministries. "It has been used as a wonderful drug to cure the maladies from defection to law and order, from agitation to voluntary resignation and from political instability to maladministration"[1]. Any abuse or misuse of this highly potential power will play havoc with our constitutional system. As such it is essential to have a machinery of control against the abuse of power[2]. A question arises, how the abuse of the power conferred under the Article can be warded off and a check can be placed on the exercise of this power.

The framers of the Constitution, in this context, relied upon the Parliament as a primary safeguard against the abuse of power and provided in the Constitution that the the Parliament should endorse the application of Article 356. This is conceived both as a check upon the power and as a vindication of the principles of Parliamentary and popular sovereignty over the executive. Parliament's power of endorsement is held to be more democratic and more flexible than the system in which the judiciary is supreme. Furthermore, the Parliamentary check makes the government accountable to the people.

The control of the Parliament in this context is to be found in clause (3) of Article 356. It provides that every such proclamation shall be laid before each House of the Parliament and shall, except where it is a proclamation revoking a previous proclamation, cease to operate at the expiration of two months[3] unless before the expiration of that period it has been approved by a resolution of both Houses of the Parliament[4]. This provides a salutary check on the executive power entrenching parliamentary supremacy over the Executive. The provision amounts in substance to a requirement that the two Houses of the Parliament shall be informed of the proclamation of emergency made by the executive and that unless the approval by resolutions of both Houses is obtained within two months, the declaration of emergency shall lapse. Provision is also made in the clause for the contingency of the Lok-Sabha having been dissolved at the time of the proclamation or the dissolution of the House taking place within a period of two months provided in the clause for the approval of both the Houses. The Constitution says that if any proclamation is issued at a time when the Lok-Sabha has been dissolved or dissolution of the House of people takes place during the period of two months, the ratification shall be done by the Rajya Sabha. However, the duration so extended by the Council of State runs at the most till the expiration of thirty days from the date on which the Lok Sabha first sits after its reconstitution unless before the expiration of the said period a resolution approving the proclamation has also been passed by the House of People[5]. Therefore, the role of the Parliament in continuing emergency beyond two months is crucial. Without such approval of the Parliament, the Presidential proclamation under this Article would cease to exist after two months. Thus, though the power of proclaiming the emergency is vested solely in the executive, the crucial decision about it is to be taken by the Parliament by its approval or disapproval within two months. The President's decision is only temporary, destined to lapse unless the Parliament wills otherwise. This position has been justified in the Bommai case thus:

> The very fact that the founding fathers have chosen to provide for approval of the proclamation by the Parliament is itself proof of the fact that the opinion or satisfaction of the President is not final or conclusive[6].

This is an important safeguard in the Constitution against an arbitrary exercise of Presidential powers. The scrutiny of the proclamation is, therefore, designed to test the validity or propriety of the proclamation of emergency. If the Parliament finds that the declaration is not proper or is not called for, it can refuse its approval.

The Parliament is also closely and intimately involved in the extension of President's Rule in the State. Once approved by the Parliament, it shall remain in force for a period of six months. If the government desires to extend it further, the executive is bound to bring the matter again before the Parliament and get an extension for a further period of six months[7]. The idea behind periodic parliamentary ratification of continuance of President's Rule is to afford an opportunity to the Parliament to review for itself the situation prevailing in the concerned state so that the central executive does not feel free to keep the proclamation in force longer than what may be absolutely necessary. The central Government is responsible and accountable for all its action to the Parliament.A safeguard against any misuse of power by the Executive is that the ultimate authority to decide whether a proclamation under Article 356 is to be continued or not lies in the Parliament.[8] The maximum period for which the President's Rule in any State may continue is three years. However, as a result of the 44th amendment Act, continuation of such rule beyond the period of one year from the date of the issue of the proclamation is dependent on two factors:

1. A proclamation of emergency under Article 352 is in operation at the time of passing such proclamation; and
2. The Election Commission certifies that the continuance in force of the proclamation is necessary on account of difficulties in holding election to the Assemblies of the State concerned. As a result of this amendment,

> ordinarily the duration of President's Rule in any State will be only one year. Under exceptional circumstances, the period may be extended. Only in rare cases, both the conditions would be fulfilled. This truth was revealed in the case of Punjab. Thus the encroachment of the Union on the autonomy of the State is now restricted to one year under ordinary circumstances.

However, it must also be noted that because of these two conditions, it became necessary to hold elections in Assam in 1983 under circumstances which were extremely unfavourable for holding election. It was also because of these conditions that the 48th, 63rd, 64th, 67th and 68th Amendment Acts were passed to continue President's Rule in Punjab beyond the period of one year to face the challenges opened up by the Akali agitation.[9] Considering these kinds of situations, the NCRWC observes:

> Circumstances may arise where even without the proclamation of Emergency under Article 352, it may be difficult to hold general elections to the state Assembly. In such a situation continuance of President's Rule may become necessary. It may, therefore, be more practicable to de-link the two conditions allowing for operation of each condition in its own specific circumstances for continuance of President's Rule. This would allow for flexibility and save the Constitution from the need to amend it from time to time.[10]

The Sarkaria Commission also recommended that in clause (5) of Article 356, the word "and" occurring between sub clause (a) and (b) should be substituted by "or" so that if either condition is satisfied, the proclamation can continue in force beyond one year. Therefore, it is suggested that at least the first condition must be removed from the Constitution.

The envisaged role of the Parliament introduces a very important Constitutional safeguard against the abuse of power. The virtual suppression of the State Government and State Legislature, which results from a declaration under this Article, beyond the initial time limit can be operative only after the approval of both Houses of the Parliament. Rajya Sabha being a representative of the State and the Lok Sabha being also comprised of members drawn from all the States, the requirement of their approval for the continuance of the proclamation of emergency is likely to operate as a powerful check against the capricious authority of the President[11].

The efficacy of this Parliamentary safeguard to prevent the abuse and misuse of this "tremendous power" with immense potential was discussed and debated by the founding fathers in the Constituent Assembly[12]. Ultimately, however, the framers in their collective wisdom were immensely satisfied with the Parliamentary "check" mechanism devised by them and as such did not provide for any alternative safeguard of direct nature.

Efficacy of the Existing Safeguards

Though the safeguards associated with Article 356 seem to be fairly effective, a close perusal of the actual working of the Parliamentary control mechanism for the last sixty years has clearly shown that the Parliament is quite ineffective in controlling the arbitrary exercise of this power. The provision has often become edentate in the hands of unscrupulous politicians. The constitutional fathers while providing for the mechanism of control could not have thought of such a contingency. If the Indian Parliament appears to have failed to act as a powerful restraint upon the arbitrary exercise of this power, then what are the reasons for it? It is mainly on account of two factors (1) constitutional lacunae in Article 356 and (2) the limitation imposed by the working of the Parliamentary system. This chapter seeks to analyse these reasons and examine how effective the Parliament has been in the matter of upholding the valid democratic rights of the State.

1. Constitutional Lacunae in Article 356

A serious analysis of the Constitutional provision brings to light the fact that the provision itself gives room for the executive to bypass the Parliamentary control. First of all, unlike some other democratic countries of the world the prior approval of the Parliament or any of its Houses is not required for the issuance of a proclamation under Article 356 of the Constitution.

The President is given the full liberty and authority to issue a proclamation even when the Parliament is in session [13]. The constitutional provision in Article 356 (3) is very clear in that respect. What the Constitution requires is that as a matter of course both Houses of the Parliament should approve it within two months. In the same way there is no obligation on the Union government under the Constitution to lay the proclamation on the table of the House on the very first day provided the Parliament is in session[14]. Since the decision to invoke Article 356 in a State has got far reaching consequence and puts in abeyance the democratic rights of the people even if it is only for a short period, it is submitted that the Parliament should be apprised of it at the very earliest possible opportunity. Our governments have often been guilty of wilfully withholding this vital information from the Parliament with ulterior motives. Therefore, it should be made statutory that the report on the introduction of President's Rule in a State should be tabled in the Parliament on the very first day itself if the Parliament is in session, or on the first day of the next session, if it is not in session.

Another weakness is that the Constitutional provisions conferring power of approval on the Parliament do not confer power to invalidate a proclamation if the Parliament wills otherwise. The proclamation in any case, is valid for an initial period of two months as per the constitutional provisions and it is so irrespective of its approval or disapproval by the two Houses of the Parliament. Its life for a period of two months cannot be cut short by the Parliament. The approval of the Parliament merely gives the proclamation further lease of life for six months. This position has been clarified by Shakdar and Kaul thus:

> The life of proclamation unless revoked earlier by the President is two months. There is no provision under which Parliament can cut it short. It is only if the proclamation is to continue in force beyond two months that Parliament has to approve of it in a manner similar to that in a case of proclamation of emergency[15].

In other words, it is a well settled principle that the initial imposition of emergency up to two months can survive without the approval of the Legislature. This is the view that has been reiterated by the various courts including the Supreme Court[16].

Quite interestingly, Chandra Chud J. in the Rajasthan case observed that if in a 'hypothetical' situation the Parliament disapproves the proclamation within two months, even though constitutionally it will not make any change in the situation, mature political judgment would lean in favour of revocation of the proclamation. This, however, has to be brushed aside as a 'non-legal' or an ethical postulate. As such, the Parliament on withholding approval to a proclamation does not sit in judgment over the 'satisfaction of the President reached on the advice of the Union Cabinet for imposing President's Rule for two months. The action of the president in imposing his rule in a State is irreversible at least for the first two months[17]. Thus, it is very clear that the Parliament only considers the desirability of the proclamation being continued beyond two months. The approval granted by the two Houses of the Parliament, therefore, does not amount to approving or disapproving the Presidential proclamation, which in any event is valid for a period of two months. Therefore the Presidential proclamation issued, for an initial period of two months can neither be validated nor be invalidated by the Parliament by its approval or disapproval. This constitutional lacuna has been said to be exploited by the ruling party at the Centre according to its political expediency. What the framers of the Constitution had in their mind while they were drafting this provision was that the Parliament should get enough time to review the situation and decide on the proper course of action. Unfortunately, this Constitutional position is often misused by the Central Government to safeguard its petty political interest. Here party politics gets the upper hand and this shows the gross inadequacy of the check mechanism.

The third reason why control by the Parliament can become ineffective is that disapproval of the proclamation does not make it unconstitutional since its inception. Article 356(3) makes it clear that the only effect of either House failing or refusing to approve the proclamation is that it ceases to operate after two months. This clearly means that it has been operative up to that time. Consequently, every act done, order made and laws passed by the government till the time the proclamation is disapproved will be quite legal and proper. That is, it cannot question, what has been done in the interim between the time when President's Rule is declared and when the Parliament refuses to ratify the proclamation. They are, however, subject to review, repeal or modification by the government/ Legislative Assembly or other competent authority. This is a lot more significant than it would appear. This constitutional provision has been used by the Union government on many occasions since the inception of the Constitution for some short term purposes, politically significant and vital for the ruling party at the Centre and its counterparts in the State and unfavourable to the opposition[18].

In this context the mass dismissal of nine State governments by the Janata Government in April 1977 becomes quite intriguing and reflects the inefficacy of the Constitutional provision. In this case, the possibility that the Congress party could use its majority in the Rajya Sabha was not a constitutional threat because Janata government had reason to believe that fresh election could be held within two months. Even if the Rajya Sabha did disapprove of the proclamation, the Janata government would have achieved the objectives. The decision to call for elections in these States was irreversible. The Parliament could not change the situation. Therefore, the Constitution is so designed that the most dubious proclamation of President's Rule can always escape the scrutiny of the Parliament. It appears that our Constitution makers failed to understand the potential danger of bypassing Parliamentary control by the executive in order to aggrandise itself and to wield power without restrictions imposed by law. This grave lacuna in the law strikes at the very root of the concept of Parliamentary check mechanism. Therefore, it should be made mandatory that no Constitutional action be taken which would be irreversible, if a particular President's Rule is not approved or revoked. Otherwise, "it would give license to the central executive to bypass the control of the Parliament"[19].

Furthermore, Parliamentary control has also been overcome by way of reissuing of the proclamation. The Central Government which becomes shy of facing the Parliament on the issue of President's Rule, revokes the proclamation within the stipulated time of two months and issues a fresh one in its place. This may happen when the proclamation issued is revoked within two months and during that period the Parliament may not be in session. Another strategy is to allow the proclamation to lapse under Article 356(3) by not placing it on the table of Parliament and issue a fresh one. Besides this, in some cases when the proclamation was about to expire after six months of the Parliamentary approval, they were revoked and fresh proclamations were issued[20].

The strategies applied by the Centre to circumvent the Constitutional provision testifies to the fact that Parliamentary approval can be conveniently avoided. In reissuing the proclamation, the government has used this power in the same way as it has issued and reissued ordinances. This practice indicates the fact that this controlling mechanism as envisaged by the Constitution becomes either meaningless or redundant. Therefore, the practice of reissuing the proclamation should be interdicted and the Union government shall be forbidden to perpetuate a fallen ordinance through reissuing it. It has already been found that it is this practice of reissuing a fallen proclamation which has often come in handy for the Central Government with some vested interests to keep the Parliament at bay. Thus it is seen that the basic postulate of the Constitution was recklessly frittered away and the Constitution was cut down to size to suit the expediency of the ruling party. This anomaly can be removed by abrogating the power of the Centre to reissue a proclamation prior to seeking the Parliamentary approval of the revoked or lapsed proclamation as the case may be. In this circumstance, the recommendation of the NCRWC is very pertinent. The Commission stated:

> 'Once the proclamation is issued, it should not be permissible to withdraw it and issue another proclamation in the same effect with a view to circumventing the requirement in clause (3). Even if a proclamation is

substituted by another proclamation, the period prescribed in clause (3) should be calculated from the date of the first proclamation'.[21] Necessary legislation should expressly be made to forbid the re-proclamation of Article 356 by the President.

2. The Limitation Imposed by the Working of the Parliamentary System

Closely allied with these Constitutional loopholes are other factors inherent in the theory and practice of Parliamentary democracy which enable the Union executive to lighten or even nullify Parliamentary safeguards as envisaged in the Constitution. The major fact is that in a Parliamentary system, any Government is normally drawn from the political party or parties which have secured a majority of seats in the Lok Sabha. Our electoral system also ensures that the leading party in the Lok Sabha gets a majority of seats even on a minority of popular votes. This majority of seats in the Lok Sabha comes to the help of the Central Government in garnering enough support for the proclamation. Under such circumstances, it is "unrealistic to rely on a government controlled majority in the Legislature to exercise effective supervision over that same government in its use of emergency power"[22]. Of course, if no party has a majority, then the Parliament's influence is more. This is vividly illustrated by the declaration and revocation of President's Rule in Bihar in 1999.

The most important occasion when the Legislature can exercise its power of control over the executive is when it is placed for discussion and approval. Unfortunately, as the imposition of Article 356 is a political move, the discussion in the Houses also is, understandably, charged with political overtones, being on party lines. Since the ruling party being safe behind its majority in the House, the debate which generally continues for a day or two or only minutes ends with the expected endorsement of government's action. The legislators of the party in power, even if they do not agree with the government, do not oppose it in the Parliament because of the fear of the party Whip. It might, therefore, be argued that Parliamentary control over the executive has, for all practical purposes, come to mean control by political parties. Thus the Parliament in general and MPs in particular are powerless in the party machine,[23] and the government control of the Parliament is absolute. The Parliament merely approves of what has already been decided by the cabinet in general and the political party in power in particular. The real power lies in the cabinet and not in the Parliament. When we talk of the supremacy of Parliament it is really the supremacy of the cabinet. As the powers and control of the cabinet are increasing, the actual independence of the members of the Parliament is becoming less and less. Ivor Jennings makes it very succinctly when he says the 'Parliamentary supremacy in the modern world is synonymous with unfettered power of the executive. The Parliament has really no control over the executive. It is a pure fiction'.[24] Further, the debate usually suffers from serious drawbacks regarding fairness, reasoning and objectivity. Conclusions on a particular proclamation are drawn well in advance on known party lines, and to support such conclusions arguments are put forth. In other words, participants and people are well aware of what a particular member is going to speak. In fact, such party positions are made clear to the media even before the actual debates start in the Parliament. Except in the rarest of the rare cases, members vote on expected lines. Ivor Jennings echoes the same sentiments when he said:

> The government determines what shall be discussed (in the Parliament), when it shall be discussed, how long the discussion shall take and what the discussion shall be[25].

Though the Legislature is charged with final authority to decide the validity or otherwise of the proclamation under Article 356, the executive branch is supported in the Legislature by a solid and disciplined party majority. In such instances, it is hardly practicable to look to the Legislature for an independent check.

A suggestion in this context for making Parliamentary control effective is to take away crucial issues like this from the purview of partisan debates on the floor of the House. In other words, members of the Parliament irrespective of their party affiliation should be allowed to vote freely according to their conscience[26]. In recent times, such freedom of voting has been allowed on many issues in the British House of Commons[27]. If this is not possible, all political parties should ensure that their members in Parliament speak freely on this most vital issue, irrespective of the party position and this is what democracy is all about. Further, a member may, after expressing his point of view, also explain his party's position if he so desires and when the matter comes up for voting he/she can abide by the party's position. Political parties should be courageous enough to bring in such a fundamental and important change in the Parliamentary behaviour. Such a step in the Indian Parliament will be immensely helpful, specially when there is a tendency to look at everything through partisan eyes[28].

It is the well considered opinion of the author that these measures, which will certainly render the central government more answerable to the parliament should be implemented. If these suggestions are put into practice both in letter and spirit, the scope of parliamentary control would be enlarged appreciably. The author, however, does not presume that the implementation of the suggestion will bring about a sea change in the present scenario where brute majority prevails over the mute minority because in a parliamentary system the writ of political party in power runs through Parliament too. However, it is hoped that this suggestion will generate discussion and be considered seriously by all concerned.

The Parliamentary control mechanism as provided by the Constitution is also affected by the inadequacy of time. We need indepth discussions on these issues. Unfortunately, a new trend has developed in our Parliament, by which the time available for discussion on the issue has become very limited. With the increasing frequency of imposition of President's Rule, the Parliament is gradually becoming incapable of any kind of worthwhile discussion on this. Mostly, discussions on President's Rule are sandwiched between discussions on other issues as pointed out by Rajeev Dhavan. As such, they are held under considerable pressure of time and members do not discuss all aspects of the issue. For instance, in the U.P debate (1996) the

Speaker reminded the House that the time allotted for discussion was over and he expressed his inability to allow time when it was demanded by Jaswant Singh and Santosh Mohan Dev. Sharing the sentiments of the members, the Speaker said:

> 'I have to sense the mood of the House .. please sit down, At four O'clock we have to take up the discussion on foreign policy. The honourable minister has also come. For U.P resolution, only four hours time was allotted. Already we have taken four hours fifteen minutes. Ten more honourable members are yet to speak on the subject. Now what is to be done.[29]

The unruly behaviour of parliamentarians is another problem which renders the Parliament incapable of transacting even its basic functions for days together. Some legislators seem to think that the legitimate and most important use of the forum of legislature is for registering protest and demonstrations and naturally this cut into the time available for enforcing accountability of the Executive to the Legislature. It has crossed all limits and reached a shocking and alarming stage where the Prime minister was not allowed to introduce his team, the Speakers were not able to speak and the Governors were obstructed from addressing the Legislatures. What started sometimes ago as a spontaneous action by a few members to make their voice heard or presences felt in the Parliament has become an ordinary form of protest. Now a days, debates and discussions on important issues like President's Rule have been overshadowed by disruptions, confrontations and such other non-democratic practices which eat into the very vitality of parliamentary behaviour. It is a matter of common knowledge that even a single parliamentary day is not passed without any walkout, dharnas, shouting, adjournments and pandemonium. The most unfortunate aspect is that even if a single member wants to disturb the proceedings, he could hold the house to ransom. It has become a fashion of some members to stall the Parliament on non-issues. While doing so, they have conveniently forgotten that the people send them to the legislatures to highlight their grievances in the Houses in a mature manner and not to disrupt the proceedings. Sometimes pernicious behaviour displayed by the members turned out to be the proportion of what could be described as 'parliamentary terrorism' and what happened in the UP debate in 2002 and more recently in the Bihar debate in 2010 remind us that it is not a mere doubt but a harsh reality. Naturally, it eats into the very limited time available for the debates on the issues in question. The above peculiarities of the functioning of the Indian Parliament allow the executive much leverage to shorten or even avoid oppositions scrutiny of the executive. Already low credibility of Indian parliamentarians will vanish if something is not done immediately to stamp out pernicious behaviour of elected representatives inside the Houses. Law makers are expected to observe certain standards so that legislative bodies which decide the destiny of millions should not be allowed to degenerates into platform for displaying muscle power. This aspects has already been discussed in the relavant pages in chapter four. It is not necessary to discuss it again.

The absence of a strong opposition further aggravates the issue. A strong opposition is the bulwark of democracy. The success and strength of parliamentary democracy depends on the effectiveness and strength of the opposition to the party in power. That is to say in a parliamentary system the opposition is as important as the government.

Unfortunately, the Indian parliamentary system lacks a strong opposition, which has to play an important role of being the *Vox populi* (voice of the people). The opposition should be a moving spirit behind any parliamentary democracy. But often, the opposition falls to pieces because of its inherent illness and vested interest like regionalism, castism and communalism. What has really weakened the position of the opposition is the fact that the opposition benches have been in a terrible state of imbalance from the point of view of numerical strength. The dominating position of the Congress party in the first five LokSabhas made the opposition totally irrelevant in the parliamentary process. The parliament in India, unlike the British Parliament, till 1989 was dominated by the Congress party which could afford to ignore the opposition. The BJP could secure a very large number of seats since 1989 elections. However, due to the ideological differences with the left parties it could not function as a corrective force. Moreover, the opposition has been largely fragmented and frustrated and lacked strong and steady support structure which resulted in diametrically opposite political trends among them. When highly important matters with far reaching implications are brought before the Parliament, some parties seek to build pressure on the government to move rightward, some seek to exert the same on the government to move leftward. Thus the major reason for the indiscriminate, arbitrary use of Article 356 by the ruling party at the Centre in its favour has been the weak position of the parties in opposition and their inability to mobilize cross sectional support so as to prevail upon the Central government to go slow in imposing President's Rule.

Another important reason why the Parliament is much weaker and much less effective in exercising control is that the Parliament is being denied of vital information about a particular President's Rule. In the absence of the relevant information how can the Parliament approve or disapprove of the action of the President? It is essential that the Parliament should be fully appraised of the reasons and circumstances which influenced the President's decision to impose President's Rule in a State.

In a democracy, the ultimate sovereignty rests with the people. Both the permanent and the political executive are meant to serve the people by looking after their interests. Therefore, the people have an inherent right to have all the information that is not declared secret or confidential in the interest of the State. Further, the Ministers have a duty to explain in Parliament their actions. They should also fully explain the grounds and details of such an action. The members can elicit information through Parliamentary questions. They can scrutinise the governmental decision, initiate debates, call Ministers to account and thereby guard the interests and liberties of the State. "If the account given by a minister to Parliament is withholding information on a matter under review, the account given is not full account and the obligation to account for what has happened has, *prima facie*, not been discharged[30]. Therefore, every scrap of information, every factor which weighed in the mind of the President or his advisors and every aspect of any advice given, including the report of the Governor and the warning issued to the State and its responses, should have been fairly and squarely placed before the Parliament and the people[31] and where necessary before the courts. The crucial decision about President's Rule is to be taken by the Parliament, not the President. The President's decision is only temporary, destined to lapse unless the Parliament wills, otherwise. The Parliament can ratify the decision of the President if it knows what the President, cabinet and the Governor know. It serves two important purposes: firstly, it informs the Legislature as to why the action was taken; and secondly, it provides an opportunity to the legislators to question or challenge the proclamation. "Such a step makes democracy more meaningful, efficient and participatory"[32]. Democratic accountability becomes meaningless if such information is not made public through the Parliament. Therefore, to make Parliamentary control over executive more effective, it is submitted that the Presidential proclamation should be stated in specific terms.

The Central Government is reluctant to part with full information because it fears that this will expose the government's action to stringent judicial scrutiny. Democratic accountability becomes meaningless if such laying of information is not made before public through the Parliament making the imposition of President's Rule a murky affair rather than the responsible exercise of the constitutional powers.

However, it would be accepted by everyone that there have always been some subjects in respect of which full information cannot be given. In S.P. Gupta v. Union of India it was held that: "disclosure of information in regard to the functioning of government must be the rule and secrecy is an exception justified only where the strictest requirement of public interest so demands"[33]. Therefore, in order that the Parliament might discharge its function properly, it is crucial and essential that the Cabinet should completely brief the Parliament on the reason or reasons for the proclamation. Otherwise, the Parliament cannot discharge the constitutional duty it owed to the people and the nation. Now, the Right to Information Act passed by the Parliament reflects a welcome realisation of the danger posed above.

The main reason for this decline, however, seems to be its present composition and quality of its debates. In particular, the Parliament has undergone a basic transformation of power from the urban middle class as represented by lawyers to the rural agricultural class. The earlier parliamentarians were remarkable in their own ways. Their visionary and sagacious leadership strengthened the very foundation of democracy. Their conduct on the floor was prim and proper, never disorderly and uproarious, who meticulously observed rules and made the debates and discussion informative. They paid attention to the opposition parties and treated them with respect as an integral part of democratic process. The opposition parties, in turn, acted responsibly abiding by the parliamentary rules, unlike the parliamentarians of today. To day it is professional politicians, trade union leaders, business magnets and industrialists and above all power-monkers and person with criminal record who are firmly rooted in the law making bodies. Their speech and behaviour inside the legislators are eroding the dignity of the Houses. The major consideration before them is to keep their political career secure rather than looking after the interests of the people and the nation. For the furtherance of their objectives, they are ready to employ any method and go to any extent. They have contributed to the break down of earlier elite consensus and conscientious style of functioning.

Closely allied with what is stated above is the growing attractiveness of politics from other professions. This in turn, attracts fortune seekers and opportunists into politics and they get elected to the law making bodies, seeing it as a means to gain authority, power, influence, money and other advantages. When the Constitution was drafted our eminent makers of the Constitution expected that only persons of high calibre, integrity and the insight would be entering the representative bodies of people. They had a visual about a true Indian and his duties as clearly envisaged in Article 51-A of the Constitution dealing with Fundamental Duties. Unfortunately all their dreams have been shattered when persons with vested interests and criminals find their way into the temples of our parliamentary democracy. It is in this occasion, Mani Shankar Iyer is perfectly justified in stating:

> 'There has been deterioration in public life as those who are unemployed are now in politics. The major difference appears to be that while earlier, serving the nation was seen as a privilege and attracted well meaning people, now it is the privilege that attracts politicians[34]

With the increase in number of vernacular and less cosmopolitan politicians, the Parliament becomes incapable of any worthwhile discussion as they are neither trained in law making process nor do they seem to have the inclination to develop the necessary skill and competence in parliamentary debates. The most animated discussion that has taken place in the Parliament in recent years concern granting of privilege to members of the Parliament during which voting was unanimous. Most of the members belonging to this breed can think only in terms of present i.e. day to day politics and they show an amazing lack of vision for the future. As things stand today, we cannot expect the Parliament to be an effective safeguard against the misuse of power under Article 356.

All the more reprehensive is low level of attendance and participation in the debates when important issues like President's Rule or resolutions on other vital issues are put up for discussion. For instance, in 1993, the defence budget for the year running in to lakhs and crores of rupees was voted and passed by the Parliament when there were less than fifty members present in the House! Too many MPs showed little or almost no interest in attending the Parliament. The statutes provide for a member of Parliament to be disqualified if absent for twenty days without previous consent, but party whip always ensure that habitual absentees sign on the twentieth day. In this connection H.V. Kamath observed: 'Heaven help us for democracy cannot go on at this rate'.[35] Therefore, it is suggested that the Speaker should give mandatory instruction to the members to be present in the House during such important discussion and take part meaningfully in its proceedings with advance preparation.

The devaluation of parliamentary authority coupled with the trivialisation of debates and the poor level of attendance would have raised question about the constitutional rationale of its existence. Parliament is the grand inquest of the nation, the platform for civilized discourse'.[36] Therefore the confidence in it must be maintained. And it should start with the members. As a first step it is suggested that political party and people should ensure stricter evaluation while nominating candidates for election to the representative bodies. A more positive approach will be needed from political parties at the time of candidate selection so that those suspected of moral turpitude, even if not convicted in a court of law, are not selected. In this contest, the latest decision of the Supreme Court is an eye opener and a corrective and rethinking force. On 13 March 2003 the Supreme Court in a mile stone judgment said that the voters have the fundamental rights to know about the criminal, financial and educational background of those they elect.[37] The Court observed that survival of democracy depends up on free and fair election. Elections would not be fair if the voters are unaware of the antecedents of candidates contesting elections. The rulings of the court serve two purposes, if implemented. Firstly, the disclosure of information makes the electorate more aware of the social and the ethical standings of the candidates; and secondly, it enables them to make a better choice and, to the extent possible, prevent or discourage persons with doubtful integrity from getting elected to the temples of democracy.

All the above factors are tending to transform the Parliament into a helpless puppet or even a rubber stamp incapable of performing even its primary function. As result proclamation of President's Rule are passed regrettably without any worth while discussion and several calling attention motion are left undiscussed. The opposition makes it impossible to hear what the Prime minister's or ministers' statements on a particular proclamations. Then, one would be tempted to ask this fundamental question, what is the relevance of parliamentary control over the executive ?.

The Positive Aspects of the Parliamentary Check

We have seen that various factors are at work in our polity to minimise effective Parliamentary control over the proclamation of emergency under Article 356. Nonetheless, the Parliament can still act as a brake on the wheels of the government. The Parliament's contribution in this regard may be discussed under three heads, viz (i) symbolic action consisting of individual members using various methods to express their disapproval, (ii) analytical assessment consisting of Parliament exposing the root cause for the successive imposition of President's Rule and (iii) institutionalization of mechanisms of control consisting of creation of procedures and institutional methods by which Parliament can control the governance of the State during President's Rule[38]. With regard to the first method, Ministers can be interrogated during question hour and information can be extracted through questions about the reasons for the proclamation of President's Rule. A skilful and determined member can use Parliamentary questions to extract much information or to conduct a campaign in favour or against a particular proclamation; as did Somnath Chatterjee over the Tamil Nadu debate in 1991, or as George Fernandes in the U.P debate in 1996. The Parliament has other means also by which it can scrutinise the actions of the executive in this regard. The members may stage walkouts, table adjournment motions and demand half an hour discussions etc. on the floor. These have the effect of diffusing political tension by permitting the expression of sentiments under the aegis of the Parliament. This may be motivated by a genuine desire to know the government's intention also. It may be also motivated by a desire to embarrass the government. Used skilfully, each of these devices is a powerful Parliamentary weapon. The doctrine of ministerial responsibility makes them so, not because Parliament may ultimately force the resignation of the government or an individual minister but because Ministers accept that they must answer Parliamentary questions and defend their actions and policies in the Parliament. "However, in the practical sense, all these Parliamentary activities contribute to the noisy environment in which government exist and politics operate"[39]. H.N. Mukherjee once reflected on the insensitivity in the debate on President's Rule in Kerala thus:

> Not even all the votes that can be registered in the House of the people could ever be an argument against an expression of the people's anger which if the government go on at this rate will burst one day (to teach the government) a lesson that they pre-eminently deserve[40].

This reflection is significantly suggestive of the failure of the political system on the whole and its incapacity to sensitively reflect the anxieties of the people who participate in it.

The second method of analytical assessment involves Parliament exposing the root cause for the successive imposition of President's Rule. The debates in the Parliament also provide occasion and opportunities to consider what exactly is wrong with the political system designed by the Constitution. In this context, several suggestions have come forth. In the Andhra debate in 1954, A.K. Gopalan's opinion on what constitutes a 'constitutional crisis' was a valuable anyalysis[41]. Similarly, in the Tamil Nadu debate in 1991, Jaswant Singh's argument that before taking the "most extreme step of invoking Article 356, the Centre should take recourse to Article 256 which empowered it to issue directive to "errant or defaulting government not acting in consonance with the interest of the security of State or on an issue relating to national security"[42] was also an argument which could be accepted.

In a number of debates, the members of the Parliament succeeded in unearthing the real reason for the imposition. For instance, when the PEPSU proclamation came up for approval in the Rajya Sabha, Ambedkar made an incisive and memorable comment that" the people have got very legitimate ground for suspicion that the government is manipulating the Article in the Constitution for the purpose of maintaining their own party. After having made this observation, he said 'those are instances of the most violent kind of rape of the constitution[43]. In the same way, the Andhra and Travancore-Cochin debate indicated that Article 356 was used by the Congress party to keep the opposition out of power[44]. The Tamil Nadu debate in 1976 also brought to light the fact that no government which was not liked by the party in power at the Centre was not safe from President's Rule, irrespective of its support in the legislature[45]. The U.P. debate in 1966 also throws much light on the bare fact that President's Rule was declared with the sole object of keeping a particular party out of power. This was described by M.M. Joshi "as the biggest rape that has been taken place on the Constitution"[46].

By describing the Centre's action in Tamil Nadu in 1991 as "nothing but a travesty of constitutional morality, a blatant abuse of power, and deliberate decimation of the fundamental principles of federalism", Somnath Chatterjee, in a way, summed up the feelings of major opposition parties. He said:

> The history of Article 356 in this country is a history of political and constitutional aberrations, and it is replete with instances of gross misuse by successive Congress governments what is astounding is the *brazen-facedness* and the effrontery of this misuse the marriage of convenience between the Congress and this motley conglomerate called the Janata Dal (S) is producing monsters[47].

The continuing unabated story of the misuse of the provision was pictured by George Fernandez in the U.P. debate in 1996, he observed:

> The position is that starting from 1959 and during the great leadership of the Congress, of Shastri, Indira Gandhi, by machinations of Centre and not because of any *bona fide* reasons, Article 356 had been used for political reasons and not for any administrative reasons. This is the experience of Article 356. It has been used indiscriminately against political opponents in West Bengal. We have been victims in Kerala, we have been victims in Orissa. Then people have been victims in U.P., Haryana and what not[48].

Replying to the discussion in Bihar debate in 2005, the Home Minister emphasised his intention to establish a democratic government in Bihar. He said 'the centre was not happy about imposing Presidents Rule and had no intention of continuing the arrangement for long'. He also advised the elected representatives to take step to ensure that a popular government may be put in place. Answering criticisms from several members that there had been undue delay in the appointment of advisors, he said, there was no provision in the constitution that required advisors to be appointed.'

In Tamil Nadu debate in 1991, Jaswant Singh made a very useful suggestion that before taking the most extreme step of invoking Article 356, the Centre should take recourse to Article 256 which empowered it to issue directives to errant or defaulting government not acting in consonance with the interest of the security of the state or on issues relating to national unity[49]. Likewise, in the Bihar debate in 1999, L.K. Advani, the Home Minister, agreed to the opposition view that breakdown of law and order or mere incompetence could not be made the basis for dismissing a democratically elected government.[50] In the Kerala debate in 1964, a useful point on the paternalistic attitude of the Union government was made by P.S. Menon when he said:

> The attitude on the part of the Union Ministers that the State Government was the part of the Union ministry, that the State Governments are their wards and that guardianship can be imposed from time to time depending upon the exigencies of the occasion, will be an obstacle for the development of democratic Constitution.[51]

By and large, Parliamentary discussion on the absence of the report of the Governor received vital attention. Somanath Chatterjee, noting the absence of Governor's report, said: "even the pretence of a Governor's report is not there". On the other hand, Congress (I) felt that it was not necessary for the Centre to wait for a report from the Governor of Tamil Nadu before acting. The party leader P.R. Kumaramangalam argued that the action under Article 356 did not depend upon "only on the report of the Governor". He elaborated that under the Article, the President could act "on receipt of a report from the Governor or otherwise" to justify the action by the Centre in the case of Tamil Nadu[52].

A perusal of the old record shows that the issue has been debated in the Parliament, but it has not been successful so far in withholding approval to a proclamation which is illegitimate or at least of doubtful legitimacy. This may be the product of Parliamentary helplessness in the face of strong, impregnable majorities in the Centre. However, an analytical assessment of this kind helps a responsible government to understand the public opinion in this regard.

As for the institutionalization of the mechanisms of control, a large number of suggestions have been made about how President's Rule can be avoided, and if imposed, controlled effectively. Parliament's most effective contribution in this regard was the Constitution of Committees of MPs to monitor the working of the President's Rule in the State. The idea was first mooted in the Punjab debate and it was incorporated in the PEPSU Legislation (delegation of powers) Act, 1953 when a Committee of Parliamentarians drawn from both the Houses and the State concerned was formed. Inevitably, the Constitution of the committee was altered so as to include members of Parliament, other than those from, the concerned State. During the Orissa proclamation, the mandatory inclusion of members from the State concerned was also dropped and a plea was made for a committee of Parliament taken as a whole[53].

The Committee now reflects, in size and shape, the political complexion of the Parliament itself. It is composed of various parties, and helps to cool down party spirit by promoting a strong corporate sense. This helps consideration of questions on their merit rather than on party line.

The meeting of the Committee is presided over by the Minister for Home Affairs. The Governor accompanied by the Chief-Secretary generally attends the meeting, giving a resume of the work done in the State during Presidents' Rule. The Committee was often ignored and in the debate on Kerala in 1964, a request was made for a genuine consultation with the committee. In the same debate, the significant point made by L.M. Singhvi that the power to legislate for the State should remain with the Parliament rather than the President was lost in the debate which concerned itself with political diatribe rather than constitutional solutions[54]. The Committee structure was stage-managed by the ruling party. H.V. Kamath proposed that the President should be mandated to consult the Committee before enacting legislation[55]. This suggestion was defeated. In order to make the Committee meaningful, it is necessary to define its status and functions and to invest it with Parliamentary privileges which enable it to function on behalf of Parliament. If the Parliament does not take such steps immediately, it will be leaving a large area of the administration outside its supervision.

The general trend of most debates was to treat institutional innovations with suspicion. This was understandable since various otherwise seemingly neutral institutions of the Constitution had, over the years, been subjected to manipulative use. The Committee was a useful suggestion. Its utility and efficacy has been diluted by the presence of the majority party's M.Ps and the fact that the Committee has been given a consultative role only. There is little that members can do. The affairs of the Parliament are stage- managed by those who have comfortable majorities in the Parliament. Debates on Presidents' Rule are not punctuated by a consistent intense concern. They merely fade in and fade out without any appreciable impact on the concerned State. The deplorable State of affairs has been aptly summed up by Rajeev Dhavan while elaborating the true role of the Parliament vis-a-vis Article 356.

> Parliament's role has been exactly what one expected it to be. Parliament expresses its anxiety but could not exert its will. With subdued passion, it has complied with the constitutional duties it has been asked to undertake by approving presidential proclamation of President's Rule. This has not been done happily; but with reservations, analysis, symbolic expressions of concern and by the use of some weak institutional control[56].

The mechanisms designed to enforce accountability are the products of an era when this problem was not quite significant. Today, the problem has grown very big and complex and is subject to multiple pressures of varying intensities, with the consequence that the conventional tools of accountability enforcement are proving to be distressingly weak and ineffective. At this juncture Shriram Maheswari observed:

> Parliament, as presently constituted, is not match for the executive... it follows... that classical mechanisms to keep the executive under control are found to be insufficient and inadequate. The fact is that the power of the present executive has enormously expanded[57].

Therefore, to prevent the scuttling of Parliamentary power by the executive as far as Article 356 is concerned, it is suggested that if a proclamation is issued, it must be deliberated upon by the Parliament, viz., if any State is placed under Article 356, the Central Government should be constitutionally bound to seek Parliamentary approval, irrespective of whether it remains in force for less than two months, or has lapsed or has been reissued or revoked. The members of the Parliament should not be denied under any circumstances, an opportunity to deliberate on the merits or otherwise of such a drastic decision.

Moreover, in compliance with the wishes of the Supreme Court in the Bommai case,[58] the Centre should not take the liberty of dissolving the State Legislature without obtaining the consent of the Parliament. It means that the application of Article 356 should be preceded by a discussion in Parliament and only after its approval it should be applied. This will have three salutary effects:

1. The country will come to know the reasons for action.
2. The State Government or party gets an opportunity to explain its conduct and defend itself.
3. The proceedings also facilitate the judicious exercise of its political predilections by the State electorate[59].

In this context, the proclamation and revocation of President's Rule in Bihar in 1999 becomes quite relevant.[60] The

Government was forced to revoke the proclamation since the ruling coalition had reason to believe that the proclamation would not be passed by the Rajya Sabha because of the numerical strength of the Congress party and other opposition groups. However, it is important to note here that this was not the first instance in which the ruling party at the Centre had lacked majority in the Rajya Sabha. The arithmetic in the Rajya Sabha was more or less the same in 1977 and 1980 when mass dismissals were made. Nevertheless, the respective ruling party could tide over this problem. Bihar (1999) was the first case of the revocation of Presidents' Rule although the emergency provision of the Constitution has been invoked in hundred cases. This has to be attributed wholly to the Bommai case verdict to the effect that it was not possible to take any irrevocable or irreversible action till the Parliament has approved the proclamation that the Legislature is to be suspended and that the order of dissolution is to be issued only after the Parliamentary approval.

This incident indicates the fact that it will no longer be easy for the Centre to contemplate dismissal of a State Government if the ruling party does not enjoy the confidence of both the Houses of the Parliament. Even though the ruling coalition has a majority in both the Houses we may not expect the coalition partners to having same opinion as happened in Bihar 1999. The different parties in the coalition may view a particular President's Rule according to the perception of loss or gain, pulls or counter pulls and conveniences. Therefore it is not likely that all the partners in the coalition would come out with whole hearted support. Till now, however it was the likelihood of judicial review that led to a restraint, even though only partial. In future, Parliament with all imponderables (given the line-up in the Lok Sabha and the differing political complexions of the two Houses) will serve as a decisive check against Centre's recklessness. Further, in the days of coalition politics, it is very difficult to get passed a proclamation of President's Rule in any State approved by both Houses of Parliament within a stipulated period of two months. Passions have always run high over Article 356, but the Congress party had, all through its years of comfortable ascendancy, no reason to believe that Parliament would actually exercise a power of scrutiny. In today's more fragmented political milieu, that can no longer be taken for granted. A certain degree of zeal in the exercise of Parliamentary scrutiny is an integral part of current realities.

However, the present mode of functioning of the Parliament brings to fore the fact that irrespective of the correctness or otherwise of the use of Article 356, the government at the Centre can get away with dismissing a State Government, provided it has the requisite majority in both Houses of Parliament, thus undermining the very essence of the Article. Here it is submitted that if a particular President's Rule declared by the government is not passed by the Parliament, it should be made a convention that the government which has declared the disapproved proclamation should resign. All political parties should whole-heartedly come forward for such a political renovation.

Another valuable suggestion is that the Parliament must create a special constitutional mechanism and procedure to deal with ratifying President's Rule and overseeing it[61]. At present the Parliament's debate on President's Rule is quite inadequate. It is also true that overseeing of President's Rule by Parliament is virtually non-existent. In this context, it is also submitted that Parliament's debate on President's Rule should be separated from Parliamentary debate on other matters, since it is a high potential power with far reaching consequences. The debate on President's Rule should not be on party lines. A free and secret ballot is an essential Constitutional requirement. A fair and balanced committee to oversee the President's Rule should be constituted and it must bring out periodic reports. But, perhaps, the most effective remedy may be evolved if all major political parties in the Legislature put their heads together and take a common stand against the increasing misuse of the provision by the executive. Unless a sincere attempt is made in this direction, the disease may escalate and ultimately reduce the Legislature to a non-entity.

These measures, if brought into operation through necessary amendments, will surely provide members of Parliament with a forum to air their views and ponder over the gravity and consequences of the excesses and misuse perpetrated by the government in the name of the failure of constitutional machinery in a particular State. The ensuing discussion and debate will deter the Central Government from going in for unilateral governance of the country and restore, to a certain extent, the authority of Parliament over the government and to that extent these suggestions strike a positive note.

References

1. J.R. Siwach, *Politics of President's Rule in India* (Shimla: Indian Institute of Advanced Study, 1979) 437.
2. *Power in a democratic society requires control and the greater the power the more the need for control. How to wrest power sufficient to the purpose in view and maintain adequate controls without crippling authority is one of the historic dilemmas of popular government.* (See L.D. White, *Introduction to the Study of Public Administration,* 4th ed. (New York : Macmillan, 1957) 495.
3. In the original Article a period of six months was provided as the period of duration of the proclamation.
4. So far as the House of Peoples is concerned, its approval within a period of first two months can be kept in abeyance if, either it has already been dissolved or if its dissolution takes place within this period.
5. It is theoretically possible for a proclamation of emergency to continue in force without the approval of the House of the people for a maximum period of nine months approximately (see Parameswara Rao, *The Role of Parliament during Emergency, Journal of Constitutional and Parliamentary Studies,* 1.2 (1967):55.
6. *S.R. Bommai v. Union of India,* A.I.R 1994, SC 1918.
7. The operation of proclamation of Emergency under Article 352 and 360 does not require the periodic approval of Parliament. The limitation of duration under Article 356 is understandable in view of the nature of the emergency contemplated in Article 356, which is different from the one provided for in Articles 352 and 360. (See Parameswara Rao 56).

8. M.P Jain, *Constitutional Law of India*, V ed (Nagpur: Wadhwa, 2003) 800
9. The 48th amendment inserted a new provision in clause (5) of Article 356, which, *provided that in the case of proclamation issued under clause (1) on 6 October 1983 with respect to the state of Punjab, the reference in this clause is to any period beyond the expiration of two years.*

   59th amendment Act was enacted for making certain changes in regard to the proclamation of emergency in Punjab and to the duration of President's Rule in the State. On reconsideration, the government decided that the special powers in regard to the proclamation of emergency in Punjab as envisaged in the said amendment is no longer required. Accordingly, the provisions to clause (5) of Article 356 and Article 359A of the Constitution have been omitted.

   The 64th amendment was made in order to provide for the extension of the President's Rule in the state of Punjab for another six months as the situation there was not favourable for holding Assembly elections. The amendment has added a new proviso after clause (4) in Article 356, which has substituted the words *three years and six months* for the words *three years and also provide that the conditions laid down in clause (5) shall not apply to the proclamation issued under clause (1) of Article 356 on II May 1987 with respect to the state of Punjab.*

   The 67th amendment has extended the period of President's Rule in the state of Punjab for a further period of six months. Accordingly, it has substituted the words *four years* for the words *three years and six months.*

   The 68th amendment amends clause (4) of Article 356 so as to further extend the period up to a total period of five years.
10. *NCRWC* see *http:/lawmin.nic.in/ncrwc/finalreport.v.1.htm.*
11. Asoka Kumar Sen, *The Parliament and Proclamation of Emergency, The Constitution and the Parliament in India,* ed. S.L. Shakdher (Delhi: National, 1976) 445.
12. *Alladi Krishna Swami Ayyar observed that "immediately after the proclamation is made, the duty is cast on the President to place it on the table of the House. It is to last only for a temporary period. Thereafter the parliament is in a position to judge the situation in the particular part of the country" I have no doubt that not merely the conscience of the representatives of the State concerned but also the conscience of the representatives of other units will be quickened*

and they will see to it that provision is properly worked (see CAD Vol. IX 151). Another stalwart S.L. Saksena stated in the same vein: *personally I feel that the powers given in the Article 278 are far too sweeping. I am glad that the ultimate authority lies with the Parliament and therefore we cannot say that these articles nullify the entire autonomy of the state. That of course is a very important safeguard, because, after all has been done, ultimately the Indian Parliament remains a sovereign body and the final authority responsible for the administration of the province.* (See Ibid. 142-43). T.D. Bhargava, another member, also expressed satisfaction with this arrangement. He said: *Parliament will decide whether the action of the cabinet was correct or not, and if Parliament agrees, then it means that the representatives of the particular state are there, and if they approve the action of the Cabinet, I do not see what possible objections can be taken.* (See Ibid. 169).

13. See The Constitution of India, Articles 356 and 357. See also the observations to this effect in *Bijayanda Patnaik v President of India* AIR 1974 Orissa 52 and *State of Rajastltan v Union of India,* AIR 1977 SC 1361.
14. Though Parliament was in session when Kerala was put under President's Rule in 1959 and 1965, the Centre placed the matter on the table of the House only after many days. In the first instance the proclamation was issued on 31 July 1959 but it was placed on the table of Rajya Sabha on 10 August 1959. When the members drew attention of the government to the fact that the proclamation should have been placed on the table of Parliament the day it was issued, because the Parliament was in session, G.B. Pant, the then Home Minister replied that it was not necessary to do so. He said that it can be done on any day, and the only limitation being that it must be approved by both the Houses of Parliament within a period of two months from the date of its issue. (See R.S.D., Vol. XXVI, Part I, Col. 93, 1959). This practice was again resorted to in Kerala in 1965. The practice provoked K. Damodaran to say that the government has failed in not only maintaining democracy in Kerala but also in safeguarding the rights of parliament as if the only duty of parliament was to okay a *fait accompli* (See RSD V.LII, No. 8, Col. 1679, 1965). Similarly the proclamation may not be placed on the table of the parliament on the first day of its session. For instance, when the proclamation imposing

President's Rule in Rajasthan was issued on 13 March 1967, the parliament was not in session. Its session started on 19 March 1967, but on that day the proclamation was not placed on the table of Rajya Sabha. When Bhupesh Gupta raised an objection in this connection, M.C. Chagla, the then leader of the House contended that *there was no obligation on the government under the constitution to lay the proclamation on the table of the House on the opening day.* (For more details see J.R. Siwach 18-19)

15. M.N. Kaul, and S.L. Shakdar, *Practice and Procedure of Parliament,* 3rd. ed., Vol. II (New Delhi: Metropolitan Books, 1972) 534-35.
16. See *Bijayananda Patnaik v President of India,* AIR 1974 Orissa 52. See also *Sunderlal Patwa v Union of India,* AIR 1993 M.P. 214.
17. This grave lacuna in the law which strikes at the very root of the concept of Parliamentary check has prompted a few learned judges in the Bommai case to express concern and to devise means to soften the blow. While Sawant, J. and Kudip Singh, J. boldly asserted that the President is barred from performing irreversible actions like the dissolution of the legislature prior to Parliamentary approval of the proclamation, Jeevan Reddy, J. and Agarwal, J. went one step further and held that in the event of Parliament withholding its approval to the proclamation *status quo ante* would be restored. (See *AIR 1994 SC 1918).*
18. In 1967, President's Rule was imposed in Rajasthan for forty four days, In 1970 it was imposed in U.P. for eighteen days. In 1990, President's Rule was imposed in Karnataka for just eight days.
19. A.K. Pandey, *Centre's Obligations and Article* 356 *of the Indian Constitution, Academy Law Review 20 (1996) : 219.*
20. The first two courses of action were followed in Orissa in 1971 and the second course of action was adopted in Bihar in 1972. Whereas, the third one was put into practice in the case of Kerala in 1965. In Orissa, President's Rule was imposed on 11 January 1971 and the Assembly was suspended. The proclamation was revoked on 23 January 1971 and a fresh proclamation was issued on the same day, which dissolved the Assembly. This time President's Rule continued till 22 March 1971, that is, for two months, after which it automatically came to an end, because it was not

placed before the parliament for approval. Then on 23 March 1971 the third proclamation was issued. It continued till 2 April 1971 and came to an end on that day when the new ministry of Biswanath Das assumed office. This shows that three proclamations were issued successively one after the other without placing them before Parliament. In Bihar, President's Rule was imposed on 9 January 1972 which lapsed on 8 March because it was not placed on the table of Parliament. As soon as it ceased to operate, a fresh proclamation was issued in its place on 9 March 1972. In Kerala, the Presidential proclamation was made on 10 September 1964 and was approved by the Lok Sabha on 23 September 1964 and by the Rajya Sabha on 30 September. This was revoked and a fresh proclamation was issued. (For detailed discussion See J.R. Siwach 24-27).

21. *NCRWC, A Consultation paper on Article 356 of the constitution, at http://lawmin.nic.in/ ncrwc/final report v.1. htm.*
22. Malcohn Smith and Lius Come, *The Power of President during Crisis,* referred to by J.R. Siwach, *Emergency Control Mechanism and Failure of Constitutional Safeguards, Journal of Constitutional and Parliamentary Studies* 12 (1978) : 375. This aspect has been dealt with by justice B.P. Jeevan Reddy in the Bommai Case (See *AIR 1994 SC 2091).*
23. Christopher Hollis observed : *Parliamentary government has already very largely perished. The member is the obedient servant of the party machine. He tramps into the division lobby voting for or against he knows not what on subject upon which as a general rule no opinion save that of the specialist is of least value...As things are now, it would really be simpler and more economical to keep a flock of tame sheep and from time to time to drive them through the division lobbies in appropriate numbers"* (See J.C. Johari, *Major Modern Political Systems,* (Jalandhar : Vishal, 1996) 226-227.
24. Jennings, Sir Ivor, *Parliament,* II ed. (New York: Cambridge University Press, 1961) p.179.
25. *Ibid* . 181.
26. During Nehru's Prime Ministership within the Congress itself there was a vocal section which performed the role of an opposition. Mahavir Tyagi, R.K. Sidhwa and Acharya Kripalani were among members who never missed an opportunity to criticise the government. The ruling party under Nehru tolerated criticism by its own members. (See

Subhash C. Kashyap, *50 Years of Opposition, The Hindu,* 22 July 1997).

27. Issues like Britain's entry in to the European Economic Community, Abortion Laws, Capital Punishment, Divorce, Censorship of Theatres etc are some of the examples. (See. Jain R.B., *Executive Accountability to Parliament, JCPS,* 15 (1981) : 67.
28. Syamasundaran, *Debates in Parliament, The Hindu,* 11 August 1999
29. *htt://alfa.nic.in/lsdeb/ls13*
30. Adam Tomkins, *Government Information and Parliament: Misleading by Design or by Default?, Public Law* (1996): 484.
31. Every scrap of advice which led to the imposition of President's Rule should be revealed to the people. Our rulers cannot abuse the Constitution and use official secrecy to hide the extent of their unconstitutionality (Rajeev Dhavan, *But who is the Governor, anyway, The Indian Express,* 5 May 1989).
32. S..P. Sathe, *Right to Know* (Bombay : N.M. Tripathi, 1991) 2.
33. (1981) Supp. SCC. 87.
34. *The Hindu,* 14 May 1997.
35. See Subhash C. Kashyap, *50 Years of Opposition, The Hindu,* 22 July 1997.
36. Shafi Rahman *'An Uncommon House, India Today,* March 2008.
37. *See Union of India v. Association for Democratic Reforms, (2002) 5 Scc 294. See also people's Union for Civil Liberties v. Union of India (2003) 4SCC 399.*
38. Rajeev Dhavan, *President's Rule in the States* (Bombay: N.M. Tripathi, 1979) 165-175.
39. Michael Rush, *Parliament and the Public* (London: Longman, 1976) 97.
40. *Lok Sabha Debates (LSD)* 6 May 1965, Col. 1355.
41. "In my opinion" he said, "*a constitutional crisis happens only when there is no confidence against a ministry, then ... there are other parties and the leaders of other parties have to be called, and they are to be given a chance to form a government. If they are not able to form a government and if either the Governor or the Crown in authority finds that there is no possibility of running the administration then and then only, there is a constitutional crisis*". (See *LSD,* 19 November 1954, Col. 434).
42. *LSD,* 25 February 1991, Col. 725.
43. *Rajya Sabha Debates (RSD),* 25 March 1953, Col. 2147.

44. In the Lok Sabha A.K. Gopalan observed: "*The practice in Travancore Cochin, pepsu and Andhrapradesh has shown that where it (Congress) was helping others, there had been a ministry, but if other parties came together and form a ministry, there could be no ministry. So it was either the Congress ministry or no ministry at all*" (*LSD*, 29 March 1956 Col. 3790).
45. *LSD*, March 1976, Cols. 95-250.
46. *LSD*, 25 February 1991, Col. 251.
47. *LSD*, 25 February 1991, Col. 251.
48. *http://alfn.nie.in/lsdeb/ls U/ses 3/c 051296. htm.*
49. *See LSD*, 4 March 1991
50. *The Hindu*, 26 February 1999. In the same debate Chandra Sekhar pointed out that if law and order were to be made the criterion for imposing President's Rule, then few State government would be safe. Every body, he pointed out, knew what was happening in Mumbai and in the North-East, violence had become endemic. Did this mean that the governments there should be dismissed, *(ibid)*.
51. *LSD*, 23 September 1964, Col. 3346.
52. See *The Indian Express*, 4 March 1991.
53. For more details see Shriram Maheswari, *Presidents' Rule in India* (Delhi: Macmillan, 1976) 142-47.
54. *LSD*, 24 September 1964, Cols. 3532-33.
55. *Ibid.* Col. 14049-54.
56. Rajeev Dhavan, 175
57. Shriram Maheswari, *Political Control over Executive Department in India, Philippine journal of Public Administration*, 25(1980): 161.
58. The Bommai judgments argue forcefully that if the presidential proclamation fails to obtain Parliamentary approval with in a stipulated period of two months, the government dismissed under Article 356 would stand reinstated and the Assembly revived. As Justice Jeevan Reddy put it : "*Disapproval or non approval means that the Houses of Parliament are saying that the President's action was not justified or warranted and that it shall no longer continue In such a case, the proclamation lapses, i.e. ceases to be in operation at the end of two months – the necessary consequences of which is that the status quo ante revives ... The dismissal of a government can not be equated to the physical death of a living being. There is no irrevocability about it. It is capable of being revived and it revives. Legislative*

Assembly which may have been kept in suspended animation also spring back to life" (AIR 1994 SC 1918).

59. Thiru Vengadam, *Agenda for the new Government, The Hindu,* 24 March 1998.

60. The opposition parties had insisted that it should be got out of the way at the earliest. The government simply responded to the opposition pressure, and exercised its constitutional obligation of getting the resolution approved by the Lok Sabha. Afterwards, the government tried to mobilise support for the resolution in the Rajya Sabha and when that did not materialise it made its assessment and took the decision to revoke President Rule.

61. Rajeev Dhavan, *A Blow Against Federalism, The Hindu, 7* February 1991.

Chapter 8

Safeguards Against Abuse of Article 356: The Courts

The Constitution of India right from its inauguration did not explicitly provide for nor did it exclude judicial review of President's power under Article 356.' The 38th Constitutional amendment enacted in the year 1975 placed the question of 'satisfaction' of the President in declaring emergency beyond judicial scrutiny. It added a new clause (clause 5) to Article 356 which reads:

> Notwithstanding anything in this Constitution the satisfaction of the President mentioned in clause (1) shall be final and conclusive and shall not be questioned in any court of law ![1]

Thus the amendment wanted to make sure constitutionally that the issue of legality of the proclamation of emergency was a political question and non-justiciable and hence beyond the purview of judicial scrutiny. This aspect has been seriously dealt with at length by a noted constitutional authority, N.K. Jayakumar.[2]

The 1975 finality clause was done away with in the year 1978 through the 44th amendment by the Janata government under the Prime Ministership of Morarji Desai. So after the 44th amendment the original position continues as regards the jurisdiction of the Court to judicially review this extraordinary power granted to the President under Article 356 of the Constitution of India. In State of Rajasthan v. Union of India the Supreme Court held:

> President's satisfaction would be open to judicial review only in those exceptional cases where on facts admitted or disclosed, it is manifest that it is *mala fide* or is based on wholly extraneous or irrelevant grounds[3]

In Sunderlal Patwa v. Union of India[4] the Jabalpur bench of the Madhya Pradesh High Court struck down the imposition of President's Rule in M.P. in 1992 on the ground of malafide and ordered the revival of the dissolved Assembly and reinstatement of the dismissed ministry. The appeal by the Union of India against the M.P. High Court judgement had led to the Constitution of a nine member constitutional bench to dispose the case. This constitutional bench of the Supreme Court in a unanimous judgement upheld the imposition of President's Rule in the three BJP ruled States of M.P., H.P. and Rajasthan[5]. The Court did not, however, hold that the findings of the M.P. High Court was erroneous. The Court referred three previous instances of President's Rule in Nagaland (1988), in Karnataka (1989) and Meghalaya (1991) where the action taken by the President was unconstitutional but nothing could be done to undo what had already taken place. Thus the position is that the Court declared in unequivocal terms that the satisfaction of the President under Article 356 is open to judicial review if it is *mala fide*. The view that exercise of power under Article 356 is open to judicial review was first laid down by the Supreme Court in 1977 followed by the M.P. High Court in 1993 and reaffirmed by the Supreme Court in 1994 and 2006 and the Allahabad High Court in 1997and again by the Supreme Court in 2006. The judiciary in India has, thus, adopted the substantive review approach rather than total ouster approach or jurisdiction approach on this issue[6]. An attempt has been made in this chapter to scan and exmine the phenomenon of judicial review of presidential proclamations under Article 356 in the light of relevant case laws.

The power to issue President's Rule in the States has been challenged several times and the question of justiciability arose for consideration on sixteen occasions: in the Kerala High Court (1965), in the Punjab High Court (1968and 1971), in the Calcutta High Court (1971 and 1973), in the A.P. High Court (1974), in the Orissa High Court (1974) in the Supreme Court of India (1977), in the Karnataka High Court (1989) in the Guwahati High Court (1988 and 1991), in the M.P. High Court (1993), in the Supreme Court (1994), in the Allahabad High Court of U.P. (1992 and 1997) and finally in the Supreme Court (2006). To get a clear understanding of the gratifying role of the judiciary, a brief analysis of the cases is highly warranted.

1. K.K. Aboo v. Union of India[7]

In this first case the Kerala High Court considered the legality and constitutionality of the Presidential proclamation of dissolving the Kerala Legislative Assembly after elections in 1965 without giving a chance to the Assembly to be convened. On behalf of Aboo, it was first of all argued that: the Governor could not recommend the imposition of President's Rule when the State was already under the rule of the President. Secondly, that the Assembly could only be dissolved after it was assembled. This would have given the Assembly an opportunity to consider the situation. The third argument was that the court and not the Parliament should consider the validity of the Presidential proclamation. The last argument was that the Governor had acted *mala fide*.

The court refused to go into the constitutionality of the proclamation. Speaking for the court M. Madhavan Nair, J., held that the remedy lay with the Parliament and not with the Court. He observed:

> When the matter comes up before, it is open to Parliament to withhold approval. If the Parliament in its supreme wisdom, is not impressed with the constitutionality, the legality or even the propriety of the proclamation, it will not give its approval to it. It requires no exposition by this Court for such an action on the part of Parliament"[8]. The court went further and found that "the Governor had made a thorough enquiry as to the possibility of the formation of a constitutional government in the State before he

submitted his report to the President as to the situation concerned". It was further held that the President had ample material for his satisfaction before he promulgated the impugned proclamation dated 10 September 1964[9].

The question regarding whether President's Rule could be imposed when a newly elected Legislature was available to form the government, the court held that: The Article (i.e. 356) of the Constitution does not prescribe any condition for the exercise of powers there under by the President, except the satisfaction of the President "that a situation has arisen"[10].

As to the last question the judge made it clear that the Governor had not acted *mala fide* even if some political leaders have been preventively detained. The court also observed that President while acting under 356 exercised power in his own right and the only sanction against him was impeachment".

It is quite interesting to note that even in this first case of judicial review the court though evading jurisdiction was eager to consider the factual legitimacy of the proclamation. Consequently the petition was dismissed without any interim relief as prayed for by the petitioner and all grounds of challenge to the proclamation was struck down thereby upholding the constitutionality of the proclamation.

2. Rao Birendra Sing v. Union of India[12]

President's Rule was imposed in Haryana on 21 November 1967 and the Legislative Assembly was dissolved. The petitioner contended that he had a majority in the Legislative Assembly and hence President's Rule could not be imposed. It was also argued that while issuing the proclamation, the satisfaction of the President in fact meant Union Council of Ministers and, therefore, it was competent for the court to enquire whether the intervention was based on facts and circumstances which were relevant to the decision of the breakdown of the constitutional machinery in the State.

This case was also not different from the first in terms of judicial response. The court dismissed the writ petition challenging the proclamation for three reasons:

Firstly, the Court held that the President while exercising his power under Article 356, did not act on behalf of the executive of the Union but in a constitutional capacity and, therefore, the exercise of power by the President was not amenable to the jurisdiction of the Court.

Secondly, reconsideration of the proclamation being specifically vested by the Constitution in Parliament, excluded the jurisdiction of the court in this regard.

Thirdly, the Court had no jurisdiction to require disclosure of material forming basis of the satisfaction of the President. Here again, though the Court dismissed the petition and out rightly rejected all the relief sought by the petitioner it did not hesitate to state that there was sufficient material in the report of the Governor to show that administration of the State had been broken down[13].

3. Jyotirmony Bose v. Union of India.[14]

In this case the Calcutta High Court rejected a writ petition challenging the President's Rule issued on 19 March 1970, under Article 356. It was argued *inter alia* that in making the proclamation, the President should have acted in his discretion and not on ministerial advice. Rejecting this plea, the Court emphasised that in the matter of making proclamation under Article 356, the President acts as a constitutional head and must act as advised by the Council of Ministers. The court said, 'to say that the power given under Article 356 is a discretionary power to the President is wholly misconceived'

4. Gokulananda v. Tarpada.[15]

The scope of judicial review of presidential proclamation was again considered by the Calcutta High Court in the case referred to above. In this case also the court observed that Article 356 enables the President to make incidental and consequential provisions to be necessary for giving effect to the objects of the proclamation. The making of such provisions is a matter entirely for the subjective satisfaction of the President. The court held that 'the validity or legality of the incidental and consequential provisions contemplated by Article

356 (1) is not justiciable' because that is a matter entirely for the satisfaction of the President.

5. Inre Sreeramulu[16]

The scope of Article 356 was, however, considered in greater detail and depth in 1974 by the A.P. High Court. Here the Presidential proclamation was challenged on the ground that President's Rule was imposed in the State without exploring the possibility for the formation of an alternative ministry when the Chief Minister resigned under the instruction of the Congress high command.

Justice Chinnappa Reddy held that a Presidential proclamation issued under Article 356 is not susceptible to judicial review because the issue of the Presidential satisfaction under Article 356 is basically a political issue, the Constitution does not enumerate a situation where President's Rule can be imposed and there are no "satisfactory criteria for judicial determination" of what are relevant consideration for invoking the power under Article 356. Consequently the question is intrinsically political and beyond the reach of the courts.

While considering the question whether there are any legal limitations to the kind of action that can be taken under Article 356 of the Constitution the judge assured that the only limitation on the exercise of power under Article 356 is political limitation. The considerations which are relevant for action under Article 356 and weighing of these considerations appear to be clearly matters of political wisdom and not of judicial scrutiny. The judge made it clear that the wide discretion allowed to the President in this regard pointed to the faith reposed by the Constitution in politics, politicians and the people. The Court observed:

> "After everything is said and done, it is the people of the country who should resist despotic tendencies on the part of the President or the majority party in the Parliament and it is scarcely a matter for the courts"[17].

The main question was whether Court could interfere if they had some doubt as to whether the action of the President was based on considerations that were not relevant to the failure of the constitutional machinery in a State. Chinnappa Reddy presumably preferred courts not to go into this question. But he suggested that in any consideration that guide to the failure of the constitutional machinery in a State, the President's discretion must be relevant'[18]. Eventually it was pointed out by the Court that even assuming that there is limited judicial review there were no circumstances in the instant case not justifying President's proclamation. Eventually the petitions were dismissed.This again points to the inner urge of the reviewers to adjudicate.

It is significant to note at this juncture that it was in Sreeramulu that for the first time the yardstick of judicial review of administrative action was sought to be invoked to test the validity of a Presidential proclamation under Article 356. Though the response of the Court was the same as before the articulation of the justification was more convincing. It is the Head of the State that is entrusted with the discharge of the duty and the fact that it is the Parliament that is the final arbiter led to the inevitable conclusion that the court can never go into the merit of the proclamation issued by the President.

In a subsequent decision in Hanumantha Rao v. State of A P.[19] the A.P. High Court reached the zenith of abdication of judicial review. It held that Court cannot examine the appropriateness or adequacy of the grounds for the taking of a decision by the President, nor any bad faith can be permitted to be attributed to him. The Court must keep a "judicial hands off" in connection with this Presidential exercise of emergency power[20].

6. Bijayananda v. President of India[21]

The constitutionality and legality of the Presidential proclamation of 3 March 1973 in Orissa was examined by the Orissa High Court in the instant case. While rejecting the challenge of the imposition, the division bench of the Orissa High Court ruled that the Presidential proclamation is not justiciable on the following grounds.

1. The wide source of information as contemplated by the expression 'or otherwise' in Article 356(1);

2. the subjective nature of satisfaction;
3. the provision of Article 72(2) and 361(1) which preclude the court from testing the ground of satisfaction;
4. the provision for the Parliamentary approval for the continuance of the proclamation beyond two months from the date of its promulgation; and;
5. the emergency provisions under Article 352, 356 and 360 in chapter XVIII of the Constitution which render the satisfaction non-justifiable[22].

However, the Orissa High Court was not totally unaware of the consequences ensuing from Central interference in situations like those involved in the case before the Court. The Court observed that: "the stability of the contemplated ministry is not to be tested by delving into antecedent and contemporaneous conduct of the legislators.... but by the physical counting of heads in the House itself." The Court also criticised the conduct of the Governor in so far as he recommended President's Rule in the State without first calling Bijayanand to form the government. By this the Governor failed to honour the conventions prevalent in Great Britain. The Court suggested that, on the fall of a ministry, the Governor should automatically ask the leader of opposition to form the government.

An incisive analysis of these decisions reveals that the courts have given support to the Central government consistently. They have taken the position that they could not review the exercise of power by the President because of the non-justiciable nature of President's satisfaction or ouster of courts jurisdiction to enquire in to the ministerial advice to the President or by treating the circumstances as sufficient to justify the Centre's conclusion that there was a breakdown of constitutional machinery in the concerned States. The Kerala and Punjab High Courts took a very restricted view on the issue. Approving the proclamation, these Courts observed that they did not have any power to go into these questions at all. The Andhra Pradesh High Court, however, explained its stand on the basis of separation of powers. Justice Chinnappa Reddy pleaded for an alternative testing of the merits of the proclamation. The

Orissa High Court also followed the total ouster approach but Gati Krushna Mishra. J. in his judgment censured the Governor for not following political conventions which ought to have been followed. Thus, in all these cases before the various High Courts, it was made known that there could be no judicial review of Presidential proclamation although the reasons for reaching the conclusions varied. None of these challenges had come before the Supreme Court. The matter came up for consideration in 1977 before the Supreme Court in the State of Rajasthan v. Union of India.

7. State of Rajasthan v. Union of India[23]

A major break through in the legal battle of Article 356 came with the epoch-making decision of the Supreme Court in the Dissolution case. The facts of the case is briefly summarized as follows. In the Parliamentary elections of March 1977 the ruling Congress party suffered a massive defeat in nine States viz. Bihar, U.P., H.P., M.P., Haryana, Orissa, Punjab, Rajasthan and West Bengal. After the elections the Janata party came to power at the Centre. On 17 April 1977 the Union Home Minister wrote a letter to the Chief Ministers of these nine States asking them to advise their Governors to dissolve the respective Assemblies and seek fresh mandate. Further, the Union Law Minister in a broadcast said that the governments in the nine Congress ruled States had forfeited confidence of the electorate and that they seek the dissolution of the State legislature[24] and obtain a fresh mandate.

Six of these nine States viz. Rajasthan, M.P., Punjab, Bihar, H.P. and Orissa in their writ petition to the Supreme Court submitted that the Home Minister's letter and the radio broadcast of the Law minister constituted a clear threat of dissolution of the Assemblies and disclosed grounds which are *prima facie* outside the purview of Article 356 of the Constitution.

The Court rejected the objections and held that the defeat of the ruling party in a State at the LokSabha elections cannot by itself, without anything more, support the inference that the government of the State cannot be carried on in accordance with the provisions of the Constitution. But the present situation was wholly different. It was not a case where just an ordinary defeat had been suffered by the ruling party in a State at the elections to the Lok Sabha but there has been a total rout of its candidates which reflected a will of estrangement and resentment and antipathy in the hearts of people against the government which may lead to instability and even the administration may be paralysed. Therefore, this ground was held to be clearly a relevant one[25].

The Court rejected the contention that judicial review of Presidential proclamation was totally barred. Bhagawati and Gupta, J.J. held that: "merely because a question of political complexion, that by itself is no ground why the court should shrink from performing its duty under the Constitution if it raises an issue of Constitutional determination" merely because a question has a political colour, the Court cannot fold its hand in despair and declare "judicial hand off"[26]. Further, they formulated the scope of Judicial review as follows.

> "But one thing is certain that if the satisfaction is *mala fide* or is based on wholly extraneous and irrelevant grounds, the Court would have jurisdiction to examine it"[27].

The court was of the view that the case did not fall within this exception. The observations made by the court are of immense significance now. This case is significant not because the Court's verdict was any different from the earlier line of cases. In fact, the Court dismissed the case unanimously, but what is significant is the assertion of all the judges that a Presidential proclamation could be challenged if the exercise of power was "*mala fide*" or on "constitutionally or legally prohibited" ground or for "extraneous or collateral purposes"[28]. The verdict assumes significance in view of the fact that the impact of the observation of the court in the later development of the law was tre-mendous and overwhelming.

In A.K. Roy v. Union of India a Constitution bench of the Supreme Court observed that after the deletion of clause (5) by the 44th constitutional Amendment, which was in existence when the Rajasthan case was decided "any observation made in the Rajasthan case on the basis of the clause cannot any longer hold good".

After the Rajasthan case the question of judicial review of Presidential proclamation under Article 356 arose for consideration in the Gauhati and Karnataka High Courts. President's Rule was imposed in Nagaland on 7 August 1988 when eight month old Congress ministry headed by Hokisha Sema was reduced to a minority due to defections. There was a difference of opinion between Chief Justice Raghaur and Justice Hansaria[29]. The former held that the Union of India cannot be compelled to tender any information to the Court because of Article 74 of the Constitution. On the other hand, Justice Hansaria held that as the material which formed part of "other information" was not before the Court and as the same did not form part of the advice tendered by the Council Ministers under Article 74(1), Union of India should be given an opportunity to disclose the information to the Court. Justice Hansaria ruled that should the Union of India fail to give the "other information" the Court would have no alternative but to decide the matter on the basis of the matter placed before it[30].

8. Kanwaljit Singh v. Union of India.[31]

In this case the petitioner challenged the 64th constitutional amendment which imposed President's Rule in Punjab in May 1987 and extension there of and dissolution of Punjab Legislative Assembly in March 1988. The 64th Amendment was challenged on the ground that the resolution for extension of President's Rule could not be passed by the Parliament a month before its expiry as the Parliament was bound to consider the material placed before it at the time of passing the resolution for continuance of President's Rule.

It was held that 64th amendment of the Constitution extending Presidents Rule in the State of Punjab neither affects the federal structure of the Constitution nor destroys the democratic process. When the alleged inbuilt safeguard in Article 356 of the Constitution for the extension of the President's rule to the effect that emergency has to be declared and a certificate from the Election Commission has to be obtained and elections cannot be held, can be dispensed with for initial imposition of President's Rule and its continuance for one year.

The court held that the law and order situation may by itself be not a ground for imposition of President's rule but as disclosed by the facts reported by the Governor to the President and he being satisfied whose satisfaction is material, that a situation has arisen that the governance of the State in accordance with the provision of the Constitution was not possible, is sufficient to impose the President's Rule. In view of the situation depicted by the report of the Governor and admitted failure of the State Government to control the law and order situation in the State of Punjab, it cannot be said that satisfaction of the President was arbitrary or was for extraneous consideration. The court also rejected the claim of the petitioner that the report of the Governor was secured malafidely and for extraneous considerations in order to deprive the Akali party of its representation in Rajya Sabha. The court held that there is no personal *mala fide* against the President or the Governor. The bold assertion of the petitioner that the report was made for extraneous considerations, *mala fide or dehorns* the Constitution would not be sustainable. There is no material placed on record to infer so. *Bona fides* of the Governor are writ large for his impartial conduct to the effect that at the initial stages only the imposition of President's Rule was sought and the Assembly was kept under suspension. The facts that report carrying the opinion along with facts, though the opinion and facts are severable, would not be sufficient to infer legal *mala fide* or any other *mala fide*, either of the Governor with respect to report or of the President with respect to his satisfaction.

9. Arun Kumar Rai Chaudhary v. Union of India.[32]

This was a case against the continuance of Mulayam Singh Yadav as the Chief Minister of Uttar Pradesh. The petitioner prayed that a writ of *quo warrant* to be issued to the Chief Minister Mulayam Singh to show cause under what authority he purports to act as Chief Minister of Uttar Pradesh. It was also prayed that he might be ordered to vacate his office as Chief Minister of U.P. as he had no constitutional mandate to hold the said office and function as such. It is not disputed that Yadav was appointed by the Governor as Chief Minister of U.P. Subsequently on the advice of the Chief Minister the Governor dissolved the Legislative Assembly and a fresh election for constituting a new Legislative Assembly was ordered. It was argued that after the dissolution of the Legislative Assembly the Chief Minister and the Council of ministers ceased to continue and in that situation the President ought to have promulgated President's rule in the State of U.P under Article 356.

After observing the facts and circumstances, the court, however, held that the question came up for consideration before the Supreme Count in the case of G.N.R Rao v. Indira Gandhi and Thiru K.N. Rai Gopal v. M. Karunamidhi. Following these decisions the court held that after the Governor of the state of U.P dissolved the Legislative Assembly and directions were issued for holding fresh poll for constituting the Legislative Assembly, the Council of Ministers continues. Further, there is being no failure of constitutional machinery with in the meaning of Article 356 of the Constitution and the president need not promulgate President's rule in the State for carrying on functions of Government.

10. S.R. Bommai v. Union of India (Karnataka High Court)

Imposition of President's rule in Karnataka on 29 April 1989 and the dissolution of the Legislative Assembly based on the Governor's report and on "other information" was challenged before the Karnataka High Court. The full Bench held[33] that Presidential proclamation was justifiable. The court said the satisfaction of the President under Article 356 which is the condition precedent for the issuance of proclamation ought to be real and genuine and it should be based on relevant facts and circumstances. The scope of judicial scrutiny is therefore confined to an examination whether the disclosed reason bear any rational nexus to the action proposed or proclamation issued. The court may examine as to whether the proclamation was based on a satisfaction which was *mala fide* for any reason, or based on wholly extraneous or irrelevant grounds. In such a situation, the stated satisfaction of the President would not be satisfaction in the constitutional sense under Article 356. However, the court declined to decide the scope of Article 74(2) with reference to the question whether "other information" could be called for. The Court ruled that recourse to floor test was neither compulsory nor obligatory on the part of the Governor to conclude that the ministry had lost the confidence of the House.

Appeals were carried to the Supreme Court from the above judgments of the Gauhati and Karnataka High Courts.

11. Sunderlal Patwa v. Union of India[34]

After the demolition of the Babri Masjid at Ayodhya, President's Rule was imposed in U.P., M.P., H.P. and Rajasthan. Imposition of President's Rule in M.P., H.P, and Rajasthan was challenged in the respective High Courts. The High Court of MP departed from the earlier decisions and held that the Presidential proclamation is open to judicial review on the ground of illegality, irrationality, impropriety or *mala fide* or in short, on the ground of abuse of power. Here to determine justifiability, the court considered the ratio in the Rajasthan case. After considering the report of the Governor and contention of parties the court came to the conclusion that in his report recommending the dismissal of Patwa ministry and dissolution of Assembly the Governor failed to substantiate how the constitutional machinery has broken. The court observed that there was no evidence to show that the state Government had defied central directions issued to the state. The court further said that failure on the part of state government to protect the life and property of a few citizens in a few cities, as a result of sudden outbreak of violence, could not reasonably lead to the conclusion that the constitutional machinery had broken down. The Court held that in the instant case there was no material to infer that the State Government could not be carried on in accordance with the provisions of the Constitution or that the Constitutional machinery had failed. Therefore the Court ordered to restore the dismissed ministry as also the dissolved Assembly. The judgment of M.P. High Court is a "significant milestone in legal history" since it is the first case where the Court struck down a Presidential proclamation as unconstitutional[35].

12. S.R. Bommai and ors.v. Union of India[36]

Appeals from the decisions of the Gauhati, Karnataka and M.P. High Courts and the writ petitions filed in the Rajasthan and HP. High Courts, which were transferred to the Supreme Court were heard by a nine member constitutional bench of the Supreme Court[37]. This is perhaps the most important case till date on the issue of judicial review and justiciability of proclamation issued under Article 356. The general principles and guidelines which have been laid down in the Bommai case are examined and analysed in the following pages under nine broad headings.

1. Interpretation of Article 356

The correct interpretation of the expression in Article 356, "a situation has arisen in which the Government of the State cannot be carried on in accordance with the provisions of the Constitution" is a constitutional breakdown and impasse which cannot be remedied through ordinary means. Article 356 can not be invoked, the court said, in situations that can be remedied, that cannot create an impasse, that do not make governance of the State in accordance with the Constitution impossible. The Court further held that, except in urgent situation a warning should be issued to the errant State and the President should use all other measures to restore the constitutional machinery in the State before having recourse to this drastic power. This view is sound and well founded. "It gives effect to the intent of the founding fathers, takes into account the experience of actual operation of Article 356 in our country, pays due regard to the principles of federalism and Centre-State relations and provides a salutary and much needed check on the deep potential for misuse of Article 356"[38].

2. Scope and Extent of Judicial Review of Article 356

The Court also considered the vital question; whether the proclamation of the President's Rule under Article 356 was subject to judicial review.[39] The Court ruled that the validity of proclamation issued by the President imposing President's Rule is "judicially reviewable"[40] to the extent of examining whether it was issued on the basis of any material at all or whether the material was relevant or whether the proclamation was issued in the *mala fide* "exercise of power"[41]. The material may be either the report of the Governor or some thing else, but it must meet the new test. The court also held that even if some part of the material is irrelevant, the court cannot interfere so long as there is some part of the material which is relevant to the action.[42] This is taken as a further modification or rather dilution of judicial interference. However, it is now established beyond legal doubt that the Presidential proclamation under Article 356 is subject to judicial review if it is found to be *mala fide* or based on wholly "irrelevant and extraneous considerations".

The majority opinion in this regard has considerably widened the scope of judicial redress available in cases involving the use of Article 356. It establishes a new constitutional position[43] which makes a significant advance over the orthodoxy that has prevailed since the 1977 ruling of the Supreme Court in the Rajasthan case. The Constitutional position then had been rendered somewhat ambiguous by the introduction of the 38th amendment of clause (5) to Article 356. The clause was later deleted by the Janata government in 1978, through the 44th amendment.

3. Scope of Article 74(2)[44]

Yet another significant fact that now emerges is whether the apex Court could call upon the Union of India to disclose materials based on which the President had formed the requisite satisfaction in taking over the administration of a State by dismissing the popular ministry. The majority judgment said that "it does not bar the court from calling up on the Union Council of Ministers to disclose to the court the material upon which the President had formed the requisite satisfaction"[45]. As Jeevan Reddy and Agarwal J.J. put it, Article 74 (2) does not mean that the Government of India need reveal the facts to the Court. Hence, the limited provision contained in Article 74 (2) cannot override the basic provision in the Constitution regarding judicial review. "If any act of President is challenged in a court of law", they continued, "it is for the Council of Ministers to justify it by disclosing the material which formed the basis"[46] of the act/order. The material placed before the President does not thereby become part of advice. Advice is what is based upon the said material. Material is not advice.

Article 74(2) and section 123 of the Evidence Act cover different fields. It may happen that while defending the proclamation, the minister or the official concerned may claim the privilege under section 123. If and when such privilege is claimed, it will be decided on its own merit in accordance with the provisions of section 123.The position all along has been that though the Court cannot compel the government to produce the advice tendered by the Council of ministers to the President or the reasons there of, there is nothing to prevent the court to compel production of material upon which the advice or its reasoning was based. This position is now further confirmed.

Now the government cannot refuse to furnish reason behind its action. However, the court will not ask 'what advice tendered to the President, what deliberation or discussion took place between President and his ministers and how the ultimate decision was arrived at'.[47] The court will enquire what was the material on the basis of which the requisite satisfaction is formed and whether it is relevant to the action. And, conclusively, it would be enough for the court to see if there are some valid reasons for imposition. 'The implications are obvious. The centre's calculations will be exposed to the glare of publicity'.[48] Here, it is not out of place to mention that if this procedure is followed it will result in difficulties to the government to carry on the administration smoothly. In this context P.P.Rao observed:

> "Disclosure of Cabinet papers may not be in public interest. As a collective expression of judicial displeasure, the judgment is justified. But as a proposition of enduring value, it is likely to run into difficulties"[49].

4. "Or otherwise" in Article 356

In this case Sawant J. has cited with approval the observation of Sidhwa J. of the Lahore High Court who held that if the government did not "choose to disclose all the material, but only some, it is their pigeon, for the case will be decided on a judicial scrutiny of the limited material placed before the court and if it happens to be totally irrelevant or extraneous, they must suffer"[50]. Justice Hansaria in the Gauhati High Court adopted the same approach. Similar trend is reflected in the Padefield case where it was observed by Lord Upjohn that if no reason was disclosed in support of the decision the Court would assume that none existed. Jeevan Reddy J. was more emphatic. He held that if "the Union" of India does not indicate or state that any other information/material was available to the President or the Union Council of Ministers other than the report of the Governor "the Court" must hold that there was no other information before the President except the report of the Governor and that the word and other information received by me "were put in the proclamation mechanically"[51]. This is a welcome development deeply heartening to the founding fathers, especially H.V. Kamath who condemned the insertion of the expression "or otherwise" in the Article as a diabolic word.

5. Dissolution of the Assembly

As regards the stage when the power to dissolve the Assembly should be exercised, the apex Court held that it would be consistent with the scheme and spirit of the constitution - particularly in the absence of specific provision in the constitution expressly empowering the President to do so - to hold that the power of dissolution can be exercised by the President only after both Houses of the Parliament have approved the proclamation and not before such approval. "This is to ensure," the Court said, "Parliamentary control of executive action in the delicate area of Centre-State relation". Once the Parliament places its seal, the Court observed, further steps may be found necessary to achieve the purpose of the proclamation i.e. dissolution of the Assembly can be ordered. As Soli. J. Sorabjee points out appreciatively:

> The plain language of the provision does not impose any such requirement. The impelling consideration for reading in to the Article such limitation was the anxiety to place a check on the executive and also to ensure that grant of final relief does not become difficult if not in fructuous. Historical realism prevailed over literalism[52].

The ruling of the Court is sound and valuable and accords with the principles of Parliamentary democracy functioning in a federal set up. However, it does not make any qualitative change. Since the party in power commands a majority in the Parliament, more often than not, approval of the Parliament by a simple majority is not difficult to obtain. Further, the government could convene the Parliament as early as possible and get its approval before dissolving the Assembly and order early elections or wait till the ground is clear for their own party to face the election. The only advantage is that the Parliament will get an opportunity to deliberate on the proclamation and the opposition could expose the government in its true colours and in this way it may be possible, sometimes, to make the situation delicate for the Central government. This also gives the State government precious time to act. Probably it is because of this reason that the check created by clause (3) of Article 356 has not proved to be effective in practice as it ought to have been.

6. Article 365.[53]

This significant provision has escaped judicial attention until the decision in the Bommai case. According to Sawant and Kuldip Singh J J. Article 356 is more in the nature of a deeming provision"[54]. Whereas to Jeevan Reddy and Aggarwal J.J. the directions given under it must be lawful and their disobedience must give rise to a situation contemplated by Article 356 (1). Furthermore.

> It is not as if each and every failure *ipso facto* gives rise to the requisite situation. The President has to judge in each case whether it has so arisen. Article 365 says it is permissible for him to say so in such a case. The discretion is still there and has to be exercised fairly[55].

The interpretation placed by the Court on Article 365 will be a progressive and far-reaching check on any tendency to have recourse to this Article for imposing President's Rule even though the situation contemplated by Article 356 (1) has not arisen.

7. Determination of the Strength of the Ministry (Floor Test)

Another important question which was considered in Bommai case was the proper method of testing the strength of the ministry and to determine whether it has lost or still retains the confidence of the House. The Court held that a ministry's strength should be tested on the floor of the House which alone "is the constitutionally ordained forum" and not by the private opinion of any individual, be he the Governor or the President". This rule can be departed from only in an extraordinary situation where because of all pervasive violence a free vote is not possible in the House. Jeevan Reddy and Agarwal. J.J. also adverted to the importance of the Tenth Schedule to the Constitution the objective of which is to prevent and discourage "floor crossing" and defection[56].

Applying this principle the Presidential proclamation dissolving Karnataka and Nagaland Assemblies were declared unconstitutional by the majority. No floor test was held by the Governor in Karnataka and Nagaland before dissolving the respective Legislative Assemblies and the presidential proclamations were based on personal assessment of the Governors about the loss of confidence by the ministries in these states. Consequently the presidential proclamations were struck down. The court's decision is a salutary development. It is a notorious fact that some of the main players in the toppling game of President's Rule have been Governors of the state. The decision of the court, however, has become a water line of a ship in view of the formation of fresh Assemblies. This situation calls for fast and timely decision by the court in the area of basic structure of the constitution. The dissolution of the Meghalaya Assembly was held to be tainted with factual and legal *mala fides*.

The affirmation by the Court is very sound and pays due regard to the principles of natural justice and democracy and prevent the dismissal of democratically elected governments on the flimsy ground that the ministry has lost the confidence of the House. Now the Court established the principle that the loss of majority like the proof of majority should be established on the floor of the House. However, we cannot underestimate the aspect of power politics. In the world of power politics it is an undisputable fact that incumbency is the key factor which decides the outcome of floor test.[57] K. Ramaswamy's J.

dissenting judgment, that "A floor test may provide impetus for corruption and rank force and violence by musclemen or wrongful confinement or volitional capacity of legislators"[58] is worth remembering. As long as the rulers of mankind are unable to suggest a more objective and manageable alternative, however, floor test continues to be the sole practical means of establishing majority-with an exception made for the rarest of rare cases, covering virtual civil war condition.

8. Relief in Case of *Mala fide* Exercise of Power

The court also considered the question of what consequential direction should be issued on the quashing of the proclamation and whether those directions should also cover within their ambit of the reinstatement of the State Governments and revival of the Sate Legislatures. The Court observed that if the Presidential proclamation is held invalid "then notwithstanding the fact that it is approved by both Houses of Parliament, it will be open to the court to restore the status quo ante"[59] and bring back to life the Legislative Assembly and ministry. The Court said it shall be open to the Supreme Court and High Court to entertain the writ petition if it is satisfied that the writ petition raises the arguable question with respect to the validity of the proclamation. Such writ petition can be entertained both before the approval of the proclamation by the Parliament as also after such approval. The Court also held that in appropriate cases and if the situation demands it, the High Court/Supreme Court have the power by an interim injunction to restrain the holding of fresh elections to the Legislative Assembly pending the final disposal of the challenge to the validity of the proclamation but not in such a manner as to allow the Assembly to continue beyond its original term. But in every such case where such an order is passed the High Court / Supreme Court shall have to dispose of the matter within two to three months Not disposing of the writ while making such an interim order would create several complications because the life of the proclamation does not exceed six months even after the approval by the Parliament and in any event the proclamation can not survive beyond one year except in the exceptional situations contemplated by clause

(5)[60] which has already been referred to in the previous chapter. In the same way it is submitted that an interim injunction can also be granted against elections being held to the Assembly pursuant to the proclamation. This it can do to avoid a *fait accompli* and to prevent "the remedy of judicial review (from) being rendered fruitless"[61]. The Pakistan Judiciary has adopted a similar approach and granted full relief without any untoward consequences.[62] In this context, it may be pointed out that if the case is taken to the Court and if the Court disapproves (even though the Parliament approves), the Legislature should not be dissolved. Here one can see that the Legislature is being made subservient to the judiciary.

The observation and direction of the court is based on sound principle and in accordance with basic fairness and common sense. Judicial review in the absence of full and effective relief would be a futile exercise. The political significance of the decision is that it will act as a bar on motivated and arbitrary dismissal of State Governments by the Centre as happened in a number of cases in the recent past. The unseating of a ministry commanding a majority in the Assembly by applying Article 356 is a virtual dismissal through back door. Now that the courts could go into the circumstances of the dismissal and declare the act as unconstitutional leading to the declaration of status quo ante, the party in power at the Centre will think twice before embarking on the adventurous course of imposing President's Rule[63]. Thus one can say with candour that the rulings of the Court is sound and in tune with the objectives of the judicial safeguards.

There may be some difference of opinion amongst political scientists and constitutional experts on the question as to whether the Supreme Court should have gone to that extent of reinstating the dismissed ministry and reviving the dissolved Assembly. In this occurance, it is useful to quote V.Y.D. Raman thus:

> The Supreme Court's assumption of authority to not only revive the dissolved Assemblies to animation but also to postpone election in a State under Central rule has raised many eyebrows. Indeed, in no part of our Constitution, is

there reference to the extraordinary situation in which Supreme Court could order or delay election to the State Assemblies[64].

A similar view has been expressed by Ramaswamy. J. in the Bommai case. His dissenting judgment expressed the view that there is no express provision in the constitution to revive the Assembly dissolved under the presidential proclamation or to re-induct the removed government of the State. Interpreting the Constitution, it is impossible to fill the gap or give the direction to revive the dissolved Assembly or to re-induct the dismissed Government of the state into office.[65] In justification of the decision of the Supreme Court it can be said that by ordering that the Court has taken the judgment to its natural conclusion. Once the Court held that the ground on which the order of the President had been assailed were well founded, the Court could in fairness to the petitioner deny him the relief sought by him.

9. Secularism – A Basic Structure

The most hotly debated issue before the Supreme Court was the validity of the Presidential proclamations and the dismissal of the BJP governments in the State of Rajasthan, M.P. and H.P. There was complete unanimity in upholding these Presidential proclamations and the Court held that violation of any basic feature of the Constitution by a State Government is a valid ground for the exercise of Article 356. Secularism[66] being part of the basic structure of the Constitution, its violation will justify use of Article 356. Thus the apex Court reiterated secularism a basic and inalienable feature of the Constitution – a feature nobody has any right to violate. Sawant and Kuldip Singh J.J. reasoned:

> 'Religion cannot be mixed with any secular activity of the State. In fact, the encroachment of religion into secular activity is strictly prohibited. The state's tolerance of religion does not make it either a religious or a theocratic state. When the State allows citizens to practice or profess their religion, it does not either explicitly or implicitly allow

> them to introduce religion into non-religious or secular activities of the State.[67]

What constitutes secularism under the constitution is spelt out in the judgment of Jeevan Reddy and Aggarwal J.J. They make it very clear that:

> Under our constitution no party or organization can simultaneously be a political and a religious party.... If a party or organization acts and or behave by word of mouth, print or in any other manner to bring about the said effect, it would equally be guilty of an act of unconstitutionality. It would have no right to function as a political party.[68] It seem that 'in deciding the Bommai case the Supreme court has enunciated the judicial and moral principles on which the practice of secularism is to be assessed.[69]

After laying down this rule, the Court considered the material before the Centre in the cases under challenge. In justification of its decision, the Court considered the following materials before its consideration. First, the BJP manifesto on which the elections were contested and won in the three States which *inter alia* declared that "the party is committed to build Shri Ram Mandir at Janmasthan by relocating the super imposed Babri structure" and similar speeches by leaders of BJP were examined. Secondly, the judges also took into account the fact that some of the Chief Ministers and ministers belonged to the R.S.S. which was a banned organisation at the relevant time and also their inability to implement the ban on R.S.S., V.H.P etc. Thirdly, the exhortation by the B.J.P ministers in these three States to join the Karseva in Ayodhya on 6 December also formed part of the material. Fourthly, the act of public send off to Karsevaks and welcoming them on their return after the destruction of the Mosque was also considered. One BJP MLA in H.P. had publicly admitted his participation in the destruction. At least in two States, namely M.P and Rajasthan there were also atrocities against the Muslims and loss of lives and destruction of property and this too was taken note of by the judges.

After considering all these facts the Court came to the reasoning that there was enough material that the government of the State could not be carried on in accordance with the provisions of the Constitution.

The Court's decision in this respect has in a way "broadened the field of Presidential proclamation"[70] under Article 356 in as much as justification for such a proclamation can be based not on some concrete act of the State Government but upon the mere apprehension that it would not implement the order of the Central government. This decision has given a new dimension and a long rope to the Central government. The dictum as such has extended the ambit and width of the power to issue Presidential Proclamation under Article 356. In this context the observation of Sahay is quite significant and relevant. He pertinently pointed out:

> By making secularism a basic feature of the Constitution but taking a rather limited view of justiciability, the Court has left the Central Government, though in a much more sophisticated way than it has done so far. Whatever material placed before the Court, in the bar of public opinion it is well known that the dismissal of the three State Governments in which the BJP was in power was an unfair act intended to hide the Center's own shortcomings in preventing the demolition of the Babri Masjid[71].

A critical analysis of the decision could now be attempted. The verdict evoked mixed reaction among politicians, journalists and constitutional experts. While recording his resentment against the decision L.K. Advani observed that "the verdict was erroneous". He said that the Judiciary had no right to set itself as an "ideological ombudsman". There was no clear rational validity for the dismissal for the three BJP governments, while all other instances of the use of Article 356 before the Court had been overturned[72]. The CPI(M) unreservedly welcomed the judgment. Prakash Karat, CPM polit bureau member, described it as a "land mark verdict" which need to be widely published and disseminated and could serve as a weapon in future struggle against the politics of communalism.

"There is a fundamental point that the judgment makes", he pointed out, "secularism can only mean that religion cannot intrude into politics"[73]. As such the judgment could be "the basis for further enactment to strengthen existing provisions of law on the separation of religion and politics"[74].

Constitutional experts also took widely divergent views of the judgment. Soli, J. Sorabjee, the former Attorney General of India, welcomed the judgment. The learned constitutional commentator observed:

> The decision in Bommai case makes the high watermark of judicial review. It is a very salutary development and will go a long way in minimising Centre's frequent onslaught on the States who, as rightly pointed out, "are neither satellite nor agent of the Centre" and "have as important role to play in the political, social educational and cultural life of the people as the Union". However, there is a genuine concern about misuse by the Centre of Article 356 on the pretext that the State Government is acting in defiance of the essential features of the Constitution. The real safeguard will be full judicial review extending to an enquiry into the truth and correctness of the basic facts relied upon in support of the action under Article 356 as indicated by Sawant and Kuldip Singh[75].

While supporting the judgment F.S Nariman, a senior Supreme Court lawyer, expressed the view that the affirmation that secularism is a basic feature of the Constitution is a welcome development. This, he said, is the single most important aspect of the judgment. The definition of the concept is reasonable and would "serve as a good starting point" for further judicial refinement[76].

However, K.K. Venugopal, the former Solicitor General of India, was not entirely convinced of the merit of the judgment, which he finds as inconsistent in parts[77]. The same view was also taken by Prashant Bhushan, a legal expert, who too was unimpressed by the status accorded to secularism as a basic feature. "Socialism too is written into the Preamble to the Constitution" he pointed out. He further posed the question:

"Does this mean that government could be dismissed on the ground that they follow policies inimical to socialism? How long would the Central Government itself with its new economic policies, survive if that were to be the case?"[78].

Here it may be stated that the general principles and guidelines which have been laid down by the Supreme Court in this case will help to strengthen national unity and integrity, to sharply limit the constitutional power vested in the Central government to dismiss State Governments and to prevent the arbitrary and whimsical use of the power of the Governors in the name of exercising their discretionary powers conferred by the Constitution and conventions. Perhaps, the most remarkable contribution of the verdict is the affirmation that secularism being one of the basic features of the Constitution, any State Government pursuing un-secular policies would be acting contrary to the constitutional mandate rendering itself amenable to action under Article 356. No doubt, it sets an example and warning to the religion oriented political parties to go slow in introducing religious fundamentalist tendencies in politics for gaining ground. It is, indeed, a new precedent set by the Supreme Court which could checkmate the ugly fundamentalist tendencies in the country. As a whole 'the Bommai judgment is water shed, perhaps the most significant, in the evolution of an organic federalism in India that surely a break with the past.[79] The verdict is, thus, strong, sound, well founded, cogent and pays due regard to the principles of federalism, and secularism as enshrined in the constitution[80].

The detailed and progressive interpretation of the Article is now the law of the land and will remain so unless the majority judgment of a larger Supreme Court bench overrules and changes it. Bommai verdict is not an absolute guarantee against the misuse of the power. Indeed after the apex Court's decision the central executive made attempts to misuse the provision again and this has led to another legal battles in Allahabad Highcourt and the Supreme Court.

The imposition of President's Rule in UP in 1996 stirred up another legal controversy. In 1996 when elections were held to the Uttar Pradesh Legislative Assembly no party secured a majority to form the government. So, President's Rule was imposed in the State and this proclamation was subsequently approved by the Parliament. Against this imposition of President's Rule five petitions were filed in the Allahabad High Court. A two member bench delivered a split verdict on 11 November 1996 necessitating the referring of the matter to a three-member bench.

The Court unanimously held that the impugned Presidential proclamation dated 17 October 1996 re-imposing President's Rule in U.P. and subsequently approved by the Parliament was unconstitutional, issued in colourable exercise of power and was based on wholly irrelevant and extraneous grounds and therefore, could not be allowed to stand. Consequently the proclamation was quashed[81]. However, to avoid any crisis as a result to the quashing of the aforesaid proclamation, the Court, by applying the doctrine of prospective overruling, directed that the judgment shall come into operation only after the pronounced date for the resumption of political process in the State.

Even though the verdict quashing the Presidential proclamation was unanimous, the three judges cited different reasons in their respective judgments. B.M. Lal, J. observed that the Governor of U.P. was constitutionally not bound to invite the single largest party to form a government, in case, it did not have the confidence of the House. But at the same time he was constitutionally bound and obliged to explore all possibilities[82].

B. Brajesh Kumar J. ruled that there is neither any convention, nor any constitutional provision under which the leader of largest single party, not in majority, must be called to form the government except where the Governor was satisfied that it would have the support of any other party in minority and would enjoy the confidence of the House. He said that the period of President's Rule could not be extended beyond one year except in the situation prevailing under Article 356(5) of the Constitution and concluded that the re-imposition of President's Rule on 19 October 1996 was not a fresh proclamation but rather an extension of a proclamation that was already a year old[83].

The Supreme Court on December 20 stayed the High Court ruling and directed the Union Government and the Governor to take measures that would enable the continuity of political process in the State.

The Allahabad High Court verdict generated enormous political interest and constitutional debate in the country. The verdict had drawn attention to certain fundamental questions involving the nature and functioning of federal system in India and its constitutional basis, in view of the exercise of Article 356 and the power of the Governor and the Union Government to use it in what way. No doubt, the judgment would pave the way for more cordial and fruitful relationship between the Centre and the States.

Rameshwar Prasad and ors. v. Union of India

Again, dissolution of the Bihar Legislative Assembly in 2005 before the elected members taking oath also led to another legal battle in the Supreme Court in the above said case. In this landmark case the Supreme Court was called upon to pronounce its verdict on the validity of the Presidential proclamation and the dissolution of the Bihar Legislative Assembly without meeting at all. On behalf of the petitioner it was argued that Governor, Butasingh, recommended the dissolution of the Assembly on the basis of subjective satisfaction - without any material - that the parties were trying to cobble up a majority in the Assembly through tainted means, and that it would not lead to a stable government.[84]

The five member constitutional bench of the Supreme Court in a majority[85] judgment held that the dissolution of the Assembly was unconstitutional and illegal.[86] The Court said that the Governor's report was based up on unascertained facts and irrelevant and extraneous consideration. The court found that the Governor's recommendation to dissolve the Assembly only to forestall the formation of a government by another political party (on the presumption that majority was cobbled through unethical and illegal means) was a *mala fide* exercise of power. His reasoning that some members of the legislature were being induced with offer of money and other allurement would seem to be just his personal *ipse dixit* (perception or opinion) without any material to substantiate. Such matter under Article 356 of the Constitution could not be decided on a mere perception. 'The drastic and extreme action under Article 356 of the Constitution can not be justified on mere *ipse-dixit,* suspicion and whims and fancies of the Governor.[87] The court further pointed out that the way the Governor misled the Union council of ministers was 'destructive of the democratic system'. His action was 'drastic and extreme' and the 'court could not remain as a silent spectator watching the subversion of the Constitution', the court forcefully made it very clear.

The majority bench while admonishing the Council of ministers for recommending dissolution, said that 'the Governor may be the main player, but the Council of ministers should have verified the facts stated in the report of the Governor before hurriedly accepting it as a gospel truth as to what the Governor stated. Though the court held the dissolution unconstitutional, yet it expressed its inability to restore the dissolved Assembly because the electoral process had been set in motion before the arguments in the case could be concluded.[88]

Apart from the issue of judicial review and justiciability, the Court had to deal with certain allied legitmate questions touching upon judicial control of President's Rule. They are discussed below:

1. ***Whether the dissolution of the Assembly under Article 356 could be ordered to prevent the staking of a claim by a political party on the ground that it has obtained a majority by illegal means?***

The majority judgment laid down that the dissolution of the Assembly cannot be ordered to 'override the majority claim on the ground that the majority was cobbled by illegal and unethical means. The court observed that such a denial was contrary to the principle of majority as enshrined in the Constitution. It was of the view that the acceptance of such a proposition as a relevant consideration to invoke the exceptional power under Article 356 of the Constitution may open up a flood gate of dissolutions and has far-reaching, alarming and dangerous consequences. It may also be a handle to reject post election alignment and realignment on the ground of the same being unethical, plunging the country or the states to another election. This aspect assumes great significance in situation of fractured verdict and in the formation of coalition governments.[89] The Court also reminded that the extraordinary power under Article 356 is not to be resorted to for good government or cleaning of politics without any authentic material. The bench opined that cleaning of politics should be left to the opposition and ultimately the electorate'. The Governor is not an autocratic political ombudsman. If such power is vested in the Governor and or the president, the consequences can be horrendous.[90] The Court also rejected the contention that if Nitish Kumar had staked the claim with the support of break-away LJP MLAs, they would have incurred disqualification under the Anti-defection law. The Court held that this argument was an extraneous consideration, because under the scheme of our Constitutions, the decision with regard to disqualification is vested in the Speaker.

The rulings of the court is good and valuable since it has sharply limited the constitutional power vested in the Governor and the Union government to dissolve state legislatures for Partisan considerations. However, with all respect to the court, it may be pertinently pointed out that political morality is no less important than constitutional propriety. Political parties should not be allowed to get legal sanction for unprincipled, unethical, ugly and devalued and dehumanized politics in the name of safeguarding Democracy and the Constitution. The unholy alliances among parties were born out of brazen political opportunism, greed and lust for power. Hence the court should have better avoided this observation. In this context, K.G. Balakrishnan's J dissenting judgment, at the time largely ignored, when not disapproved of, had a prescient quality. He was of the view that:

> If by any foul means the government is formed, it cannot be said to be a democratically elected government. If Governor has got a reasonable apprehension and reliable

information that such unethical means are being adopted by the political parties to get majority, they are certainly matters to be brought to the notice of the President and at least they are not irrelevant matters, [91]

2. ***Whether it is permissible to dissolve Legislative Assembly before the Assembly met for the first time after its due constitution and members took their Oath?***

The majority judgment held that Assembly can be dissolved under Article 174(2) even before its first meeting is held as postulated by Article 172 of the Constitution. The court said that Assembly is duly constituted on the issuance of notification under section 73 of the Representation of the Peoples' Act. The court found, therefore, nothing wrong in dissolving an elected Assembly immediately after its due constitution, even before it was allowed to meet for the first time.

If holding of first meeting is held to be essential in such an eventuality, the court observed, the Governor will neither be able to appoint executive government nor be able to exercise power of dissolution under Article 174(2) b. Therefore, the full court implicitly agrees that 'if there are no claims, the Governor has no option but to dissolve the Assembly, even before it meets for the first time, and such dissolution would be valid'.[92] Further, it was also said that no where in the Constitution lays down that the dissolution can only be made after the first meeting of the legislature. They concluded that the Constitution did not postulate a live Assembly without an executive government. The court's observation in this regard is also realistic, pragmatic, constitutional and parliamentary in spirit.

3. ***What is the scope of Article 361 granting immunity to the Governor?***

Article 361(1) of the Constitution says that no Court can compel the President or Governor to exercise any power or to perform any duty nor can a court compel him to forbear from exercising his power or performing his duties. He is not amenable to the writ or directions issued by any court.

The court, however, was of the view that despite the stringent mandate of Article 361, the Court could determine the actions of the Governor on the touch stone of *mala fideness.* The court observed that the immunity granted does not, however, take away the power of the court to examine the validity of the action on the ground of *mala fides*. Even in the case where personal *mala fides* is alleged and established, it would not be open to the Governor to urge that the same cannot be satisfactorily answered because of the immunity granted. In such an eventuality, the court observed, it is for the respondent defending the action to satisfy the court either on the basis of material on record or even by filing of an affidavit. The bar is only against the power of the court to issue notice or making the President or Governor answerable. No doubt, the observation of the court is a welcome realization of the danger of the immunity granted under Article 361. By delivering this break-through observation, the court, once again, reminded that the actions and decisions of the Governor have to be non-political.

From the above analysis it is very clear that the epoch-making judgment is a major break through in the annals of judicial review of President's Rule. No doubt, the decision will act as a check and limit the scope of arbitrary action by the Governor and the Union Government in the matter of dissolving legislatures[93] . The dissolution of the Assembly by applying Article 356 is the virtual denial of the democratic right of the people to have a representative government. In the light of the verdict, it is hoped that, the Centre should apply its mind and think more than once before taking recourse to the extreme step of the dissolution of the Assembly. Thus the verdict is a scathing indictment of not only the Governor but also the council of ministers presided over by the Prime minister.[94] It is hoped that in future the Governor should also base his report on material evidence and will always permit the majority party to stake claim and how the majority was cobbled should not be the concern of the Governor. The decision, no doubt, is a blow to the arbitrary action of midnight dissolution.[95]

The Court's observation is significant in another perspective also. It has also drawn attention to the misuse of the office of the Governor and recommended a national policy for the appointment of Governors. The bench suggested that political parties debate and evolve a national policy on choosing a non-partisan Governor, with common parameters acceptable and applicable to all parties. The observation is realistic pragmatic and master minded and has great relevance in the context of current political situations.

The case is relevant from another point of view as well for it is the case in which the Court makes it very clear that Governor's action can be examined on the ground of *mala fides*. The court established the fact that the immunity granted to the Governor under Article 361 can also be reviewed by the Court to the extent of examining its constitutionality. The Court was of the view that while the Governor's authority to exercise his discretion can not be questioned in any court of law, whether such exercise is in keeping with the spirit of the Constitution can be reviewed.

In the final analysis, it seems that the 'apex Court's orders were vindication of constitutionalism, democracy and federalism and has far reaching impact on our parliamentary democracy.[96] The subsequent developments on the legal and political planes bear ample testimony to the legitimacy and potency of these decisions. It is to be noted that in all the subsequent proclamations the state legislatures were kept in a suspended animation as mandated by the Bommai case. The aborted attempt of the Union government to dismiss Mulayam Singh Yadav in U.P. in 2007 was also the result of the judicial norms evolved in the Bommai and the Rameshwer Prasad cases. Thus the panacea for the abuse of President's Rule lies in a judicious blend of activism and restraint commensurate with control the politically exuberant constitutional exercise.[97]

References

1. *The Constitution of India, Article 356* (5) which has been deleted by the 44th Constitutional Amendment Act of 1978.

2. The doctrine of political questions originates from an awareness of the institutional and functional limitation of the judicial process. The doctrine defies precise definition; though several versions have been offered by judges and jurists. Explaining the scope of the doctrine a judge of the U.S. Supreme Court observed: Prominent on the surface of any case held to involve in political question is found a textually demonstrable constitutional commitment of the issue to a coordinate political department; or a lack of judicially discoverable and manageable standards for resolving it; or the impossibility of deciding without an initial policy determination of a kind clear for non-judicial discretions; or the impossibility of a Courts undertaking independent resolution without expressing lack of the respect due coordinate branches of Government; or an unusual need for questioning adherence to a political decision already made; or the potentiality of embarrassment from multifarious pronouncements by various departments on one question [per Brennan, J. in Baker v. Carr 369 U.S. 186, 217(1962). (See N.K. Jayakumar, *Judicial Process in India: Limitations and Leeways* (New Delhi: A.P.H., 1997) 257-265.
3. *AIR 1977 SC 1361*. This decision was given before the 44th amendment **Act.**
4. *AIR 1993 MP* 214.
5. *S.R. Bommai v Union of India,* AIR 1994 SC 1918.
6. See Rajeev Dhavan, *Presidents Rule in the States* (Bombay: N.M. Tripathi, 1979) 126-158. See also Shivaraj B. Nakade, *Emergency in the Indian Constitution* (New Delhi: Cosmo Publication, 1990) 119-217.
7. *AIR 1965 Ker 229.*
8. *Ibid.*
9. *Ibid.*
10. *Ibid.*
11. *Ibid.*
12. *AIR 1968 P. and H. 441.*
13. *Ibid.*
14. *AIR* 1971 Cal. 122
15. *AIR* 1973 Cal. 233
16. *AIR 1974 AP. 106.*
17. *Ibid.* 111.
18. *Ibid.*
19. (1975) 2 *AWR* 277.
20. *Ibid.* 301.
21. *AIR 1974 Ori.* 52.

22. The Court hled that in sending his report to the President the Governor act directly and not with the aid and advice of the Council of ministers. Whether the Governor's report is *mala fide* or based on any extraneous facts cannot be questioned in the court of law under Article 356(1). The Court also held that the President's action under Article 356 could also not be challenged and that, proving that the President was acting *mala fide* was very difficult and was not made out in the case concerned. The aspect of objective determination of the satisfaction of the President was raised and ruled out for the first time in this case. In order to substantiate the non justiciability of the proclamation under Article 356 the Court relied on the non-justiciability of the other emergency provision. (See *ibid.).*
23. *AIR 1977 SC 1361.*
24. It was quite clear that if the suggestion was not acted upon, the Union government would invoke emergency powers under Article 356 and impose President's Rule and dissolve the State legislatures though this was not mentioned in the letter.
25. *Ibid.* 665.
26. *Ibid.*
27. *Ibid.* 663.
28. The Presidential proclamation under Article 356 had been outside the purview of judicial review till the decision in the Rajasthan case where in the Supreme Court while recognising that the satisfaction of the President was a subjective one which could be guided by political factors still stressed that the political colour of the question would not cause the court to declare a "judicial hands off". The scope of judicial review was narrowly constructed in the Rajasthan case has been expanded in Bommai case. (For a critical evaluation of the case see. (Alice Jacob and Rajeev Dhavan, *The Dissolution Case Politics at the Bar of the Supreme Court, Journal of Indian Law Institute,* 19 (1977).
29. (1982) 2 *Gauh 468.*
30. *Ibid.* 517.
31. *AIR* 1991 P&H. 55
32. *AIR 1992 All. 1*
33. *AIR 1990 Kart.* 5 (F.B) The Court followed the Rajasthan case.
34. *AIR 1993 MP.* 214.
35. D. Nagasaila, and V. Suresh, *Will the Supreme Court break new ground?, The Hindu,* 9 May 1993. The Court upheld the federal principles enshrined under the Constitution of India. The Court totally discarded the concept that presidential proclamation is a political decision and it could not be challenged before any

court of law. The Court also refused the doctrine of "Political Ticket" adopted by Supreme Court in the Rajasthan case.

36. *S.R. Bommai v. Union of India,* (1994) 3 SCC 1.
37. Separate judgements have been delivered by S.R. Pandyan, J. A.M. Ahamadi J. and K. Ramaswamy J.. Judgements were also delivered by Verma J. for himself and Dayal J. by Sawant J. for himself and Kuldip Singh J. and by Jeevan Reddy J. for himself and Agarwal J. The majority judgements are of Sawant, Kuldip Singh, Jeevan Reddy Agarwal and Pandyan J.J. The majority judgment constitutes the law of the land under Article 141 of the Constitution of India, (See *Ibid.* 2-3).
38. Soli, J. Sorabjee, *Decision of the Supreme Court in S.R. Bommai v Union of India : A Critique (1994)* 3 SCC (J) 11.
39. Justice Jeevan Reddy observed, *Regarding scope and reach of judicial review it must be said at the very outset that there is not and there cannot be a uniform rule applicable to all cases. It is bound to vary depending on the subject matter, nature of the rights and various other factors". (AIR 1994 SC 2075)*
40. Ahmadi J. showed the greatest sense of restraint, treating the President's decision as an almost purely political question. The learned judge said that since the President is not expected to record his reason for his subjective satisfaction it would be equally different for the Court to enter the political ticket. The opinion which the President would form on the basis of the Governor's report or otherwise would be based on his political judgement and it is difficult to evolve judicially manageable norms to scrutinise such political decisions. To do so, according to him, would be entering political ticket and questioning the political wisdom which the Court of Law must avoid. *(1994) 3 SCC 81-82).* Verma and Yogeshwara Dayal, J.J. also were in agreement with the above view.
41. *(1994) 3 SCC 93.*
42. *Ibid.* 268.
43. A judge being a part and parcel of society is invariably influenced by the compulsions and yearnings of society. These demands of society consciously and unconsciously influence the judgement which in rum reflect it in his judgement. (For more insight in to this topic (see Benjamin Cardozo, *The Nature of Judicial Process* (New Delhi: Universal Book Traders, 1921).
44. *Article 74* (2) clearly states that the question whether any and what advice was tendered by the ministers to the President "Shall not" be enquired in to by any Court.

45. *(1994) 3 SCC 80.* Justice K. Rameswamy observed: By operation of Article 74(2) only the actual advice tendered by the Council of ministers gets immunity from production and court shall not inquire into the question whether and if so what advice was tendered by the minister. In other words, the records other than the advice tendered by the minister to the President, if found necessary, may be required to be produced before the constitutional court *((1994) 3 SCC 182).*
46. *Ibid.*
47. Khanna H R, *Supreme Court Judgment on Article 356. AIR* Sept:1994 (J)
48. Noorani AG, *Constitutional Questions in India* (New Delhi: OUP, 2000) 282
49. See Sukumar Muralidharan and V. Venkatesan, *Article 356, For and Against: A Range of Reflection, Frontline, 1 April 1994:*120.
50. *Muhammed Shariff v. Federation of Pakistan,* 1988 Lah 725.
51. *(1994) 3 SCC 278.*
52. Soli. J, Sorabjee 24.
53. Where any State has failed to comply with or to give effect to, any direction given in the exercise of the executive power of the Union under any of the provisions of this Constitution, it shall be lawful for the President to hold that a situation has arisen in which government of the State cannot be carried on in accordance with the provisions of the Constitution.
54. *(1994) 3 SCC 104.*
55. *Ibid.* 273.
56. *Ibid.* 278.
57. The decline and fall of the Suresh Mehta ministry in Gujarat in 1996 reveals this. Here Suresh Mehta ministry won the confidence of the House amidst violence in the Assembly. One month later, many of the MLAs who had voted for Suresh Mehta started supporting the Shankar Singh Vaghela ministry.
58. *AIR 1994 SC 2004.*
59. (1994) 3 *SCC 298;* 149.
60. Khanna H R, *Supreme Court Judgment on Article 356, AIR* 1994 (Journal)
61. *Ibid* 149.
62. TheSupremeCourt of Pakistan by an unprecedented judgement set aside the President Gulam Ishak Khan's dismissal of the Nawaz Sharif government and the National Assembly and reinstated him. The tense judgment was delivered with a 10-1 majority on 26 May 1993. In the *obiter dicta* of the judgment the

Court charged the President for dismissing the elected government in a fit of anger. It was the first time in Pakistan's history that the Supreme Court had ailed against the Establishment. In the 46 years of Pakistan's existence, seven National Assemblies were dissolved but never was one restored. Significantly, the court also denied the care-taker government the right to appeal against the decision. (See *India Today,* 15 June 1993).

63. *A Landmark Verdict,* editorial, *The Hindu,* 14 March 1994.
64. . Raman V.Y.D, *Need for Judiciary to uphold Popular Sovereignty, The Hindu,* 15 November 1994.
65. *AIR 1994 SC 1918.*
66. An excellent exposition of secularism is offered by Jeevan Reddy and Agrawal J.J. "*While freedom of religion is guaranteed to all persons in India, from the point of view of the state, the religion, faith or belief of a person is immaterial. To the state, all are equal and are entitled to be treated equally. In matters of state, religion has no place. No political party can simultaneously be a religious party. Politics and religion cannot be mixed*". {AIR 1944 SC 2064).
67. *(1994) 3 SCC 148.*
68. *AIR 1994 SC 1918.*
69. *Frontline,* 8 April 1994:13.
70. . Khanna H.R, *Secularism and Judicial Review, The Hindu,* 31 May 1994.
71. S. Sahay, *Secularism is Basic Structure, Mainstream,* 26 March 1994: 4.
72. See *Frontline.* 8 April 1994.
73. *Ibid.*
74. *Ibid.*
75. Soli. J, Sorabjee 30-31.
76. *Frontline* 8 April 1994.
77. *Ibid.*
78. *Ibid.*
79. Bidyut Chakrabarty, *Indian Politics and Society since Independence* (London: Routledge, 2009) 178
80. K.Surya Prasad and V.K. Ramjeev, *President's Rule and the Courts* (Mal),

Vijnana Knirali, 27 (1996): 489.

81. *The Hindustan Times,* 20 December 1996.
82. *Ibid.*
83. *UNI Backgrounder, 22.18 (1997):4.*
84. See *Frontline,* 24 February 2006.

85. The majority judgment was delivered by Y.K. Sabharwal C.J and B.N. Agarwal. J. and Ashok Bhan. J. Arijit pasayat and K.G. Balakrishnan J.J. dissented and held the dissolution constitutional.
86. *2006 AIR SCW 494.*
87. *Ibid.*
88. *Ibid.*
89. *Ibid.*
90. *Ibid.*
91. *Ibid.*
92. *Ibid.*
93. *No more brazening it out* ,editorial, *The Hindu,* 25 Jan 2006.
94. Arun Jaitley, See *The Hindu,* 8 Oct. 2005.
95. Soli, J.Sorabjee, see the *The Hindu, Ibid.*
96. *Ibid.*
97. Mohit, C.S. *Aboo to Bommai, The Fall and Rise of Judicial Control over President's Rule - Quo Vadis?, The Academy Law Review,* Vol.XXII, No 1 and 2 (1998) :158-159.

Chapter 9

Conclusion: The Need for a Fresh Look

The Constitution of a State is a formal legal contrivance for its governance. It is the embodiment of the aspirations of the people as understood and interpreted by its makers whose views and attitudes themselves are inspired by their ideology A Constitution is made to mould the future on the basis of the present which has its roots deep in the past. In this sense, a Constitution symbolises a historical continuity. Naturally, it reflects the society for which it is made. It does not operate in a vacuum or in some higher region cut off from the world of existing political and social realities. It operates in a political system which in turn is immensely influenced by its cultural milieu. It follows that the entire societal system and Constitution interact with each other. The Constitutional process is very much moulded by the entire gamut of the political process which in turn is determined by the political culture as presented by the party system, ideology of the political leadership and the stage of development of the political consciousness of the people.

Indian Constitution is a federal Constitution. In an ideal federation, the constituent units enjoy maximum autonomy consistent with the notions of nation's unity. Such a federation is the result of a contract among the States which are independent. But the Indian federation was imposed from above. It drew heavily from the Government of India Act of 1935 which was a gift of the British Parliament for her Indian colony. The very fact that the Act of 1935 was the archetype of the draft Constitution led to the conferring of more powers on the federal government at the cost of the constituent units. Some provisions have gone to the extent of even destroying the limited autonomy of the States. Article 356 empowers the Union Government to dismiss a State Government, dissolve a State Legislature and bring the State under President's Rule. The *raison d'etre* for invoking Article 356 is provided by Article 355 which casts a duty on the Union Government to protect every State against external aggression and internal disturbances. In jurisprudence, the concept of duty is linked with the concept of power or authority. Thus Article 356 becomes relevant only in the light of Article 355 and hence the relevance of Article 355. The founding fathers of the Constitution had incorporated Article 356 in the Constitution with a view to meeting extraordinary situations. Certain safeguards were also provided to prevent its misuse.

The picture will be complete only when it is noted that Article 356 of the Indian Constitution is similar to section 93 of the Government of India Act of 1935, which conferred on the Governor the sole responsibility for the administration of the provinces in case of breakdown of the Constitutional machinery of the provincial government in whole or in part. However, the dimension of the provision regarding breakdown of Constitutional machinery under the Act of 1935 was quite different from the dimension of the provision of Article 356. Under the Act of 1935, the Governor General and Governors were not Constitutional heads of the State as they are under the present Constitution. They exercised real powers in their own right. Again, under the 1935 Act, breakdown of Constitutional machinery was visualised both at the Centre and State levels. But under the Constitutional provision, the position is entirely different. The power can be exercised only against the State and that too by the President and not by the Governor. Thus it will be seen that entire Constitutional philosophy concerning the breakdown of the Constitutional machinery is different from its archetype. It is in this context, D.D. Basu himself observed that 'the provision in the constitution is a measure of 'federal coercion' while the corresponding provisions in the Act of 1935 had no such implication. The object of the Act, 1935, was simply to withdraw power from popular control to the irresponsible Executive.[1]

The provision of Article 356 was not readily accepted in the Constituent Assembly. Serious objections were raised against its incorporation by several members on the ground that it would be an invasion into the field reserved for the States. All the objections were over-ridden by Ambedkar with the argument that he was conscious of the fact that these provisions were liable to be abused or employed for political purpose. But he brushed aside the objections by stating that no provision is immune from being abused and expressed the hope that it might remain a dead letter and might never be used except as a last resort, after everything fails.

The framers of the Constitution were certain that there was no alternative to a strong Central government. They could not help being influenced by the turbulence of partition, the precarious integration of the princely states and the armed challenge to the new Indian States on account of communist insurgency in some parts of the country. Consequently, it was only natural that they enjoined upon the Centre the duty to take care of the federal units, protect them and ensure that the States remained faithful to the Constitution. Hence the Centre was armed with an impressive and imposing array of emergency powers.

Though the provisions relating to President's Rule have been inserted in part XVIII dealing with Emergency provisions, it is qualitatively different from other emergencies dealt with in the part. Yet, the breakdown of Constitutional machinery in a State does give rise to a situation of emergency. Hence, Article 356 should be interpreted as an emergency provision like Article 352 and Article 360.

An examination of Article 355 and 356 with reference to other federal Constitutions would reveal that even though provisions approximating to Article 355 can be found in a few federal Constitutions, there is no Constitution containing a provision exactly parallel to Article 356. The only other constitution that contained a somewhat similar provision which has already been repealed is the Constitution of Pakistan. As such Article 356 is a unique and extraordinary provision in the history of federal Constitutions.

No particular condition is laid down to impose President's Rule under Article 356. However, a close analysis of the Constitutional provision identifies four elements, such as, 'report of the Governor', the clause 'or otherwise', 'satisfaction of the President' and the expression 'failure of the Constitutional machinery in a State'.

A Constitutional functionary, who has a crucial role to play in the arena of Article 356 is the Governor. The President invokes Article 356 on a report from the Governor. Thus the assessment of the situation that necessitates Central intervention is primarily a Constitutional function of the Governor. In this context, he acts as the President's advisor on the spot. The report which the Governor is expected to send must be a 'speaking report'. It should contain clear and specific facts. The Governor exercises personal discretion while sending a report. The Governor's report, the net result of the discretionary exercises, assumes immense significance as in most cases the President acts solely on facts and opinion disclosed in it.

A close perusal of the imposition of President's Rule under the Article in various States shows that in quite a number of instances, the office and services of the Governors were utilised as a tool to get rid of Chief Ministers who were politically inconvenient or belonging to other parties. The framers of the Constitution intended that the Governor should be a person above party politics and one who can give an impartial advice and that care should be taken to appoint people of undoubted integrity as Governors. But, unfortunately, their hopes were not fulfilled. The remedy lies in the Constitution of a committee of impartial persons without any party affiliation for recommending the name of persons to be appointed as

Governers. Therefore, it is submitted that Article 155 should be so amended as to give effect to this change in the mode of appointment of Governors.

The words 'or otherwise' indicate that the President may act under Article 356 on information received from sources other than the Governor's report. The source of information on which the President can reach his satisfaction is very wide. The words 'or otherwise' imposes no restriction or limitation on the source of information. The President might have the information on failure of Constitutional machinery from secret sources like the intelligence wing of the executive. Theoretically, the word otherwise shifts the whole burden of responsibility from the Governor's shoulders to those of the President and Governor's role pales into insignificance.

In most cases, barring four instances, President's Rule was imposed on the recommendation of the Governor. Thus, a precedent has been set that it is the Governor who recommends President's Rule in the State. This practice is significant in the sense that it has transferred the responsibility back to the Governor from the President, and thus the Governor becomes duty bound.

A cursory glance through the Constitutional provision pertaining to the imposition of President's Rule will reveal that the President of India is the central character in the exercise. The functions of the President under Article 356 come within the ambit of his executive power to be exercised by him in accordance with the aid and advice of the Council of Ministers. However, he is not totally helpless. The proviso to Article 74(1) and the mandate of Article 78 and above all, the deliberations in the Constituent Assembly would suggest that he can exert pressure on the Prime Minister and his Council regarding the proclamation. This leverage that was belatedly granted to the President is truly in keeping with his Constitutional role. The widely prevalent view that the President is totally helpless in the Constitutional exercise of President's Rule is not wholly true. The recent action of President Narayanan in U.P. in 1997 and in Bihar in 1998 bears testimony to this fact. But if, after reconsideration, the same recommendation is sent back to the

President (this is what happened in Bihar in 1999) he is Constitutionally obliged to act in accordance with the mandate of Article 74. Nevertheless, when the President is a person of integrity and is widely believed to be non-partisan, his action is bound to produce an impact on public opinion which no democratic government can afford to ignore.

The expression 'failure of Constitutional machinery' does not permit of a precise definition. The Constitution is silent about the circumstances that can be construed to mean the 'failure of Constitutional machinery'. It was definitely the intention of the founding fathers of the Constitution that the use of the Article should be confined only to cases of actual breakdown of the Constitutional machinery and that the provision was an exceptional one. The words "government of the State cannot be carried on in accordance with the provisions of the Constitution" should not be taken to convey failure to comply with any particular provision of the Constitution or inability to maintain law and order in a part of the State. It should be clearly a case of failure to maintain the form of the Constitution, which in relation to the provincial part of the Constitution means the form of responsible government. Though it is impossible to catalogue the envisaged situations falling within its ambit, there is unanimous opinion among constitutionalists that the Article should be used only in rare and exceptional cases wherein the Centre is compelled by the dictates of good conscience and its duty to uphold the Constitution.

During sixty years since the inauguration of the Constitution in 1950, President's Rule was proclaimed one hundred and eleven times, which amounts to an average of 1.85 times a year. The State of Punjab was the first State in the Union where President's Rule was necessitated within two years of the commencement of the Constitution. The maximum number of President's Rule was declared in the State of UP (10 times). Kerala, Punjab and Bihar have come under President's Rule as many as nine times each. The longest spell of President's Rule was witnessed in Jammu and Kashmir followed by Punjab and the shortest in Karnataka and Bihar for only eight days. There were only sixteen years during the period 1950-2010 when no President's Rule was proclaimed in any State. The number of imposition of President's Rule went up to twelve a year. An analysis of the table of President's Rule in chronological order shows that hundred instances out of hundred and eleven have taken place since the year 1967. In one way the founding fathers were justified in incorporating Articles 355 and 356 in the Constitution; in the absence of which, the political process in many States could not have been controlled, especially when we were confronted with the developments in Punjab, Jammu and Kashmir, North-Eastern States etc. But this contention is not a Constitutional or political green signal to all the President's Rule proclamations because no political analyst, no constitutional expert, no politician, no jurist could wholeheartedly support or justify all cases of President's Rule proclamation. Even the Sarkaria Commission has found only twenty six cases inevitable out of seventy five instances during the thirty seven years from 1950 to 1987.

It may be stated that on most of the occasions, there was no justification for invoking Article 356 and imposing President's Rule. It is seen that the ruling party at the Centre has wantonly misused the Article for its petty political ends. It is true that with few exceptions, the Article maintained its genuine spirit till 1967, after which political pluralism began to dominate the scene. In the altered political set up, Article 356 began to acquire a different complexion. The position shifted from "as the last resort of the President" to "the first resort of the ruling party at the Centre". In 1977, the first non-congress government headed by Morarji Desai came to power at the Centre on the basis of a mandate against the excesses committed during emergency. It wasted no time in toppling down Congress governments in all the States where the party had been routed in the Parliamentary polls. An analysis of the cases of imposition of Article 356 has shown that this Article has not been used for legitimate purposes. More often than not, the provision has been misused to promote the political interests of the party in power at the Centre.

Virtually, all political parties or coalitions that came to power at the Centre have manipulated the Article to suit their political interests. From a comparative analysis of the frequency with which both the Congress and the various non-Congress governments invoked the provision, it becomes evident that the average frequency was greater during the non-Congress regimes. What is true of frequency is equally true of the justifiability of the proclamations.

The reasons for the imposition of President's Rule are as varied and perplexing, as defeat of the ruling party in the Parliamentary elections, State Governments run by a political party failing to effectively implement the Central ordinances banning certain communal organisation, hung Assemblies, corruption and maladministration, breakdown of law and order, party wranglings, paralysis of Parliamentary process, delay in electoral process, absence of Legislature in newly formed States, failure to honour the assurance to the nation and Court, resort to violence in the Assembly when the non-confidence motion is to be voted, getting the interim budget of the State passed in the Parliament and party splits defections and break up of coalitions.

It is to be noted that in forty -one cases President's Rule was imposed even though the ministry enjoyed the confidence of the State Legislatures[2]. These include instances where provisions of Article 356 were invoked to deal with intra-party problems, or for considerations not relevant to the purpose of the Article. There were fifty -eight instances in which the Legislative Assembly of the State concerned was dissolved simultaneously with the proclamation. In fourty- five cases, the State Assembly, instead of being dissolved, was kept in a state of suspended animation. In fouteen cases where the respective State Assemblies were initially suspended, the possibility of its revival later was thwarted by subsequently dissolving them. In other nine cases, the Legislative Assemblies were dissolved by the respective Governors before the Presidential proclamation came. In as many as sixteen cases where the ministry had resigned, the other claimants were not given a chance to form an alternative government. It may also be recalled that on five occasions President's Rule was declared without ascertaining the opinion of the Legislature on whether the sacked Chief Minister had majority or not. It is seen that in seventy one cases, the decision to impose President's Rule was motivated by the political consideration of the Centre and not inspired by the responsibility and obligation to uphold the Constitution. Thus, it becomes quite clear that in a large number of instances, the invoking of Article 356 has not been in accordance with the assurance given by Ambedkar in the Constituent Assembly, though in a few cases the power has been properly used.

Thus, the apprehension and doubt expressed by the founding fathers regarding the possibility of this Article "being abused or employed for political purposes" proved prophetic. All these point to the deficiencies, inaccuracies, inconsistencies and the violation of the norms and healthy practices surrounding the imposition of Article 356.

In order to prevent the misuse of power, the Constitution has incorporated certain safeguarding mechanisms. The greatest safeguard against any unjustifiable imposition is the President of India himself. It is true that no such express power is conferred on the President. However, the President is duty-bound to ask the Cabinet to reconsider its suggestion if he disagrees with it, and ask for information or refuse to sign the proclamation if he is insufficiently informed. Of course, it is open to the Cabinet to reject the advice and send back the proposal, in which case, the President is constitutionally bound to give his assent. Further, we should not forget that the President is also, in fact, part and parcel of the executive system and also the party system. In this context, it would not be realistic to expect that his decisions will always be fool proof.

The framers of the Constitution had reposed immense faith in the Parliamentary control mechanism devised by them to prevent the abuse. The control mechanism through the political process was envisaged keeping in view the salient features of democracy. However, in practice, the Parliamentary check over the abuse of power is minimal and ineffective. So far no Presidential proclamation has been voted down by the

Parliament. The Bommai judgment, however strengthened the role of Parliament to check the centre's onslaught. The court's ruling that the centre cannot dissolve State legislatures until the proclamation is approved by the Lok Sabha and the Rajyasabha has served as an effective restraint during the period when no party or combination of parties has enjoyed a majority in both the Houses of the Parliament. This pronouncement has forced the Vajpaye government to revoke President's Rule in Bihar in 1999 and deterred the Manmohan Singh government from its attempt to unseat Mulayam government in Uttar Pradesh in 2007.

The judiciary, which was initially reluctant to interfere in and to review the exercise of power under Article 356, asserted its power to do so in 1977 in the Rajasthan case. Thereafter the impression was that the 1977 judgment would remain a mere symbolic assertion of judicial power. But this was shattered in 1993 when the MP. High Court invalidated the proclamation of the President dismissing Sunderlal Patwa ministry under Article 356. In the Bommai case, the Supreme Court went further and more emphatically asserted the power of judicial review. It examined whether the power under Article 356 was exercised *mala fide* or on extraneous considerations, and consequently, the Court struck down the dismissal of ministries and the dissolution of Assemblies in Karnataka, Meghalaya and Nagaland. In the light of this judgment, there is a possibility that in future, the unwarranted use of Article 356 might be struck down by the Court as happendend in the Bihar Assembly dissolution case. In the Bommai case, the majority view was emphatic and was an open renunciation of the "judicial hands off" approach. It is heartening to note that striking down of these proclamations has clearly shown that imposition of President's Rule under Article 356 is justiciable. This indeed is the judicial answer to the politically *mala fide* abuse of the Article. Any decision of the Court, however may take time. The Union government can after seeking the approval of the Parliament can dissolve Assembly and order fresh elections as in the case of in Bihar in 2005. If the case taken to the court promptly, will the court issue an injunction preventing the conduct of elections?

As whole even after the Bommai and Rameshwar Prasad judgments the danger abuse of the Article is not substantially diluted.

Despite the Constitutional safeguards, all the political parties which came to power at the Centre used the Article indiscriminately or misused on number of occasions and in most cases it appeared to be of doubtful constitutional validity. In a majority of cases, it seems the power was exercised to dismiss state government controlled by political parties opposed to the ruling party at the centre. Thus "the provision which was included as a life saving device by the framers of the Constitution, has become poison for our political system"[3]. Two important questions, therefore, arise for consideration: whether the Article should be deleted. In case the answer is in the negative, should it be retained as it is or amended?

As regards the first question, P.V. Rajamannar Committee on Centre - State Relations has observed that 'Article 356 is an unusual provision not found in other federations and the union after all is one of the parties to the federal compact and vesting such unguided description in the Union is bound to work to the detriment of the State'. Therefore, the committee recommended that 'Article 356 and 357 may be entirely repealed'.[4] Constitutional experts like Rajeev Dhavan and V.R Krishna Iyer J. also seemed to express severe doubts about its relevance. The regional parties like DMK, Telugu Desam and National Conference have also made appeal to the centre to move an amendment for the deletion of this Article. However, it may be argued that in view of the situation prevailing in India, the responsibility of the Centre to protect the unity and integrity of the country is all the greater. Terrorism and militancy are raising their ugly faces more than ever before. Ethnic minority movements are putting forth demands which can endanger the unity of the country. The tribals, especially of the North-Eastern sector feel neglected as a result of being cut off from the national mainstream. Some movements are even voicing their demand for independence or creation of a separate state. In this grave situation it may be necessary to preserve this over-riding powers. Further, what is the possible solution in a situation where a State Government directly or indirectly supports an armed rebellion or a government goes beyond control and turns almost totalitarian? Any government can flout the norms and there may be virtual dictatorship in the State. It is the bounden duty of the Centre in such instances to intervene and see that the State is governed in accordance with the Constitutional provisions. There are also other situations where Article 356 becomes relevant. It provides a temporary solution in the event of a total Constitutional deadlock wherein no combination of Assembly members is in a position to constitute a government. A similar situation would also arise when a party commanding majority declines to form a ministry. Moreover, one cannot conceive of all the situations which may arise in future and necessitate the Central government to interfere in the larger interest of the nation. Over and above, this exceptional power is an effective weapon which act as check on any corrupt intention of state governments. It is pointed out that 'power corrupts and absolute power corrupts absolutely' Our experience and wisdom do not encourage the deletion of the provision because it may lead to a steady weakening of the centre and strengthening of the states. This, sometimes, results balkanization of the already weakened federal polity. Definitely, our founding fathers discussed, debated and deliberated on every article of the Constitution before adopting the same. Certainly, they would not have included Article 356 without valid and cogent reasons.

Different Committees and Commissions, such as, the Administrative Reforms Commission, the Governor's Committee, the Sarkaria Commission and finally the National Commission to Review the working of the Constitution strongly advised against the repeal of the Article from the Constitution. The Sarkaria Commission felt that in view of the growth of sub nationalism which has tended to strengthen the divisive and secessionist forces and weaken the unity and integrity of the country, it will not be prudent to scrap the Article. After having stated this the Commission observed:

> We are firmly of the view that Article 356 should remain as an ultimate Constitutional weapon to cope with extreme situations[5].

A similar view has been expressed by NCRWC. According to the Commission: 'Article should not be deleted' stating that this would create an imbalance in Union-State Relations in upholding Constitutional governance through out India and that in many more instances than not the use of Article 356 was inevitable. However, the Commission warn that 'it must be used sparingly and only as remedy of last resort and after exhausting action under other Articles like 256, 257 and 355[6]. In this connection Sawant J. said 'just because Article 356 is often misused, it should not be deleted. 'It serves a constitutional purpose, and must be retained'. 'At the same time', 'he observed, 'precautions should be taken to prevent it from being abused. The Governor, the Cabinet, the President, the Court and above all people, all have a duty to prevent its abuse' [7]

Here it is certainly needs to be mentioned that the powerful weapon of President's Rule should not be discarded from the Constitutional armoury. Article 356 is highly desirable in our country keeping in view the innumerable threats and dangers faced by the Republic within and without, to the integrity of Indian States. If we do not have a strong Centre with adequate powers, we can not face and overcome such contingencies succesfully. It is unfortunate that the government in power at the centre, sometimes use this provision for the furtherance of their partisan interests. Despite its misuse on certain occasions, Article 356 will continue to be more a necessity rather than a liability and can be positively used to ensure that the State Government is carried on in accordance with the provisions of the Constitution, given the fact that our Parliamentary democracy has entered the coalition age and that at present the regional parties are emerging stronger. The motivating factor for Presidential take-over of a State administration under Article 356 should never be petty party gains, rather it must be the objective satisfaction that the Constitutional machinery has failed. Frequent elections would detract from the faith of the people in the efficacy of elected governments apart from incurring huge election expenditure, which could be used for other developmental and welfare measures. Therefore, this power should be wielded only in extreme cases where the Union Government having no other option to restore the spirit of the Constitution.[8] For this, we must develop a Constitutional culture imbibing federal spirit. 'in which any power given by the constitution to any authority should be used only for the purposes intended, and not to achieve some other extraneous purpose.[9] If sufficient safeguards are fostered as conventions the provision can play a useful, inevitable and vital role in the constitutional scheme of India. As has already been noted before, the constitution operates not in a vacuum. It works in the context of the given political system. In the context of the given political system the Article is essential for our country. In fact, it is not a constitutional problem, on the contrary it is question of political culture and morality of its practitioners. There fore, what is desirable is to do away with the possibilities of misinterpretation and misuse and not to do away with the Article.

The Congress, the Janata, the UF, the BJP, the NDA and the UPA governments that have come to power in India stand for the retention of Article 356. The Left parties, in principle, oppose the retention of the Article. But they have supported the imposition of President's Rule on some occasions. The point is that most political parties make use of the provision when it suits them, otherwise, they want it to be deleted. On a closer examination, it appears that neither deletion nor dilution is the answer to the vexed question of the misuse and abuse of the Article. For, Article 356 is not an isolated nor severable provision of the Constitution, it verily constitutes the crux of the entire Centre-State relationship. Remove it, and there goes along with it the rubric of federal design which has been erected with a great sense of responsibility by the founding fathers of the Constitution[10]. Naturally, the question arises when and how to use if the Article is to be retained? In its present shape, the Article may be interpreted differently in similar situations and could be used in dubious ways, arbitrarily and for the sake of political interest of the party in power at the Centre. Some suggest that Article 356 may be amended so as to give a clear definition of 'Constitutional breakdown' in the State. But it is difficult and impossible to envisage all the circumstances which lead to the failure of Constitutional machinery in a State. It is, therefore, better to leave the expression as it is and to decide in each case whether there is a failure of Constitutional machinery or whether the State is unable to carry on the government in accordance with the provisions of the Constitution. It is also difficult to drop the expression "or otherwise" in view of the changing nature of our polity. In the same way, Article 355 also can not be deleted. Then the only way is to incorporate effective safeguards apart from the existing Constitutional checks keeping in view the federal nature of our society.

The Administrative Reforms Commission Report (1969), the Rajamannar Committee Report (1969), the Sarkaria Commission Report (1988) and finally the National Commission to Review the working of the Constitution (2002) while recommending suitable changes in the Centre-State relations also looked into the problems of misuse of Article 356.

The ARC (1969) recommended setting up of a machinery at the Centre to advise the President on possible intervention in the affairs of the State[11]. This "high status and standing body", the Commission observed, should advise the President as to "when, where, and how" the Central government may intervene in the law and order matter in the State. Its functions should be purely of advisory nature and a report should be placed before the Parliament. The Commission called for some restraint in the exercise of the Presidential powers under Article 356.

The Rajamannar Committee on the other hand recommended the deletion of Article 356 and 357[12]. In case the Union Government wanted to retain the present provision, the Committee suggested that sufficient safeguards should be provided in the Constitution itself to secure the interest of the States against the arbitrary use of Article 356.

A brief account of Sarkaria Commission recommendations (1988), with reference to the use of Article 356 would be valuable[13] in this part of discussion. The Commission is emphatic in recommending that Article 356 should be used very sparingly in extreme cases as a measure of last resort, when all available alternatives fail to prevent or rectify a Constitutional breakdown in a State. "All attempts should be made to resolve the crisis at the State level" before taking recourse to the provisions of Article 356, the commission pointed out. After having made the above observation, the Commission also suggested that a warning should be issued to the errant State, in specific terms that it is not carrying on the government of the State in accordance with the Constitution and the explanation given by the State should be taken into account before taking action under Article 356.

In a situation of political breakdown, the Commission observed that the Governor should explore all possibilities of having a government with a majority support in the Legislature. If it is not possible to install such a government and if fresh elections can be held without avoidable delay, he should ask the outgoing ministry to continue as a caretaker government if the ministry was defeated in a major policy issue, unconnected with any allegations of maladministration or corruption, and is agreeable to continue. The Governor then should dissolve the Legislature leaving the resolution of the Constitutional crisis to the electorate.

The Commission has also recommended the course of action to be taken consequent on the proclamation of President's Rule. Every proclamation should be placed before each House of the Parliament at the earliest. But since the Constitutional provision in clause (3) of Article 356 lays down that this should be done before the expiry of two months period, it comes to the rescue of the Central government and this recommendation is practically rendered ineffective.

Another recommendation of the Commission is significant. The State Legislative Assembly should not be dissolved either by the Governor or by the President before the proclamation has been laid before the Parliament and it has an opportunity to consider it. The Commission recommended that Article 356 should be suitably amended to ensure this. The novelty in this recommendation is that it enables the Parliament to discuss the issues involved in the proclamation and it is published in the media. After the discussion, it might not be possible for the government to dissolve the Assembly if the State Government has a strong case against the dismissal of the ministry and the dissolution of the Assembly and public opinion affirms this. But if the Central government enjoys a safe majority, nothing tangible would happen, yet this gives an opportunity to the Parliament to discuss the issue in all its ramifications.

Another significant recommendation of the Commission is that "the safeguards corresponding, in principle, to clauses (7) and (8) of Article 352 should be incorporated in Article 356" to enable the Parliament to review the continuance in force of the proclamation periodically.

The heart of the remedy suggested by the Commission is that the material facts and grounds on which Article 356(1) is invoked should be made an integral part of the proclamation. This would make the remedy of judicial review "a little more meaningful". The Commission suggested that this should be provided, through an appropriate amendment, notwith-standing anything in clause(2) of Article 74 of the Constitution. This will enable the aggrieved party to approach the Supreme Court and High Courts to determine whether the proclamation is well founded. And because of the logic of the decision will be written into the proclamation, the Supreme Court will be able to pronounce on the Constitutional validity of the proclamation without invading the Constitutional domain of the executive.

The Commission has recommended that the report of the Governor on the basis of which the President acts under Article 356 normally should be "a speaking document" and should contain a precise and clear statement of all material facts and ground on the basis of which the President has satisfied himself as to the existence or otherwise of the situation contemplated in Article 356. Further, the Governor's report should be given wide publicity in all the media and in full.

No doubt, the Sarkaria Commission has gone beyond the framers of the Constitution and their predecessors in suggesting certain recommendations with regard to the use of Article 356. Of course, these suggestions are not radical. They are appendages to the existing Constitutional provisions to suit the political system which has undergone much transformation since 1967[14]. They cover the past and make useful observations and suggestions with regard to the clear and specific malpractices. However, they hesitate to venture into the future and they take shelter in the original Constitutional provisions and in the wisdom and ingenuity of the founding fathers of the Constitution. In the place of concrete suggestion to remedy the weakness, the Commission restricted its observation to giving advice on how to use the Article, on what occasion to use it, how to treat ministries backed with majority, how to understand the breakdown of Constitutional machinery etc. Role of conventions in the democratic framework is another area on which the Sarkaria Commission was not eloquent. Many of the issues linked with the imposition of Article 356 genuinely need the support of conventions. The Commission's suggestions are good and valuable. But no one would follow them without concrete legal sanctions. The attempt of Sarkaria Commission, however small and limited, was a good step and served as a corrective or rethinking element in the political process.

The Inter-State Council constituted a standing committee to look into the matter relating to Centre-State relations including abuse of Article 356. The committee recommended the issue of warning or showcause notice with seven days time to reply to it and the proclamation be issued only after considering the reply of the concerned State Government. The committee went a little further than the Sarkaria Commission by stating that the proclamation should contain the text of the notice as well as the reply of the State Government thereto. The proclamation is not in the nature of a Court judgment to contain all these ingredients. The committee suggested that the period of two months for obtaining the approval of

Parliament might be reduced to one month. The period of two months is a fairly short period and there is no reason to reduce it to one month. The committee further recommended that the proclamation be approved by a two-third majority in the Parliament. Here it may be point out that in this days of fractured verdicts and coalition government, where no party has even a majority, the condition that the proclamation be approved by a two-third majority would completely nullify the objective and effectiveness of Article 356[15]. The basic problem is that no political party has a definite stand on the utility of Article 356. It is precisely for this reason that despite several meetings, the standing committee of the Inter-State Council could not reach an effective consensus on Article 356.

In this connection, it seems worthwhile to consider the suggestions put forth by a few leading Constitutional experts. H.M. Seervai has suggested that before resorting to action under Article 356, a written warning should be issued to the State concerned and if the warning is challenged by the State it would be consistent with the principle of representative government to ask for the advisory opinion of the Supreme Court under Article 143[16]. This suggestion seems to be good and valuable and is in accordance with democratic principles and the principles of natural justice. However, inview of the conditions prevailing in this country it will be difficult to apply this suggestion in all cases. As an example one can very well point out the sacking of the U.P. government in the aftermath of the demolition of Babri Masjid.

Khanna J. suggested an amendment to the Constitution to provide that the proclamation of Article 356 be required to be approved by the Parliament by a majority of the total membership of each House and by a majority of not less than two-thirds of the members of each House present and voting[17]. Krishna Iyer J. said: "In my view, Article 356 must be abolished and an alternative provision found for the check on the power of the State Government when it runs berserk and turns tyrannical."[18].

However, it is submitted that the suggestions made by both the jurists to minimise the abuse of power are not very practical, and with the decline in the national character of the polity, it will be ineffective. In this context, certain suggestions are submitted here regarding the exercise of this awesome power. First of all, it is submitted that, all the steps suggested by the founding fathers should be observed by the Union government before embarking on the imposition of President's Rule. Ambedkar had clearly pointed out in the Constituent Assembly that before resorting to Article 356 the first thing the President will do would be to issue a mere warning to the province that has erred, that things were not happening in the way in which they were intended to happen in the Constitution. If the warning fails, the second thing for him to do will be to order an election allowing the people of the State to settle matters by themselves. It is only when those two remedies fail that he would resort to this Article. It is hoped that the President of India will not limit his attention to the Constitution only, but also to the proceedings of the Constituent Assembly. The ideas contained in the debate should be incorporated in Article 356. It may be argued that this may not be possible under all circumstances. It may be true that such circumstances (communal, religious disharmony anti-national activities etc.) can also be incorporated where warning and ordering of elections may not be resorted to. It is necessary that these pre-proclamation steps should be incorporated in the Constitution, because so far since the inception of the Constitution, friendly warnings were hardly given, so called conventions were not evolved, and public opinion was not mobilised by the power oriented political parties.

The Inter-State Council may be further expanded by co-opting former Presidents, former Chief Justices of the Supreme Court, Attorney General etc. and this Council may be endowed with the advisory function of discussing each and every proclamation of President's Rule and the measures taken by the President in pursuance of such proclamation. The result of these deliberations may be placed before the Parliament and also before the general public. If implemented, it will make our federations vibrant reality and minimise the scope for partisan action. The Council could have a permanent standing committee which could constantly monitor issues relating to Centre-State relations and the imposition of Article 356 in a State.

Another valuable and practical suggestion in this regard is that whenever President's Rule is imposed on a state for the political privilege of the ruling party at the centre, the electorates of the concerned state must organise themselves on non-party basis and agitate against the arbitrariness of the centre in interpreting and applying the provision. Political parties often view a President's Rule from the point of view of the problem of power, position, privileges and prestige but non-party organization could cut across power interest of the parties and deal with any President's Rule proclamation in a democratic federal perspective centred around the welfare of people at large. Along with the evolution of the vigilant public opinion, a strong and healthy opposition and above all the existence of a free press can also act as a deterrent against the possible abuse of power and go a long way in ensuring that Article 356 is used as was intended by the founding fathers of the Constitution. It was the combined force of these three institutions which enabled to correct the wrong decisions of the Centre and the same resulted in the reinstatement of Rama-Rao in Andhra in 1984, Kalyan Singh in U.P. in 1998 and Rabri Devi in Bihar in 1999. But unfortunately, the Indian Parliamentary system lacks a strong opposition, vigilant public opinion and an independent press. These agencies should be the moving spirit behind any Parliamentary system. But very often, these institutions cater to their vested interests only and look at problems from factional and communal angles. Ancient India's master political craftsman, Chanakya once remarked, 'indifference and inertia of the honest people would inflict more harm on the society and country than by the wrong doers'.

The Administrative Reforms Commission, the Rajamannar Committee, the Sarkaria Commission, the NCRWC and finally the Supreme Court verdicts in the Bommai and Rameshwar Prasad cases which went into the thorny problem have put forward several suggestions, recommendations and rulings. So far no substantial recommendation of these Commissions or the rulings of the Court were accepted, nor were they incorporated in the Constitution by way of amendment to Article 356. It is ironical to note that Article 356 has been misused twenty-one times since the Sarkaria's recommendations, eight times after the Bommai judgement and six times since the executive activism displayed by President Narayanan. All these show that no safeguards, whether Constitutional or conventional or even judicial will ensure a cent percent guarantee against misuse or abuse of the Constitutional provisions unless the political parties are committed to democratic ideology, principles and practices. Further, no existing party has consistently demanded the deletion of Article 356. Neither the Congress nor the non-Congress parties have so far seriously tried to bring in the required changes in the provision. This means that there is every possibility for Article 356 being misused so long as the political process of the country remains the same. The political process of today will continue to be so until any of the major parties in India is capable of or has the political will to bring about a radical transformation in the political process of the country resulting in the rise of a new political culture.

In the context of the existing federal structure, the States cannot take any initiative in bringing about a Constitutional amendment. Therefore, the initiative should come from the Centre or the States should be able to prevail upon the Union Government to review the Constitution. The Constitution must be restored to what its framers intended it to be. For this, suitable amendments should be made in the light of the intention of the founding fathers, the recommendations of the Sarkaria Commission, the observation of the NCRWC, the decisions of the Supreme Court in Bommai and Rameshwar Prasad cases and the suggestions submitted here. Such an amendment must ensure that the recourse to Article 356 must be a last resort after exhausting the options under Articles 256, 257, and more importantly, 355. It is very important that such a review should be undertaken by a body established after effective consultation with the States so that it commands their confidence as well. Its recommendations must be implemented properly.

All said and done, ultimately, the Constitutional and political process depends on the political leadership, their ideology and their way of doing things. In this context, the following observation of Ambedkar in the Constituent Assembly seems to be quite relevant and significant. He observed:

> I feel however good a Constitution may be, it is sure to turn out bad because those who are called to work it, happen to be a bad lot. However bad a Constitution may be, it may turn out to be good if those who are called to work it happened to be a good lot. The working of the Constitution does not depend wholly upon the nature of the Constitution[19].

The Constitution alone is never a guarantee of good government, howsoever,well framed and well phrased it may be. Infact, success or failure of the Constitution depends more on the participants and less on the words used in the Constitution. So what is needed is good statesmanship and respect for democratic and federal principles. Only this can prevent the desire to lynch the opposition party controlled State Governments. But this is easier said than done. It may take some more time to realise it. Till we achieve this, it is essential that we should have severe restraint and invigilatory mechanism before this horrendous power is made operational.

However, as things stand today the only effective safeguard against the misuse of the Article appears to be the Judiciary. As and when the power is unilaterally used against a State Government the Courts apart from considering the case should also be able to come out with a verdict within a short period of time. 'Justice delayed is justice denied' is a proverbial saying which should be followed by the Courts in cases like this. Hence, it is suggested that the power to issue writs in this regard will enable the Supreme Court and the High Courts to deliver timely verdicts. This will help to put the Constitutional process back on the rails without further damage.

References

1. Basu D.D, *Commentary on the Constitution of India,* 6th ed., Vol. O (Calcutta: Kamal Law House, 1989) P. 13
2. *See Appendix VI.*
3. J.R. Siwach, *Polities of President's Rule in India* (Simla: Indian Institute of Advanced Study, 1979) 437.
4. See *Report of the Centre-State Relations Inquiry Committee (1971)* 135-37
5. *The Sarkaria Commission Report, 178.*
6. *htt://law min nic in/ncrwc/final report volume 1 htm 2004*
7. Sawant P.B J., interview, *Frontline,* 17 July 1988
8. See *AIR 1994, SC 1918*
9. Sawant P.B J., interview
10. RLM, Patel, *Why Deletion is no Solution, Vidya Bharathi,* 10 (1995): 59.
11. See *The Administrative Reforms Commission Report (1969).*
12 See *The Rajamannar Committee Report (1971).*
13. See *The Sarkaria Commission Report, 179-180.*
14 Surya Prasad K., *Discretionary Power of the Governor: A Critique of the Sarkaria Commission Report, ISDA Journal,* 3 (1993): 252.
15. See the observation of Alladi Kuppuswami, *Does Article 356 Need Amendment, The Hindu,* 26 November 1997.
16. H.M. Seervai, *Emergency, Future Safeguards and Habeas Corpus Case:* A Criticism (Bombay: N.M. Tripathi, 1978) 116.
17. H.R. Khanna, *Article 356 and its Misuse, 'The Hindu,* 15 November 1997.
18. V.R. Krishna *Iyer, Indian Federalism Dialectics and Dynamics* (Guwahati: Ashok Publishing House, 1992) 94.
19. *CAD, Vol X-XII, 975*

Appendices

APPENDIX I

Text of Sections 45 and 93 of the Government of India Act of 1935

Section 45

If at anytime the Governor-General is satisfied that a situation has arisen in which the government of the Federation can not be carried on in accordance with the provisions of this Act, he may by proclamation—

a. declare that his functions shall, to such extent as may be specified in the proclamation, be exercised by him in his discretion;
b. assume to himself all or any of the powers vested in or exercisable by any Federal body or authority, and any such proclamation may contain such incidental and consequential provisions as may appear to him to be necessary or desirable for giving effect to the objects of the proclamation, including the provisions for suspending in whole or in part the operation of any provisions of this Act relating to any Federal body or authority:

Provided that nothing in this sub section shall authorise the Governor General to assume to himself any of powers vested in or exercisable by the Federal Court or to suspend, either in whole or in part, the operation of any provision of this Act relating to the Federal Court.

Any such proclamation may be revoked or varied by a subsequent proclamation.

A proclamation issued under this section—

> *(a)* Shall be communicated forthwith to the secretary of state and shall be laid by him before each House of parliament; *(b)* Unless it is a proclamation revoking a previous proclamation, shall cease to operate at the expiration of six months:

provided that, if and so often as a resolution approving the continuance in force of such a proclamation is passed by both Houses of parliament, the proclamation shall, unless revoked, continue in force for a further period of twelve months on which under this subsection it would otherwise have ceased to operate. 4. If at any time the government the Federation has for a continuous period of three years been carried on under and by virtue of a proclamation issued under this section, then at the expiration of that period, the proclamation shall cease to have effect and the government of the Federation shall be carried on in accordance with the other provisions of this Act, subject to any amendment there of which parliament may deem it necessary to make, but nothing in this subsection shall be construed as extending the power of parliament to make amendments in this Act without affecting the accession of a state. 5. If the Governor General, by a proclamation under this section, assumes to himself any power of the Federal legislature to make laws, any law made by him in the exercise of that power shall, subject to the term thereof, continue to have effect until two years have elapsed from the date on which the proclamation ceases to have effect,

unless sooner repealed or re-enacted by Act of the appropriate Legislature, any reference in this Act to Federal Acts, Federal laws, or Acts or Laws of the Federal Legislature shall be construed as including a reference to such a law.

The functions, of the Governor-General under this section shall be exercised by him in his discretion.

Similarly Section 93 dealt with the failure of constitutional machinery in the provinces as given below:

1. If at any time the Governor of the province is satisfied that a situation has arisen in which the government of

the province cannot be carried on in accordance with the provisions of this Act, he may by proclamation—

a. declare that his function shall, to such extent, as may be specified in the proclamation be exercised by him in his discretion;
b. assume to himself all or any of the powers vested in or exercisable by any provincial body or authority;
c. and any such proclamation may contain such incidental and consequential provisions as any appear to him to be necessary or desirable for giving effect to the object of the proclamation, including provisions for suspending in whole or in part the operation of any provisions of this Act relating to any provincial body or authority. Provided that nothing in the subsection shall authorise the Governor to assume to himself any of the powers vested in or exercisable by a High Court or to suspend, either in whole or in part, the operation of any provisions of this Act to High Courts.

2. Any such proclamation may be revoked or varied by a subsequent proclamation; A proclamation under this section:—

a. Shall be communicated forth with to the secretary of states and shall be laid by him before each House of parliament.
b. Unless it is a proclamation revoking a previous proclamation, shall cease to operated at the expiration of six months.

Provided that, if and so often as a resolution so approving the continuance in force of such proclamation is passed by both the Houses of parliament, the proclamation shall unless revoked, continue in force for a further period of 12 (twelve) months from the date on which under this subsection it would authorise have ceased to operate, but no such proclamation shall in any case remain in force for more than three years.

4. If the Governor, by a proclamation under this section, assumes to himself any power of provincial legislature to make laws, any law made by him in the exercise of that power shall, subject to the term thereof, continue to have effect until two years have elapsed from the date on which the proclamation ceased to have effect, unless sooner replaced or re-enacted by Act of the appropriate legislature and any reference in this Act to provincial Acts, provincial laws, or Acts or Laws of a provincial legislature shall be constructed as including a reference to such a law.

5. The functions of the Governor under this section shall be exercised by him in his discretion and no proclamation shall be made by a governor under this section without the concurrence of the Governor-General in his discretion.

APPENDIX II

Text of Articles 356 and 357 of the Constitution of India

[As amended up to and including the Constitution (Forty-eighty Amendment) Act, 1984]

356. *Provisions in case of failure of Constitutional Machinery in States*—(1) If the President on receipt of a report from the Governor[1] of a State or otherwise, is satisfied that a situation has arisen in which the Government of the State cannot be carried on in accordance with the Provisions of this Constitution, the President may by Proclamation—

a. assume to himself all or any of the functions of the Government of the State and all or any of the powers vested in or exercisable by the Governor[2] or any body or authority in the State other than the Legislature of the State;
b. declare that the powers of the Legislature of the State shall be exercisable by or under the authority of Parliament;
c. make such incidental and consequential previsions as appear to the President to be necessary or desirable for giving effect to the objects of the proclamation, including provisions for suspending in whole or in part the operation of any provisions of this Constitution relating to any body or authority in the State;

Provided that nothing in this clause shall authorise the President to assume to himself any of the powers vested in or exercisable by a High Court, or to suspend in whole or in part the operation of any provision of this Constitution relating to High Courts.

2. Any such Proclamation may be revoked or varied by a subsequent Proclamation.

3. Every Proclamation issued under this article shall be laid before each House of Parliament and shall, except where it is a Proclamation revoking a previous Proclamation, cease to operate at the expiration of two months unless before the expiration of that period it has been approved by resolutions of both Houses of Parliament;

Provided that if any such Proclamation (not being a Proclamation revoking a previous Proclamation) is issued at a time when the House of the People is dissolved, or the dissolution of the House of the People takes place during the period of two months referred to in this clause, and if a resolution approving the Proclamation has been passed by the Council of States, but no resolution with respect to such Proclamation has been passed by the House of the People before the expiration of that period, the Proclamation shall cease to operate at the expiration of thirty days from the date on which the House of the People first sits after its reconstitution unless before the expiration of the said period of thirty days as resolution approving the Proclamation has been also passed by the House of the People. (4) A Proclamation so approved shall, unless revoked, cease to operate on the expiration of period of (six months from the date of issue of the Proclamation)[3].

Provided that if and so often as a resolution approving the continuance in force of such a Proclamation is passed by both Houses of Parliament, the Proclamation shall, unless revoked, continues in force for a further period of (six months)[4] from the date on which under this clause it would otherwise have ceased to operate, but no such Proclamation shall in any case remain in force for more than three years: Provided further that if the dissolution of the House of the People takes place during any such period of (six months) and a resolution approving the continuance in force of such Proclamation has been passed by the Council of States, but no resolution with respect of the continuance in force of such Proclamation has been passed by the House of the People during the said period, the Proclamation shall cease to operate at the expiration of thirty days from the date on which the House of the People first sits after its reconstitution unless before the expiration of the said period of thirty days a resolution approving the continuance in force of the Proclamation has been also passed by the House of the People.

[Provide also that in the case of Proclamation issued under clause (1) on the 11th day of May 1987 with respect to the State of Punjab, the reference in the first proviso to this clause to "three years" shall be construed as a reference to "five years"][5]. [(5) Notwithstanding anything contained in clause (4), a resolution with respect to the continuance in force of a Proclamation approved under clause (3) for any period beyond the expiration of one year from the date of issue of such Proclamation shall not be passed by either House of Parliament unless—

a. Proclamation of Emergency is in operation, in the whole of India or, as the case may be, in the whole or any part of the State, at the time of the passing of such resolution, and
b. the Election Commission, certifies that the continuance in force of the Proclamation approved under clause (3) during the period specified in such resolution is necessary on account of difficulties in holding general elections to the Legislative Assembly of the State concerned.][6]

[Provided that nothing in this clause shall apply to the Proclamation issued under clause (1) on the 11th day of May, 1987 with respect to the State of Punjab.][7] 357. *Exercise of Legislative powers under Proclamation issued under Article* 356-(1) Where by a Proclamation issued under clause (1) of Article 356, it has been declared that the powers of the Legislature of the State shall be exercisable by or under the authority of Parliament it shall be competent:—

a. for Parliament to confer on the President the power of the Legislature of the State to make laws, and to authorise the President to delegate, subject to such

b. conditions as he may think fit to impose, the power so conferred to any other authority to be specified by him in that behalf;
c. for Parliament, or for the President or other authority in whom such power to make laws is vested under sub-clause (a), to make laws conferring powers and imposing duties, or authorising the conferring of powers and the imposition of duties, upon the Union or officers and authorities thereof;
d. for the President to authorise when the House of the People is not in session expenditure from the Consolidated Fund of the State pending the sanction of such expenditure by Parliament.
e. [(2) Any law made in exercise of the power of Legislature of the State by Parliament or the President or other authority referred to in sub-clause (a) of clause (1) which Parliament or the President or such other authority would not, but for the issue of a Proclamation under Article 356, have been competent to make shall, after the Proclamation has ceased to operate, continue in force until altered or repealed or amended by a competent legislature or other authority.][8]

APPENDIX III

Text of Articles 58 (2) b and 112 (2) b of the Constitution of Pakistan

Article 58 of the Constitution of Pakistan, 1973 provides for dissolution of National Assembly. Clause (1) says that the President shall dissolve the National Assembly if so advised by the Prime-minister. It further provides that in any event on the expiry of forty-eight hours after the Prime-minister has advised the dissolution, the National Assembly stands dissolved.

Clause (2) provides:

"Notwithstanding anything contained in clause (2) of Article 48, the President may also dissolve the National Assembly in his discretion. Where in his opinion"

a. a vote of nonconfidence having been passed against the Prime-minister, no other member of the National Assembly is likely to command the confidence of majority of the members of the National Assembly in accordance with the provisions of the Constitution as ascertained in a session of the National Assembly summoned for the purposes, **or**
b. a situation has arisen in which the government of the Federation cannot be carried on in accordance with the provisions of the Constitution and an appeal to the electorate is necessary.

There is a similar provision in Article 112 (2) (b) empowering the provincial Governor to dissolve the Assembly of the province.

APPENDIX IV

Text of Section 92 of the Constitution of Jammu and Kashmir

92. Provision in case of failure of constitutional machin-ery in the State:—

(1) If at any time the 'Governor is satisfied that a situation has arisen in which the Government of the State cannot be carried on in accordance with the provisions of this Constitution, the 'Governor may by Proclamation—

a. assume to himself all or any of the functions of the Government of the State and all or any of the powers vested in or exercisable by any body or authority in the State;

b. make such incidental and consequential provisions as appear to the 'Governor to be necessary or desirable for giving effect to the objects of the Proclamation, including provisions for suspending in whole or in part the operation of any provision of this Constitution relating to any body or authority in the State:— Provided that nothing in this section shall authorise the 'Governor to assume to himself any of the powers vested in or exercisable by the High Court or to suspend in whole or in part the operation of any provision of this Constitution relating to the High Court.

2. Any such Proclamation may be revoked or varied by a subsequent Proclamation.

3. Any such Proclamation whether varied under sub-section (2) or not, shall except where it is Proclamation revoking a previous Proclamation cease to operate on the expiration of six months from the date on which it was first issued, if the

4. 'Governor by a Proclamation under this section assumes to himself any of the powers of the Legislature to

make laws, any law made by him in the exercise of that power shall subject to the terms thereof, continue to have effect until two years have elapsed from the date on which the Proclamation ceases to have effect, unless sooner repealed or re-enacted by an Act of the Legislature constructed as including a reference to such law.

5. No Proclamation under sub-section (1) shall be issued except with the concurrence of President of India.

6. Every Proclamation under this section shall, except where it is a Proclamation revoking a previous Proclamation, be laid before each House of the Legislature as soon as it is convened.

APPENDIX V

Text of Presidential Proclamation, Ministry of Home Affairs

NOTIFICATION
New Delhi, the 31st January 1976

G.S.R. 55 (E)—The following Proclamation by the President is published for general information:

Whereas, I, Fakhruddin Ali Ahmed, President of India, have received a report from the Governor of the State of Tamil Nadu and after considering the report and other information received by me, I am satisfied that a situation has arisen in which the Government of that State cannot be carried on in accordance with the provisions of the Constitution of India (hereinafter referred to as "the Constitution");

Now, therefore, in exercise of the powers conferred by Article 356 of the Constitution and of all other powers enabling me in that behalf, I hereby proclaim that I:

a. assume to myself as President of India all functions of the Government of the said State and all powers vested in or exercisable by the Governor of that **State;**
b. declare that the powers of the Legislature of the said State shall be exercisable by or under the authority of Parliament; and
c. make the following incidental and consequential provisions which appear to me to be necessary or desirable for giving effect to the objects of this proclamation, namely:

(i) in the exercise of the functions and powers assumed to myself by virtue of Clause (a) of this Proclamation as aforesaid, it shall be lawful for me as President of India to act to such extent as I think fit through the such extent as I think fit through the Governor of the said State; *(ii)* the operation of the following provisions of the Constitution in relation to that State is hereby suspended, namely;

so much of the proviso to Article 3 as relates to the reference by the President to the Legislature of the State;

so much of Clause (2) of Article 151 as relates to the laying before the Legislature of the State of the report submitted to the Governor by the comptroller and Auditor-General of India;

Articles 163 and 164;
Clause (3) of Article 166;
Article 167;
so much of Clause (1) of Article 169 as relates to the passing of a resolution by the Legislative Assembly of a State;
Clause (1) and Sub-Clause (a) of Clause (2) of Article 174;
Articles 175 to 178 (both inclusive);
Clauses (b) and (c) of Article 179 and the first proviso to that Article;
Articles 180, 181 and 182, Clause (c) of Article and the proviso thereto;
Articles 183 and 185;
so much of Article 186 as relates to the salaries and allowances of the Deputy Speaker of the Legislative Assembly;
so much of Article 188 as relates to a member of the Legislative Assembly;
Articles 189,193 and 194;
so much of Article 195 as relates to the salaries and allowances of Members of the Legislative Assembly;
Articles 196 to 198 (both inclusive);
Clauses (3) and (4) of Article 199;
so much of Clause (3) of Article 202 as relates to the salaries and allowances of the Deputy Speaker of the Legislative Assembly;
Articles 208 to 211 (both inclusive); the proviso to Clause (1) and the proviso to Clause (3) of Article 213; and

so much of Clause (2) of Article 323 as relates to the laying of the report with a memorandum before the Legislature of the State; *(Hi)* the Legislative Assembly of the said State is hereby dissolved; *(iv)* any reference in the Constitution to the Governor shall in relation to the said State be construed as a reference to the President, and any reference therein to the Legislature of the State or the Houses thereof shall insofar as it relates to the functions and powers thereof, be construed, unless the context otherwise requires, as a reference to Parliament, and, in particular, references in Article 213 to the Governor and to the Legislature of the State or the Houses thereof, shall be construed as references to the President and to Parliament or to the Houses thereof respectively;

Provided that nothing herein shall affect the provisions of Article 153, Articles 155 to 159 (both inclusive), Article 299 and Article 361 and paragraphs 1 to 4 (both inclusive) of the Second Schedule or prevent the President from acting under Sub-clause (i) of this Clause to such extent as he thinks fit through the Governor of the said State; *(v)* any reference in the Constitution to Acts or laws of or made by the Legislature of the State shall be construed as including a reference to Acts or laws made in exercise of the powers of the Legislature of the State, by Parliament by virtue of this Proclamation, or by the President or other authority referred to in sub-clause (a) of Clause (1) of Article 357 of the Constitution and the Madras General Clauses Act, 1891 (Madras Act 1 of 1891) as in force in the State of Tamil Nadu, and so much of the General Clauses Act. 1897 (10 of 1897), as applies to State laws, shall have effect in relation to any such Act or law as if it were an Act of the Legislature of the State.

Fakhruddin Ali Ahmed
President
New Delhi

31 January 1976
[No. V/11013/2/TN/76-S&P (DV)]
S.L. Khurana, Secy.
New Delhi
31 January 1976

ORDER New Delhi, the 31st January 1976

G.S.R. 56 (E)—The following Order by the President is published for general information:

In pursuance of Sub-Clause (i) of Clause (c) of the Proclamation issued on this the 31st day of January, 1976 by me under Article 356 of the Constitution of India. I hereby direct that all the functions of the Government of the State of Tamil Nadu and all the powers vested in or exercisable by the Governor of the State under the Constitution or under any law in force in that State, which have been assumed by the President by virtue of Clause (a) of the said Proclamation, shall, subject to the superintendence, direction and control of the President, be exercisable also by the Governor of the said State.

New Delhi
31 January 1976
New Delhi
31 January 1976

Fakhruddin Ali Ahmed
President
S.L. Khurana, Secy.

Source: Shiram Maheshwari, President s *Rule in India* (New Delhi: Mac Millan, 1979) 209-213.

APPENDIX VI

Details of President's Rule Imposed when the Ministry Commanded Majority in the Legislature (1950-2010)

Sl. No.	State	Year	Reason	Whether justifiable or not
1	Haryana	1977	Government in these states no longer represented the will of the people	No
2.	Punjab	1977	"	"
3.	H.P.	1977	"	"
4.	U.P.	1977	"	"
5.	Bihar	1977	"	"
6.	Orissa	1977	"	"
7.	M.P.	1977	"	"
8.	West Bengal	1977	"	"
9.	Rajasthan	1977	"	"
10.	Punjab	1980	"	"
11.	Rajasthan	1980	"	"
12.	Orissa	1980	"	"
13.	M.P.	1980	"	"
14.	U.P.	1980	"	"
15.	Maharashtra	1980	"	"
16.	Bihar	1980	"	"
17.	Gujarat	1980	"	"
18.	Tamil Nadu	1980	"	"
19.	MP.	1992	State governments run by a political party failed to effectively implement the central ordinances	No
20.	H.P.	1992	"	"
21.	Rajasthan	1992	"	"
22.	Tamil Nadu	1976	Corruption and maladministration.	No
23.	Manipur	1979	"	"
24.	U.P.	1992	Failure to honour the assurance to the nation and the Courts	Yes

25	Gujarat	1996	Resort Violence within The Assembly when non-confidence motion was taken up for voting.	No
26.	Kerala	1959	Break down of law and order	No
27.	Punjab	1983	"	No
28.	Punjab	1987	"	Yes
29.	Assam	1990	"	No
30.	Jammu & Kashmir	1990	"	Yes
31.	Tamil Nadu	1991	"	No
32.	Bihar	1999	"	No
33.	Manipur	1993	"	Yes
34.	Punjab	1951	Party Wrangling	No
35.	Punjab	1966	"	"
36.	Uttar Pradesh	1973	"	"
37.	Uttar Pradesh	1975	"	"
38	Andhra Pradesh	1973	"	
39.	Gujarat	1974	"	"
40.	Orissa	1976	"	"
41.	Kamataka	1990	"	"

Source: Computed from various secondary sources.

Explanation

As the table shows out of total 111 instances, President's Rule was imposed 41 times when the respective ministries enjoyed the confidence of the House. Out of the 41 instances only in nine instances the ruling party at the centre and the respective states were the same and that too except one (Punjab 1983) were resorted to with suspended Assemblies for solving the internal problem of ruling party and form a new Government under new Chief Ministers. In this regard of instances in which the intention of the ruling party at the centre was materialised. It would appear that out of the 41 instances we reviewed under this heading only five declarations may be placed under the category of justifiable cases.

APPENDIX VII

Detailed Classification of President's Rule According to Reason (1950-2010)

Sl.No	Category of President's Rule	No.	State and Year	Whether justifiable or not
I	1. Mass dismissals	21 (18+3)		
	A. Governments in the State nolonger represented the will of the people		Haryana(1977)	No
			Punjab (1977)	No
			HP.(1977)	No
			UP.(1977)	No
			Bihar (1977)	No
			Orissa(1977)	No
			MP.(1977)West	No
			Bengal(1977)	No
			Rajasthan(1977)	No
			Punjab(1980)	No
			Rajasthan (1980)	No
			Orissa(1980)	No
			MP.(1980)	No
			UP.(1980)	No
			Maharashtra(1980)	No
			Bihar(1980)	No
			Gujarat(1980)	No
			Tamil Nadu(1980)	No
	B. State Governments run by a political party failed to effectively implement the central ordinances banning certain communal organizations		MP.(1992)	No
			HP.(1992)	no
			Rajasthan(1992)	No
II	Hung Assemblies	6	Kerala (1965)	No
			Rajasthan(1967)	No
			Orissa(1971)	No
			Uttar Pradesh(1996)	No
			Uttar Pradesh(2002)	Yes
			Bihar (2005)	No
III	Corruption and Maladministration	2	Tamil Nadu (1976)	No
			Manipur(1979)	No
IV	Break down of Law and order	8	Kerala(1959)	No
			Punjab(1983)	Yes
			Punjab(1987)	yes
			Assam(1990)	no
			Jammu and	

			Kashmir(1990)	Yes
			Tamil Nadu(1991)	No
			Manipur(1993)	Yes
			Bihar(1999)	No
V	Party Wranglings	8	Punjab(1951)	No
			Punjab(1966)	No
			UP.(1973)	No
			UP.(1975)	No
			AP.(1973)	No
			Gujarat(1974)	No
			Orissa(1976)	No
			Karnataka(1990)	No
VI	Paralysis of parliamentary Process	9	West Bengal (1968)	No
			Nagaland (1975)	No
			Tamil Nadu(1988)	No
			Mizoram(1988)	No
			Meghalaya(1991)	No
			Nagaland(1992)	No
			Goa(2005)	No
			Nagaland(2008)	No
			Meghalaya(2009)	No
VII	To deal with delay in electoralprocess	3	Sikkim(1979)	Yes
			Tripura(1993)	Yes
			Bihar(1995)	Yes
VIII	In the context of State Reorganization	3	Kerala(1956)	Yes
			Manipur(1972)	Yes
			Tripura(1972)	Yes
IX	Failure to honour the assurance to the Nation and the Court	1	Uttar Pradesh(1992)	Yes
X	Resort to violence with in the precinct of assembly when confidence motion was taken up for voting	1	Gujarat (196)	No
XI	To get the interim budget of the State passed in the Parliament	7	Bihar(1968)	Yes
			My sore(1971)	Yes
			Gujarat(1971)	Yes
			Punjab(1971)	Yes
			WB.(1971)	Yes
			Manipur(1973)	Yes
			Gujarat(1976)	Yes
XII	Political instability as a result of party splits Defection etc.	42	Pepsu(1953)	No
			AP(1954)	No
			Travacore Cohin(1956)	No
			Orissa(1961)	Yes
			Kerala(1964)	Yes
			Haryana(1967)	No
			UP(1968)	No
			Punjab(1968)	Yes
			Bihar(1969)	No
			WB(1970)	No
			Kerala(1970)	Yes

	UP(1970)	No
	Orissa(1971)	Yes
	Orissa(1971)	No
	Bihar(1972)	No
	Bihar(1972)	No
	Orissa(1973)	Yes
	Manipur(1977)	Yes
	Tripura (1977)	Yes
	Karnataka(1977)	No
	Kerala(1979)	No
	Assam (1979)	Yes
	Manipur(1981)	No
	Assam(1981)	Yes
	Kerala(1981)	Yes
	Kerala(1982)	No
	Assam(1982)	Yes
	Sikkim(1984)	Yes
	Jamu &Kashmir(1986)	No
	Nagaland(1988)	No
	Karnataka (1989)	No
	Goa (1990)	Yes
	Haryana (1991)	Yes
	Manipur(1992)	No
	UP(1995)	No
	Goa(1999)	Yes
	Manipur (2001)	No
	Karnataka(2007)	Yes
	Karnataka(2007)	Yes
	Jammu &Kashmir(2008)	Yes
	Jharkhand(2008)	Yes
	Jharkhand(2010)	Yes

Source: Computed from various primary and secondary sources.

APPENDIX VIII
Summary Table of President's Rule in the States (1950-2010)

SL No	Year	No	States	Date of Proclamation	Date of Revocation	Duration	Whether Assembly Suspended/ Dissolved	Remarks
1	1951	1	Punjab	20.06.1951	17.04.1951	00.09 3S	Assembly	
	1952	0	NIL			Suspended		
2	1953	1	Pepsu	04.03.1953	07.03.1954	01.00.03	Dissolved	
							Assembly	
3	1954	2	Andhra	15.11.1954	28.03.1955	00.04.09	Dissolved	
	1955	0	NIL					
4	1956	1	Travancore-Cochin	23.03.1956	01.11.1956	00.07.09	Dissolved	
5	1956		Kerala	01.11.1956	05.04.1957	00.05.04 of States	Reorganization	Justiiable
	1957	0	NIL					
	1958	0	NIL					
6	1959	1	Kerala	31.07.1959	22.02.1960	00.0622	Dissolved	
	1960	0	NIL					
7	1961	1	Orissa	25.02.1961	23.06.1961	00.03.29	Dissolved	Justifiable
	1962	1	NIL					
	1963	0	Nil					
8	1964	1	Kerala	10.09.1964	24.03.1965	00.06.14	Dissolved	Justifiable
							Dissolved	
9	1965	1	Kerala	24.03.1965	06.03.1967	01.11.10		

10	1966	1	Punjab	05.07.1966	01.11.1966	0003.27	Reorganisation of State	11
1967	2		Rajasthan	13.03.1967	26.04.1967	00.01.13	Suspended	
12	1967		Haryana	21.11.1967	21.05.1968	00.06.00	Dissolved	
13	1968	4	West Bengal	20.02.1968	25.02.1969	01.00.05	Dissolved	Justifiable
14	1968		Uttar Pradesh	25.02.1968	26.02.1969	01.00.01	Suspended andsubsequently Dissolved	
15	1968		Bihar	29.06.1968	26.02.1969	00.07.28	justifiable	
16	1968		Punjab	23.08.1968	17.02.1969	00.05.25	justifiable	
17	1969	1	Bihar	04.07.1969	16.02.1970	00.07.12	Suspended	
18	1970	3	West Bengal	19.03.1970	02.04.1971	01.00.14	Suspended and subsequently dissolved on 30.07.70	
19	1970		Kerala	04.08.1970	03.10.1970	00.02.00	Assembly dissolved on 26.6.70 by the Governor Justifiable	
20	1970		Uttar Pradesh	01.10.1970	18.10.1970	00.00.17	Suspended	
21	1971	7	Orissa	11.01.1971	23.01.1971	00.00.12	Suspended	Justifiable
22	1971		Orissa	23.01.1971	22.02.1971	00.02.00	Dissolved	Justifiable
23	1971		Orissa	23.03.1971	03.04.1971	00.00.11	Suspended	
24	1971		Mysore	27.03.1971	20.03.1971	00.1122	Suspendedand Subsequently dissolved 14.04.1971	Justifiable
25	1971		Gujarat	13.05.1971	17.03.1972	00.10.04	Dissolved	Justifiable

26	1971		Punjab	15.06.1971	17.03.1972	00.09.02	Dissolved by Governor on 13.06.1971	Justifiable
27	1971		West Bengal	29.06.1971	20.03.1972	00.0822	Dissolved on 25.6.1971 by Governor	Justifiable
28	1972	4	Bihar	09.01.1972	08.03.1972	00.0129	Dissolved on 29.12.1971 by Governor	
29	1972		Bihar	09.03.1972	19-.03.1972	00.00.10	Freshproclamation was issued as earlier one earlier one ceased to operate on 8.3.1972	
30	1972		Manipur	21.01.1972	20.03.1972	00.02.00	Reorganization of State	Justifiable
31	1972		Tripura	21.01.1972	20.03.1972	00.02.00	Reorganization of State	Justifiable
32	1973	4	Andhra Pradesh	18.01.1973	10.12.1973	00.10.22	Suspended	
33	1973		Orissa	03.03.1973	06.03.1974	01.00.03	Dissolved	
34	1973		Manipur	28.03.1973	04.03.1974	00.11.04	justifiable	
35	1973		Uttar Pradesh	13.06.1973	08.11.1973	00.04.26	Suspended	
36	1974	1	Gujarat	09.02.1974	18.06.1975	01.04.09	Assembly suspended and subsequently dissolved	
37	1975	2	Nagaland	22.03.1975	25.11.1977	02.08.03	Suspended and dissolved	
38	1975		Uttar Pradesh	30.11.1975	21.01.1976	00.0122	Suspended	
39	1976	3	Tamil Nadu	31.01.1976	30.06.1977	01.04.29	Dissolved	
40	1976		Gujarat	12.03.1976	24.12.1976	00.09.12	Suspended	Justifiable
41	1976		Orissa	16.12.1976	29.12.1976	00.00.13	Suspended	
42	1977	12	Punjab	30.04.1977	20.06.1977	00.01.21	Dissolved	
43	1977		Rajasthan	30.04.1977	22.06.1977	00.0123	Dissolved	
44	1977		Orissa	30.04.1977	26.06.1977	00.0127	Dissolved	

45	1977		Haryana	30.04.1977	21.06.1977	00.0122	Dissolved	
46	1977		Himachal Pradesh	30.04.1977	22.06.1977	00.0123	Dissolved	
47	1977		Madhya Pradesh	30.04.1977	23.06.1977	00.0124	Dissolved	
48	1977		Uttar Pradesh	30.04.1977	23.06.1977	00.0124	Dissolved	
49	1977		West Bengal	30.04.1977	21.06.1977	00.0122	Dissolved	
50	1977		Bihar	30.04.1977	24.06.1977	00.0125	Dissolved	
51	1977		Manipur	16.05.1977	29.06.1977	00.01.13	Suspended	Justifiable
52	1977		Tripura	05.11.1977	04.01.1978	00.02.00	Dissolved justifiable	
53	1977		Kamataka	31.12.1977	27.02.1978	00.0127	Dissolved	
	1978		NIL					
54	1979	4	Sikkim	10.08.1979	17.10.1979	0020.00	Dissolved by Governor on 13.08.1979	Justifiable
55	1979		Manipur	14.11.1979	13.01.1980	00.0129	Dissolved	
56	1979		Kerala	05.12.1979	25.01.1980	00.0121	Dissolved by the Governor on 30.11.1979	
57	1979		Assam	1112.1979	06.12.1980	00.1114	Suspended	Justifiable
58	1980	9	Rajasthan	17.02.1980	06.06.1980	00.03.18	Dissolved	
59	1980		Gujarat	17.02.1980	07.06.1980	00.03.19	Dissolved	
60	1980		Punjab	17.02.1980	07.06.1980	00.03.19	Dissolved	
61	1980		Bihar	17.02.1980	08.06.1980	00.0310	Dissolved	
62	1980		Tamil Nadu	17.02.1980	09.06.1980	00.0311	Dissolved	
63	1980		Orissa	17.02.1980	09.06.1980	00.0311	Dissolved	
64	1980		Madhya Pradesh	17.011980	09.06.1980	00.0311	Dissolved	
65	1980		Maharasthra;	17.02.1980	09.06.1980	00.0311	Dissolved	
66	1980		Uttar Pradesh	17.02.1980	09.06.1980	00.0311	Dissolved	
67	1981	3	Manipur	28.02.1981	19.06.1981	00.0311	Suspended	

68	1981		Assam	30.06.1981	13.01.1982	00.06.13	Suspended	Justifiable
69	1981		Kerala	21.10.1981	28.111981	00.02.07	justifiable	
70	1982	2	Kerala	17.03.1982	24.05.1982	00.02.07	Dissolved	
71	1982		Assam	19.03.1982	27.02.1983	00.01.09	justifiable	
70	1983	1	Punjab	06.10.1983	29.09.1985	011114 26.06.1985	Suspended and dissolved on	Justifiable
73	1984	1	Sikkim	25.05.1984	08.03.1985	00.09.14	Dissolved	Justifiable
	1985		Nil					
74	1986	1	Jammu and Kashmir		07.19.1986	06.11.1986	00.02.00 Assembly suspended	justifiable
75	1987	1	Punjab	11.05.1987	23.02.1992	04.09.19	Suspended and subsequently dissolved	
76	1988	3	Tamil Nadu	30.01.1988	27.01.1989	00.1118	Assembly dissolved	
77	1988		Nagaland	07.08.1988	25.01.1989	00.05.19	Dissolved	
78	1988		Mizoram	07.09.1988	24.01.1989	00.03.18	Dissolved	
79	1989	1	Kamataka	21.04.1989	30.11.1989	00.07.10	Dissolved	Justifiable
80	1990	4	Jammu and Kashmir		18.07.1990		Assembly was Dissolved during Governor's Rule	
81	1990		Kamataka	10.10.1990	17.10.1990	00.00.08	Suspended	
82	1990		Assam	27.11.1990	30.06.1991	00.07.04	Dissolved	
83	1990		Goa	14.12.1990	25.01.1991	00.01.12	Suspended	Justifiable
84	1991	3	Tamil Nadu	30.01.1991	24.06.1991	00.0516	Dissolved	

85	1991		Haryana	06.04.1991	23.06.1991	00.02.18	Dissolved	Justifiable
86	1991		Meghalaya	11.10.1991	05.02.1992	00.0316	Suspended	
87	1992	6	Manipur	07.01.1992	08.04.1992	00.03.02	Suspended	
88	1992		Nagaland	0104.1992	22.02.1993	00.1011	Assembly was dissolved by the Governor	
89	1992		Uttar Pradesh	06.111992	04.111993	00.1119	Dissolved	Justifiable
90	1992		Madhya Pradesh	15.111992	07.12.1993	00.1114	Dissolved	
91	1992		Himachal Pradesh	15.111992	03.111993	00.1110	Dissolved	
92	1992		Rajasthan	15.111992	04.111993	00.1111	Dissolved	
93	1993	2	Tripura	11.03.1993	10.04.1993	oim.00	Dissolved	Justifiable
94	1993		Manipur	31.111993	13.111994	00.11.13	Suspended	Justifiable
	1994	0	Nil					
95	1995	2	Bihar	28.03.1995	04.04.1995	00.00.08	Term of the assembly expired	justifiable
96	1995		Uttar Pradesh	18.10.1995	16.10.1996	00.11.29	Suspended and dissolved	
97	1996	2	Gujarat	19.09.1996			Suspended	
98	1996		Uttar Pradesh	17.10.1996	21.03.1997	00.05.05	Suspended	
	1997	0	Nil					
	1998	0	Nil					
99	1999	2	Goa	10.02.1999	07.06.1999	00.03.28	Dissolved	Justifiable
100	1999		Bihar	12.02.1999	08.03.1999	00.00.25	Suspended	
	2000	0	Nil					
101	2001	1	Manipur	26.02.2001	06.03.2002	01.00.09	Suspended	
102	2002	1	Uttar Pradesh	04.03.2002	29.04.2002	00.01.27	Suspended	Justifiable

	2003	0	Nil					
	2004	0	Nil					
103	2005	2	Goa	07.03.2005	06.06.2005	00.03.01	Suspended	
							and dissolved	
104	2005		Bihar	07.03.2005	06.11.2006	00.08.07	"	
	2006	0	Nil					
105	2007	2	Karnataka	09.10.2007	12.11.2007	00.01.02	Suspended	Justifiable
106	2007		Karnataka	20.11.2007	30.05.2008	00.06.19	Suspended and	
						dissolved		Justifiable
107	2008	2	Nagaland	03.01.2008	12.03.2008	00.02.12	"	Justifiable
108	2008		Jammu & Kashmir	23.07.2008	05.01.2009		"	
109	2009	2	Jharkhand	19.01.2008	13.12.2009	00.11.08	Suspended	
							and dissolved	Justifiable
110	2009		Meghalaya	25.03.2009	08.05.2009	00.01.15	Suspended	
111	2010	1	Jharkhand	01.06.2010			Suspended	Justifiable

Source: Computed from various primary and secondary sources.

APPENDIX IX

Details of President's Rule under Article 356 in Each State and the Year of Imposition (1950-2010)

SL. No	Name of State	1	2	3	4	5	6	7	8	9	10	No of times	Justifiable
1	Andhra Pradesh	1954	1973									2	0
2	Assam	1979	1981	1982	1990							4	3
3	Bihar	1968	1969	1972	1973	1977	1980	1995	1999	2005		9	3
4	Goa	1990	1999	2005								3	2
5	Gujarat	1971	1974	1976	1980	1996						5	2
6	Haryana	1967	1977	1991								3	2
7	Himachal Pradesh	1977	1992									2	0
8	Jammu & Kashmir	1986	1990	2008								3	2
9	Jharkhand	2009	2010									2	2
10	Karnataka	1971	1977	1989	1990	2007	2007					6	3
11	Kerala	1956	1956	1959	1964	1965	1970	1979	1981	1982		9	4
12	Madhya Pradesh	1977	1980	1992								3	0
13	Maharashtra	1980										1	0
14	Manipur	1972	1973	1977	1979	1981	1992	1993	2001			8	3
15	Meghalaya	1991	2009									2	0
16	Mizoram			1988								1	0
17	Nagaland	1975	1988	1992	2008							4	0

18	Orissa	1961	1971	1971	1971	1973	1976	1977	1980			8	3
19	Punjab	1951	1953	1966	1968	1971	1977	1980	1983	1987		9	4
20	Rajasthan	1967	1977	1980	1992							4	0
21	Sikkim	1979	1940									2	2
22	Tamil Nadu	1976	1980	1987	1991							4	0
23	Tripura	1972	1977	1993								3	3
24	Uttar Pradesh	1968	1970	1973	1975	1977	1980	1992	1995	1996	2002	10	2
25	West Bengal	1968	1970	1971	1977							4	0
	Total											111	40

Source: Computed from various primary and secondary sources.

Bibliography

Primary Sources

A. Reports

1. *Indian Statutory Commission (Simon Commission)* (1930).
2. *Administrative Reforms Commission Report* (1969).
3. *The Report of Centre-State Relations Inquiry Committee (Rajamannar Committee Report)* (1971).
4. *The Report of the Committee of Governors* (1971).
5. *The Report of the Commission on Centre-State Relation (Sarkaria Commission Report)* (1988).
6. *President's Rule in the States and Union Territories, Lok Sabha Secretariat* (1996).
7. *The Report of the National Commission to Review the Working of the Constitusion (NCRWC)* (2002)

B. Statutes

1. *The Government of India Act,* 1909.
2. *The Government of India Act,* 1919.
3. *The Government of India Act, 1935.*
4. *The Indian Independence Act,* 1947.
5. *The Constitution of India.*

C. State Government Publications

1. *Statement on Centre – State Relations Released at Sringar in October,* 1983, *Calcutta, Government of West Bengal* (1983).
2. *White paper on the Office of the Governor, Government of Karnataka,* (1983)
3. *Seminar on Centre – State Relations, Government of Karnataka,* (1984)

D. Debates

1. *Constituent Assembly Debates. (CAD)*
2. *Lok Sabha Debates. (LSD)*
3. *Rajya Sabha Debates. (RSD)*
4. *http://alfa.nie.in/lsdeb/lsll/ses3/c 051296. htm.*

E. Dictionaries

1. *Shorter Oxford English Dictionary.*

F. Judicial Dicisions

1. *A.K. Roy v. Union of India, AIR 1982 SC 710.*
2. *Arun Kumar Rai Chaudhary v. Union of India, AIR 1992 All. 1*
3. *B.R. Kapur v. State of Tamil Nadu and Anr, AIR 2001 SC 3435*
4. *Barium Chemical Ltd and Anr v. Company Law Board and Ors (1966) Supl SCC 311*
5. *Bijayananda v. President of India, AIR 1974 Ori. 52.*
6. *Bimanchandra v. Governor, west Bengal, AIR 1952 cal.799.*
7. *Capt. Kanwaljit Singh v. Union of India, AIR 1991 Pand. H. 54 Nagaland v. Union of India,*
8. *Dhronamaraju Sataya Narayana v. NT Rama Rao, AIR 1988 AP.69.*
9. *Election Commission of India and Anr.v.Dr.Subrahmaniam Swamy and Anr.(1996) 4SCC 104.*
10. *Gokulananda. v. Tarpada, AIR 1973 Cal 233*
11. *Golak Behari v. State of Orissa, AIR 1972 Ori.*
12. *Hanumantha Rao v. State of AP, (1975) 2 AWR 277.*
13. *Hargovind Pant v. Raghukul Tilak, and ors. AIR 1979 SC 1109.*
14. *Inre Sreeramulu, AIR 1974 AP106.*
15. *Jyotirmony Bose v. Union of India, AIR 1971 cal 122*
16. *K.K. Aboo v. Union of India, AIR 1965 Ker 229.*
17. *Kallada Sukumaran. v. Union of India, AIR 1987 Ker. 212*
18. *K.A Mathialagan and Ors. v. The Governor of Tamil Nadu and Ors.AIR 1973 Mad.198.*
19. *Kanwaljit Singh v. Union of India, AIR 1991 P and H 55*
20. *Kehar Singh and Anr v. Union of India, and Anr. (1989) I SCC 204.*
21. *Kihoto Hollohan v., Zachillhu and Ors (1992) Supp (2) SCC 651.*

22. *M.P. V. Sundararamier v. State of AP, (1958) SCR 1422.*
23. *M.R Deke v. N.E. Frontier Railways, AIR 1964, SC600*
24. *Mahabir Prasad Sharma v. Prafullachandra, AIR 1969 cal.198*
25. *Maru Ram v. Union of India, (1989) I SCC107*
26. *MSM Sharma v. S.K Sinha, AIR 1960, SC 1186*
27. *Muhammed Sharif v. Federation of Pakistan, PLD 1988 (Lah) 725.*
28. *People's Union for Civil Liberties (PUCL) and Anr. v. Union of India and Anr. (2003) 4 SCC 399.*
29. *Rameshwar Prasad and Ors v. Union of India, 2006 AIR SCW 494.*
30. *Rao Birendra Singh v. Union of India, AIR 1968 P and H 441.*
31. *S.P. Gupta v. Union of India (1981) supp. SCC 87.*
32. *S.R. Bommai and ors. v. Union of India (1994) 3 SCC 1.; AIR 1994 SC 1918.*
33. *S.R. Bommai and ors. v. Union of India and ors. AIR 1989 Kart 5.*
34. *Shamsher Singh v. State of Punjab, AIR 1974 SC 2192.*
35. *Shri Pratapsingh Raojirao Rane and ors v. The Governor of Goa and ors, AIR 1999 Bom 53.*
36. *State of Punjab v. Satpal Dange, AIR 1969 SC 903*
37. *State of Rajasthan and Ors. v. Union of India and Ors., AIR 1977 SC 1361.*
38. *Sunderlal Patwa v. Union of India, AIR 1993 MP 214.*
39. *Sunil Kumar v. Government of West Bengal, AIR 1950 cal. 274.*
40. *Union of India v.Association for Democratic Reforms, (2002)5 SCC 294.*
41. *Vamuzo v. Union of India, (1988) 2 Gahu LJ 468*

II . SECONDARY SOURCES

A. Books

Aditya Mukherjee : *India After Independence* (New Delhi: Penguin, 2000).

Alladi Aruna : *Unfederal Features of Indian Constitution* (Chennai: Muthivan, 2001)

Alexander, P.G : *India in the New Millennium* (New Delhi: Somariya, 2001)

Anil Mishra, Ed. : *Coalition Politics in India: Problem and prospectus* (New Delhi: Manohar, 2006)

Arun Shourie : *The Parliamentary System what we have made of it, what we can make of it?* (New Delhi: Rupa, 2007).

Atual Kohli : *Democracy and Discontent* (Cambridge: Cambridge Uni. Press, 1990)

Atul Kohli : *India's Democracy* (Princeton: Princeton Uni. press, 1988)

Atul Kohli : *The Success of India's Democracy* (New Delhi: Cambridge, 2002)

Akbar, M.J : *India: The Siege Within: Challenges to a Nation's Unity* (New Delhi: Harmonds worth: Penguin).

Akhtar Majeed : *Federation within the Union: Distribution of Responsibilities in Indian system* (New Delhi: Manak Publications, 2004)

Alexandrowiez, C.A.: *Constitutional Development in India* (London : OUP, 1957).

Alice Jacob, Ed. : *Constitutional Development since Independence* (Bombay: N.M. Tripathi, 1975).

Anirudh Prasad : *Centre and State Powers under the Indian Constitution* (New Delhi: Deep and Deep, 1981).

Anirudh Prasad : *Centre-State Relations in India* (New Delhi: Deep and Deep,1985).

Aric De Ruijter : *The Purse and the Power : Aspects of Centre-State Relations in India* (Delhi: BR Publishing Co., 1998).

Arora, S.C. : *President's Rule in Indian States* (N e w Delhi: Mittal, 1990).

Austin, Granville : *The Indian Constitution : Corner Stone of a Nation* (Madras: Oxford University Press, 1966).

Austin, Granville : *Working a Democratic Constitution* (New Delhi : OUP, 1999).

Ball, T. : *Transforming Political Discourse* (New Delhi: OUP, 1998)

Basu, D.D. : *Comparative Constitutional Law* (New Delhi: Prentice-Hall, 1984).

Basu, D.D. : *Commentary on the Constitution of India,* 6th ed.. Vol. O (Calcutta: Kamal Law House, 1989).

Basu, D.D. : *Shorter Constitution of India,* 12th ed., New Delhi: Prentice Hall, 1996).

Bidyut Chakrabarthy : *Indian Politics and Society since Independence* (New York: Routledge, 2008).

Bipan Chandra and others : *India After Independence* (New Delhi: Viking, 1999)

Brass, Paul R. : *The Politics of India since Independence* (Cambridge: Cambridge Uni. Press, 1990)

Brazier, Rodney : *Constitutional Practice,* 2nd ed. (Oxford: Clarendon Press, 1994).

Brazier, Rodney : *Constitutional Reform,* 2nd ed.(Oxford: OUP, 1998).

Cardozo, Benjamin : *The Nature of Judicial Process* (New Delhi: Universal Book Traders, 1921).

Chandrapal : *State Autonomy in Indian Federalism* (New Delhi: Deep and Deep, 1984).

Chandrapal : *Centre State Relation and Co-operative Federalism* (New Delhi: Deep and Deep, 1985).

Crowin, Edwards : *The Constitution What it Means Today* (Princeton: Princeton University Press, 1973).

Copland, Ian and Richard john : *Federalism: Compartivie perspective from India and Australia* (New Delhi: Manohar, 2001)

Dau, B.D. : *President's Rule in India 1950-1974, A Study in Crisis Politics* (New Delhi: S. Chand and Co., 1979).

Dicey, A.V. : *An Introduction to the Study of the Law of the Constitution, 10th ed.* (New Delhi: Macmillon, 1994).

Forguscn and Mc Hendry : *The American Federal Government*, 4th ed. (New York, 1956).

Gani, H.A. : Centre-State Relations and Sarkaria Commission: Issues, Institutions, Challenges (New Delhi: Deep and Deep, 1990).

Gehlot, N.S. : *Indian Government and Politics* (Jaipur: Rawat, 1996).

Gert Kueek and Others : *Federalism and Decentralization Centre - State Relations in India and Germany* (New Delhi: Mudrit, 1998)

Govinda Rao Nirvikar Singh : *Political Economy of Federalism in India* (Delhi: OUP, 2005)

Hansaria, B.L. : *Does India need a New Constitution?* (Calcutta: Eastern Law House, 1998).

Harbirsingh Kathuria : *President's Rule in India* (New Delhi: Uppal, 1990).

Hardgrave, Robert and : *India: Government and Politics in a Developing Nation, V Ed.* Kochanck, Stanley (New York: Harcourt Brace Jovan Ovich,1993)

Iqbal Narayan : *Twilignt or Dawn : The Political Change in India* 1967-71 (Agra: S.L. Agarwal, 1972).

Iqbal Narayan : *State Politics in India* (Meerut: Meenakshi Prakashan, 1976).

Jain, M.P. : *Indian Constitutional Law,* 4th ed. (Nagpur :Wadhwa and Co., 1994).

Jaya Kumar, N.K. : *Judicial Process in India: Limitations and Lee Ways* (New Delhi: APH, 1997).

Jawaharlal Nehru : *The Discovery of India* (New York: Doubleddy and Co., 1960).

Jennings, Sir Ivor : *Parliament,* 2nd ed. (New York: Cambridge, 1961).

Jennings, Sir Ivor : *Cabinet Government,* 3rd ed. (New York: Cambridge, 1961).

Kaul, M.N. and Shakdar, S.L. : *Practice and Procedure of Parliament with Particular Reference to Lok- Sabha,* 3rd ed., Vol. II (New Delhi: Metropolitan Books, 1972).

Khanna, H.R : *Neither Rose Nor Thorns* (Lucknow: Eastern Book, 1985)

Kothari, Rajani : *Rethinking Democracy* (New Delhi: Orient Longman, 2005).

Kothari, Rajni : *State Against Democracy* (Delhi: Ajanta, 1988)

Krishna Iyer, VR. : *A Constitutional Miscellany* (Lucknow: Eastern Books, 1988).

Krishna Iyer, V.R. : *Indian Federalism Dialectics and Dynamics* (Gauhati: Ashok Publishing, 1992).

Krishna Iyer, V.R. : *The Indian Presidency* (New Delhi: Duporal Dup, 1988).

Krishna Shetty, K.P.: The *Law of Union-State Relation and Indian Federalism* (Madras: Sainag, 1981).

Lumb, RD. and Yan, K.W. : *The Constitution of Common Wealth of Australia—Annotated* (London: Buttor-Worths, 1974).

Madhav Godbole : *Unfinished Innings* (New Delhi: Orient Longman, 1996)

Madhulimaya : *President VS Prime Minister* (Bomaby: Cambridge, 2002)

Markandan, K.C. : *Centre-State Relations: The Perspective* (Qalandhur: ABS, 1986).

Mathur, PL. : Role of Governor in Non-Congress States (Jaipur: Rawat, 1988).

Meera Srivastava : *Constitutional Crisis in the Indian States* (New Delhi: Concept, 1979).

Meena Verma : *Centre-State Relations : Economi and Political Dimensions* (New Delhi: Deep and Deep, 1994).

Michael, Breecher : *Nehru—A Political Biography* (London: OUP, 1959).

Morris-Jones, W.H. : *The Government and Politics of India* (New Delhi: Universal Book Stall, 1994).

Mridual Mukherjee andAditya Mukherjee: *India after Independence* (New Delhi: penguin, 2000)

Nainta, R.P. : *Governor under the Indian Constitution* (New Delhi: Deep and Deep, 1992).

Nani A. Palkhivala : *We, the Nation—The Lost Decades* (New Delhi : UBSPD, 1994).

Nani A. Palkhivala : *Selected Writings,* ed. L.M. Singhvi and others (New Delhi: Penguin, 1999).

Noorani, A.G. : *India's Constitution and Politics* (Bombay: Jaico, 1970).

Noorani, A.G. : *Constitutional Questions in India* (New Delhi: OUP, 2000).

Noorani, A. G : The Presidential System: The Indian Debate (New Delhi: Sage, 1989).

Nossiter, Tom : *Marxist State Governments in India* (London: Pinter Press, 1988)

Palkhivala N.A : *We, the Nation* (New Delhi: UBS, 1994).

Pandhy, K.S. : *Press and Pliant Governors* (New Delhi: Kanishka, 1996).

Pandey, J.N. : *Constitutional Law of India* (Allahabad: Central Law Agency, 1998).

Partha, Chatterjee, Ed. : *State and Politics India* (Delhi: OUP, 1997)

Perival, Spear : *The Oxford History of Modern India* (Oxford: Clarendon Press, 1965).

Pylee, M.V. : *Constitutional Government in India* (Bomaby: Asia Publishing House, 1977).

Pylee, M.V : *The Constitution of India* (Mal), (Thiruvananthapuram: Kerala Language Institute, 1999).

Pylee, M.V : *Our Constitution, Government and Politics* (Delhi: Universal publishing Co, 2000)

Rajeev Dhavan : *President's Rule in the States* (Bombay: N.M. Tripathi, 1979).

Randhir Singh : *Indian politics Today* (Delhi: Aakar, 2009).

Rajni Kothari : *Politics in India* (New Delhi: Orient Longman, 1972).

Rao, K.Y. : Parliamentary Democracy of India : A Critical Commentary (Calcutta: World Press, 1965).

Retna Swamy : *Political Question and Article 356* (New Delhi: Manas, 1988).

Rush, Michael : *Parliament and the Public* (London: Longman, 1976).

Rickard, John, Ed : *Federalism: Comparative perspective from India and Australia.*(New Delhi: Manohar, 2001)

Sathe, S.P. : *Right to Know* (Bombay: N.M. Tripathi, 1991).

Sarkar RCS, : *Union - State Relation in India* (New Delhi: Institute of const. and parlia: Studies, 1986).

Sathyamurthy, T.V, Ed. : *Class Formation and Political transformation in Post – Colonial India, 4 Vols,* (New Delhi: OUP, 1996).

Seervai, H.M. : *The Emergency, Future Safeguards and the Habeascorpus Case: A Criticism* (Bombay: N.M. Tripathi, 1978).

Seervai, H.M. : *Constitutional Law of India,* 4th ed., Vol. 2 (Bombay: N.M. Tripathi, 1993).

Seervai, H.M. : *Constitutional Law of India,* 4th ed., Vol. 3 (Bombay: N.M. Tripathi, 1996).

Setalvad, M.C. : *Grave Emergency and Emergency Arising out of the Failure of the Constitutional Machinery in a State* (Madras: University of Madras, 1966).

Setalvad, M.C. : *Union and State Relations Under the Indian Constitution* (Calcutta: Eastern Law House, 1974).

Shakder, Ed. : *The Constitution and the Parliament in India: The 25 Years of the Republic* (Delhi: National, 1976).

Shiram Maheswari : *President's Rule in India* (New Delhi: Macmillan, 1977).

Shivaraj B. Nakada : *Emergency in Indian Constitution,* (New Delhi: Cosmo, 1990).

Shiva Rao, Ed. : *Framing of India's Constitution: Select Documents,* 5 vols. (Bombay: N.M. Tripathi, 1966).

Shiva Rao : *The Framing of India's Constitution—A Study* (New Delhi: EPA, 1968).

Shukla, VN. : *V.N Shukla's Constitution of India,* 9th ed., Mahendra P. Singh (Eastern: Lucknow, 1994).

Singh M.P : *Constitutional Law of India, 2 Vols* (Delhi: Universal Law publishing Co, 2008).

Singh, M.P. and Chaube, *Ed.* : *Indian Constitution : A Review* (New Delhi: Har-Anand, 1997).

Siwach, J.R. : *The Indian Presidency* (Delhi: Hariyana Prakashan, 1971).

Siwach, J.R. : *Office of the Governor : A Critical Study* 1950-1973 (New Delhi: Sterling, 1977).

Siwach, J.R. : *Politics of President's Rule in India* (Shimla: Indian Institute of Advanced Study, 1979).

Soli. J. Sorabjee : *The Governor : sage or saboteur* (New Delhi: Roli Books , 1985)

Subash C. Kashyap : *Politics of Power* (Delhi : National, 1974).

Subash C. Kashyap : *Union-States Relations in India* (New Delhi, The Institute of const: and parlia: studies, 1983).

Subash C. Kashyap : *History of Parliamentary Democracy* (New Delhi: SHIPRA, 1991).

Subba Rao : *Constitutional Development in India* (New Delhi: Deep and Deep, 1992).

Sudipto Kaviraj, Ed. : *Politics in India* (New Delhi: OUP, 1997).

Sukhbir Bhatnagar : *Constitutional Law and Governance* (New Delhi: Mittal, 2008)

Sunil Deshta : *President's Rule in the States: Constitutional Provision and Practices* (New Delhi: Deep and Deep, 1993).

Sunil Deshta : *President's Rule in the States: Constitutional Provision and Practices* (New Delhi: Deep and Deep, 1993).

Taneja, S.P : *Society and politics in India* (Delhi: Swastik publishers,2009).

Tiwari, O.P. : *Federalism and Centre State Relations in India : Towards a New Era of Mutual Co-operation,* (New Delhi: Deep and Deep, 1996).

Tope, T.K. : *The Constitutional Law of India,* 2nd ed. (Luknow: Eastern Books, 1922).

Tope, T.K. : *The Constitutional Law of India,* 2nd ed. (Luknow: Eastern Books, 1992).

Venkata Raman, R. : *My Presidential Years* (New Delhi: Harper Collins, 1994).

Verinder Grover, Ed, : *Federal System, Centre-State Relations and State Autonomy* (New Delhi: Deep and Deep, 1977).

Vibhuti, K.L Ed. : *Ambedkar and Empowerment: Constitutional Vicissitudes* (Bombay: N.M. Tripathi, 1993).

Verney, D. Ed. : *Multiple Identities in a Single State* (New Delhi: Konark, 1995)

Wheare, K.C. : *Federal Government,* (London: OUP, 1968).

Weiner, Myron : *The Politics of Scarcity* (New Delhi: Asia Publishing House, 1962).

White, L.D : *Introduction to the Study of Public Administration,* 4th ed. (New York: Macmillan and Co., 1955).

Yadav,B.R. Ed. : *Indian Politics in comparative perspective* (New Delhi: Murai Lal and Sons, 2009).

Zoya Hasan E and others, Ed. : *India's Living Constitution, Ideas, Practices, Controversies* (Delhi: Permanent Black, 2002)

B. Articles

Ajith Bhattacharjee : *Decline of Federalism : Ruling the State in a Viceregal Style, The Indian Express, 6 May 1993.*

Akhtar Majeed : *India's Federal structure: Some inbuilt strains, in India Federalism in the New Millennium Ed. by Dua B.D and M.P* Singh *(New Delhi: Manohar, 2003)*

Alexandro Wiez : *Development in Indian Federalism, Asian Journal of Political Science, 15.2 (2007).*

Alice Jacob and Rajeev Dhavan : *The Dissolution Case : Politics at the Bar of the Supreme Court, Journal of Indian Law Institute, 19 (1977).*

Alladi Kuppuswami: *Article 356: To Delete or to Retain, The Hindu, 21 October 1998*

Alladi Kuppuswami: *Does Article 356 need Amendment, The Hindu, 26 November 1997.*

Alladi Kuppuswami: *Was the Patna High Court Right, The Hindu, 13 August 1997.*

Anand ST Das : *Ugly Coalition: Independents lust for power.* http://www.tehelka.com

Anjali Mody : *When will the Centre Intervene, The Hindu, 26 April 2002*

Aravind : *Article 356: Pros and Cons (Mal),The Mathrubhumi,10 October 1997.*

Arshikhan : *Triumph of Federalism, Mainstream, 13 March 1999*

Arun Ghosh : *Article 356 of the Constitution and the Bihar Scenario, Mainstream, 20 February 1999*

Arvind P. Datar : *Debates in Parliamen,. The Hindu, 16 August 2004.*

Arvind, P. Datar : *Article which was expected to remain a dead letter, The Hindu, 7 July, 1998.*

Asoka Kumar : *The Parliament and Proclamation of Emergency in the Constitution and parliament in India, ed. by Shakdher (Delhi: National, 1976)*

Alladi Aruna : *Use of Article 356, The Hindu, 25 June 1998*

Bhambhri, CP. : *The Governor in Theory and Practice,* Mainstream, 4 May 1966

Binoy Viswam : *Right and Wrong of the Political History (Mal), The Mathrubhumi, 10 October 1997.*

BJP Coalition Failed: *Article ID = 126878* http://www.merinews.com./eatfull-jsp

Chandra Das, CP. : *Governor vis-a-vis Council of Ministers (Mal), The Mathrubhumi, 31 July 1999.*

Chandrapal : *Demand for Greater Autonomy and National Integration: A Review of Constitutional Experiences, Journal of*

		Constitutional and Parliamentary Studies, 27 (1993).
Chatterjee	:	*Articles 356 must be Removed, Mainstream, 18 Nov 2005*
Chatterjee	:	*How to Safeguard Article 356 from Abuse and Misuse, The Hindu, 19 November 1996.*
David Annoussamy	:	*Scanning of Article 356, Politics India, 2.9 (1998).*
Dharmadan	:	*How to root out Pernicious practice in Parliament?Indian Law Reports, (Kerala series) 24 December 2008*
Dholakia, H.C.	:	*Rethinking on Emergency Provisions, JCPS, 12 (1978)*
Dilip, K. Chatterjee	:	*President's Rule and Union-States Relations in India, JCPS, 14 (1980).*
Don't Dismiss Mulayam	:	*http://retributions. nationalinterest. indon'tdismissmulayam*
Era Sezhiyan	:	*Parliament under suspension, The Hindu 4 September 2004.*
Fali. S. Nariman	:	*The Jharkhand Case: with Retrospect, Mainstream, 25 March 2005.*
Girglani J.M	:	*Free the President, The Hindu, 2 December 1997.*
Gopakumar, G.	:	*Article 356: The Unending Debate (Mal), The Mathrubhumi, 10 March 1999.*
Gopalakrishnan, P.	:	*Dominance of the Centre : Need for Co-operative and Co-ordinate Federalism, The Indian Express, 29 April 1993.*
Gopalakrishnan, P.	:	*The Constitutional Implications of President's Rule in Kerala, The Supreme Court Journal, 22 (1959).*
Guhan	:	*Constitutional Collapse: InTamil Nadu or in Delhi, Frontline, 16 February 1991.*
Hande, H. V	:	*Limitations of Article 356, The Hindu, 6May 2003*
Hande, H.V,	:	*Genesis of Presidential Activism, The New Indian Express, 16 June 2006.*

Hareendranadhan : *Presidential Prerogatives (Mal), The Mathrubhumi, 30 October 1997.*

Harish Khara : *Protecting the Constitutional Edifice, The Hindu, 4 October 1998.*

Jain, C.K. : *Crime on the Floor, JCPS 33 (1999).*

Jain, R.B. : *Executive Accountability to Parliament, JCPS, 15 (1981)*

Jain, S.K. : *Article 356 and Centre-State Relations, Mainstream, 2* ***April*** *1993.*

Jaya Raina : *Role of the Governor, The Hindustan Times, 27 April 1998.*

Jayasudha Reddy : *Executive Discretion and Article 356 of the Constitution of and* Joy V. Joseph India: *A comparative critique EJCL, 8. 1 (2004)*

Jena, B.B. : *The Case of Hung Parliament, Politics India, 2.4 (1997).*

Kamala Prasad : *Governor's Rule and Governance in Uttar Pradesh, Mainstream, 8 February 1997.*

Kamala Prasad : *President's Rule and Bihar Politics, Mainstream, 27 March 1999.*

Kameswari, G. : *Article 356 of the Constitution – A boon or a ban to Federalism, AIR 1999 (J).*

Karunakaran, K.P. : *Governor, Chief Minister and Coalitions, EPW, 10 (1970).*

Katyal K.K : *Ambiguity of Article 355, The Hindu, 13 May 2002*

Katyal K.K, : *President unhappy with Governor, The Hindu,22 February 1999.*

Katyal, K.K : *Use of Article 355, The Hindu, 15 May 2002*

Katyal, K.K. : *Presidential Intervention, The Hindu, 29 September 1998.*

Katyal, K.K. : *The Role of Governors, The Hindu, 1 January 1996.*

Katyal, K.K. : *Two Faces of Indian Polity, The Hindu, 2 November 1997.*

Kaushik, P.D. : *The Constituent Assembly and the Governor, Journal of the Society for the Study of State Governments, 4 (1971).*

Khanna, H R : *Supreme Court judgment on Article 356, AIR 1994, September (J)*

Khanna, H.R. : *Article 356, and its Use and Misuse I* ***and*** *II, The Hindu, 14 and 15 November 1997.*

Khanna, H.R. : *Article 356 and the Courts, The Hindu, 12 April 1993.*

Khanna, H.R. : *Dismissal of the BJP Governments, The Hindu, 1 June 1994.*

Khanna, H.R. : *Secularism and Judicial Review, The Hindu, 31 May 1994.*

Khanna, H.R. : *Use of Article 356, The Hindu, 30 May 1994.*

Koladi Govindan Kutty : *Challenges against Federalism (Mal) The Kerala Kaumudi, 24 November 1994.*

Koticha, K.K. : *Presidential Intervention under Article 356 of the Constitution of India, Journal of Indian Law Institute, 2 (1960).*

Krishana Iyer V.R. : *Radical Restructuring Needed, The Hindu 4 April 1992.*

Krishna Iyer V.R : *Constitutional Condurum, The Hindu, 21 June 1999*

Krishna Iyer V.R. : *The Chemistry of Raj Bhavan, The Hindu 24 and 25 April 1992*

Krishna Iyer, V.R : *Governor's Reign and President's Rule: A Constitutional- Political Critique", Essays on Constitutional Law, ed. Venkataramanaiah (New Delhi: Concept, 1986).*

Krishna Mohan Mathur : *Centre – State Relations: Lessons and Prospectus, The Indian Journal of Public Administration (2001)*

Krishna Shetty, K.P.: *Hung Parliament and Volatile Governments: A Constitutional Riddle, The Hindu, 4 June 1996.*

Kuldip Nayar : *Abuse of Article 356 – Secularism cannot be Subject to Legal Definition, The Indian Express, 21 March 1994.*

Kuldip Nayar : *Article 356 in the Age of Coalition politics, The Mathrubhumi (Malayalam) 21 December. 2007*

Madhakarrao Chaudhari : *Four Decades of Indian Democracy, JCPS, 27 (1993).*

Madhav Godbole : *Reform of political system, EPW, 10 July 2004*

Madhavan Kutty : *Behind the Leak, Frontline, 19 February 1999*

Madhavankutty,V.K. : *The President at Centre Stage, The Hindu, 10 August 1999.*

Madhu Limaya . *Ambedkar and Constitution Making, The Hindu, 2 January 1995.*

Madhusudhana Rao : *Power of the President to dissolve the Legislative Assembly under Article 356(1), (2001) 4 SCC (J).*

Madhusudhana Rao : *The scope of Article 365 of the constitution, (2000) 4 SCC (J)*

Madhusudhana Rao : *The scope of Judicial Review of Presidential proclamation issued under Article 356 of the Constitution, AIR 2006 (J)*

Malhotra : *Safeguarding Democracy: Role of opposition in Indian Parliament, The Journal of Parliamentary Information, 57(2001)*

Manishankar Aiyar : *Article 356 in the Age of Gowda: Stick to Beat Secessionists, The Indian Express, 23 September 1996*

Manoj Mitta : *If NHRC Indicts Modi, He must be sacked, The New Indian Express, 31 March 2002, at http://www.indianexpress.com/ic2002033i/op/.htm/*

Mohit, C.S. : *Aboo to Bommai: The Fall and Rise of Judicial Control Over President's Rule – Quo Vadis; ACLR 22 (1998).*

Mukund Padmanabhan : *Dealing with Hung Legislatures, The Hindu, 18 June 1997.*

Mukund Padmanabhan : *The President and Bihar, The Hindu, 24 October 1998.*

Nagasailan D. and Suresh, V. : *Will the Supreme Court Break New Grounds?, The Hindu, 9 May 1993*

Nagindas Sanghav : *President's Rule – Temporary Quiet, EPW, 31 (1996).*

Nalini Pant : *The Governor and Article 356 : Problems and Challenges, Journal of the Society for the Study of State Governments, 4 (1971).*

Narayanan, V.N. : *An Article of Bad Faith, News Week, 27 September 1988.*

NC's Writings : *President's Moral standings, Mainstream, 1 November 1997.*

Nikhil Chakravarthy : *Whither Parliamentary Democracy, The Hindu, 14 December 1997.*

Nilay Vipin Chandran : *Article 356: viewing in a Right perspective, AIR 1999, (J)*

Nilay, V. Anjaria : *Clause 'or otherwise' in Article 356, AIR, 1991 (J)*

Nirmal Mukarjee : *For a More Federal India, EPW, 27 (1992).*

Nirmal Mukarjee : *Resolving Centre-State Conflicts, EPW, 30 (1995).*

Pandey, A.K. : *Centre's Obligation and Article 356 of the Indian Constitution, Academy Law Review (AcLR), 20 (1996).*

Pandya, B.P. : *The Role of Governor, JCPS, 30 (1996).*

Parameswara Rao, P : *The Role of Parliament During the Emergency, JCPS, 1.2 (1967).* Partha Sarathy, G.: *Federalism and Constitutional Process in India, Mainstream, 17 Aug. 1996.*

Parvathi Menon : *Coalition quake, Frontline, 19 October 2007*

Patil, RLM : *Article 356 of the Indian Constitution: Why Deletion is no Solution, Vidya Bharathi, 10 (1995).*

Patil, RLM : *Presidency under the Indian Constitution, Deccan Herald, 6 Nov. 1994.*

Pattabhiram : *The Genesis of Article 356, The Hindu, 26 June 1997.*

Philip, A.J. : *Limitations of the Presidency, The New Indian Express, 21 March 1998.*

Praful Bidwail : *Beyond the obvious http://www.prafulbidwai.net/archives/20070302.ft.htm*

Prakash : *Judicial Review of Presidential Proclamation under Article 356,(1988) 3 SCC (J).*

Purnima S. Tripathi : *In suspended animation, Frontline, 29 March 2002.*

Purnima S. Tripathi : *A Role for the Governor, Frontline, 12 May 2005.*

Putta Swamy : *Article 356 of the Constitution-oral Observation of Patna High Court: Legality and Propriety, Politics India 2.4 (1997).*

Pylee, M.V : *Ambedkar's Momentous Contribution, The Indian Express, 17 January 1991.*

Pylee, M.V. : *The Governor and the Constitution, EPW, 2 (1967).*

Pylee, M.V : *The States under Constitutional Emergency, JCPS, 1.2 (1967).*

Radhakrishna Menon KP : *Article 356 and the President – The limits of power, The Indian Express, 20 October 1998*

RadhaN.K : *Presidents Rule under Indian Constitution, AIR 1997 (J)*

Raghavan C : *The Exit of a friendly Governor, The Indian Express, 30 May 1993.*

Rahim Macheri : *Article 356: Always Controversial (Mal), Maadhyamam, 5 May 1998.*

Raja Sekahara, H.M. : *It is Times to Stop Misuse of Article 356, The Hindu, 4 March 1997.*

Raja Sekahara, H.M. : *President's Rule in the Indian State, The Indian Journal of Political Science, 48 (1987).*

Raja Sekahara, H.M. : *The Indian Presidency: Plea for a Second Look, JCPS, 31 (1997).*

Rajani Kothari : *Rethinking Centre-State Relations: A Struggle for Power EPW,18 (1983).*

Rajeev Dhavan : *Activist Governors, The Hindu, 24 January 2003*

Rajeev Dhavan : *But Who is the Governor, The Indian Express, 5 May 1989.*

Rajeev Dhavan : *Beyond Parliament, The Hindu, 3 May 2002*

Rajeev Dhavan : *Politician, Heal Thyself, The Times of India, 29 February 2000.*

Rajeev Dhavan : *President's Rule in the States, JCPS,3(1969).*

Rajeev Dhavan : *The Gujarat Imbraglio, The Hindu,19 April 2002*

Rajeev Dhavan : *Choosing a Prime Minister, The Hindu 13 May 2004.*

Rajeev Dhavan : *Power without Responsibility, The Indian Express, 15 January 1989.*

Rajeev Dhavan : *President's Rule : Recent Trends, Journal of Indian Law Institute, 31 (1989).*

Rajeev Dhavan : *Judicial Surgery in UP, The Hindu, 26 February 1997.*

Rajeev Dhavan : *A Requiem for Democracy, Mainstream, 2 November 1996.*

Rajeev Dhavan : *A Blow against Federalism, The Hindu, 7 February 1991.*

Rajeev Dhavan : *A President Demurs, The Hindu, 28 September 1997.*

Rajeev Dhavan : *Democracy for Sale, The Hindu, 8 November 1997.*

Rajeev Dhavan : *Subverting Federalism, The Hindu, 3 July 1998.*

Rajeev Dhavan : *The BJP or the Constitutions, The Hindu, 24 September 1998.*

Rajendra Sachar : *Judiciary Vs Legislative, EPW, 28 May 2005*

RajeshPandey : *What Matter Most is the Constitution's Spirit, National Herald, 28 November 1996.*

Rajesh Ramachandran : *First of its Kind, The week, 2 November 1997.*

Rakshit : *Constitutional Review Committee and the Governor, EPW, 13 April 2002*

Raman, V.Y.D. : *Need for Judiciary to uphold Popular Sovereignty, The Hindu, 15 November 1994.*

Ramanujan, TCA and: *Sangeetha, TCA* *Article 356: Competency of Judiciary to Advise the President, (1988) 3 SCC (J)-*

Ramasharma : *Evaluating Jharkhand Governor's Indiscretion, Mainstream, 25 March 2005.*

Ramaswami R Iyer : *Some Constitutional Dilemmas,*

Ramjith Melani : *The President Shall..., The Indian Express, 30 October 1990.*

Ranadive, B.T. : *The Sarkaria Commission Report: Empty Rhetoric, The Marxist, January-March 1988.*

Range Rao, K. and Ravi Teja : *Article 356 and President's Rule in the State, JCPS, 25 (1991).*

Rao, K.V. : *Guidelines for the Governors, Journal of the Society for the Study of State Governments, 4 (1971).*

Rao, K.V : *Dissolution of Assembly and Article 356, JCPS, 4 (1970)*

Rao, UNR : *Tamil Nadu Governor's Action, The Hindu, 29 May 2001.*

Rasheeda Bhagat : *President does a UP in Bihar, Business Line, 28 September 1988.*

Ravi. P. Bhatia : *Federation in India and the Supreme Court Rulings, in Indian Federalism in the New Millennium, Ed. By Dua and M.P Singh.*

Ravisharma : *Another Government in Goa, Frontline, 18 June 2005.*

Roshni Sengupta : *Communal Violence in India, EPW, 14 May 2005*

Rubinoff, Arthur G : *The Decline of Parliament. Legal and Constitutional Digest 15 (2001)*

Sachidananda Murthy : *Fair play, The week, 2 November 1997.*

Sahay, S. : *Governor VS Speaker, The Hindustan Times, 6 June 1995.*

Sahay, S. : *Secularism is Basic Structure, Mainstream, 26 May 1994.*

Sandeep Shastri : *Victim of Political Opportunism, Mainstream, 2 January 1993.*

Sathya Murthy : *Impact of Centre-State Relations of Indian Politics An Interpretive Reckoning 1947-87,EPW, 24 (1989).*

Satyapal Dang : *House Dissolution, Code of Conduct, Free and Fair polls, Mainstream, 28 February 2004*

Satyaprakash Malviya : *Constitution of India in Precept and Practice (Article 355 and 356 of the Constitution), JCPS, 27 (1993).*

Saumyajit Ray : *Politics of Black Mail, Mainstream, (1991).*

Sen, S.R : *Centre-State Relations in India, EPW, 23 (1988)*

Shafi Rahman : *An Uncommon House, India Today, March 2008.*

Shanti Bhushan : *What are the Indian Presidents Power, The Hindu, 6 June 2006.*

Shenoy, TVR. : *The Misunderstood Article : Majority gives no Immunity The New Indian Express, 24 September 1998.*

Sher R.K : *Importance of Article 356, Kashmir Sentinel, 16 July 1999.*

Shivaraj Nakade : *Article 356 of the Indian Constitution: Its Uses and Misuse, JCPS, 2 (1969).*

Shrawan K. Singh : *Governor's Role in Indian Democracy, Legal and Constitutional Digest, 20 (2006)*

Shriram Maheswari : *Coercive Federalism: Three Out of Ten People do not Live under a Popular Government, The Indian Express, 20 May 1993.*

Shriram Maheswari : *Political Control over Executive Department in India, Philippine Journal of Public Administration, 25 (1980).*

Shyamanand Singh : *Imposition and Revocation of President's Rule, Mainstream, 16 November 1996.*

Sing, K.P. : *Governor in the Constituent Assembly, The Indian Journal of Political Science, 26 (1965).*

Singh, L.S. and Nanda Kumar, V.K. : *Restructuring Indian Federalsim with Special Reference to Article 356, UP. Journal of Political Science, 2 (1990).*

Singh, MP : *Towards a more Federalized parliamentary System in India, in Indian Federalism in the New Millennium Ed. by Dua and Singh.*

Singh, S.K. : *Role of President under Article 356, CULR, 22 (1998).*

Siwach, J.R. : *Emergency Control Mechanism and Failure of Constitutional Safeguards in India, JCPS, 12 (1978).*

Siwach, J.R. : *State Autonomy and the President's Rule, in Federalism, Centre-State Relations and State Autonomy, Ed. Grover (New Delhi: Deep and Deep, 1997).*

Siwach, JR. : *President's Rule and Politics of Suspending and Dissolving State Assemblies, JCPS, 11 (1977).*

Soli J. Sorabjee : *Constitutional Morality Violated in Gujarat, The Indian Express, 21 September 1996.*

Soli, J. Sorabjee : *An Active Judiciary, Mainstream, 26 March 1994.*

Soli, J. Sorabjee : *Decision of the Supreme Court in S.R. Bommai v. Union of India : A Critique, (1994) 3 SCC (J).*

Somanath Chatterjee : *Parliamentary Democracy and Some Challenges, The Hindu, 15 November 2007.*

Subhash C. Jain : *Governor's Responsibility for his address, Legal and Constitutional Digest, 16. 3 (2002)*

Subash, C. Kashyap : *Minority Government is not Freak Phenomenon, The Indian Express, 22 October 1996.*

Subash, C. Kashyap : *50 Years of Opposition, The Hindu, 22 July 1997.*

Subash, C. Kashyap : *Failure of Constitution in Bihar, The Hindu, 22 September 1998.*

Subash, C. Kashyap : *President's Rule is Illegal, The Indian Express, 18 October 1996.*

Subhash C. Kashyap : *President's Powers, The Hindu, 25 July 2002*

Subodh Kumar : *Role of Governor in Indian Democracy, Mainstream, March 2005*

Subramanian C : *Should Governors Change with change of Government, The Indian Express, 23 January 1990.*

Subramanian : *Reforming the Legislature, The Hindu, 11 April 1998.*

Sudama Singh : *Changing Concept of Article 356: The Tamil Nadu Experiment, U.P. Journal of Political Science, 2 (1990).*

Sudha Pai : *Electoral Identity Politics in Uttar Pradesh: Hung Assembly Again, EPW, 6 April 2002*

Sudhanshu Ranjan : *President's Rule in States How to Tackle the Problem at the* Centre.

Sukhjindersingh Tiwana : *Centre-State Relations in India : A Critique of Governor's Role, ISDA Journal, 3 (1993).*

Sukumar Muralidharan : *Appeasing the Hindu Right, Frontline,29 March 2002*

Sukumar Muralidharan : *Un warranted intervention, Frontline, 12 February 1999.*

Sukumar Muralidharan : *Watershed Verdict, Frontline, 8 April 1994.*

Sukumaran Nayar, V.K : *New Challenges before Indian Federalism, Kerala Journal of Political Studies, 2 (1985).*

Sumanta Banerjee : *Salvaging an endangered Institution, EPW, 9 Sept. 2006.*

Sura Redy : *Judicial Review vis – a - vis Article 356, Supreme Court Journal 2 (1994).*

Surya Prasad, K. : *President's Rule in Kerala : A Historical Overview, Journal of Kerala Studies, 15 (1988).*

Surya Prasad, K. and Ramjeev, V.K : *Pleasure of the Governor and Life of the Ministry (Coverstory) (Mal) The Mathrubhumi Weekly, 6 December 1995.*

Surya Prasad, K. and: Ramjeev, V.K *President's Rule and the Courts (Mal), Vtjnana Kairali, 27 (1996)*

Surya Prasad, K. and : Santhosh, C.R *Article 356 of the Constitution of India (Coverstory) (Mal) The Mathrubhumi Weekly, 26 September 1999.*

Suryaprasad, K. : *Discretionary Power of the Governor: A Critique of the Sarkaria Commission Report, ISDA Journal, 3 (1993).*

Suryaprasad K. : *Judicial review of Presidential proclamation under Article 356 of the Constitution of India – A Critical Study, JCPS, 33 (1999)*

Suryaprasad K. : *Electoral Reforms: Plea for a Fresh Look, JCPS, 35 (2001)*

Suyraprasad K. : *Dealing with Hung Legislatures, JCPS, 40 (2006)*

Suyraprasad K. : *Presidential Activism, UCJPS, 3 (2008)*

Suyraprasad K. : *Pernicious Behaviour of Elected Representatives, UCJPS, 4 (2009)*

Syma Sundaran : *Debates in Parliament, The Hindu, 11 August 1998.*

Thiruvengadam : *Agenda for the New Government, The Hindu, 24 March 1998.*

Tiwana, S.S : *Article 356 and Centre – State Relations in India, see Legal and Constitutional Digest, 18 (2004)*

Tomkuns, Adam : *Government Information and Parliament: Misleading by Design or by Default? Public Law, (1996).*

Tope, T.K. : *Dr. Ambedkar and President's Rule in a State: Some Reflections in Dr. Ambedkar and Empowerment : Constitutional Vicissitudes Ed. Vibhuti (Poona: U of Poona, 1993)*

Venkataramaiah : *Greater Autonomy : All States will Benefit, The Indian Express, 30 November 1997.*

Venkatesan : *Unresolved Questions, Frontline, 24 February 2006*

Venkatesan : *Governor's Choice, Frontline, 16 November 2007*

Venkatesan V : *The Dissolution and the Law, Frontline, 17 June 2005.*

Venketesh Rama Krishanan : *The judicial Verdict : Question of Constitutionality and Federalism, Frontline, 10 January 1997.*

Venkitesh Ramakrishnan : *Theoretical blunder, Frontline, 9 March 2007*

Verma, O.P. and

Sharma, M.L. : *Failure of Constitutional Machinery in Tamil Nadu, JCPS, 22 (1988).*

Verney, Doughlas V.: *Federalism, Federative Systems, and Federations: The United States, Canada and India, Publics, 25 (1995).*

Vidya Subrahmanian : *Who is guilty party in Uttar Pradesh, The Hindu, 21 February 2007.*

Viswam, S : *Outcome of President's Initiatives, Mainstream, 21 June 1997.*

Winterton, George : *Tasmania's Hung Parliament, 1989, Public Law, (1992).*

C. Editorials

Is Governor the lackey of the Centre (Mal): The Kerala Kaumudi, 14 April 1992

For a better Centre- State Relations (Mal): The Mathrubhumi, 15 April 1992.

States need more powers (Mal): The Kerala Kaumudi, 26 May 1992.

Dominating attitudes of the Centre (Mal): The Kerala Kaumudi, 28 December1992.

Article 356 (Mal): The Kerala Kaumudi, 5 April 1993.

Centre in a spot, The Hindu, 5 April 1993.

A landmark verdict: The Hindu, 14 March 1994.

A pragmatic decision: The Hindu, 30 October 1995.

Greater Autonomy for the States (Mal): The Mangalam, 5 September1996.

Inter-state Council and Article 356 The Hindu, 17 October 1996.

Presidential Activism Politics India, 2.5(1997).

A remarkable verdict of the Judiciary (Mal) The Mathrubhumi, 14 July 1997.

Historic milestone: (Mal) The Kerala Kaumudi, 23 October 1997

Constitutional Activism of the President (Mal) The Mathrubhumi, 23 October 1997.

Article 356 and Bihar (Mal) The Maadhyamam, 26 October 1997.

Judiciary again to the rescue of	*The Deepika, 25 February 1998. democracy (Mal)*
Political sabre-rattling	*The Hindu, 4 April 1998.*
Article 356, Bommai and fair play	*Frontline, 17 July 1998.*
Unreasonable demand	*The Hindu, 22 July 1998.*
Ill-timed, unwise 1998.	*Hindustan Times, 24 September*
An unwanted step	*The Hindu, 24 September 1998.*
The President speaks	*The Sunday Statesman, 27 Septem-ber 1998.*
Well done Mr. Narayanan	*The Hindu, 27 September 1998.*
Article 356: whether debates serve	*The Malayala Manorama, 29 October any purpose (Mal) 1998.*
Triumph of democracy (Mal)	*The Kerala Kaumudi, 29 October1998.*
Article 356 and Misuse	*The Hindu, 25 January 1999.*
Democracy under siege	*Mainstream, 20 February 1999.*
Percept and Practice:	*The New Indian Express, 27February 1999.*
Meaning of BJP- Samata 's Ignominious Retreat	*Mainstream, 13 March 1999.*

Partisan move /The Times of India, 1 February 1991.
Manipur Conundrum/ The Hindu, 30 May 2001.
An Inevitable Step /The Hindu, 6 June 2001.
Horror in Gujarat /The Hindu, 2 March 2002.
Central Rule in UP/ The Hindu, 8 March 2002.
Stigma of Gujarat /The Times of India, 1 May 2002.
Winning the vote and Losing the Debate / The Hindu, 2 May 2002.
Misplaced Article /The Times of India, 9 May 2002.
Army and Deployment /The Hindu, 15 May 2003.
Amending Article 356 /The Hindu, 30 August 2003.
A Flawed Institution /The Hindu, 5 July 2004.

Short – Circuiting the Democratic Process *Mainstream, 27 May 2005.*

A Farcical Vote of Confidence The Hindu, 4 February 2005.
A Rule to the bottom *The Hindu, 5 March 2005.*
Unavoidable, For a while, in Bihar The Hindu, 9 March 2005.
Democracy Traumatized *Mainstream, 10 March 2005.*
A whiff of fresh Air Mainstream, 11 March 2005.
No alternative to Dissolution The Hindu, 24 May 2005.
No more brazening it out *The Hindu, 25 January 2006.*
At the helm, Until voters decide *The Hindu, 27 January 2007.*
Desist from Article 356 Fraud The Hindu, 19 February 2007.
Constitutionally Off- track The Hindu, 3 October 2007.
End of a Sordid political chapter The Hindu, 21 November 2007
Humiliating Defeat The Hindu, 12 January 2009.
A Dream gone Sour *The Hindu, 20 January 2009.*

D.News Papers

The Deepika (Mal)
The Desabhimani (Mal)
The Hindu
The Hindustan Times
The Kerala Kaumudi (Mal)
The Maadhyamam (Mal)
The Malayala Manorama (Mal)
The Mangalam (Mal)
The Mathrubhumi (Mal)
The New Indian Express
The Times of India
UNI Backgrounder.

E.Magazines

1. *The Economic and Political Weekly*

2. *Frontline*
3. *India Today*
4. *Mainstream*
5. *The statesman*
6. *The week*